BIRDS
of
MICHIGAN

Ted Black
Gregory Kennedy

with contributions from
John Acorn, Chris Fisher,
Andy Bezener, Marke Ambard
& Amanda Joynt

Lone Pine Publishing International

The Distributor:
Lone Pine Publishing
1808 B Street NW, Suite 140
Auburn, WA, USA 98001

Website: www.lonepinepublishing.com

National Library of Canada Cataloguing in Publication Data

Black, Ted, 1914–
    Birds of Michigan / Ted Black and Gregory Kennedy.

    Includes bibliographical references and index.
    ISBN-13: 978-1-55105-336-3
    ISBN-10: 1-55105-336-5

    1. Birds—Michigan—Identification. I. Kennedy, Gregory, 1956–   II. Title.
QL684.M5B52 2003   598'.07'234774   C2003-910240-8

Cover Illustration: Great Horned Owl, by Gary Ross
Illustrations: Gary Ross, Ted Nordhagen
Separations & Film: Elite Lithographers Co.

PC: P13

CONTENTS

ACKNOWLEDGMENTS

I t is not possible to mention all the individuals who have contributed to this book. Nevertheless, there is a critical cast that has played an essential part. Thanks are extended to the growing family of ornithologists and dedicated birders who have offered their inspiration and expertise to help build Lone Pine's expanding library of field guides. Special thanks go to Gail McPeek and Raymond Adams for their recent monumental *The Birds of Michigan,* and to its contributing authors James Granlund, Philip Chu, Jack Reinoehl, Charles Nelson, Richard Schinkel, Michael Kielb, Stephen Allen and Andrea Trautman. Also to Richard Brewer, McPeek and Adams and the thousand or more birders who made possible *The Atlas of Breeding Birds of Michigan* that forms a solid basis for many of the range maps in this book. In the current book, particular appreciation goes to the work of the artists Gary Ross and Ted Nordhagen. Especially helpful have been the Lone Pine staff of Nancy Foulds, Genevieve Boyer, Gary Whyte, Curtis Pillipow, Nicholle Carriere and Carol Woo. Thanks also go to John Acorn, Chris Fisher, Andy Bezener and Ross James for their contributions to previous books in this series. Additional thanks go to Adam Byrne, Chair of the Michigan Audubon Society's Michigan Bird Records Committee for his kind assistance in providing the updated official checklist and other advice on current Michigan rare bird status as the basis for our checklist. Finally, Ted extends his grateful thanks to his family who permitted a high school city boy to explore the avian world and achieve a lifetime satisfaction in the pursuit of birds and the natural world, and to his wife Marijane, whose vigorous support was essential to the success of this project.

Red-throated Loon
size 25 in • p. 33

Common Loon
size 32 in • p. 34

Pied-billed Grebe
size 13 in • p. 35

Horned Grebe
size 13 in • p. 36

Red-necked Grebe
size 20 in • p. 37

Eared Grebe
size 13 in • p. 38

American White Pelican
size 62 in • p. 39

Double-crested Cormorant
size 29 in • p. 40

American Bittern
size 25 in • p. 41

Least Bittern
size 13 in • p. 42

Great Blue Heron
size 52 in • p. 43

Great Egret
size 39 in • p. 44

Snowy Egret
size 24 in • p. 45

Little Blue Heron
size 24 in • p. 46

Cattle Egret
size 20 in • p. 47

Green Heron
size 18 in • p. 48

Black-crowned Night-Heron
size 25 in • p. 49

Turkey Vulture
size 29 in • p. 50

Greater White-fronted Goose
size 30 in • p. 51

Snow Goose
size 31 in • p. 52

Canada Goose
size 36 in • p. 53

Mute Swan
size 60 in • p. 54

Trumpeter Swan
size 65 in • p. 55

Tundra Swan
size 54 in • p. 56

Wood Duck
size 18 in • p. 57

Gadwall
size 20 in • p. 58

American Wigeon
size 20 in • p. 59

American Black Duck
size 22 in • p. 60

Mallard
size 24 in • p. 61

Blue-winged Teal
size 15 in • p. 62

Northern Shoveler
size 19 in • p. 63

Northern Pintail
size 23 in • p. 64

Green-winged Teal
size 14 in • p. 65

Canvasback
size 20 in • p. 66

Redhead
size 20 in • p. 67

Ring-necked Duck
size 16 in • p. 68

Greater Scaup
size 18 in • p. 69

Lesser Scaup
size 16 in • p. 70

Harlequin Duck
size 16 in • p. 71

Surf Scoter
size 18 in • p. 72

White-winged Scoter
size 21 in • p. 73

Black Scoter
size 19 in • p. 74

Long-tailed Duck
size 19 in • p. 75

Bufflehead
size 14 in • p. 76

Common Goldeneye
size 18 in • p. 77

Hooded Merganser
size 17 in • p. 78

Common Merganser
size 25 in • p. 79

Red-breasted Merganser
size 22 in • p. 80

Ruddy Duck
size 15 in • p. 81

Osprey
size 24 in • p. 82

Bald Eagle
size 36 in • p. 83

Northern Harrier
size 20 in • p. 84

Sharp-shinned Hawk
size 13 in • p. 85

Cooper's Hawk
size 17 in • p. 86

Northern Goshawk
size 23 in • p. 87

Red-shouldered Hawk
size 19 in • p. 88

Broad-winged Hawk
size 16 in • p. 89

Swainson's Hawk
size 21 in • p. 90

Red-tailed Hawk
size 21 in • p. 91

Rough-legged Hawk
size 22 in • p. 92

Golden Eagle
size 35 in • p. 93

American Kestrel
size 8 in • p. 94

Merlin
size 11 in • p. 95

Gyrfalcon
size 22 in • p. 96

Peregrine Falcon
size 17 in • p. 97

Ring-necked Pheasant
size 30 in • p. 98

Ruffed Grouse
size 17 in • p. 99

Spruce Grouse
size 15 in • p. 100

Sharp-tailed Grouse
size 17 in • p. 101

Wild Turkey
size 39 in • p. 102

Northern Bobwhite
size 10 in • p. 103

Yellow Rail
size 7 in • p. 104

Virginia Rail
size 10 in • p. 105

Sora
size 9 in • p. 106

Common Moorhen
size 13 in • p. 107

RAILS, COOTS & CRANES

American Coot
size 14 in • p. 108

Sandhill Crane
size 45 in • p. 109

Black-bellied Plover
size 12 in • p. 110

American Golden Plover
size 10 in • p. 111

SHOREBIRDS

Semipalmated Plover
size 7 in • p. 112

Piping Plover
size 7 in • p. 113

Killdeer
size 10 in • p. 114

American Avocet
size 17 in • p. 115

Greater Yellowlegs
size 14 in • p. 116

Lesser Yellowlegs
size 10 in • p. 117

Solitary Sandpiper
size 8 in • p. 118

Willet
size 15 in • p. 119

Spotted Sandpiper
size 7 in • p. 120

Upland Sandpiper
size 11 in • p. 121

Whimbrel
size 18 in • p. 122

Hudsonian Godwit
size 14 in • p. 123

Marbled Godwit
size 18 in • p. 124

Ruddy Turnstone
size 9 in • p. 125

Red Knot
size 10 in • p. 126

Sanderling
size 8 in • p. 127

Semipalmated Sandpiper
size 6 in • p. 128

Western Sandpiper
size 6 in • p. 129

Least Sandpiper
size 5 in • p. 130

White-rumped Sandpiper
size 7 in • p. 131

Baird's Sandpiper
size 7 in • p. 132

Pectoral Sandpiper
size 9 in • p. 133

Purple Sandpiper
size 9 in • p. 134

Dunlin
size 8 in • p. 135

Stilt Sandpiper
size 8 in • p. 136

Buff-breasted Sandpiper
size 8 in • p. 137

Short-billed Dowitcher
size 11 in • p. 138

Long-billed Dowitcher
size 11 in • p. 139

Wilson's Snipe
size 11 in • p. 140

American Woodcock
size 11 in • p. 141

Wilson's Phalarope
size 9 in • p. 142

Red-necked Phalarope
size 7 in • p. 143

Pomarine Jaeger
size 21 in • p. 144

Parasitic Jaeger
size 18 in • p. 145

Laughing Gull
size 16 in • p. 146

Franklin's Gull
size 14 in • p. 147

Little Gull
size 10 in • p. 148

Bonaparte's Gull
size 13 in • p. 149

Ring-billed Gull
size 19 in • p. 150

Herring Gull
size 24 in • p. 151

Thayer's Gull
size 23 in • p. 152

Iceland Gull
size 22 in • p. 153

Lesser Black-backed Gull
size 21 in • p. 154

Glaucous Gull
size 27 in • p. 155

Great Black-backed Gull
size 30 in • p. 156

Sabine's Gull
size 13 in • p. 157

Black-legged Kittiwake
size 17 in • p. 158

Caspian Tern
size 21 in • p. 159

Common Tern
size 15 in • p. 160

Forster's Tern
size 15 in • p. 161

Black Tern
size 9 in • p. 162

Rock Dove
size 12 in • p. 163

Mourning Dove
size 12 in • p. 164

Black-billed Cuckoo
size 12 in • p. 165

Yellow-billed Cuckoo
size 12 in • p. 166

Eastern Screech-Owl
size 8 in • p. 167

Great Horned Owl
size 21 in • p. 168

Snowy Owl
size 23 in • p. 169

Northern Hawk Owl
size 16 in • p. 170

Barred Owl
size 20 in • p. 171

Great Gray Owl
size 28 in • p. 172

Long-eared Owl
size 15 in • p. 173

Short-eared Owl
size 14 in • p. 174

Boreal Owl
size 10 in • p. 175

Northern Saw-whet Owl
size 8 in • p. 176

Common Nighthawk
size 9 in • p. 177

Whip-poor-will
size 9 in • p. 178

Chimney Swift
size 5 in • p. 179

Ruby-throated Hummingbird
size 4 in • p. 180

Belted Kingfisher
size 12 in • p. 181

Red-headed Woodpecker
size 9 in • p. 182

Red-bellied Woodpecker
size 10 in • p. 183

Yellow-bellied Sapsucker
size 8 in • p. 184

Downy Woodpecker
size 6 in • p. 185

Hairy Woodpecker
size 8 in • p. 186

Black-backed Woodpecker
size 9 in • p. 187

Northern Flicker
size 13 in • p. 188

Pileated Woodpecker
size 17 in • p. 189

FLYCATCHERS

Olive-sided Flycatcher
size 7 in • p. 191

Eastern Wood-Pewee
size 6 in • p. 192

Yellow-bellied Flycatcher
size 6 in • p. 193

Acadian Flycatcher
size 6 in • p. 194

Alder Flycatcher
size 6 in • p. 195

Willow Flycatcher
size 6 in • p. 196

Least Flycatcher
size 5 in • p. 197

Eastern Phoebe
size 7 in • p. 198

SHRIKES & VIREOS

Great Crested Flycatcher
size 8 in • p. 199

Western Kingbird
size 8 in • p. 200

Eastern Kingbird
size 8 in • p. 201

Loggerhead Shrike
size 9 in • p. 202

Northern Shrike
size 10 in • p. 203

White-eyed Vireo
size 5 in • p. 204

Yellow-throated Vireo
size 5 in • p. 205

Blue-headed Vireo
size 5 in • p. 206

JAYS & CROWS

Warbling Vireo
size 5 in • p. 207

Philadelphia Vireo
size 5 in • p. 208

Red-eyed Vireo
size 6 in • p. 209

Gray Jay
size 12 in • p. 210

LARKS & SWALLOWS

Blue Jay
size 12 in • p. 211

American Crow
size 18 in • p. 212

Common Raven
size 20 in • p. 213

Horned Lark
size 7 in • p. 214

Purple Martin
size 7 in • p. 215

Tree Swallow
size 5 in • p. 216

Northern Rough-winged Swallow
size 5 in • p. 217

Bank Swallow
size 5 in • p. 218

Cliff Swallow
size 5 in • p. 219

Barn Swallow
size 7 in • p. 220

Black-capped Chickadee
size 5 in • p. 221

Boreal Chickadee
size 5 in • p. 222

Tufted Titmouse
size 6 in • p. 223

Red-breasted Nuthatch
size 5 in • p. 224

White-breasted Nuthatch
size 6 in • p. 225

Brown Creeper
size 5 in • p. 226

Carolina Wren
size 5 in • p. 227

House Wren
size 5 in • p. 228

Winter Wren
size 4 in • p. 229

Sedge Wren
size 4 in • p. 230

Marsh Wren
size 5 in • p. 231

Golden-crowned Kinglet
size 4 in • p. 232

Ruby-crowned Kinglet
size 4 in • p. 233

Blue-gray Gnatcatcher
size 5 in • p. 234

Eastern Bluebird
size 7 in • p. 235

Townsend's Solitaire
size 8 in • p. 236

Veery
size 7 in • p. 237

Gray-cheeked Thrush
size 7 in • p. 238

Swainson's Thrush
size 7 in • p. 239

Hermit Thrush
size 7 in • p. 240

Wood Thrush
size 8 in • p. 241

American Robin
size 10 in • p. 242

Varied Thrush
size 9 in • p. 243

Gray Catbird
size 9 in • p. 244

Northern Mockingbird
size 10 in • p. 245

Brown Thrasher
size 11 in • p. 246

European Starling
size 8 in • p. 247

American Pipit
size 6 in • p. 248

Bohemian Waxwing
size 8 in • p. 249

Cedar Waxwing
size 7 in • p. 250

Blue-winged Warbler
size 5 in • p. 251

Golden-winged Warbler
size 5 in • p. 252

Tennessee Warbler
size 5 in • p. 253

Orange-crowned Warbler
size 5 in • p. 254

Nashville Warbler
size 5 in • p. 255

Northern Parula
size 5 in • p. 256

Yellow Warbler
size 5 in • p. 257

Chestnut-sided Warbler
size 5 in • p. 258

Magnolia Warbler
size 5 in • p. 259

Cape May Warbler
size 5 in • p. 260

Black-throated Blue Warbler
size 5 in • p. 261

Yellow-rumped Warbler
size 5 in • p. 262

Black-throated Green Warbler
size 5 in • p. 263

Blackburnian Warbler
size 5 in • p. 264

Yellow-throated Warbler
size 5 in • p. 265

Pine Warbler
size 5 in • p. 266

Kirtland's Warbler
size 6 in • p. 267

Prairie Warbler
size 5 in • p. 268

WOOD-WARBLERS & TANAGERS

Palm Warbler
size 5 in • p. 269

Bay-breasted Warbler
size 5 in • p. 270

Blackpoll Warbler
size 5 in • p. 271

Cerulean Warbler
size 5 in • p. 272

Black-and-white Warbler
size 5 in • p. 273

American Redstart
size 5 in • p. 274

Prothonotary Warbler
size 5 in • p. 275

Worm-eating Warbler
size 5 in • p. 276

Ovenbird
size 6 in • p. 277

Northern Waterthrush
size 6 in • p. 278

Louisiana Waterthrush
size 6 in • p. 279

Kentucky Warbler
size 5 in • p. 280

Connecticut Warbler
size 5 in • p. 281

Mourning Warbler
size 5 in • p. 282

Common Yellowthroat
size 5 in • p. 283

Hooded Warbler
size 5 in • p. 284

Wilson's Warbler
size 5 in • p. 285

Canada Warbler
size 5 in • p. 286

Yellow-breasted Chat
size 7 in • p. 287

Summer Tanager
size 7 in • p. 288

Scarlet Tanager
size 7 in • p. 289

Eastern Towhee
size 8 in • p. 290

American Tree Sparrow
size 6 in • p. 291

Chipping Sparrow
size 6 in • p. 292

Clay-colored Sparrow
size 6 in • p. 293

Field Sparrow
size 6 in • p. 294

Vesper Sparrow
size 6 in • p. 295

Savannah Sparrow
size 6 in • p. 296

Grasshopper Sparrow
size 5 in • p. 297

Henslow's Sparrow
size 5 in • p. 298

Le Conte's Sparrow
size 5 in • p. 299

Fox Sparrow
size 7 in • p. 300

Song Sparrow
size 6 in • p. 301

Lincoln's Sparrow
size 5 in • p. 302

Swamp Sparrow
size 6 in • p. 303

White-throated Sparrow
size 7 in • p. 304

Harris's Sparrow
size 7 in • p. 305

White-crowned Sparrow
size 6 in • p. 306

Dark-eyed Junco
size 6 in • p. 307

Lapland Longspur
size 6 in • p. 308

Snow Bunting
size 7 in • p. 309

Northern Cardinal
size 8 in • p. 310

Rose-breasted Grosbeak
size 8 in • p. 311

Indigo Bunting
size 5 in • p. 312

Dickcissel
size 6 in • p. 313

15

Bobolink
size 7 in • p. 314

Red-winged Blackbird
size 9 in • p. 315

Eastern Meadowlark
size 9 in • p. 316

Western Meadowlark
size 9 in • p. 317

Yellow-headed Blackbird
size 9 in • p. 318

Rusty Blackbird
size 9 in • p. 319

Brewer's Blackbird
size 9 in • p. 320

Common Grackle
size 12 in • p. 321

Brown-headed Cowbird
size 7 in • p. 322

Orchard Oriole
size 7 in • p. 323

Baltimore Oriole
size 7 in • p. 324

Pine Grosbeak
size 9 in • p. 325

Purple Finch
size 6 in • p. 326

House Finch
size 6 in • p. 327

Red Crossbill
size 6 in • p. 328

White-winged Crossbill
size 6 in • p. 329

Common Redpoll
size 5 in • p. 330

Hoary Redpoll
size 5 in • p. 331

Pine Siskin
size 5 in • p. 332

American Goldfinch
size 5 in • p. 333

Evening Grosbeak
size 8 in • p. 334

House Sparrow
size 6 in • p. 335

INTRODUCTION

BIRDING IN MICHIGAN

In recent decades, birding has evolved from an eccentric pursuit practiced by a few dedicated individuals to a continent-wide activity that boasts millions of professional and amateur participants. There are many good reasons why birding has become so popular. Many people find it simple and relaxing, while others enjoy the outdoor exercise that it affords. Some see it as a rewarding learning experience, an opportunity to socialize with like-minded people and a way to monitor the health of the local environment. Still others watch birds to reconnect with nature. A visit to any of our region's premier birding locations, such as the Monroe Marsh Preserve, Nayanquing Point Wildlife Area, Muskegon Wastewater System and Whitefish Point Bird Observatory, would doubtless uncover still more reasons why people watch birds.

Osprey

We are truly blessed by the geographical and biological diversity of Michigan. In addition to supporting a wide range of breeding birds and year-round residents, our state hosts a large number of spring and fall migrants that move through our area on the way to their breeding and wintering grounds. In all, 415 bird species have been seen and recorded in Michigan. Out of these, 302 species make regular appearances in the state.

Spring and fall are the busiest birding times. Temperatures are moderate, and a great number of birds are on the move, often heavily populating small patches of habitat before moving on. Male songbirds are easy to identify on spring mornings as they belt out their courtship songs. Throughout much of the year, diurnal birds are most visible in the early morning hours when they are foraging, but during winter they are often more active in the day when milder temperatures prevail. Timing is crucial because summer foliage often conceals birds and cold weather drives many species south of our region for winter.

Christmas bird counts, breeding bird surveys, nest box programs, migration monitoring and birding lectures and workshops all provide a chance for novice, intermediate and expert birdwatchers to interact and share their enthusiasm for the wonder of birds. So, whatever your level, there is ample opportunity for you to get involved!

BIRDING BY HABITAT

Michigan can be separated into three biophysical regions or "bioregions": Southern Deciduous Forest, Transition Forest and Northern Hardwoods–Conifer Forest. Each bioregion is composed of a number of different habitats. Each habitat is a community of plants and animals supported by water and soil infrastructure and regulated by constraints of topography, climate and elevation.

Least Bittern

Simply put, a bird's habitat is the place in which it normally lives. Some birds prefer the open water, some are found in cattail marshes, others like mature coniferous forest, and still others prefer abandoned agricultural fields overgrown with tall grass and shrubs. Knowledge of a bird's habitat increases the chances of identifying the bird correctly. If you are birding in wetlands, you will not be identifying tanagers or towhees; if you are wandering among the leafy trees of the Southern Deciduous Forest, do not expect to meet Boreal Owls or Tundra Swans.

Habitats are just like neighborhoods: if you associate friends with the suburb in which they live, you can just as easily learn to associate specific birds with their preferred habitats. Only in migration, especially during inclement weather, do some birds leave their usual habitat.

Boreal Owl

BIRD LISTING

Many birders list the species they have seen during excursions or at home. You can keep systematic or casual lists in a field notebook with personalized sketches or observations or you may choose not to make lists at all. However, lists may prove rewarding in unexpected ways. For example, after you visit a new area, your list becomes a souvenir of your experiences. It can be interesting to compare the arrival dates and last sightings of seasonal visitors, or to note the first sighting of a new visitor to your area.

BIRDING ACTIVITIES

Birding Groups

We recommend that you join in on such activities as Christmas bird counts, birding festivals and the meetings of your local birding or natural history club. Meeting other people with the same interests can make birding even more pleasurable, and there is always something to be learned when birders of all levels gather. If you are interested in bird conservation and environmental issues, natural history groups and conscientious birding stores can keep you informed about the situation in your area and what you can do to help. Bird hotlines provide up-to-date information on the sightings of rarities, which are often easier to relocate than you might think. The following is a brief list of contacts that will help you get involved:

Cattle Egret

Organizations

Michigan Audubon Society
6011 West St Joseph Hwy
Suite 403, P.O. Box 80527
Lansing, MI 48908-0527
Phone: 517-886-9144
E-mail: mas@michiganaudubon.org
Website: www.michiganaudubon.org

Michigan Nature Association
326 E Grand River Avenue
Williamston, MI 48895
Phone: 517-655-5655
E-mail: michigannature@michigannature.org
Website: www.michigannature.org

Michigan Environmental Council
Suite 2A, 119 Pere Marquette Drive
Lansing, MI 48912
Phone: 517-487-9539
E-mail: mec@voyager.net
Website: www.mecprotects.org

The Wilderness Society
1615 M St, NW
Washington, DC 20036
1-800-THE-WILD (800-843-9453)
E-mail: member@tws.org
Website: www.wilderness.org

Nature Conservancy–Michigan Field Office
101 E Grand River
Lansing, MI 48906
Phone: 517-316-0300
Melissa Soule, Communications
E-mail: msoule@tnc.org

Sierra Club–Michigan Mackinac Chapter
109 E Grand River
Lansing, MI 48906
Phone: 517-484-2372
E-mail: mackinac.chapter@sierraclub.org
Website: michigan.sierraclub.org

Bird Conservation

Michigan abounds with bird life. There are still large areas of wilderness here, including parks, wildlife refuges and public lands. Nevertheless, agriculture, forestry and development for housing threaten viable bird habitat throughout the region. We hope that more people will learn to appreciate nature through birding, and that those people will do their best to protect the natural areas that remain. Many bird enthusiasts support groups such as the Michigan Audubon Society and Michigan Nature Association, which help birds by providing sanctuaries or promoting conservation of the natural world.

Landscaping your own property to provide native plant cover and natural foods for birds is an immediate way to ensure the conservation of bird habitat. The cumulative effects of such urban "nature-scaping" can be significant. If your yard is to become a bird sanctuary, you may want to keep the neighborhood cats out—cats kill millions of birds each year. Check with the local Humane Society for methods of protecting both your feline friends and wild birds. Ultimately, for protection of birds, cats are best kept indoors.

Bird Feeding

Many people set up backyard bird feeders or plant native berry- or seed-producing plants in their garden to attract birds to their yard. The kinds of food available will determine which birds visit your yard. Staff at birding stores can suggest which foods will attract specific birds.

Contrary to popular opinion, birds do not become dependent on feeders, nor do they subsequently forget to forage naturally. Winter is when birds appreciate feeders the most, but it is also difficult to find food in spring before flowers bloom, seeds develop and insects hatch. Birdbaths will also entice birds to your yard at any time of year, and heated birdbaths are particularly appreciated in the colder months. Avoid birdbaths that have exposed metal parts because wet birds can accidentally freeze to them in winter. There are many good books written about feeding birds and landscaping your yard to provide natural foods and nest sites.

Nest Boxes

Another popular way to attract birds is to set out nest boxes, especially for House Wrens, Eastern Bluebirds, Tree Swallows and Purple Martins. Not all birds will use nest boxes: only species that normally use cavities in trees are comfortable in such confined spaces. Larger nest boxes can attract kestrels, owls and cavity-nesting ducks.

Cleaning Feeders and Nest Boxes

Nest boxes and feeding stations must be kept clean to prevent birds from becoming ill or spreading disease. Old nesting material may harbor parasites and their eggs. Once the birds have left for the season, remove the old nesting material and wash and scrub the nest box with detergent or a 10 percent bleach solution (1 part bleach to 9 parts water). You can also scald the nest box with boiling water. Rinse it well and let it dry thoroughly before you remount it.

Eastern Bluebird

Feeding stations should be cleaned monthly. Feeders can become moldy and any seed, fruit or suet that is moldy or spoiled must be removed. Unclean bird feeders can also be contaminated with salmonellosis and possibly other avian diseases. Clean and disinfect feeding stations with a 10 percent bleach solution, scrubbing thoroughly. Rinse the feeder well and allow it to dry completely before refilling it. Discarded seed and feces on the ground under the feeding station should also be removed.

We advise that you wear rubber gloves and a mask when cleaning nest boxes or feeders.

West Nile Virus

Since the West Nile Virus first surfaced in North America in 1999, it has caused fear and misunderstanding—some people have become afraid of contracting the disease from birds, and health departments in some communities have advised residents to eliminate feeding stations and birdbaths. The virus is transmitted to birds and to humans (as well as some other mammals) by mosquitoes that have bitten infected birds. Not all mosquito species can carry the disease and birds do not get the disease from other birds. As well, humans cannot contract the disease from casual contact with infected birds. According to the Centers for Disease Control and Prevention (CDC), only about 20 percent of people who are bitten and become infected will develop any symptoms at all and less than 1 percent will become severely ill.

Because mosquitoes breed in standing water, birdbaths have the potential to become mosquito breeding grounds. Birdbaths should be emptied and the water changed at least weekly. Drippers, circulating pumps, fountains or waterfalls that keep water moving will prevent mosquitoes from laying their eggs in the water.

American Crow

MICHIGAN'S TOP BIRDING SITES

There are hundreds, if not thousands, of good birding areas throughout Michigan. The following areas have been selected to represent a broad range of bird communities and habitats, with an emphasis on accessibility. Common birds are included in these accounts, as well as exciting rarities.

Lake Erie Marshes

Because of their strategic locations on Lake Erie and their miles of walkable dikes for gaining easy access to the shores, the 2000-acre Erie Marsh Preserve and the 4000-acre Pointe Mouillee State Game Area rank at the top of the list for finding waterfowl, marsh birds and shorebirds. At Pointe Mouillee, alternate flooding and draining of many compartments produce a variety of water levels favoring a wide range of shorebirds, herons and waterfowl. Late spring, summer and early fall are the best times to visit these extensive wetlands to view Great, Snowy and Cattle egrets, Yellow-crowned Night-Herons, Wilson's Phalaropes, Red

Great Egret

Phalaropes, Western Sandpipers, Least Bitterns, Hudsonian Godwits, Marbled Godwits, Glaucous, Iceland, Franklin's and Little gulls, Willets, Whimbrels and many more.

Erie Metropark

This park, occupying two miles of Lake Erie shoreline across from southeastern Ontario, offers the best fall hawk-watching in Michigan. In mid to late September you can view more than 50,000 hawks in a single day, mostly Broadwings with some Red-tails and Sharp-shins, plus Peregrine Falcons and Golden Eagles. The greatest variety of raptors pass through in October but volunteers count daily from September 1 to November 30.

The best times for hawk watching are between mid-morning and mid-afternoon, on a day with broken clouds or clear skies and light to moderate winds from a northerly quadrant. Most hawk watching is from the Great Wave Parking Lot. Also, the waterfront is kept open in winter by hot water from the Trenton Power Plant, and this attracts large numbers of Greater Scaups, Redheads, Canvasbacks and some Bald Eagles.

Metro Beach Metropark and St. Clair Flats Wildlife Area

Despite being a heavily developed recreational beach and park, 750-acre Metro Beach Metropark is one of the best birding spots in Michigan. Extensive marshes, open water and woods plus the park's location on a major migration route are the reasons that 260 species have been spotted here. During October, and into winter on Lake St. Clair, you may see tens of thousands of Redheads, Canvasbacks, scaups and Double-crested Cormorants. Least Bitterns and Black-crowned Night-Herons frequent the marshes and wetlands. Other birds include Red-throated Loons, Red-necked Grebes, Tundra Swans, Snowy Owls, Long-tailed Ducks, Ospreys, Water Pipits, Prothonotary Warblers, Northern Parulas, Cerulean Warblers, Lapland Longspurs, Virginia Rails, Yellow-billed Cuckoos and Glaucous, California, Iceland and Franklin's gulls.

Virginia Rail

Saginaw Bay Wildlife Area

A long chain of great birdwatching spots rings Saginaw Bay from Port Crescent State Park to Tawas Point State Park. The flat landscape of diked and ditched farmlands, marshes and lagoons and the open waters of Saginaw Bay make this an unequalled area to observe shorebirds and waterfowl. At the 3400-acre Fish Point State Game Area, you can see a stunning number of waterfowl from your car without disturbing the birds, or you can walk a mile-long dike nature trail. Up to 5000 Tundra Swans stop here in late March, and shorebirds can be numerous in wet springs and in fall. Huge numbers of dabbling ducks are in the fields, flooded areas and on the bay, along with some Snow Geese and White-fronted Geese. Yellow-headed Blackbirds nest here. Rare species include Brants, Cinnamon Teals, Eurasian Wigeons, Long-tailed Ducks, Whimbrels and Ruffs. The Nayanquing Point Wildlife Area on the west side of Saginaw Bay is similar. At the north end of Saginaw Bay is Tawas Point State Park, a 175-acre peninsula. Over 200 species of birds have been tallied here, and spring migration brings songbirds and 31 species of warblers, including a recent nesting of the endangered Piping Plover.

Shiawassee River Wetlands

Twenty-five thousand Canada Geese, some Snow Geese, 50,000 ducks, and 7000 Tundra Swans annually visit the managed wetlands of the 9000-acre Shiawassee National Wildlife Refuge and the adjoining 8490-acre Shiawassee River State Game Area. Diked pools are mechanically flooded to add to the natural habitats, and in extensive cropped lands, a third of the crop area is left standing as food for wildlife. The refuge has been named one of the top 25 birding sites in America. Over 200 bird species have been tallied here, including two pairs of Bald Eagles and a rookery of 200 pairs of Great Blue Herons. Prothonotary Warblers and Brown Creepers nest here. Peak migration times for waterfowl are March to April and September to November. Regularly occurring are Double-crested Cormorants, Great Egrets, Black-crowned Night-Herons, Least Bitterns, American Bitterns, Red-shouldered Hawks, Sandhill Cranes, rails, shorebirds, Short-eared Owls and Snow Buntings. Rare birds may turn up each year, including White Pelicans, Yellow-crowned Night-Herons, Glossy Ibis, Ross's Geese, White-fronted Geese and Black-necked Stilts.

Great Blue Heron

Huron–Clinton Metropolitan Parks and State Recreation Areas

In addition to the Lake Erie marshes, the Detroit River, Lake St. Clair and the St. Clair River, birdwatchers of the Detroit Metropolitan Area have available a ring of superb birding areas in ten natural parks replete with woodlands, marshes, meadows and rivers, all within less than an hour's drive. Outstanding are Stony Creek and Kensington Metroparks and Pinckney and Waterloo State Recreation Areas. Ranging from 3000 to 18,000 acres, these parks are distributed along the Huron and Clinton rivers and across a wide area of morainal hilly areas with scattered lakes. The woodlands host Chestnut-sided, Cerulean and Hooded warblers and Louisiana Waterthrushes. Marshes have nesting Sandhill Cranes, American Bitterns, Least Bitterns, Black Terns, coots and dabbling ducks. The meadows attract Grasshopper Sparrows and Henslow's Sparrows.

Haehnle and Baker Sanctuaries

In southcentral Michigan, the Phyllis Haehnle and Bernard Baker Sanctuaries host the largest fall flocking of the Sandhill Crane in Michigan. In October and November, 3000 to 4000 cranes gather nightly at each sanctuary before migrating to Florida for the winter. These 900-acre marsh preserves have ample viewing opportunities both at the marshes and in surrounding farmland where the cranes feed by day. Owned by the Michigan Audubon Society, these marshes present an unparalleled extravaganza. In summer, these sanctuaries host a wide variety of nesting marsh birds including Sandhill Cranes, American Bitterns, Least Bitterns, Black Terns, American Coots, Marsh Wrens, Swamp Sparrows and Common Yellowthroats.

Sandhill Crane

Southwest Lake Michigan Shore

The waterfronts of New Buffalo, St. Joseph and Benton Harbor offer some of the most spectacular birding in Michigan. The sandy beaches, open water, small marshes and harbors with rocky breakwaters provide the backdrop for an amazing variety of waterfowl, shorebirds, gulls, terns and marsh birds. You can gain access to most of the areas if you use common sense. Tiscornia Park and Silver Beach in St. Joseph and Jean Klock Park in Benton Harbor are the best sites. Among the less common birds are Red-necked, Eared and Western grebes, Red-throated Loons, Harlequin Ducks, all three scoters and six kinds of gulls. Hundreds of Common Loons occur in migration. The sandy beaches produce Piping Plovers, Willets, Buff-breasted, Purple and Western sandpipers, American Avocets, Red Knots and Red Phalaropes. Riverview Park on the St. Joseph River is an excellent wooded area for warblers in migration.

Warren Woods and Russ Forest

Southwest Michigan provides two of the best preserved, nearly virgin examples of the primitive Oak–Hickory Forest, here liberally sprinkled with sugar maple. The Warren Woods Natural Area (a 200-acre Michigan State Park) and the 600-acre Fred Russ Forest (Newton Woods) of Michigan State University offer insights into birds of primitive times. The Galien River in Warren Woods and a small stream at Russ Forest add to the avian variety. Both woodlands are excellent places for birds generally found farther south and, during migration, great places for warblers. In summer, Cerulean and Hooded Warblers, Louisiana Waterthrushes and Acadian Flycatchers are common at Warren Woods, with Yellow-throated Warblers farther downstream on the Galien River. At both forests, summer specialties include Great-crested Flycatchers, Least Flycatchers, Blue-gray Gnatcatchers, Wood Thrushes, Ovenbirds, Red-eyed Vireos, Common Yellowthroats, Yellow Warblers and Blue-winged Warblers. Pileated Woodpeckers and Barred Owls are common. Occasionally sighted are Kentucky Warblers, Carolina Wrens, White-eyed Vireos, Yellow-breasted Chats, Northern Mockingbirds and Orchard Orioles.

Hooded Warbler

Allegan State Game Area

This 50,000-acre tract is one of the largest and most diverse wildland expanses in southern Michigan and provides some of the best and most varied birding in the state. The woodlands have northern and southern elements. The more northern Black-throated Green, Blackburnian, Chestnut-sided, Canada, Northern Parula and Black-and-white warblers nest here, along with the southern Cerulean Warblers, Hooded Warblers, Louisiana Waterthrushes and Northern Mockingbirds. Henslow's, Grasshopper and Savannah sparrows are in the few meadows. The Swan Creek and Ottawa marshes have their quota of herons, egrets, Ospreys and even some Trumpeter Swans and Bald Eagles. The farm unit on the west side holds thousands of Canada Geese and hundreds of Snow Geese each fall and winter along with a few White-fronted and Ross's Geese, and occasional Bald Eagles and Golden Eagles.

Muskegon Area Birding

Few Michigan birding areas have the variety found around Muskegon—Lake Michigan sandy beaches, a river-mouth lake, forested lakeshore dunes, a woody, swampy river valley, and a manmade municipal waste-water pool system. Muskegon Lake, Muskegon State Park, P.J. Hoffmaster State Park, Muskegon State Game Area, and Muskegon County Wastewater System with its two large lagoons attract an unbelievable number and variety of birds. The wastewater lagoons alone host 50,000 waterfowl in the fall, and may hold 30 species of shorebirds in spring and fall migration. Raptors follow—Peregrine Falcons, Gyrfalcons and Golden Eagles. The forested state parks have hordes of migrating warblers following the Lake Michigan shore. The swamp forest of the state game area is home to Marsh Wrens, Prothonotary Warblers, Black-crowned Night-Heron, Yellow-crowned Night-Herons, Pileated Woodpeckers and Barred Owls.

Gyrfalcon

Jack Pine Plains Birding

The Kirtland's Warbler is the most sought-after bird in Michigan, and it nests only in the jack pine plains of the northcentral Lower Peninsula in Crawford, Oscoda, Ogemaw, Kalkaska, Iosco, Roscommon and Montmorency counties. The Kirtland's Warbler is definitely endangered—the annual summer census of the entire population registers barely over 1000 pairs— and a considerable amount of money and effort is being expended to save it from extinction. Entry into nesting areas is strictly prohibited, so the urge to search the jack pines on your own should be strongly resisted. The warbler is easy to find on free warbler tours conducted from May 15 to July 4 at Grayling and Mio. While in the jack pine plains, look for Upland Sandpipers, Clay-colored Sparrows and Lincoln's Sparrows.

Kirtland's Warbler

Houghton Lake Area and Hartwick Pines

The Dead Stream Flooding and the Houghton Lake Flats are two water-fowl areas well worth a visit. West of Houghton Lake, Muskegon River's Reedsburg Dam creates one of the largest managed wetlands in the northern Lower Peninsula. The flooding is teeming with birdlife, and using a non-motorized boat you can explore the veritable wilderness of the 30,000-acre Dead-Stream Swamp. An active Bald Eagle nest is here, five nesting platforms for Ospreys are usually occupied, and Mallards, Blue-winged Teals, goldeneyes and Black Terns also nest here. Closer to Houghton Lake is the Houghton Lake Flats marsh between Hwy 27 and Old Hwy 27. Here are two Osprey nests plus many Black Terns and other marsh birds. Farther north near Grayling is the 9000-acre Hartwick Pines State Park with a 50-acre stand of virgin pine. Here you can see Pileated Woodpeckers, Solitary Vireos, Pine Warblers, Winter Wrens, Red-breasted Nuthatches, Golden-crowned Kinglets and Evening Grosbeaks. Nearby are Cape May Warblers, Golden-winged Warblers and Olive-sided Flycatchers.

Red-breasted Nuthatch

Sleeping Bear Dunes National Lakeshore

This scenic area along 31 miles of Lake Michigan's northwest shore offers a variety of birding opportunities. The Platte Plains at the southern portion of the area is the best place in Michigan to see the endangered Prairie Warbler. Here, mixed pine and oak woods with old beach lines and low swales end in low dunes and Lake Michigan. Prairie Warblers nest in the pines at the edge of the dunes. Other birds here are Olive-sided Flycatchers, Hermit Thrushes and Pine and Magnolia Warblers. Farther north at Otter Creek are pine–oak and beech–maple woods, cedar swamp, marsh and sand dunes, with more Prairie Warblers along the dunes. Also look for Alder Flycatchers and Mourning, Chestnut-sided, Blackburnian and Black-throated Blue warblers. On the Old Grade Nature Trail in wetland woods are Winter Wrens, Warbling Vireos, Black-and-white Warblers and Northern Waterthrushes. In old fields and marshes along Kelderhouse Road are Grasshopper Sparrows, Upland Sandpipers, Bluebirds, Soras and Virginia Rails. In the mixed pines of Good Harbor Bay at the north end are nesting Olive-sided Flycatchers, Red-breasted Nuthatches, Purple Finches and Pine, Yellow-rumped and Prairie warblers.

Whitefish Point Bird Observatory

Spring migration at Whitefish Point at the east end of the Upper Peninsula is possibly more exciting than anywhere else in Michigan. Common birds are seen in large numbers and accidental birds turn up with remarkable regularity. The "Point" is a peninsula that extends into Lake Superior to within a few miles of Canada. Waterfowl pass close to the Point with a few passing over. Hawks circle before crossing over to Canada or going back around Whitefish Bay to avoid the overwater route. As many as 25,000 hawks pass through the Point each spring. Most are Sharpshins, Broadwings and Red-tails, but Northern Goshawks, Golden Eagles and Peregrine Falcons occur regularly. Red-throated Loons are frequent and Common Loons pass by in the thousands. Over 100 owls are banded each spring, including the irruptive Boreal Owl from Canada. Northern birds recorded in numbers here are Boreal Chickadees, Bohemian Waxwings, Pine Grosbeaks, crossbills, redpolls and Evening Grosbeaks. Fall migration is equally exciting—most notable is an early fall movement of 10,000 Red-necked Grebes.

Seney National Wildlife Refuge

This 95,000-acre refuge is now recognized as one of the best birding spots in the Upper Peninsula. It encompasses 7000 acres of managed wetlands (diked pools), a 9500-acre bog and 25,000 acres of wilderness, affording a wide variety of birdwatching. Birding is done from two nature trails or from a 7-mile-long, self-guided auto tour. The Marshland Wildlife Drive has three observation decks and is constructed on the tops of water-control dikes so wetland wildlife can be seen at close range on both sides of the road. Commonly viewed are Canada Geese, Sandhill Cranes, Trumpeter Swans, Ospreys, Bald Eagles, Merlins and Pileated Woodpeckers. Persistent searching, by sight or by ear, will locate the elusive Yellow Rail. Major accomplishments here were the re-establishing of the Canada Goose and Trumpeter Swan as breeding species in the Upper Peninsula. Many other waterfowl nest here—Mallards, Blue-winged Teals, Green-winged Teals, Common Mergansers, Red-breasted Mergansers, Black Ducks and Wood Ducks.

Pileated Woodpecker

Sylvania Wilderness and Recreation Area

This 21,000-acre area of pristine wilderness in the Ottawa National Forest in the far western Upper Peninsula is unequalled in mainland Michigan. Countless clear lakes and vast stands of virgin northern hardwoods offer top birding opportunities. Sylvania is a roadless park except for the Clark Lake Access area—most birding is done by canoe and overnight camping. Bald Eagles, Ospreys and Common Loons are hallmarks of Sylvania. Barred Owls and Pileated Woodpeckers are commonly seen and heard. Other bird specialties include northern nesting warblers and flycatchers, crossbills, Black-backed Woodpeckers, Gray Jays, Boreal Chickadees and Goshawks.

Porcupine Mountains Wilderness State Park

The Porcupine Mountains' 60,000 acres of untamed rivers, spectacular waterfalls, rapids, gorges, crystal clear lakes and rugged Lake Superior coastline presents the ultimate in wilderness birding in mainland Michigan. Porcupine Mountains Wilderness State Park, a wilderness gem purchased from a lumbering company in 1948, offers most kinds of native wildlife. This is a roadless area so birding must be done on perimeter day-long hikes or from rental cabins in the interior. Northern breeding warblers, Pileated Woodpeckers, Common Ravens and Barred Owls are specialties, with Pine Grosbeaks, crossbills and redpolls in winter when birding must be done on snowshoes or snowmobiles.

Pine Grosbeak

Keweenaw Peninsula–Brockway Mountain Drive

The heavily forested Keweenaw Peninsula, which is the northernmost portion of the Michigan mainland, reaches almost halfway across Lake Superior toward Canada. The peninsula includes the primitive Estivant Pines Sanctuary of virgin white pines and the Brockway Mountain Drive—the highest American road between the Appalachians and the Rocky Mountains. All this adds up to unequaled wilderness birding and rarely equaled hawkwatching. The Brockway Mountain Drive has frequent pullouts for observation so you can safely watch the spring hawk migration from early May to early June, a sight that equals the migration at Whitefish Point. Tallies of 1000 hawks daily are frequent, with Broadwings, Sharpshins and Roughlegs predominating. Redtails, Goshawks, Turkey Vultures and Bald Eagles are regular, and Peregrine Falcons, Merlins and Golden Eagles are frequent. In the extensive boreal forest are Yellow-bellied Flycatchers, Olive-sided Flycatchers, a good variety of northern warblers, crossbills, Pileated Woodpeckers, Northern Goshawks and Saw-whet Owls.

Isle Royale National Park

The 210-square-mile Isle Royale National Park is a pristine, roadless, island wilderness that at 45 miles long and 9 miles wide is the largest island in Lake Superior. Only 15 miles from Canada, its birdlife is characteristic of the Canadian boreal forest, though it is quite similar to the birdlife of the Keweenaw Peninsula. Birding must be done on foot on an excellent trail system. Room and meal accommodations are available on the island, but camping is necessary for remote area birding. Isle Royale may be reached only in summer, by boat from Houghton and Copper Harbor in Michigan and from Grand Portage, Minnesota, or by seaplane from Houghton, Michigan. The island is not accessible in winter. Among the most interesting summer birds are Northern Goshawks, Bald Eagles, Ospreys, Merlins, Saw-whet Owls, Black-backed Woodpeckers, Gray Jays, Boreal Chickadees, Pine Grosbeaks, crossbills, Yellow-bellied Flycatchers and Yellow-bellied Sapsuckers.

Boreal Chickadee

MICHIGAN'S TOP 100 BIRDING SITES

SOUTHERN DECIDUOUS FOREST

1. Erie Marsh Preserve
2. Sterling SP
3. Pointe Mouillee SGA
4. Lake Erie Metropark
5. Dearborn Environmental Study Area
6. Metrobeach Metropark
7. St. Clair Flats WA
8. St. Clair River
9. Port Huron SGA
10. Stony Creek Metropark
11. Seven Ponds Nature Center
12. For-Mar Nature Center
13. Holly SRA
14. Indian Springs Metropark
15. Highland SRA
16. Kensington Metropark
17. Pinckney SRA
18. Waterloo SRA and Haehnle Sanctuary
19. Thorn Lake
20. Lost Nation SGA
21. Fenner Nature Center
22. Rose Lake WA
23. Sleepy Hollow SP
24. Baker Sanctuary
25. Fort Custer SRA
26. Yankee Springs SRA and Barry County SGA
27. Kalamazoo Nature Center
28. Russ Forest (Newton's Woods)
29. Warren Woods Natural Area
30. New Buffalo Lakefront
31. Warren Dunes and Grand Mere State Parks
32. St. Joseph Lakefront
33. Sarett Nature Center
34. Saugatuck SP
35. Allegan SGA
36. Maple River SGA
37. Gratiot–Saginaw SGA
38. Shiawassee Flats NWR and SGA
39. Tobico Marsh WA
40. Fish Point SGA
41. Tuscola SGA

TRANSITION FOREST

42. Minden City SGA
43. Port Crescent SP
44. Sleeper SP
45. Nayanquing Point WA
46. Chippewa Nature Center
47. Big Rapids—Muskegon River
48. Rogue River SGA
49. Muskegon Wastewater System
50. P.J. Hoffmaster SP
51. Muskegon SP
52. Ludington SP
53. Nordhouse Dunes—Michigan Recreation Area
54. East Lake Marsh
55. Arcadia Lake Marsh
56. Grass Lake Flooding
57. Sleeping Bear Dunes National Lakeshore
58. Traverse City Nature Education Reserve
59. Skegemog Lake WA
60. Jordan River Valley
61. Leelanau SP
62. Fisherman's Island SP

NORTHERN HARDWOOD–CONIFER FOREST

63. Hartwick Pines SP
64. Kirtland Warbler Tours
65. Grass Lake WA
66. Dead Stream Flooding
67. Gladwin Field Trial Area
68. Rifle River SRA
69. Tawas Point SP
70. Lovell Forest
71. Sturgeon Point SP Vicinity
72. Whitefish Bay Area
73. Peninsula Point
74. Colonial Point Forest
75. Wilderness SP
76. Sault Ste. Marie—St. Mary's River
77. Betchler Lakes
78. Hulbert Corner Bog
79. Whitefish Point Bird Observatory

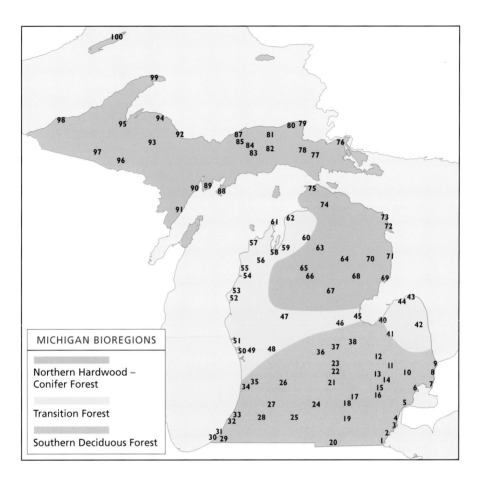

MICHIGAN BIOREGIONS

Northern Hardwood –
Conifer Forest

Transition Forest

Southern Deciduous Forest

80. Tahquamenon Falls SP
81. Sleeper Lake Bog
82. Tahquamenon Bog
83. Seney NWR
84. Adams Trail—Driggs River Bog
85. Adams Trail—Log Lake Bog
86. Grand Marais Harbor area
87. Pictured Rocks National Lakeshore
88. Garden Peninsula
89. Little Bay De Noc
90. Portage Point Marsh
91. J.W. Wells SP
92. Marquette Harbor—Peninsula Park
93. Van Riper SP

94. Yellow Dog Plains
95. Baraga Jack Pine Plains
96. Ottawa Recreation Area
97. Sylvania Recreation Area
98. Porcupine Mountains
    Wilderness SP
99. Brockway Mountain Drive
100. Isle Royale NP

NP = National Park
NWR = National Wildlife Refuge
SGA = State Game Area
SP = State Park
SRA = State Recreation Area
WA = Wildlife Area

ABOUT THE SPECIES ACCOUNTS

This book gives detailed accounts of the 302 species of birds that are listed as regular by the *Michigan Bird Records Committee;* these species can be expected on an annual basis. Thirty-two occasional species and species of special note are briefly mentioned in an illustrated appendix. Michigan birders can expect to see small numbers of these species every few years, brought here either because of anticipated range expansion, migration or well-documented wandering tendencies. The order of the birds and their common and scientific names follow the American Ornithologists' Union's *Check-list of North American Birds* (7th edition, July 1998 and *The Forty-third Supplement 2002*).

As well as discussing the identifying features of a bird, each species account also attempts to bring a bird to life by describing its various character traits. Personifying a bird helps us to relate to it on a personal level. However, the characterizations presented in this book are based on the human experience and most likely fall short of truly defining the way birds perceive the world. The characterizations should not be mistaken for scientific propositions. Nonetheless, we hope that a lively, engaging text will communicate our scientific knowledge as smoothly and effectively as possible.

One of the challenges of birding is that many species look different in spring and summer than they do in fall and winter. Many birds have breeding and nonbreeding plumages, and immature birds often look different from their parents. This book does not try to describe or illustrate all the different plumages of a species; instead, it focuses on the forms that are most likely to be seen in our area.

ID: It is difficult to describe the features of a bird without being able to visualize it, so this section is best used in combination with the illustrations. Where appropriate, the description is subdivided to highlight the differences between male and female birds, breeding and nonbreeding birds and immature and adult birds. The descriptions use as few technical terms as possible, and favor easily understood language. Birds may not have "jaw lines," "eyebrows" or "chins," but these, and other scientifically inaccurate terms are easily understood by all readers. Some of the most common features of birds are pointed out in the Glossary illustration (p. 346).

Size: The size measurement, the average length of the bird's body from bill to tail, is an approximate measurement of the bird as it is seen in nature. The size of larger birds is often given as a range, because there is variation among individuals. In addition, wingspan (from wing tip to wing tip) is given for all birds in the book. Please note that birds with long tails often have large measurements that do not necessarily reflect "body" size.

Status: A general comment, such as "common," "uncommon" or "rare" is usually sufficient to describe the relative abundance of a species. Wherever possible, we have also indicated status at different times of the year. Situations are bound to vary somewhat since migratory pulses, seasonal changes and centers of activity tend to concentrate or disperse birds.

Habitat: The habitats we have listed describe where each species is most commonly found. In most cases, it is a generalized description, but if a bird is restricted to a specific habitat, the habitat is described precisely. Because of the freedom flight gives them, birds can turn up in almost any type of habitat. However, they will usually be found in environments that provide the specific food, water, cover, and in some cases, nesting habitat, they need to survive.

Nesting: The reproductive strategies used by different bird species vary: in each species account, nest location and structure, clutch size, incubation period and parental duties are discussed. Remember that birding ethics discourage the disturbance of active bird nests. If you disturb a nest, you may drive off the parents during a critical period or expose defenseless young to predators. The nesting behavior of birds that do not nest in our region is not described.

Feeding: Birds spend a great deal of time foraging for food. If you know what a bird eats and where the food is found, you will have a good chance of finding the bird you are looking for. Birds are frequently encountered while they are foraging; we hope that our description of their feeding styles and diets provides valuable identifying characteristics, as well as interesting dietary facts.

Voice: You will hear many birds, particularly songbirds, which may remain hidden from view. Memorable paraphrases of distinctive sounds will aid you in identifying a species. These paraphrases only loosely resemble the call, song or sound produced by the bird. Should one of our paraphrases not work for you, feel free to make up your own—the creative exercise will reinforce your memory of the bird's vocalizations.

Similar Species: Easily confused species are discussed briefly. If you concentrate on the most relevant field marks, the subtle differences between species can be reduced to easily identifiable traits. You might find it useful to consult this section when finalizing your identification; knowing the most relevant field marks will speed up the identification process. Even experienced birders can mistake one species for another.

Selected Sites: If you are looking for a particular bird, you will have more luck in some locations than in others, even within the range shown on the range map. There are many excellent sites in Michigan; unfortunately we cannot list them all. We have listed places that, besides providing a good chance of seeing a species, are easily accessible. As a result, many nature centers, state game areas, national lakeshores and state and national parks are mentioned.

Range Maps: The range map for each species represents the overall range of the species in an average year. Most birds will confine their annual movements to this range, although each year some birds wander beyond their traditional boundaries. These maps do not show differences in abundance within the range—areas of a range with good habitat will support a denser population than areas with poorer habitat. These maps also cannot show small pockets within the range where the species may actually be absent, or how the range may change from year to year. Unlike most other field guides, we have attempted to show migratory pathways—areas of the region where birds may appear while en route to nesting or winter habitat. Many of these migratory routes are "best guesses," which will no doubt be refined as new discoveries are made. The representations of the pathways do not distinguish high-use migration corridors from areas that are seldom used. Although most migratory birds will migrate over the Great Lakes, usually at high altitude, their migration patterns over these large expanses of water are not well known.

Range Map Symbols

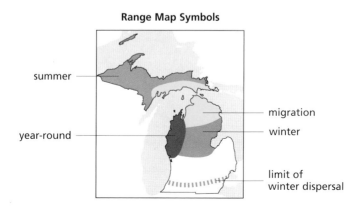

summer

migration

year-round

winter

limit of
winter dispersal

NONPASSERINES

Nonpasserine birds represent 17 of the 18 orders of birds found in Michigan, but only about 55 percent of the species in our region. They are grouped together and called "nonpasserines" because, with few exceptions, they are easily distinguished from the "passerines," or "perching birds," which make up the 18th order. Being from 17 different orders, however, means that our nonpasserines vary considerably in their appearance and habits—they include everything from the 5-foot-tall Great Blue Heron to the 3 ¾-inch-long Rufous Hummingbird.

Generally speaking, nonpasserines do not "sing." Instead, their vocalizations are referred to as "calls." There are also other morphological differences. For example, the muscles and tendons in the legs of passerines are adapted to grip a perch, and the toes of passerines are never webbed. Many non-passerines are large, so they are among our most notable birds. Waterfowl, raptors, gulls, shorebirds and woodpeckers are easily identified by most people. Some of the smaller non-passerines, such as doves, swifts and hummingbirds, are frequently thought of as passerines by novice birders, and can cause those beginners some identification problems. With a little practice, however, they will become recognizable as nonpasserines. By learning to separate the nonpasserines from the passerines at a glance, birders effectively reduce by half the number of possible species for an unidentified bird.

Eastern Screech-Owl

Broad-winged Hawk

RED-THROATED LOON
Gavia stellata

The Red-throated Loon typically swims low in the water with its bill held high, as if trying to accentuate its maroon throat in breeding plumage. Our smallest loon, the Red-throat is able to leap up from the water directly into flight, stand upright on land and even take off from land. No other loon has these abilities—other loons require 330 feet or more of runway on open water to gain flight. • Your best chance of seeing a Red-throated Loon is in spring and fall at Whitefish Point, where up to 300 birds may pass through. These loons breed in the Arctic and winter along the Atlantic and Pacific coasts and occasionally on the Great Lakes. • Native Americans have long considered Red-throated Loons as reliable meteorologists— these birds often become very noisy before the onset of foul weather, possibly sensing changes in barometric pressure. • The scientific name *stellata* refers to the starlike, white speckles on this bird's back in its nonbreeding plumage.

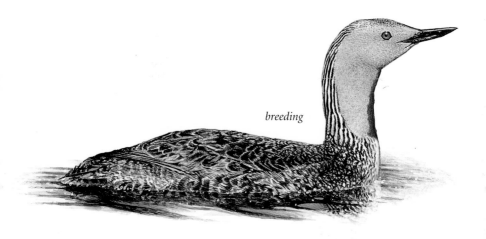

breeding

ID: slim bill is held upward. *Breeding:* red throat; gray face and neck; black and white stripes from nape to back of head; plain, brownish back. *Nonbreeding:* white-speckled back; white face; dark gray on crown and back of head. *In flight:* hunched back; legs trail behind tail; rapid wingbeats.
Size: *L* 23–27 in; *W* 3½ ft.
Status: rare migrant and winter resident.
Habitat: large freshwater lakes.
Nesting: does not nest in Michigan.

Feeding: dives deeply and captures small fish; occasionally eats aquatic insects and amphibians; may eat aquatic vegetation in early spring.
Voice: Mallard-like *kwuk-kwuk-kwuk-kwuk* in flight; distraction call is a loud *gayorwork*.
Similar Species: *Common Loon* (p. 34): larger; heavier bill; lacks white speckling on back in nonbreeding plumage. *Pacific Loon* (p. 336): larger; purple throat and white speckling on back in breeding plumage; all-dark back in nonbreeding plumage.
Selected Sites: Whitefish Point; Tawas Point SP; Muskegon SP; New Buffalo lakeshore; Grand Traverse Bay.

COMMON LOON

Gavia immer

The quavering wail of the Common Loon pierces the stillness of quiet nights, its haunting call alerting cottagers that summer has begun. Loons float very low on the water, disappearing behind swells, then reappearing like ethereal guardians of the lakes. • Common Loons are well adapted to their aquatic lifestyle. These divers have nearly solid bones that make them less buoyant (most birds have hollow bones), and their feet are placed well back on their bodies for underwater propulsion. Small bass, perch, sunfish, pike and whitefish are all fair game for these excellent underwater hunters. On land, however, their rear-placed legs make walking seem difficult, and their heavy bodies and small wing size means they require a lengthy sprint over water before taking off. • It is thought that "loon" is derived from the Scandinavian word *lom*, meaning "clumsy person," in reference to this bird's clumsiness on land. • The Common Loon is no longer common in Michigan—it is listed as a threatened native species in our area.

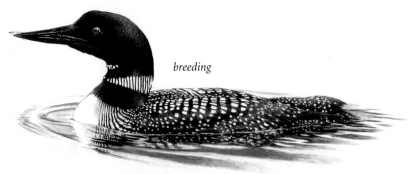

breeding

ID: *Breeding:* green black head; stout, thick, black bill; white "necklace"; white breast and underparts; black-and-white "checkerboard" upperparts; red eyes. *Nonbreeding:* much duller plumage; sandy brown back; light underparts. *In flight:* long wings beat constantly; hunchbacked appearance; legs trail behind tail.

Size: *L* 28–35 in; *W* 4–5 ft.

Status: threatened; common migrant; uncommon breeder; rare winter resident.

Habitat: *Breeding:* large lakes, often with islands that provide undisturbed shorelines for nesting. *Winter:* lakes with open water.

Nesting: on a muskrat lodge, small island or projecting shoreline; always very near water; nest mound is built from aquatic vegetation; pair incubates 1–3 dark-spotted, olive eggs for 24–31 days; pair shares all parental duties, including nest building, egg incubation and rearing of the young.

Feeding: pursues small fish underwater to depths of 180 ft; occasionally eats large, aquatic invertebrates and larval and adult amphibians.

Voice: alarm call is a quavering tremolo, often called "loon laughter"; contact call is a long but simple wailing note *where aaare you?*; breeding notes are soft, short hoots; male territorial call is an undulating, complex yodel.

Similar Species: *Red-throated Loon* (p. 33): smaller; slender bill; red throat in breeding plumage; sharply defined white face and white-spotted back in nonbreeding plumage. *Pacific Loon* (p. 336): smaller; dusty gray head often looks silver; dark "cap" extends down over eye and is lighter than back in nonbreeding plumage.

Selected Sites: Whitefish Point; Marquette Harbor; Presque Isle; Tawas Point SP; Saginaw Bay; Lake St. Clair; Muskegon SP; Houghton L.; Great Lakes shores.

PIED-BILLED GREBE

Podilymbus podiceps

The odd, exuberant chortle of the Pied-billed Grebe fits right in with the boisterous cacophony of this region's wetland communities. Heard more frequently than seen, the Pied-billed Grebe is the smallest, shyest and least colorful of our grebes. • The Pied-billed Grebe is an extremely wary bird and is far more common than encounters would lead you to believe. It tends to swim inconspicuously in shallow waters of quiet bays and rivers, only occasionally voicing its strange chuckle or whinny. • These grebes build their floating nests among sparse vegetation, so that they can see predators approaching from far away. When frightened by an intruder, they cover their eggs and slide underwater, leaving a nest that looks like nothing more than a mat of debris. A Pied-billed Grebe can slowly submerge up to its head, so that only its nostrils and eyes remain above the water. • The scientific name *podiceps*, which means "rump foot," refers to the way the bird's feet are located toward the back of its body. In flight, the feet extend beyond the tail and help the bird to steer.

breeding

ID: *Breeding:* all-brown body; black ring on pale bill; laterally compressed "chicken bill"; black throat; very short tail; white undertail coverts; pale belly; pale eye ring. *Nonbreeding:* yellow eye ring; yellow bill lacks black ring; white "chin" and throat; brownish crown.

Size: *L* 12–15 in; *W* 16 in.

Status: fairly common migrant; uncommon local breeder; rare winter resident.

Habitat: ponds, marshes and backwaters with sparse emergent vegetation.

Nesting: among sparse vegetation in sheltered bays, ponds and marshes; floating platform nest, made of wet and decaying plants, is anchored to or placed among emergent vegetation; pair incubates 4–5 white to buff eggs for about 23 days and raises the striped young together.

Feeding: makes shallow dives and gleans the water's surface for aquatic invertebrates, small fish and adult and larval amphibians; occasionally eats aquatic plants.

Voice: loud, whooping call begins quickly, then slows down: *kuk-kuk-kuk cow cow cow cowp cowp cowp.*

Similar Species: *Eared Grebe* (p. 38): red eyes; black-and-white head; golden "ear" tufts and chestnut flanks in breeding plumage; seldom seen in summer. *Horned Grebe* (p. 36): seldom seen in summer; red eyes; black-and-white head; golden "ear" tufts and red neck in breeding plumage. *American Coot* (p. 108): all-black body; pale bill extends onto forehead.

Selected Sites: Erie Marsh Preserve; St. Clair Flats WA; Fish Point SGA; Muskegon Wastewater System; Thorn L.; Allegan SGA; Maple River SGA.

HORNED GREBE

Podiceps auritus

A trip to the Great Lakes will provide the best opportunity for observing Horned Grebes in migration and in winter, although these birds can also be seen on large inland lakes. • This compact little bird rides high in the water and has a rounded head outline with slightly puffed "cheeks." The neck is somewhat curved or thrust forward when swimming. • The Horned Grebe flies more readily than most grebes, with a strong, direct, loonlike flight that reveals a large white patch at the rear of the inner wing. • Grebes catch their food in long dives that may last up to three minutes and they can travel as far as 400 feet under water. The bird starts the dive with a pronounced upward and forward leap, and propels itself under water solely with its feet. • Unlike the fully webbed front toes of most swimming birds, grebe toes are individually webbed, or "lobed"—the three forward-facing toes have individual flanges that are not connected to the other toes. • This bird's common name and its scientific name, *auritus* (eared), refer to the golden feather tufts, or "horns," that these grebes acquire in breeding plumage.

breeding

ID: *Breeding:* rufous neck and flanks; black head; golden "ear" tufts ("horns"); black back; white underparts; red eyes; flat crown. *Nonbreeding:* lacks "ear" tufts; black upperparts; white "cheek," foreneck and underparts. *In flight:* wings beat constantly; hunchbacked appearance; legs trail behind tail.
Size: *L* 12–15 in; *W* 18 in.
Status: locally common migrant from mid-March to early June and from early August to November; rare in winter.
Habitat: Great Lakes; wetlands and large lakes.

Nesting: does not nest in Michigan.
Feeding: makes shallow dives and gleans the water's surface for aquatic insects, crustaceans, mollusks, small fish and adult and larval amphibians.
Voice: silent in migration.
Similar Species: *Eared Grebe* (p. 38): black neck in breeding plumage; black "cheek" and darker neck in nonbreeding plumage. *Pied-billed Grebe* (p. 35): thicker, stubbier bill; mostly brown body. *Red-necked Grebe* (p. 37): larger; dark eyes; lacks "ear" tufts; white "cheek" in breeding plumage.
Selected Sites: Whitefish Point; Tawas Point SP; Lake St. Clair; St. Clair R.; Pointe Mouillee SGA; Thorn L.; Allegan SGA; Erie Marsh Preserve; Grand Traverse Bay.

RED-NECKED GREBE

Podiceps grisegena

The Red-necked Grebe, a regular fall migrant in Michigan, rarely summers here. Rare breeders in Michigan, Red-necks are usually quiet and retiring when away from their breeding grounds, so they may be easily overlooked here. They can be seen reliably at Whitefish Point during fall migration, as early as late July. • This short-bodied bird has a long, slim neck and a triangular head, which is carried erect. When on the wing it resembles a miniature loon—in flight it stretches its neck and legs to their full extent—but with conspicuous white areas on the leading and rear edges of the inner wing. • The Red-necked Grebe is generally shy. Ordinarily it rides high in the water with its head nodding back and forth as it swims. To escape attention, it can compress its feathers, reducing its buoyancy, and sink out of sight before it is noticed. • The scientific name *grisegena* means "gray cheek"—a distinctive field mark of this bird in winter plumage.

breeding

ID: *Breeding:* rusty neck; whitish "cheek"; black crown; straight, heavy bill is dark above and yellow underneath; black upperparts; light underparts; dark eyes. *Nonbreeding:* grayish white foreneck, "chin" and "cheek."
Size: *L* 17–22 in; *W* 24 in.
Status: locally common migrant from late March to May and from late July to November; rare winter resident; very rare breeder.
Habitat: open, deep lakes.
Nesting: floating platform nest of aquatic vegetation is anchored to submerged plants; pair incubates 4–5 white eggs for 20–23 days; eggs often become stained by wet vegetation.

Feeding: dives and gleans the water's surface for small fish, aquatic invertebrates and amphibians.
Voice: silent in migration.
Similar Species: *Horned Grebe* (p. 36): smaller; dark "cheek" and golden "horns" in breeding plumage; red eyes, all-dark bill and bright white "cheek" in nonbreeding plumage. *Eared Grebe* (p. 38): smaller; black neck in breeding plumage; black "cheek" in nonbreeding plumage. *Pied-billed Grebe* (p. 35): smaller; thicker, stubbier bill; mostly brown body. *Western Grebe* (p. 336): red eyes; black-and-white neck in breeding plumage. *Ducks* (pp. 57–81): all lack the combination of white "cheek" and red neck.
Selected Sites: Whitefish Point; Muskegon Wastewater System; New Buffalo and St. Joseph waterfronts.

EARED GREBE

Podiceps nigricollis

This little grebe is typically found farther west, but each year small numbers make their way into Michigan. The Eared Grebe also inhabits parts of Europe, Asia, Central Africa and South America, making it the most abundant grebe not only in North America, but also the world. • Eared Grebes undergo cyclical periods of atrophy and hypertrophy throughout the year, meaning that their internal organs and pectoral muscles shrink or swell, depending on whether or not the birds need to migrate. This strategy leaves Eared Grebes flightless for a longer period—nine to ten months per year—than any other flying bird in the world. • Like other grebes, the Eared Grebe eats feathers. The feathers often pack the digestive tract, and it is thought that they protect the stomach lining and intestines from sharp fish bones or parasites, or perhaps slow the passage of food, allowing more time for complete digestion. • The scientific name *nigricollis* means "black neck," a characteristic of this bird's breeding plumage.

breeding

ID: *Breeding:* black neck, "cheek," forehead and back; red flanks; fanned-out, golden "ear" tufts; white underparts; thin, straight bill; red eyes; slightly raised crown. *Nonbreeding:* dark "cheek" and upperparts; light underparts; dusky upper foreneck and flanks. *In flight:* wings beat constantly; hunchbacked appearance; legs trail behind tail.

Size: *L* 11½–14 in; *W* 16 in.

Status: very rare migrant from April to November.

Habitat: wetlands, larger lakes, sewage disposal ponds.

Nesting: does not nest in Michigan.

Feeding: makes shallow dives and gleans the water's surface for aquatic insects, crustaceans, mollusks, small fish and larval and adult amphibians.

Voice: usually quiet outside the breeding season.

Similar Species: *Horned Grebe* (p. 36): rufous neck in breeding plumage; white "cheek" in nonbreeding plumage. *Pied-billed Grebe* (p. 35): thicker, stubbier bill; mostly brown body. *Red-necked Grebe* (p. 37): larger overall; longer bill; red neck and whitish "cheek" in breeding plumage; dusky white "cheek" in nonbreeding plumage.

Selected Sites: Muskegon Wastewater System.

AMERICAN WHITE PELICAN
Pelecanus erythrorhynchos

Pelicans are a majestic wetland presence with a wingspan only a foot shy of the height of a basketball hoop. Their porous, bucketlike bills are dramatically adapted for feeding. Groups of foraging pelicans deliberately herd fish into schools, then dip their bills and scoop up the prey. As the pelican lifts its bill from the water, the fish are held within its flexible pouch while the water drains out. In a single scoop, a pelican can hold over 3 gallons of water and fish, which is about two to three times as much as its stomach can hold. This impressive feat confirms Dixon Lanier Merritt's quotation: "A wonderful bird is a pelican, His bill will hold more than his belican!" • American White Pelicans eat about 4 pounds of fish per day, but because they prefer nongame fish they do not pose a threat to the potential catches of fishermen. All other large, white birds with black wing tips fly with their necks extended—the American White Pelican is the only one to fly with its neck pulled back toward its wings.

nonbreeding

ID: very large, stocky, white bird; long, orange bill and throat pouch; black primary and secondary wing feathers; short tail; naked orange skin patch around eye. *Breeding:* small, keeled plate develops on upper mandible; pale yellow crest on back of head. *Nonbreeding* and *immature:* white plumage is tinged with brown. **Size:** *L* 4½–6 ft; *W* 9 ft.
Status: rare spring migrant; summer and fall post-breeding wanderer.
Habitat: large lakes or rivers.
Nesting: does not nest in Michigan.
Feeding: surface dips for small fish and amphibians; small groups of pelicans often feed cooperatively by herding fish into large concentrations.
Voice: generally quiet; adults rarely issue piglike grunts.
Similar Species: no other large, white bird has a long bill with a pouch.
Selected Sites: Pointe Mouillee SGA; Nayanquing Point WA; Whitefish Point; Muskegon Wastewater System.

DOUBLE-CRESTED CORMORANT

Phalacrocorax auritus

The Double-crested Cormorant's beauty can take longer to appreciate than that of other birds. This slick-feathered bird often appears disheveled, and extra-close encounters typically reveal the foul stench of fish oil. Nevertheless, its mastery of the aquatic environment is virtually unsurpassed. The Double-crested Cormorant lacks oil glands, and this lack of waterproofing helps it during underwater dives by decreasing the bird's buoyancy. Instead of floating upon the water after a bout of diving, the Double-crested Cormorant is often seen perched in a tree with its wings partially spread in an attempt to dry its feathers. The cormorant's long, rudderlike tail, excellent underwater vision and sealed nostrils also contribute to the success of its aquatic lifestyle. Once believed to compete with fishermen for the same fish, it is now known that cormorants take undesirables such as alewives, sticklebacks and sculpins.

breeding

ID: all-black body; long, crooked neck; thin bill, hooked at tip; blue eyes. *Breeding:* throat pouch becomes intense orange yellow; fine, black plumes trail from "eyebrows." *Immature:* brown upperparts; buff throat and breast; yellowish throat patch. *In flight:* rapid wingbeats; kinked neck.

Size: *L* 26–32 in; *W* 4½ ft.

Status: uncommon migrant from April to November; locally common breeder; rare winter resident.

Habitat: large lakes and large, meandering rivers; Great Lakes.

Nesting: colonial; on the ground on a low-lying island, often with terns and gulls, or precariously high in a tree; nest platform is made of sticks, aquatic vegetation and guano; pair incubates 3–6 bluish white eggs for 25–33 days; young are fed by regurgitation.

Feeding: long underwater dives to depths of 30 ft or more when after small schooling fish or, rarely, amphibians and invertebrates; uses its bill to grasp prey and bring it to the surface.

Voice: generally quiet; may issue piglike grunts or croaks, especially near nesting colonies.

Similar Species: *Canada Goose* (p. 53): white "cheek"; brown overall.

Selected Sites: Whitefish Point; offshore islands in the northern parts of L. Michigan and L. Huron; Dead Stream Flooding; Charity Islands in Saginaw Bay; Pointe Mouillee SGA; Erie Marsh Preserve; Muskegon Wastewater System.

AMERICAN BITTERN

Botaurus lentiginosus

If you are lucky enough to see an American Bittern, you might think its girth would make it difficult for this bird to blend in with the wetland reeds. On the contrary, the bittern depends on its camouflage to both hide and hunt. The American Bittern is common around productive marsh habitat, but it is uncommon or even rare to actually see one. Late mornings and early afternoons are the best times to try to catch a glimpse of this secretive bird.

• At the approach of an intruder, a bittern's first reaction is to freeze with its bill pointed skyward—its vertically streaked, brown plumage blends perfectly with the surroundings. An American Bittern will always face an intruder, moving ever so slowly to keep its camouflaged breast toward danger. In most cases, intruders simply pass by without ever noticing the bird. This defensive reaction can sometimes result in an unfortunate comical turn for the bittern—it will try to mimic a reed even in an entirely open field. Although its camouflage fools potential predators, its cryptic plumage is most likely an adaptation to reduce the bird's visibility to prey while hunting. It prefers to hunt in dim light situations, at dawn or dusk, when its camouflage is most effective.

ID: brown upperparts; brown streaking from "chin" through breast; straight, stout bill; yellow legs and feet; black outer wings; black streaks from bill down neck to shoulder; short tail.

Size: *L* 23–27 in; *W* 3½ ft.

Status: special concern; uncommon migrant from April to November; rare to fairly common breeder; rare winter resident.

Habitat: marshes, wetlands and lake edges with tall, dense grass, sedges, bulrushes and cattails.

Nesting: singly; above the waterline in dense vegetation; nest platform is made of grass, sedges and dead reeds; nest often has separate entrance and exit paths; female incubates 3–5 pale olive or buff eggs for 24–28 days.

Feeding: patient stand-and-wait predator; strikes at small fish, crayfish, amphibians, reptiles, mammals and insects.

Voice: deep, slow, resonant, repetitive *pomp-er-lunk* or *onk-a-BLONK;* most often heard in the evening or at night.

Similar Species: *Black-crowned Night-Heron* (p. 49), *Yellow-crowned Night-Heron* (p. 337), *Least Bittern* (p. 42) and *Green Heron* (p. 48): immatures lack dark streak from bill to shoulder; immature night-herons have white-flecked upperparts.

Selected Sites: Pointe Mouillee SGA; Erie Marsh Preserve; St. Clair Flats WA; Fish Point SGA; Maple River SGA; Allegan SGA.

LEAST BITTERN

Ixobrychus exilis

The Least Bittern is the smallest of the herons and one of the most seclusive marsh birds in North America. It inhabits marshes where tall, impenetrable stands of cattails conceal most of its movements. This bird moves about with ease, its slender body passing freely and unnoticed through dense marshland habitat. An expert climber, it can often be seen 3 feet or more above water, clinging to vertical stems and hopping about without getting its feet wet. This technique allows it to forage over much deeper water, although only at the water's surface. • In Michigan, where this species approaches the northern limit of its North American range, the Least Bittern pushes the boundaries of its adaptability, particularly its tolerance to chilly summer nights. Least Bitterns are uncommon here and sightings are rare, owing in part to this bird's secretive behavior and solitary lifestyle.

ID: rich buff flanks and sides; streaking on foreneck; white underparts; mostly pale bill; yellowish legs; short tail; dark primary and secondary feathers. *Male:* black crown and back. *Female* and *immature:* chestnut brown head and back; immature has darker streaking on breast and back. *In flight:* large, buffy shoulder patches.

Size: *L* 11–14½ in; *W* 17 in.

Status: threatened; uncommon migrant from late April to October; rare to uncommon breeder.

Habitat: freshwater marshes with cattails and other dense emergent vegetation.

Nesting: mostly the male constructs a platform of dry plant stalks on top of bent marsh vegetation; nest site is usually well concealed within dense vegetation; pair incubates 4–5 pale green or blue eggs for 17–20 days; pair feeds the young by regurgitation.

Feeding: stabs prey with its bill; eats mostly small fish; also takes large insects, tadpoles, frogs, small snakes, leeches and crayfish; may build a hunting platform.

Voice: *Male:* guttural *uh-uh-uh-oo-oo-oo-ooah. Female:* a ticking sound. Both issue a *tut-tut* call or a *koh* alarm call.

Similar Species: *American Bittern* (p. 41): larger; bold brown streaking on underparts; black streak from bill to shoulder. *Black-crowned Night-Heron* (p. 49) and *Yellow-crowned Night-Heron* (p. 337): immatures have dark brown upperparts with white flecking. *Green Heron* (p. 48): immature has dark brown upperparts.

Selected Sites: Erie Marsh Preserve; Pointe Mouillee SGA; Maple River SGA; Allegan SGA; Waterloo SRA; Dead Stream Flooding.

GREAT BLUE HERON

Ardea herodias

The sight of a majestic Great Blue Heron is always memorable, whether you are observing its stealthy, often motionless hunting strategy or tracking its graceful wingbeats. The Great Blue Heron nests in large colonies. Its communal treetop nests, known as rookeries, are sensitive to human disturbance, so it is best to observe the birds' behavior from a distance. • It is rare for a few Great Blue Herons to successfully survive a Michigan winter. Spotting one would highlight your local Christmas bird count. • This heron is often mistaken for a crane, but unlike a crane, which holds its neck outstretched in flight, the Great Blue folds its neck back over its shoulders in an S-shape. Though mostly a fish eater, this bird may also be found stalking fields and meadows in search of rodents.

breeding

ID: large, blue gray bird; long, curving neck; long, dark legs; blue gray back and wing coverts; straight, yellow bill; chestnut brown thighs. *Breeding:* richer colors; plumes streak from crown and throat. *In flight:* neck folds back over shoulders; legs trail behind body; slow, steady wingbeats.
Size: *L* 4–4½ ft; *W* 6 ft.
Status: common migrant from late March to late November; common breeder; rare winter resident.
Habitat: forages along edges of rivers, lakes, marshes, fields and wet meadows.
Nesting: colonial; usually in a tree but occasionally on the ground; flimsy to elaborate stick-and-twig platform, added onto over years, can be up to 4 ft in diameter; pair incubates 4–7 pale blue eggs for about 28 days.

Feeding: patient stand-and-wait predator; strikes at small fish, amphibians, small mammals, aquatic invertebrates and reptiles; rarely scavenges.
Voice: usually quiet away from the nest; occasionally a deep, harsh *frahnk frahnk frahnk,* usually during takeoff.
Similar Species: *Green Heron* (p. 48), *Black-crowned Night-Heron* (p. 49) and *Yellow-crowned Night-Heron* (p. 337): much smaller; shorter legs. *Great* (p. 44), *Snowy* (p. 45) and *Cattle* (p. 47) *egrets:* all are predominately white. *Sandhill Crane* (p. 109): red "cap"; flies with neck outstretched. *Little Blue Heron* (p. 46): dark overall; purplish head; lacks yellow on bill. *Tricolored Heron* (p. 336): smaller; darker upperparts; white underparts.
Selected Sites: Erie Marsh Preserve; Pointe Mouillee SGA; St. Clair Flats WA; Maple River SGA; Thorn L.; Waterloo SRA.

GREAT EGRET

Ardea alba

The Great Egret was first recorded in Michigan in 1929, though nesting was not officially confirmed until the 1950s. Today it is a rare breeder in shore areas of Lake Erie and Saginaw Bay. • The plumes of the Great Egret and Snowy Egret were widely used to decorate hats in the early 20th century. An ounce of egret feathers cost as much as $32—more than an ounce of gold at that time—and, as a result, egret populations began to disappear. Some of the first conservation legislation in North America was enacted to outlaw the hunting of Great Egrets. These egrets are now recovering and expanding their range, probably to where they formerly nested. • Egrets are actually herons, but were given their name for their impressive breeding plumes, referred to as "aigrettes." • The Great Egret is the symbol for the National Audubon Society, one of the oldest conservation organizations in the United States.

breeding

ID: all-white plumage; black legs; yellow bill. *Breeding:* white plumes trail from throat and rump; green skin patch between eyes and base of bill. *In flight:* neck folds back over shoulders; legs extend backward.
Size: *L* 3–3½ ft; *W* 4 ft.
Status: uncommon migrant from April to mid-October; rare to uncommon breeder; uncommon post-breeding wanderer from the south from June to October.
Habitat: marshes, open riverbanks, irrigation canals and lakeshores.

Nesting: colonial, but may nest in isolated pairs; in a tree or tall shrub; pair builds a platform of sticks and incubates 3–5 pale blue green eggs for 23–26 days.
Feeding: patient stand-and-wait predator; occasionally stalks slowly, stabbing at frogs, lizards, snakes and small mammals.
Voice: rapid, low-pitched, loud *cuk-cuk-cuk*.
Similar Species: *Snowy Egret* (p. 45): smaller; black bill; yellow feet. *Cattle Egret* (p. 47): smaller; stockier; orange bill and legs. *Whooping Crane:* extremely rare; much larger; red crown; black-and-red facial mask; black primaries.
Selected Sites: Erie Marsh Preserve; Sterling SP; Pointe Mouillee SGA; St. Clair Flats WA; Waterloo SRA; Shiawassee Flats NWR.

SNOWY EGRET

Egretta thula

The Snowy Egret is distinguished by its small size and spotless white plumage. When it reaches adulthood, its black legs with yellow feet make it stand out even more. • The Snowy Egret was even more affected by plume hunters than the Great Egret, because it was more abundant and widespread, and because its plumes were softer and more delicate. Today, a few Snowy Egrets are regular visitors to Michigan as post-breeding wanderers from the south. • Herons and egrets, particularly Snowy Egrets, use a variety of feeding techniques. By poking their bright yellow feet in the muck of shallow wetlands, these birds spook potential prey out of hiding places. In an even more devious hunting strategy, Snowy Egrets are known to create shade by extending their wings over open water. When a fish succumbs to the attraction of the cooler shaded spot, it is promptly seized and eaten. Some paleontologists have even suggested that this was one of the original functions of bird wings.

breeding

VAGRANT

ID: white plumage; black bill and legs; bright yellow feet. *Breeding:* long plumes on throat and rump; erect crown; red orange lores. *Immature:* similar to adult but with more yellow on legs. *In flight:* yellow feet are obvious.
Size: *L* 22–26 in; *W* 3½ ft.
Status: rare post-breeding wanderer from the south from mid-April to October.

Habitat: open edges of rivers, lakes and marshes.
Nesting: does not nest in Michigan.
Feeding: stirs wetland muck with its feet; stands and waits with wings held open; occasionally hovers and stabs; eats small fish, amphibians and invertebrates.
Voice: low croaks.
Similar Species: *Great Egret* (p. 44): larger; yellow bill; black feet. *Cattle Egret* (p. 47): yellow orange legs and bill.
Selected Sites: southern regions of the state.

LITTLE BLUE HERON

Egretta caerulea

A few Little Blue Herons wander into Michigan each year, most often in the southeastern region. Although adults of the species are quite distinct, immature Little Blues are white like Snowy Egrets and Cattle Egrets, making identification confusing. It takes two years for Little Blue Herons to reach the completely dark plumage of adult birds. • Feeding behavior is often the best way to distinguish herons. Larger herons seem graceful even while lunging for a fish, whereas the Little Blue Heron often seems tentative and stiff in its hunting maneuvers, as it awkwardly jabs at prey. • Because of its dark plumage and lack of aigrettes plumes, the Little Blue Heron was only occasionally taken by hunters in the early 20th century and did not suffer the same population decimation as many of its close relatives.

immature

VAGRANT

ID: medium-sized heron; slate blue overall. *Breeding:* shaggy, maroon-colored head and neck; black legs and feet. *Nonbreeding:* smooth, purple head and neck; dull green legs and feet. *Immature:* white, dusky-tipped primaries; yellowish olive legs; blue gray bill; spotted blue and white when molting to adult plumage.
Size: *L* 24 in; *W* 3½ ft.
Status: rare post-breeding wanderer from the south from April to May and from July to October.
Habitat: marshes, ponds, lakes, streams and meadows.

Nesting: does not nest in Michigan.
Feeding: patient stand-and-wait predator but may wade slowly to stalk prey; eats mostly fish, crabs and crayfish; also takes grasshoppers and other insects, frogs, lizards, snakes and turtles.
Voice: generally silent.
Similar Species: *Snowy Egret* (p. 45): black bill; black legs; bright yellow feet; immature has yellow lores, entirely dark bill, black legs, greenish yellow feet and lacks dusky primary tips. *Cattle Egret* (p. 47): short, yellow bill; yellow legs and feet; immature is similar to adult but has black feet.
Selected Sites: Erie Marsh Preserve; Pointe Mouillee SGA; St. Clair Flats WA.

CATTLE EGRET
Bubulcus ibis

Over the last century—and without help from humans—the Cattle Egret has dispersed from Africa to inhabit every continent except Antarctica. Like most herons, the Cattle Egret is a natural wanderer. It spread from Africa to Brazil, through the Caribbean and, by 1950, to Florida, then across the U.S. • The Cattle Egret gets its name from its habit of following grazing animals. Unlike other egrets, its diet consists of terrestrial invertebrates—it feeds on the insects and other small creatures found around ungulates. When foraging, the Cattle Egret sometimes uses a "leapfrog" feeding strategy in which birds leapfrog over one another, stirring up insects for the birds that follow. • This bird's scientific name *Bubulcus,* means "belonging to or concerning cattle."

breeding

ID: mostly white; yellow orange bill and legs. *Breeding:* long plumes on the throat and rump; buff orange throat, rump and crown; orange red legs and bill; purple lores. *Immature:* similar to adult but with black feet and dark bill.
Size: *L* 19–21 in; *W* 35–37 in.
Status: uncommon migrant and post-breeding wanderer from the south from April to November; rare breeder.
Habitat: agricultural fields, ranchlands and marshes.
Nesting: colonial; often among other herons; in a tree or tall shrub; male supplies sticks for the female who builds a platform or shallow bowl; pair incubates 3–4 pale blue eggs for 21–26 days.
Feeding: picks grasshoppers, other insects, worms, small vertebrates and spiders from fields; often associated with livestock.
Voice: generally silent.
Similar Species: *Great Egret* (p. 44): larger; black legs and feet. *Snowy Egret* (p. 45): black legs; yellow feet. *Little Blue Heron* (p. 46): immature has blue gray bill and yellowish olive legs. *Gulls* (pp. 146–157): do not stand as erect; generally have gray mantle.
Selected Sites: Erie Marsh Preserve; Pointe Mouillee SGA; Nayanquing Point WA; mouth of the Saginaw R.

GREEN HERON

Butorides virescens

This crow-sized heron is far less conspicuous than its Great Blue cousin. • The Green Heron prefers to hunt for frogs and small fish in shallow, weedy wetlands, where it often perches just above the water's surface. While hunting, Green Herons sometimes drop small debris, including twigs, vegetation and feathers, onto the water's surface as a form of bait to attract fish within striking range. • If the light is just right, you may be fortunate enough to see a glimmer of green on the back and outer wings of this bird. Most of the time, however, this magical shine is not apparent, especially when the Green Heron stands frozen under the shade of dense marshland vegetation. • Unlike most herons, the Green Heron nests singly rather than communally, although they can sometimes be found in loose colonies. • The scientific name *virescens* is Latin for "growing or becoming green," and refers to this bird's transition from a streaky brown juvenile to a greenish adult.

ID: stocky; green black crown; chestnut face and neck; white foreneck and belly; blue gray back and wings mixed with iridescent green; relatively short, yellow green legs; bill is dark above and greenish below; short tail. *Breeding male:* bright orange legs. *Immature:* heavy streaking along neck and underparts; dark brown upperparts.

Size: *L* 15–22 in; *W* 26 in.

Status: rare to locally common migrant from April to November; rare to locally common breeder.

Habitat: marshes, lakes and streams with dense shoreline or emergent vegetation.

Nesting: nests singly or in small, loose groups; male begins and female completes construction of a stick platform in a tree or shrub, usually very close to water; pair incubates 3–5 pale blue green to green eggs for 19–21 days; young are fed by regurgitation.

Feeding: stabs prey with its bill after slowly stalking or standing and waiting; eats mostly small fish; also takes frogs, tadpoles, crayfish, aquatic and terrestrial insects, small rodents, snakes, snails and worms.

Voice: generally silent; alarm and flight call are a loud *kowp, kyow* or *skow;* aggression call is a harsh *raah.*

Similar Species: *Black-crowned Night-Heron* (p. 49): larger; white "cheek"; pale gray-and-white neck; 2 long, white plumes trail down from crown; immature has streaked face and white flecking on upperparts. *Least Bittern* (p. 42): buffy yellow shoulder patches, sides and flanks. *American Bittern* (p. 41): larger; more tan overall; black streak from bill to shoulder.

Selected Sites: Erie Marsh Preserve; Pointe Mouillee SGA; Maple River SGA; Muskegon Wastewater System; Shiawassee Flats NWR.

BLACK-CROWNED NIGHT-HERON

Nycticorax nycticorax

When the setting sun has sent most wetland waders to their nightly roosts, Black-crowned Night-Herons arrive to hunt the marshy waters and to voice their hoarse squawks. These herons patrol the shallows for prey, which they can see in the dim light with their large, light-sensitive eyes. They remain alongside water until morning, when they flap off to treetop roosts. • A popular hunting strategy for day-active Black-crowned Night-Herons is to sit motionless atop a few bent-over cattails. Anything passing below the perch becomes fair game—even ducklings, small shorebirds or young muskrats. • Young night-herons are commonly seen around large cattail marshes in fall. Because of their heavily streaked underparts, they are easily confused with American Bitterns and other immature herons. Although somewhat local in Michigan, the Black-crowned Night-Heron is the most abundant heron in the world, occurring virtually worldwide. • *Nycticorax,* meaning "night raven," refers to this bird's distinctive nighttime calls.

breeding

ID: black "cap" and back; white "cheek," foreneck and underparts; gray neck and wings; dull yellow legs; stout black bill; large, red eyes. *Breeding:* 2 white plumes trail down from crown. *Immature:* lightly streaked underparts; brown upperparts with white flecking.
Size: *L* 23–26 in; *W* 3½ ft.
Status: special concern; uncommon migrant from April to November; locally common breeder.
Habitat: shallow cattail and bulrush marshes, lakeshores and along slow rivers.
Nesting: colonial; in a tree or shrub; male gathers the nest material; female builds a loose nest platform of twigs and sticks and lines it with finer materials; pair incubates 3–4 pale green eggs for 21–26 days.

Feeding: often at dusk; patient stand-and-wait predator; stabs for small fish, amphibians, aquatic invertebrates, reptiles, young birds and small mammals.
Voice: deep, guttural *quark* or *wok,* often heard as the bird takes flight.
Similar Species: *Great Blue Heron* (p. 43): much larger; longer legs; blue gray back. *Yellow-crowned Night-Heron* (p. 337): white crown and "cheek" patch, otherwise black head; gray back; immature is very similar to Black-crowned immature. *Green Heron* (p. 48): chestnut brown face and neck; blue gray back with green iridescence; immature has heavily streaked underparts. *American Bittern* (p. 41): similar to immature night-heron, but bittern has black streak from bill to shoulder and is lighter tan overall.
Selected Sites: Erie Marsh Preserve; Sterling SP; Pointe Mouillee SGA; St. Clair Flats WA; Nayanquing Point WA; Thunder Bay.

TURKEY VULTURE

Cathartes aura

Turkey Vultures are unmatched in this region at using updrafts and thermals—they can tease lift from the slightest pocket of rising air and patrol the skies when other soaring birds are grounded. • The Turkey Vulture eats carrion almost exclusively, so its bill and feet are not nearly as powerful as those of eagles, hawks and falcons, which kill live prey. Its red, featherless head may appear grotesque, but this adaptation allows it to remain relatively clean while feeding on messy carcasses. • Vultures seem to have mastered the art of regurgitation. This ability allows parents to transport food over long distances to their young and also enables engorged birds to repulse an attacker or "lighten up" for an emergency takeoff. • Recent studies have shown that American vultures are most closely related to storks, not to hawks and falcons as was previously thought. Molecular similarities with storks, and the shared tendency to defecate on their own legs to cool down, strongly support this taxonomic reclassification.

ID: all black; bare, red head. *Immature:* gray head. *In flight:* head appears small; silver gray flight feathers; black wing linings; wings are held in a shallow "V"; rocks from side-to-side when soaring.
Size: *L* 26–32 in; *W* 5½–6 ft.
Status: uncommon to common migrant from late March to November; uncommon breeder; very rare winter resident.
Habitat: usually seen flying over open country, shorelines or roads; rarely seen over forested areas.
Nesting: in a cave crevice or among boulders; sometimes in a hollow stump or log;

no nest material is used; female lays 2 dull white eggs, spotted and blotched with reddish brown, on bare ground; pair incubates the eggs for up to 41 days; young are fed by regurgitation.
Feeding: entirely on carrion (mostly mammalian); not commonly seen at roadkills.
Voice: generally silent; occasionally produces a hiss or grunt if threatened.
Similar Species: *Golden Eagle* (p. 93) and *Bald Eagle* (p. 83): lack silvery gray wing linings; wings are held flat in flight; do not rock when soaring. *Black Vulture* (p. 337): rare visitor; gray head; silvery tips on otherwise black wings.
Selected Sites: Lake Erie Metropark; Whitefish Point; Allegan SGA; Muskegon SP; Grand Mere SP; Waterloo SRA; Maple River SGA.

GREATER WHITE-FRONTED GOOSE
Anser albifrons

Greater White-fronted Geese are typically birds of the West, but they are occasionally spotted in Michigan. These geese are best seen during spring and fall migration, when they stop to refuel on aquatic plants in shallow ponds and marshes or on freshly sprouted grains in fields and pastures. The small numbers that occasionally migrate through Michigan often travel among flocks of Canada Geese. The slightly smaller White-fronted Geese can best be distinguished by their bright orange feet, which shine like beacons as the birds stand on frozen spring wetlands and fields. • Like most geese, the White-front is a long-lived bird that mates for life, with both parents caring for the young. • The Greater White-fronted Goose is probably most familiar to hunters, who know it as "Speckle Belly."

ID: brown overall; black speckling on belly; pinkish bill; white around bill and on forehead; white hindquarters; black band on upper tail; orange feet. *Immature:* pale belly without speckles; little or no white on face.
Size: *L* 27–33 in; *W* 4½–5 ft.
Status: rare migrant from March to early May and from September to November.
Habitat: croplands, fields, open areas and shallow marshes.

Nesting: does not nest in Michigan.
Feeding: dabbles in water and gleans the ground for grass shoots, sprouting and waste grain and occasionally aquatic invertebrates.
Voice: high-pitched "laugh."
Similar Species: *Canada Goose* (p. 53): white "chin strap"; black neck; pale belly lacks speckling. *Snow Goose* (p. 52): blue morph has white head and upper neck and all-dark breast and belly.
Selected Sites: Pointe Mouillee SGA; Thorn L.; Maple River SGA; Muskegon Wastewater System; Fish Point SGA; Allegan SGA.

SNOW GOOSE
Chen caerulescens

Michigan does not receive the staggering numbers of migrating Snow Geese found in other areas, but they are still sure to come in spring and fall. Landing in farmers' fields, these cackling geese fuel up on waste grain from the previous year's crops. In recent years, Snow Goose populations have increased dramatically in North America, as they take advantage of human-induced changes in the landscape and in the food supply. • Snow Geese grub for their food, often targeting the belowground parts of plants. Their strong, serrated bills are well designed for pulling up the root stalks of marsh plants and gripping slippery grasses. Because of their large numbers, there is concern that they may be degrading the sensitive tundra environment that they use for nesting. • Unlike Canada Geese, which fly in "V" formations, migrating Snow Geese usually form oscillating, wavy lines. • Snow Goose plumage, like that of the Sandhill Crane, is often stained rusty red from iron in the water. • Until 1983, this species' two color morphs, a white and a blue, were considered different species. The scientific name *caerulescens* means "bluish" in Latin and was coined to describe the blue morph.

ID: white overall; black wing tips; pink feet and bill; dark "grinning patch" on bill; plumage is occasionally stained rusty red. *Blue morph:* white head and upper neck; dark blue gray body. *Immature:* gray or dusty white plumage; dark bill and feet.
Size: *L* 28–33 in; *W* 4½–5 ft.
Status: rare to locally common migrant from March to May and from late September to mid-November.
Habitat: shallow wetlands, lakes and fields.

Nesting: does not nest in Michigan.
Feeding: grazes on waste grain and new sprouts; also eats aquatic vegetation, grasses, sedges and roots.
Voice: loud, nasal, constant *houk-houk* in flight.
Similar Species: *Ross's Goose* (p. 338): smaller; shorter neck; lacks black "grinning patch." *Tundra* (p. 56), *Trumpeter* (p. 55) and *Mute* (p. 54) *swans:* larger; white wing tips. *American White Pelican* (p. 39): much larger bill and body.
Selected Sites: Allegan SGA; Waterloo SRA; Thorn L.; Muskegon Wastewater System; Grand Mere SP; Fish Point SGA; Tawas Point SP; Shiawassee Flats NWR.

CANADA GOOSE
Branta canadensis

Canada Geese are among the most recognizable birds in Michigan, but they are also among the least valued. Few people realize that at one time birds of the now-common midwestern subspecies of Greater Canada Goose were hunted almost to extinction. Populations have since been reestablished and, in recent decades, these large, bold geese have inundated urban waterfronts, picnic sites, golf courses and city parks. Today many people even consider them pests. • Fuzzy goslings seem to compel people, especially children, to get closer. Unfortunately, Canada Goose parents can cause harm to unwelcome strangers. Hissing sounds and low, outstretched necks are signs that you should give these birds some space. Unlike most birds, Canada Goose parents do not sever bonds with their young until the beginning of the next year's nesting, almost a year after the young are hatched.

ID: long, black neck; white "chin strap"; white undertail coverts; light brown underparts; dark brown upperparts; short, black tail. **Size:** *L* 21–48 in; *W* 3½–5 ft.

Status: common migrant from March to May and from September to November; common breeder; common year-round resident.
Habitat: lakeshores, riverbanks, ponds, farmlands and city parks.
Nesting: on an island or shoreline; usually on the ground but may use a heron rookery; female builds a nest of plant materials lined with down; female incubates 3–8 white eggs for 25–28 days while the male stands guard.

Feeding: grazes on new sprouts, aquatic vegetation, grass and roots; tips up for aquatic roots and tubers.
Voice: loud, familiar *ah-honk,* often answered by other Canada Geese.
Similar Species: *Greater White-fronted Goose* (p. 51): brown neck and head; lacks white "chin strap"; orange legs; white around base of bill; dark speckling on belly. *Brant* (p. 338): lacks white "chin strap"; white "necklace"; black upper breast. *Snow Goose* (p. 52): blue morph has white head and upper neck. *Double-crested Cormorant* (p. 40): lacks white "chin strap" and undertail coverts; crooked neck in flight.
Selected Sites: suburban areas, marshy state game areas and most state parks with open terrain and water frontage; Allegan SGA; Thorn L.; Haehnle Sanctuary; Shiawassee Flats NWR.

MUTE SWAN

Cygnus olor

Admired for its grace and beauty, this Eurasian native was introduced to eastern North America in the mid-1800s to adorn estates and city parks. Over the years, Mute Swans have adapted well to the Michigan environment. They have continued to expand their feral populations, and although they are not usually migratory, more northerly nesters have established short migratory routes to milder wintering areas. • Like many nonnative species, Mute Swans are often fierce competitors for nesting areas and food sources. They can be very aggressive toward geese and ducks, often displacing many native species. Of particular concern is the negative influence Mute Swans have on the Common Loon and Trumpeter Swan—both endangered, native species in Michigan. • A reliable long-distance characteristic for distinguishing a Mute Swan from a native swan is the way a Mute Swan holds its neck in a graceful curve with its orange bill hanging down.

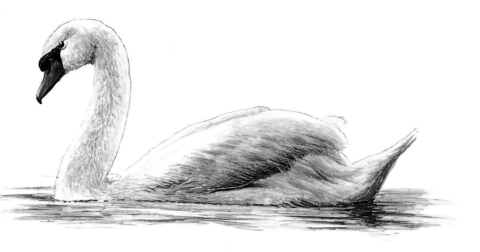

ID: all-white plumage; orange bill with downturned tip; bulbous, black knob at base of bill; neck is usually held in an S-shape; wings are often held in an arch over back while swimming. *Immature:* plumage may be white to grayish brown.

Size: *L* 5 ft; *W* 7–8 ft.

Status: uncommon year-round resident.

Habitat: marshes, lakes and ponds.

Nesting: on the ground along a shoreline; male helps gather nest material; female builds a mound of vegetation and incubates 5–10 pale green eggs for about 36 days; pair tends the young.

Feeding: tips up or dips its head below the water's surface for aquatic plants; grazes on land.

Voice: generally silent; may hiss or issue hoarse barking notes; loud wingbeats can be heard from up to half a mile away.

Similar Species: *Tundra Swan* (p. 56) and *Trumpeter Swan* (p. 55): lack orange bill with black knob at base; neck usually held straight.

Selected Sites: Traverse City Nature Education Reserve; Erie Marsh Preserve; Pointe Mouillee SGA; Huron–Clinton Metroparks.

TRUMPETER SWAN

Cygnus buccinator

The Trumpeter Swan was hunted nearly to extinction for its meat and feathers in the early 20th century. Although some populations in Alaska and western Canada persisted, eastern populations were less fortunate and the Trumpeter Swan is listed as a threatened native species in Michigan. Throughout North America attempts have been made to reintroduce this species to its former range. A program to reestablish Trumpeters in Michigan started in 1986. With the release of subadults raised at the Kellogg Bird Sanctuary and the Detroit Zoo to wildlife areas around our state, there are now three small, established populations. By respecting the sensitivity of Trumpeter Swan nesting sites and protecting Trumpeter habitat across our state, we may once again hear the resonant notes of this magnificent bird. • Both "trumpeter" and *buccinator* refer to this bird's loud, bugling voice, which is produced when air is forced through the long windpipe that runs through the keel of the bird's breast bone. • The neck of a Trumpeter Swan is twice the length of its body. This magnificent bird measures in as the world's largest species of waterfowl.

ID: all-white plumage; large, solid black bill; black skin extends from bill to eyes; black feet; neck is kinked at base when standing or swimming. *Immature:* gray brown plumage; gray bill.
Size: *L* 5–6 ft; *W* 6–7 ft.
Status: threatened; rare, year-round resident; some northern populations are locally migratory.
Habitat: lakes and large wetlands; extremely local.
Nesting: always close to water; on shore, on a small island or on a muskrat or beaver lodge; male gathers marsh plants such as cattails, bulrushes, sedges and grasses; female constructs a nest mound and lines it

with down; mostly the female incubates 4–6 creamy white to dull white eggs for 32–37 days.
Feeding: tips up, surface gleans and occasionally grazes for vegetation; primarily eats pondweeds, duckweed, aquatic tubers and roots.
Voice: loud, resonant, buglelike *koh-hoh.*
Similar Species: *Tundra Swan* (p. 56): smaller; more common; often shows yellow lores; rounder neck and head; softer, more nasal voice. *Mute Swan* (p. 54): down-pointed, orange bill with black knob on upper base; neck usually held in an S-shape; wings often held in an arch over back while swimming. *Snow Goose* (p. 52): smaller; black wing tips; shorter neck; pinkish bill.
Selected Sites: Seney NWR; Kalamazoo vicinity; northeastern Lower Peninsula; Baker Sanctuary.

TUNDRA SWAN

Cygnus columbianus

Before the last of the winter's snows have melted into the fields, Tundra Swans return to Michigan, bringing us the first whispers of spring. In early March, massive flocks of these swans pause in Lake Erie marshes, then Saginaw Bay, stopping to refuel before continuing on to their arctic breeding grounds. • Of the three species of swans in Michigan, the Tundra Swan is the one most likely to be seen in the wild. Distinguishing among swan species comes down to the bill: the bright orange bill of the Mute Swan is hard to mistake, while the subtle difference in slope between the bills of the Tundra Swan and the Trumpeter Swan, and the yellow at the base of the Tundra's bill, can be more difficult to discern. • In the early 19th century, members of the Lewis and Clark expedition found this bird near the Columbia River, thus its scientific name *columbianus*.

ID: white plumage; large, black bill; black feet; often shows yellow lores; neck is held straight up; neck and head show rounded, slightly curving profile. *Immature:* gray brown plumage; gray bill.

Size: *L* 4–5 ft; *W* 6–7 ft.

Status: uncommon to abundant migrant from late February to mid-April and from late October to early December; rare winter resident.

Habitat: shallow areas of lakes and wetlands, agricultural fields and flooded pastures.

Nesting: does not nest in Michigan.

Feeding: tips up, dabbles and surface gleans for aquatic vegetation and aquatic invertebrates; grazes for tubers, roots and waste grain.

Voice: high-pitched, quivering *oo-oo-whoo* is constantly repeated by migrating flocks.

Similar Species: *Trumpeter Swan* (p. 55): extremely rare; larger; loud, buglelike voice; lacks yellow lores; neck and head show more angular profile. *Mute Swan* (p. 54): orange bill with black knob on upper base; neck is usually held in an S-shape; downpointed bill; wings are often held in an arch over back while swimming. *Snow Goose* (p. 52): smaller; black wing tips; shorter neck; pinkish bill.

Selected Sites: Baker Sanctuary; Seney NWR; Shiawassee Flats NWR; Fish Point SGA; Pointe Mouillee SGA; Lake Erie Metropark; Erie Marsh Preserve; St. Clair Flats WA; Maple River SGA.

WOOD DUCK

Aix sponsa

The male Wood Duck is one of the most colorful waterbirds in North America, and books, magazines, postcards and calendars routinely celebrate its beauty. • Truly birds of the forest, Wood Ducks will nest in trees that are a mile or more from the nearest body of water. Forced into the adventures of life at an early age, newly hatched ducklings often jump 20 feet or more out of their nest cavity in a tree to follow their mother to the nearest body of water. The little bundles of down are not exactly feather light, but they bounce fairly well and seldom sustain injury. • Landowners with a tree-lined small pond or other suitable wetland may attract a family of Wood Ducks by building a nest box with a predator guard and lining it with sawdust. The nest box should be erected close to the wetland shoreline at a reasonable height, usually at least 5 feet from the ground. • The scientific name *sponsa* is Latin for "promised bride," suggesting that the male appears formally dressed for a wedding.

ID: *Male:* glossy, green head with some white streaks; crest is slicked back from crown; white "chin" and throat; white-spotted, purplish chestnut breast; black-and-white shoulder slash; golden sides; dark back and hindquarters. *Female:* white, teardrop-shaped eye patch; mottled brown breast is streaked with white; gray brown upperparts; white belly.

Size: *L* 15–20 in; *W* 30 in.

Status: common migrant from mid-March to late October; uncommon to common breeder; rare winter resident.

Habitat: swamps, ponds, marshes and lakeshores with wooded edges.

Nesting: in a hollow or tree cavity; may be as high as 30 ft up; also in an artificial nest box; usually near water; cavity is lined with down; female incubates 9–14 white to buff eggs for 25–35 days.

Feeding: gleans the water's surface and tips up for aquatic vegetation, especially duckweed, aquatic sedges and grasses; eats more fruits and nuts than other ducks.

Voice: *Male:* ascending *ter-wee-wee.* *Female:* squeaky *woo-e-e-k.*

Similar Species: *Hooded Merganser* (p. 78): slim, black bill; black-and-white breast; male has black head with white crest patch. *Harlequin Duck* (p. 71): very rare; male is blue gray overall with black-and-white patches; female has unstreaked breast and white "ear" patch.

Selected Sites: Seney NWR; Shiawassee Flats NWR; Pointe Mouillee SGA; Erie Marsh Preserve; St. Clair Flats WA; Waterloo SRA.

GADWALL

Anas strepera

Male Gadwalls lack the striking plumage of most other male ducks, but they nevertheless have a dignified appearance and a subtle beauty. Once you learn their field marks—a black rump and white wing patches—Gadwalls are surprisingly easy to identify. • Ducks in the genus *Anas*, the dabbling ducks, are most often observed tipping up their hindquarters and submerging their heads to feed, but Gadwalls dive more often than others of this group. These ducks feed equally during the day and night, a strategy that reduces the risk of predation because the birds avoid spending long periods of time sleeping or feeding. • Gadwall numbers have greatly increased in Michigan since the 1950s, and this duck has expanded its range throughout North America. The majority of Gadwalls winter on the Gulf Coast of the United States and Mexico, although a few birds over-winter in Michigan.

ID: white speculum; white belly. *Male:* mostly gray; black hindquarters; dark bill. *Female:* mottled brown; brown bill with orange sides.
Size: *L* 18–22 in; *W* 33 in.

Status: common migrant from late March to mid-May and from mid-September to mid-November; rare breeder and winter resident.
Habitat: shallow wetlands, lake borders and beaver ponds.
Nesting: in tall vegetation, sometimes far from water; nest is well concealed in a scraped-out hollow, often with grass arching overhead; nest is made of grass and other dry vegetation and lined with down; female incubates 8–11 white eggs for 24–27 days.

Feeding: dabbles and tips up for aquatic plants; also eats aquatic invertebrates, tadpoles and small fish; grazes on grass and waste grain during migration; one of the few dabblers to dive routinely for food.
Voice: *Male:* simple, singular quack; often whistles harshly. *Female:* high *kaak kaaak kak-kak-kak,* in series and oscillating in volume.
Similar Species: *American Wigeon* (p. 59): green speculum; male has white forehead and green swipe trailing from each eye; female lacks black hindquarters. *Mallard* (p. 61), *Northern Pintail* (p. 64) and *other dabbling ducks* (pp. 57–65): generally lack white speculum, black hindquarters of male Gadwall, and orange-sided bill of female.
Selected Sites: Erie Marsh Preserve; St. Clair Flats WA; Waterloo SRA; Maple River SGA; Nayanquing Point WA.

AMERICAN WIGEON

Anas americana

The male American Wigeon's characteristic, piping, three-syllable whistle sets it apart from the wetland orchestra of buzzes, quacks and ticks. Listen carefully, however, and you'll realize where toy makers got the sound for rubber duckies. • Although this bird frequently dabbles for food, nothing seems to please a wigeon more than the succulent stems and leaves of pond-bottom plants. These plants grow far too deep for a dabbling duck, so wigeons often pirate from accomplished divers, such as American Coots, Canvasbacks, Redheads and scaups. In contrast to other ducks, the American Wigeon is a good walker and is commonly observed grazing on shore. • The American Wigeon nests farther north than any other dabbling duck with the exception of the Northern Pintail. Pair bonds are strong and last well into incubation. • Because of the male's bright white crown and forehead, some people call this bird "Baldpate."

ID: large, white upperwing patch; cinnamon breast and sides; white belly; black-tipped, blue gray bill; green speculum; white "wing pits." *Male:* white forehead; green swipe extends back from eye. *Female:* grayish head; brown underparts.
Size: *L* 18–22½ in; *W* 32 in.
Status: common migrant from early March to late May and from early September to late November; rare breeder and winter resident.
Habitat: shallow wetlands, lake edges and ponds.
Nesting: always on dry ground, often far from water; nest is well concealed in tall vegetation and is built with grass, leaves and down; female incubates 8–11 white eggs for 23–25 days.

Feeding: dabbles and tips up for the leaves and stems of pondweeds and other aquatic plants; also grazes and uproots young shoots in fields; may eat some invertebrates; occasionally pirates food from other birds.
Voice: *Male:* nasal, frequently repeated whistle: *whee WHEE wheew.* *Female:* soft, seldom heard quack.
Similar Species: *Gadwall* (p. 58): white speculum; lacks large, white wing patch; male lacks green eye swipe; female has orange swipes on bill. *Eurasian Wigeon* (p. 338): gray "wing pits"; male has rufous head, cream forehead and rosy breast; lacks green eye swipe; female usually has browner head.
Selected Sites: Pointe Mouillee SGA; Erie Marsh Preserve; Thorn L.; Baker Sanctuary; Maple River SGA; Muskegon Wastewater System; Allegan SGA.

AMERICAN BLACK DUCK

Anas rubripes

At one time, the American Black Duck was the most common and widely distributed duck in the region. In recent years, the eastern expansion of the Mallard has come at the expense of this dark dabbler. A male Mallard will aggressively pursue a female American Black Duck, and if unable to find a male of her own kind, she will often accept the offer. Hybrid offspring are less fertile and are usually unable to reproduce. To the abundant Mallard, it is not a loss, but to the American Black Duck it is a further set back. • This duck usually feeds in shallows where it is able to probe the mud by dabbling, searching below the water's surface with only its rump left exposed. In summer, the Black Duck will eat aquatic insects, salamanders, small frogs and anything else that it is able to snatch up. • Male and female American Black Ducks are remarkably similar in appearance, which is unusual for waterfowl. The scientific name *rubripes* means "red foot" in Latin.

ID: dark brownish black body; light brown head and neck; bright orange feet; violet speculum. *Male:* yellow olive bill. *Female:* dull green bill mottled with gray or black.
In flight: whitish underwings; dark body.
Size: *L* 20–24 in; *W* 35 in.
Status: common migrant from late March to late May and from August to November; uncommon breeder and winter resident.
Habitat: lakes, wetlands, rivers and agricultural areas.
Nesting: usually on the ground among clumps of dense vegetation near water; female fills a shallow depression with plant material and lines it with down;

female incubates 7–11 white to greenish buff eggs for 23–33 days; second clutches are common, especially to replace lost broods.
Feeding: tips up and dabbles in shallows for the seeds and roots of pondweeds; also eats aquatic invertebrates, larval amphibians and fish eggs.
Voice: *Male:* a croak. *Female:* a loud quack.
Similar Species: *Mallard* (p. 61): white belly; blue speculum bordered with white; female is lighter overall and has white outer tail feathers. *Gadwall* (p. 58): black hindquarters; white speculum.
Selected Sites: Erie Marsh Preserve; Pointe Mouillee SGA; St. Clair Flats WA; Thorn L.; Maple River SGA; Allegan SGA; Fish Point SGA.

MALLARD
Anas platyrhynchos

The male Mallard, with his iridescent, green head and chestnut brown breast, is the classic wild duck. Mallards can be seen almost any day of the year, often in flocks and always near open water. These confident ducks have even been known to take up residence in local swimming pools. • Wild Mallards will freely hybridize with domestic ducks, which were originally derived from Mallards in Europe. The resulting offspring, often seen in city parks, are a confusing blend of both parents. • Male ducks molt after breeding, losing much of their extravagant plumage. This "eclipse" plumage camouflages them during their flightless period and they usually molt again into their breeding colors by early fall. • Most people think of the Mallard's quack as the classic duck call, and in fact, the Mallard is the only duck that really "quacks." • The body heat generated by a brooding hen is enough to increase the growth rate of nearby grasses, which she will then manipulate to further conceal her precious nest. • The scientific name *platyrhynchos* is Greek for "broad, flat bill."

ID: dark blue speculum bordered by white; orange feet. *Male:* glossy, green head; yellow bill; chestnut brown breast; white "necklace"; gray body plumage; black tail feathers curl upward. *Female:* mottled brown overall; orange bill is spattered with black.
Size: *L* 20–27½ in; *W* 35 in.
Status: common migrant and breeder; common winter resident.
Habitat: lakes, wetlands, rivers, city parks, agricultural areas and sewage lagoons.
Nesting: in tall vegetation or under a bush, often near water; nest of grass and other plant material is lined with down;

female incubates 7–10 light green to white eggs for 26–30 days.
Feeding: tips up and dabbles in shallows for the seeds of sedges, willows and pondweeds; also eats insects, aquatic invertebrates, larval amphibians and fish eggs.
Voice: *Male:* deep, quiet quacks. *Female:* loud quacks; very vocal.
Similar Species: *Northern Shoveler* (p. 63): much larger bill; male has white breast. *American Black Duck* (p. 60): darker than female Mallard; purple speculum lacks white border. *Common Merganser* (p. 79): blood red bill and white underparts; male lacks chestnut breast.
Selected Sites: widely distributed across any habitats with access to water, including urban and agricultural areas, marshes, lakes and ponds.

BLUE-WINGED TEAL

Anas discors

The small, speedy Blue-winged Teal is renowned for its aviation skills. These teals can be identified in flight by their small size and by the sharp twists and turns that they execute with precision. • Despite the similarity of their names, the Green-winged Teal is not the Blue-winged Teal's closest relative. The Blue-winged Teal is more closely related to the Northern Shoveler and the Cinnamon Teal *(A. cyanoptera).* These birds all have broad, flat bills, pale blue forewings and green speculums. Female Cinnamon Teals and Blue-winged Teals are so similar in appearance that even expert birders and ornithologists have difficulty distinguishing them in the field. • Blue-winged Teals migrate farther than most ducks, summering as far north as the Canadian tundra and wintering mainly in Central and South America. • The scientific name *discors* is Latin for "without harmony," which might refer to this bird's call as it takes flight, or to its contrasting plumage.

ID: *Male:* blue gray head; white crescent on face; darker bill than female; black-spotted breast and sides. *Female:* mottled brown overall; white throat. *In flight:* blue forewing patch; green speculum.

Size: *L* 14–16 in; *W* 23 in.

Status: common migrant from early April to early October; common breeder.

Habitat: shallow lake edges and wetlands; prefers areas of short but dense emergent vegetation.

Nesting: in grass along a shoreline or in a meadow; nest is built with grass and considerable amounts of down; female incubates 8–13 white eggs, sometimes tinged with olive, for 23–27 days.

Feeding: gleans the water's surface for sedge and grass seeds, pondweeds, duckweeds and aquatic invertebrates.

Voice: *Male:* soft *keck-keck-keck. Female:* soft quacks.

Similar Species: *Cinnamon Teal:* female is virtually identical to female Blue-winged Teal, but brown is richer and eye line is less distinct. *Green-winged Teal* (p. 65): female has smaller bill, black-and-green speculum and lacks blue forewing patch. *Northern Shoveler* (p. 63): much larger bill with paler base; male has green head and lacks spotting on body. *Harlequin Duck* (p. 71): very rare; male is blue gray overall with many black-and-white patches.

Selected Sites: Erie Marsh Preserve; Pointe Mouillee SGA; St. Clair Flats WA; Thorn L.; Waterloo SRA; Muskegon Wastewater System; Maple River SGA; Arcadia Lake Marsh.

NORTHERN SHOVELER

Anas clypeata

The initial reaction upon meeting this bird for the first time is often, "Wow, look at the big honker on that Mallard!" A closer look, however, will reveal a completely different bird altogether—the Northern Shoveler. An extra large, spoonlike bill allows this strangely handsome duck to strain small invertebrates from the water and from the bottoms of ponds. The Northern Shoveler eats much smaller organisms than do most other waterfowl, and its intestines are elongated to prolong the digestion of these hard-bodied invertebrates. The shoveler's specialized feeding strategy means that it is rarely seen tipping up, but is more often found in the shallows of ponds and marshes where the mucky bottom is easiest to access. • The scientific name *clypeata*, Latin for "furnished with a shield," possibly refers to the chestnut patches on the flanks of the male. This species was once placed in its own genus, *Spatula*, the meaning of which needs no explanation.

ID: large, spatulate bill; blue forewing patch; green speculum. *Male:* green head; yellow eyes; white breast; chestnut brown flanks. *Female:* mottled brown overall; orange-tinged bill.

Size: *L* 18–20 in; *W* 30 in.

Status: common migrant from mid-March to mid-May and from September to November; rare breeder and winter resident.

Habitat: shallow marshes, bogs and lakes with muddy bottoms and emergent vegetation, usually in open and semi-open areas.

Nesting: in a shallow hollow on dry ground, usually within 150 ft of water; female builds a nest of dry grass and down and incubates 10–12 pale greenish buff eggs for 21–28 days.

Feeding: dabbles in shallow and often muddy water; strains out plant and animal matter, especially aquatic crustaceans, insect larvae and seeds; rarely tips up.

Voice: generally quiet; occasionally a raspy chuckle or quack; most often heard during spring courtship.

Similar Species: *Mallard* (p. 61): blue speculum bordered by white; lacks pale blue forewing patch; male has chestnut brown breast and white flanks. *Blue-winged Teal* (p. 62): much smaller bill; smaller overall; male has spotted breast and sides.

Selected Sites: Erie Marsh Preserve; St. Clair Flats WA; Fish Point SGA; Shiawassee Flats NWR; Maple R. SGA; Sleepy Hollow SP; Allegan SGA.

NORTHERN PINTAIL

Anas acuta

The trademark of the elegant and graceful male Northern Pintail is its long, tapering tail feathers, which are easily seen in flight and point skyward when the bird dabbles. In Michigan, only the male Long-tailed Duck shares this pintail feature. • Migrating pintails are often seen in flocks of 20 to 40 birds, but some early spring flocks have been known to consist of nearly 10,000 individuals. In spring, flooded agricultural fields tend to attract the largest pintail flocks. Pintails breed earlier than most waterfowl, and in Michigan they begin nesting in mid-April. • Although the Michigan pintail population seems to be increasing slightly, this widespread duck appears to be in an overall decline across its range in central and western North America.

ID: long, slender neck; dark, glossy bill. *Male:* chocolate brown head; long, tapering tail feathers; white of breast extends up sides of neck; dusty gray body plumage; black-and-white hindquarters. *Female:* mottled light brown overall.
In flight: slender body; brownish speculum with white trailing edge.
Size: *L* 21–25 in; *W* 34 in.
Status: common migrant from mid-March to May and from September to November; uncommon breeder; rare winter resident.
Habitat: shallow wetlands, fields and lake edges.
Nesting: in a small depression in low vegetation; nest of grass, leaves and moss is lined with down; female incubates 6–12 greenish buff eggs for 22–25 days.

Feeding: tips up and dabbles in shallows for the seeds of sedges, willows and pondweeds; also eats aquatic invertebrates and larval amphibians; eats waste grain in agricultural areas during migration; diet is more varied than that of other dabbling ducks.
Voice: *Male:* soft, whistling call. *Female:* rough quack.
Similar Species: male is distinctive. *Mallard* (p. 61) and *Gadwall* (p. 58): females are chunkier, usually have dark or 2-tone bills and lack tapering tail and long, slender neck. *Blue-winged Teal* (p. 62): green speculum; blue forewing patch; female is smaller. *Long-tailed Duck* (p. 75): head is not uniformly dark; all-dark wings.
Selected Sites: Fish Point SGA; Nayanquing Point WA; Muskegon Wastewater System; Thorn L.; Erie Marsh Preserve; Maple River SGA; Little Bay de Noc; Pointe Mouillee SGA.

GREEN-WINGED TEAL

Anas crecca

One of the speediest and most maneuverable of waterfowl, the Green-winged Teal, with its red head, green "mask" and amazing flying speed, might bring to mind a comic book superhero. • When intruders cause these small ducks to rocket up from the wetland's surface, the birds circle quickly overhead in small, tight-flying flocks, returning to the water only when the threat has departed. A predator's only chance of catching a healthy teal is to snatch it from the water or from a nest. Although female Green-wings go to great lengths to conceal their nests within the protective cover of grasses and brush, some nests may still be discovered by hungry predators. • Green-winged Teals often undertake a partial migration before molting into their post-breeding, "eclipse" plumage. In this plumage they are unable to fly because they do not possess a full set of flight feathers. • Few Green-wings remain here to breed because they are on the periphery of their range in Michigan. They are a common migrant, though, and these lovely little teals often loiter on ponds and marshy wetlands until cold winter weather freezes the water's surface.

ID: small bill; green-and-black speculum. *Male:* chestnut brown head; green swipe extends back from eye; white shoulder slash; creamy breast is spotted with black; pale gray sides. *Female:* mottled brown overall; light belly.
Size: *L* 12–16 in; *W* 23 in.
Status: common migrant from mid-March to mid-May and from late August to November; rare breeder and winter resident.
Habitat: shallow lakes, wetlands, beaver ponds and meandering rivers.

Nesting: well concealed in tall vegetation; nest is built of grass and leaves and lined with down; female incubates 6–14 cream to pale buff eggs for 20–24 days.
Feeding: dabbles in shallows, particularly on mudflats, for aquatic invertebrates, larval amphibians, marsh plant seeds and pondweeds.
Voice: *Male:* crisp whistle. *Female:* soft quack.
Similar Species: *American Wigeon* (p. 59): male lacks white shoulder slash and chestnut brown head. *Blue-winged Teal* (p. 62) and *Cinnamon Teal:* female has blue forewing patch.
Selected Sites: Shiawassee Flats NWR; Pointe Mouillee SGA; Nayanquing Point WA; Erie Marsh Preserve; Maple River SGA.

65

CANVASBACK

Aythya valisineria

Most male ducks sport richly decorated backs, but the male Canvasback has a bright, clean back that, appropriately, appears to be wrapped in white canvas. In profile, the Canvasback casts a noble image—the long bill meets the forecrown with no apparent break in angle, allowing birds of either sex to be distinguished at long range. This bird's back and unique profile are unmistakable field marks. • Canvasbacks are diving ducks that are typically found on large areas of open water. Because these birds prefer large lakes and bays and the deepest areas of wetlands, birders often need binoculars to admire the male's wild red eyes and mahogany head.

Canvasbacks are most likely to be seen during spring and fall migration, when flocks composed of more than 10,000 individuals occasionally converge on a suitable wetland. • The scientific name *valisineria* refers to one of the Canvasback's favorite foods, wild celery *(Vallisneria americana)*. The abundance of this plant in southeastern Michigan border waters explains the large flotillas of Canvasbacks that can be seen refueling there in migration and in winter.

ID: head slopes upward from bill to forehead. *Male:* canvas white back and sides; chestnut brown head; black breast and hindquarters; red eyes. *Female:* profile is similar to male's; duller brown head and neck; gray back and sides.

Size: *L* 19–22 in; *W* 29 in.

Status: common migrant from mid-March to mid-May and from October to December; very rare breeder; locally common winter resident in the southeast.

Habitat: marshes, ponds, shallow lakes and other wetlands; large lakes in migration.

Nesting: basket nest of reeds and grass is lined with down and suspended above shallow water in dense stands of cattails and bulrushes; may also nest on dry ground; female incubates 7–9 olive green eggs for up to 29 days.

Feeding: dives to depths of up to 30 ft (average is 10–15 ft); feeds on roots, tubers, the basal stems of plants, including pondweeds and wild celery, and bulrush seeds; occasionally eats aquatic invertebrates.

Voice: generally quiet. *Male:* occasional coos and "growls" during courtship. *Female:* low, soft, "purring" quack or *kuck;* also "growls."

Similar Species: *Redhead* (p. 67): rounded rather than sloped forehead; male has gray back and bluish bill.

Selected Sites: Anchor Bay in Lake St. Clair; lower Detroit R.; Pointe Mouillee SGA; Muskegon Wastewater System; Whitefish Point.

REDHEAD
Aythya americana

L ike the Canvasback, the Redhead is most abundant as a migrant and winter resident. To distinguish a Canvasback from a Redhead, most birders will tell you
to contrast the birds' profiles, but the most obvious difference between them is
the color of their backs— the Canvasback has a white back, while the Redhead's is
gray. • Redheads prefer large marshes for nesting, where they easily blend into the busy
goings-on of woodland summer life. • Female Redheads usually incubate their own
eggs and brood their young as other ducks do, but they occasionally lay their eggs in
the nests of other ducks. In Michigan, the Blue-winged Teal and the
Ring-necked Duck may be rare victims of Redhead egg dumping,
also known as "brood parasitism." • The Redhead is a diving duck, but it will occasionally feed on the surface of a wetland like a dabbler.

ID: black-tipped, blue gray bill. *Male:* rounded, red head; black breast and hindquarters; gray back and sides. *Female:* dark brown overall; lighter "chin" and "cheek" patches.
Size: *L* 18–22 in; *W* 29 in.
Status: common migrant from March to April and from October to mid-December; rare breeder; locally common winter resident in the southeast.
Habitat: large wetlands, ponds, lakes, bays and rivers.
Nesting: usually in shallow water; sometimes on dry ground; deep basket nest of reeds and grass is suspended over water at the base of emergent vegetation and lined with fine white down; female incubates 9–14 greenish eggs for 23–29 days; female may lay eggs in other ducks' nests.

Feeding: dives to depths of 10 ft; primarily eats aquatic vegetation, especially pond-weeds, duckweeds and the leaves and stems of plants; occasionally eats aquatic invertebrates.
Voice: generally quiet. *Male:* catlike meow in courtship. *Female:* rolling *kurr-kurr-kurr; squak* when alarmed.
Similar Species: *Canvasback* (p. 66): clean white back; bill slopes onto forehead. *Ring-necked Duck* (p. 68): female has a more prominent white eye ring, white ring on bill and peaked head. *Lesser Scaup* (p. 70) and *Greater Scaup* (p. 69): male has dark head and whiter sides; female has more white at base of bill.
Selected Sites: Anchor Bay in Lake St. Clair; Metrobeach Metropark; Belle Isle in Detroit; lower Detroit R.; Muskegon Wastewater System; Houghton L.; Lake Erie Metropark; Little Bay de Noc; St. Clair R.

RING-NECKED DUCK

Aythya collaris

The Ring-necked Duck's distinctive white bill markings and angular head are field marks that immediately strike an observer. After seeing the Ring-necked Duck in the wild, you may wonder why it was not named the "Ring-billed Duck," and you would not be the first birder to ponder this perplexing puzzle. The official appellation is derived from the scientific name *collaris* (collar), which originated with an ornithologist looking at an indistinct cinnamon "collar" on a museum specimen, not a birder looking at a live duck through binoculars. • Ring-necked Ducks are diving ducks, like scaups, Redheads and Canvasbacks, but they prefer to feed in shallower shoreline waters, frequently tipping up for food like a dabbler. They ride high on the water and tend to carry their tails clear of the water's surface. Ring-necks are generalized feeders, allowing them to capitalize on the low resources found in the subarctic and boreal settings where they commonly nest. Ring-necks are even able to nest in boggy areas where a more picky eater would find it hard to eke out a living.

ID: *Male:* angular, dark purple head; black breast, back and hindquarters; white shoulder slash; gray sides; blue gray bill with black and white bands at tip; thin, white border around base of bill. *Female:* dark brown overall; white eye ring; dark bill with black and white bands at tip; pale crescent on front of face.

Size: *L* 14–18 in; *W* 25 in.

Status: common migrant from late February to late May; uncommon migrant from mid-September to November; fairly common breeder; rare winter resident.

Habitat: wooded ponds, swamps, marshes and sloughs with emergent vegetation; small lakes.

Nesting: on a hummock or shoreline; frequently over water; bulky nest of grass and moss is lined with down; female incubates 8–10 olive tan eggs for 25–29 days.

Feeding: dives underwater for aquatic vegetation, including seeds, tubers and pondweed leaves; also eats aquatic invertebrates and mollusks.

Voice: seldom heard. *Male:* low-pitched, hissing whistle. *Female:* growling *churr.*

Similar Species: *Lesser Scaup* (p. 70): lacks white ring near tip of bill; male lacks white shoulder slash and black back; female has broad, clearly defined white border around base of bill. *Greater Scaup* (p. 69): lacks white ring near tip of bill; male has greenish black head and white sides; female has broad, clearly defined white border around base of bill. *Redhead* (p. 67): rounded rather than peaked head; less white on front of face; female has a less prominent eye ring.

Selected Sites: Erie Marsh Preserve; Pointe Mouillee SGA; Lake Erie Metropark; Metrobeach Metropark; Whitefish Point.

GREATER SCAUP

Aythya marila

The Greater Scaup has assumed an important ecological role in Great Lakes waters by feeding on the recently introduced pest, the zebra mussel. • Greater Scaup are abundant throughout much of the region during spring and fall migration, and some locations boast concentrations of more than 27,000 individuals. • Look for the rounder, not peaked, more greenish head of the Greater Scaup to distinguish it from its Lesser relative. The Lesser Scaup has a lavender iridescence on its head. This feature makes it easy to remember which scaup is which by correlating the color of each duck's head with the corresponding first letter of its name. However, scaups usually raft so far out in the water that specific identification is often not possible. • Scaups are diving ducks, which have a heavier bone structure, and they require a running start across the surface of the water to take off.

ID: rounded head; golden eyes. *Male:* dark, iridescent green head (may appear black); black breast; white belly, sides and flanks; light gray back; dark hindquarters; black-tipped, blue bill. *Female:* brown overall; well-defined white patch at base of bill. *In flight:* white flash through wing extends well into primary feathers.

Size: *L* 16–19 in; *W* 28 in.

Status: common migrant from early February to May and from September to November; locally common winter resident in the southeast.

Habitat: lakes, large marshes and reservoirs; usually far from shore.

Nesting: does not nest in Michigan.

Feeding: dives underwater, to greater depths than other *Aythya* ducks, for aquatic invertebrates and vegetation; favors freshwater mollusks in winter.

Voice: generally quiet in migration; alarm call is a deep *scaup*. *Male:* may issue a 3-note whistle and a soft *wah-hooo*. *Female:* may give a subtle "growl."

Similar Species: *Lesser Scaup* (p. 70): slightly smaller; shorter white wing-flash in flight; slightly smaller bill; male has peaked, purplish black head; female has peaked head. *Ring-necked Duck* (p. 68): black back; white shoulder slash; white ring around base of bill. *Redhead* (p. 67): female has less white at base of bill; male has red head and darker sides.

Selected Sites: Pointe Mouillee SGA; Lake Erie Metropark; Belle Isle Park in Detroit; St. Clair R.; Muskegon Wastewater System; Tawas Point SP; Little Bay de Noc; Whitefish Point.

LESSER SCAUP

Aythya affinis

The male Lesser Scaup and its close relative, the Greater Scaup, mirror the color pattern of an Oreo cookie: they are black at both ends and light in the middle. Although Greater Scaups and Lesser Scaups may occur together on larger lakes during migration, they tend not to mingle. • The Lesser Scaup, which nests in Michigan, is most at home among the lakes of forested areas, but can also be found nesting in marshes. • A member of the *Aythya* genus of diving ducks, the Lesser Scaup leaps up neatly before diving underwater, where it propels itself with powerful strokes of its feet. • The scientific name *affinis* is Latin for "adjacent" or "allied"—a reference to this scaup's close association to other diving ducks. "Scaup" might refer to a preferred winter food of this duck—shellfish beds are called "scalps" in Scotland—or it might be a phonetic imitation of one of its calls. • Both the Lesser Scaup and the Greater Scaup are known by the nickname "Bluebill."

ID: yellow eyes. *Male:* purplish black head; black breast and hindquarters; dusty white sides; grayish back; black-tipped, blue gray bill. *Female:* dark brown overall; well-defined white patch at base of bill.

Size: *L* 15–18 in; *W* 25 in.

Status: common migrant from late February to late May and from late August to November; very rare breeder; uncommon winter resident.

Habitat: *Breeding:* woodland ponds, wetlands and lake edges with grassy margins. *In migration:* lakes, large marshes and rivers.

Nesting: in tall, concealing vegetation, generally close to water and occasionally on an island; nest hollow is built of grass and lined with down; female incubates 8–14 olive buff eggs for about 21–27 days.

Feeding: dives underwater for aquatic invertebrates, mostly mollusks, amphipods and insect larvae; occasionally eats aquatic vegetation.

Voice: alarm call is a deep *scaup*. *Male:* soft *whee-oooh* in courtship. *Female:* purring *kwah*.

Similar Species: *Greater Scaup* (p. 69): rounded head; slightly larger bill; longer, white wing-flash; male's head is greenish black. *Ring-necked Duck* (p. 68): male has white shoulder slash and black back; female has white-ringed bill. *Redhead* (p. 67): female has less white at base of bill; male has red head and darker sides.

Selected Sites: Pointe Mouillee SGA; Lake Erie Metropark; Metrobeach Metropark; St. Clair R.; Fish Point SGA; Shiawassee Flats NWR.

HARLEQUIN DUCK
Histrionicus histrionicus

The small, surf-loving Harlequin Duck is a scarce but regular migrant and winter visitor to Michigan, and its numbers have declined over the years. Eastern Harlequin populations have dwindled to only about 1000 birds, but there seems to have been an increase in sightings—though by only a few each year. Although the Harlequins' stay in Michigan is usually brief, their dynamic appearance never fails to excite and impress fortunate onlookers. • In eastern North America, Harlequins breed along the northeastern Atlantic Coast of Canada, favoring fast-flowing, coastal mountain streams as breeding habitat. After a short breeding season, flocks of Harlequins move south to winter along the coast from Newfoundland to New York State, with some of these flocks wandering to the Great Lakes.

• This duck is named after a character from traditional Italian comedy and pantomime, the Harlequin, who wore a diamond-patterned costume and performed "histrionics," or tricks. Some people refer to Harlequins as "Lords and Ladies."

ID: small, rounded duck; blocky head; short bill; raises and lowers its tail while swimming. *Male:* gray blue body; chestnut brown sides; white spots and stripes outlined in black on head, neck and flanks. *Female:* dusky brown overall; light underparts; 2–3 light-colored patches on head.
Size: *L* 14–19 in; *W* 26 in.
Status: very rare migrant and winter visitor from October to March.
Habitat: Great Lakes shores; rocky jetties.
Nesting: does not nest in Michigan.

Feeding: dabbles and dives for aquatic invertebrates, mostly crustaceans and mollusks in freshwater lakes.
Voice: generally silent outside the breeding season.
Similar Species: male is distinctive. *Bufflehead* (p. 76): smaller; never found on fast-flowing water; female lacks white between eye and bill. *Surf Scoter* (p. 72): female has bulbous bill. *White-winged Scoter* (p. 73): female has white wing patch and bulbous bill.
Selected Sites: harbor entrances at New Buffalo, St. Joseph, Holland, Saugatuck, Muskegon, Alpena and Rogers City; Sault Ste. Marie; Whitefish Point; Port Huron.

SURF SCOTER

Melanitta perspicillata

When spring storms whip up whitecaps on our big lakes, migrating Surf Scoters ride comfortably among the crashing waves. These scoters are most often seen during spring and fall migration, when tired flocks settle upon open water in large, dark rafts. Most scoters spend their winters just beyond the breaking surf on both the Atlantic and Pacific coasts, and they are well adapted to life on rough water. The Surf Scoter is the only scoter that breeds and winters exclusively in North America. • Like other far northern breeders, Surf Scoters pair up before arriving on their summer breeding grounds to take advantage of the precious little summer available to them. • The Surf Scoter has the unfortunate distinction of being one of the least-studied waterbirds in North America. Much of the information that is known of its behavior and distribution was documented for the first time only in the latter part of the 20th century. • The scientific name *Melanitta* means "black duck"; *perspicillata* is Latin for "spectacular," which refers to this bird's colorful, bulbous bill.

ID: large, stocky duck; large bill; sloping forehead; all-black wings. *Male:* black overall; white forehead and nape; orange bill and legs; black spot, outlined in white, at base of bill. *Female:* brown overall; dark gray bill; 2 whitish patches on sides of head.
Size: *L* 16–20 in; *W* 30 in.
Status: common migrant from mid-April to late May and from September to early December; very rare winter resident.
Habitat: large, deep lakes and large rivers; Great Lakes.

Nesting: does not nest in Michigan.
Feeding: dives to depths of 30 ft; eats mostly mollusks; also takes aquatic insect larvae, crustaceans and some aquatic vegetation.
Voice: generally quiet; infrequently utters low, harsh croaks. *Male:* occasionally gives a low, clear whistle. *Female:* guttural *krraak krraak.*
Similar Species: *White-winged Scoter* (p. 73): white wing patches; male lacks white on forehead and nape. *Black Scoter* (p. 74): male is all black; female has well-defined, pale "cheek."
Selected Sites: Whitefish Point; Thunder Bay; Port Huron; Metrobeach Metropark; L. Michigan harbor entrances.

WHITE-WINGED SCOTER

Melanitta fusca

As White-winged Scoters race across lakes, their flapping wings reveal a key identifying feature—the white inner-wing patches strike a sharp contrast to the bird's otherwise black plumage. Scoters have small wings relative to the weight of their bodies, so they require long stretches of water for takeoff. • The White-winged Scoter is the largest and most abundant of the three species of scoters seen in Michigan, and it is the only scoter seen consistently in moderate numbers throughout winter, usually along Great Lakes shores. • The White-winged Scoter often eats hard-shelled clams and shellfishes whole. It relies upon its remarkably powerful gizzard to crush shells that would require a hammer for us to open. • The name "scoter" may be derived from the way this bird scoots across the water's surface. Scooting can be a means of traveling quickly from one foraging site to another. The name "coot" has also been incorrectly applied to all three species of scoter because of their superficial resemblance to this totally unrelated species.

ID: stocky body; large, bulbous bill; sloping forehead; base of bill is fully feathered. *Male:* black overall; white patch below eye. *Female:* brown overall; gray brown bill; 2 whitish patches on sides of head. *In flight:* white wing patches.
Size: *L* 18–24 in; *W* 34 in.
Status: common migrant from late April to late May and from early October to early November; uncommon winter resident.
Habitat: large, deep lakes and large rivers; Great Lakes.
Nesting: does not nest in Michigan.

Feeding: deep, underwater dives last up to 1 minute; eats mostly mollusks; may also take crustaceans, aquatic insects and some small fish.
Voice: courting pair produces harsh, guttural noises, between a *crook* and a quack.
Similar Species: *Surf Scoter* (p. 72): lacks white wing patches; male has white forehead and nape. *Black Scoter* (p. 74): lacks white patches on wings and around eyes. *American Coot* (p. 108): whitish bill and nasal shield; lacks white patches on wings and around red eyes.
Selected Sites: Great Lakes waterfronts at New Buffalo, St. Joseph, Holland, Muskegon, Manistee, Cheboygan, Rogers City and Alpena.

BLACK SCOTER
Melanitta nigra

Migration is a lengthy and tiring journey, especially after a rigorous breeding season, so many Black Scoters make rest stops on the Great Lakes and on other large bodies of water as they travel south through Michigan. Some of these handsome scoters begin arriving as early as September, but the majority arrive through late fall and early winter, just when the frigid cold beckons at our doors. • While floating on the water's surface, Black Scoters tend to hold their heads high, unlike other scoters, which generally look downward. The male is the only North American duck that is uniformly black. • Black Scoters are the most vocal of the scoters, and often reveal their presence with their plaintive, mellow whistling calls from far out on open water. • Of the three species of scoters in the region, the Black Scoter is the least common. This rarity belies its earlier designation of Common Scoter, the name still given to the Eurasian *nigra* subspecies.

ID: *Male:* black overall; large orange knob on bill. *Female:* light "cheek"; dark "cap"; brown overall; dark gray bill. **Size:** *L* 17–20 in; *W* 28 in. **Status:** casual migrant from March to May; more common from September to January; rare winter resident. **Habitat:** large, deep lakes, large rivers and sewage lagoons.

Nesting: does not nest in Michigan. **Feeding:** dives underwater; eats mostly mollusks and aquatic insect larvae; occasionally eats aquatic vegetation and small fish. **Voice:** generally quiet; infrequently an unusual *cour-loo;* wings whistle in flight. **Similar Species:** *White-winged Scoter* (p. 73): white wing patches; male has white slash below eye. *Surf Scoter* (p. 72): male has white on head; female has 2 whitish patches on sides of head. **Selected Sites:** Whitefish Point; Port Huron; St. Clair R.; Muskegon SP; New Buffalo and St. Joseph waterfronts.

LONG-TAILED DUCK
Clangula hyemalis

This ancient mariner of the Great Lakes is able to survive violent winter gales on the scale of the great storm that scuttled the unfortunate *Edmund Fitzgerald*. Long-tailed Ducks tend to remain in deeper waters, well away from shore, limiting observers to brief glimpses of their winter finery and the long, slender tail feathers for which the bird is named. • Long-tailed Ducks are among the noisiest breeders on the arctic tundra, but during migration and over winter they remain relatively silent. • The breeding and nonbreeding plumages of these arctic-nesting sea ducks are like photo-negatives of each other: their spring breeding plumage is mostly dark with white highlights, while their winter plumage is mostly white with dark patches. • Long-tailed Ducks are among the world's deepest diving waterfowl—they make regular dives to depths of more than 200 feet. • Until recently, this duck was officially called "Oldsquaw," a name that many people still use.

breeding

nonbreeding

ID: *Breeding male:* dark head with white "eye patch"; dark neck and upperparts; white belly; dark bill; long, dark central tail feathers. *Breeding female:* short tail feathers; gray bill; dark crown, throat patch, wings and back; white underparts. *Nonbreeding male:* pale head with dark patch; pale neck and belly; dark breast; long, white patches on back; pink bill with dark base; long, dark central tail feathers. *Nonbreeding female:* similar to breeding female, but generally lighter, especially on head.
Size: *L* 17–20 in; *W* 28 in.

Status: common migrant and winter resident on the Great Lakes from late October to April or May.
Habitat: large, deep lakes and wetlands.
Nesting: does not nest in Michigan.
Feeding: dives for mollusks, crustaceans and aquatic insects; occasionally eats roots and young shoots; may also take some small fish.
Voice: courtship call is *owl-owl-owlet,* but is rarely heard outside breeding range.
Similar Species: *Northern Pintail* (p. 64): thin, white line extends up sides of neck; gray sides.
Selected Sites: Muskegon SP; Ludington SP; Saugatuck SP; Sleeping Bear Dunes National Lakeshore; Leelanau SP; Wilderness SP.

BUFFLEHEAD

Bucephala albeola

Every winter, the open waters of the Great Lakes become an avian battleground of sorts. Dozens of species of waterfowl patrol the waters in huge flotillas that are often composed of thousands of birds. Winter imposes many limiting factors on birds, so food and suitable habitat may be scarce at times. Fortunately for the tiny Bufflehead, it is right at home on lakes amid its larger relatives. • In migration and in winter, the Bufflehead dives for mollusks, mostly snails. If you are lucky, you may even see a whole flock dive at the same time for these tasty morsels. • The scientific name *Bucephala*, meaning "ox-headed" in Greek, refers to the shape of this bird's head; *albeola* is Latin for "white," a reference to the male's plumage.

ID: very small, rounded duck; white speculum in flight; short gray bill; short neck. *Male:* white wedge on back of head; head is otherwise iridescent, dark green or purple, usually appearing black; dark back; white neck and underparts. *Female:* dark brown head; white, oval ear patch; light brown sides.
Size: *L* 13–15 in; *W* 21 in.
Status: common migrant from early March to early May and from late September to early November; rare summer visitor; uncommon winter resident.
Habitat: open water of lakes, large ponds and rivers.

Nesting: does not nest in Michigan.
Feeding: dives for aquatic invertebrates; takes water boatmen and mayfly and damselfly larvae in summer; favors mollusks, particularly snails, and crustaceans in winter; also eats some small fish and pondweeds.
Voice: *Male:* growling call. *Female:* harsh quack.
Similar Species: *Hooded Merganser* (p. 78): white crest is outlined in black. *Harlequin Duck* (p. 71): female has several light-colored spots on head. *Common Goldeneye* (p. 77) and *Barrow's Goldeneye* (p. 339): males are larger and have white patch between eye and bill. *Other diving ducks* (pp. 66–81): females are much larger.
Selected Sites: Erie Marsh Preserve; Pointe Mouillee SGA; Lake Erie Metropark; Anchor Bay; St. Clair R.; Maple River SGA; Thorn L.

COMMON GOLDENEYE

Bucephala clangula

The courtship display of the male Common Goldeneye looks much like an avian slapstick routine, although to the bird itself it is surely a serious matter. Courtship begins in winter, when the male performs a number of odd postures and vocalizations, often in front of apparently disinterested females. In one common routine, he arches his puffy, iridescent head backward until his forehead seems to touch his back. Next, he catapults his neck forward like a coiled spring while producing a seemingly painful *peent* sound. • Common Goldeneye females often lay their eggs in the nests of other goldeneyes and cavity-nesting ducks. After hatching, duck-

lings remain in the nest for one to three days before jumping out of the tree cavity, often falling a long distance to the ground below. • The Common Goldeneye breeds around the world in northern forests, usually choosing to nest near lakes that have no fish. These lakes are well stocked with the Common Goldeneye's food of choice, aquatic invertebrates. • Common Goldeneyes are frequently called "Whistlers," because the wind whistles through their wings when they fly.

ID: steep forehead with peaked crown; black wings with large, white patches; golden eyes. *Male:* dark, iridescent green head; round, white "cheek" patch; dark bill; dark back; white sides and belly. *Female:* chocolate brown head; lighter breast and belly; gray brown body plumage; dark bill is tipped with yellow in spring and summer.
Size: *L* 16–20 in; *W* 26 in.
Status: common migrant and winter resident from mid-October to mid-April; uncommon breeder.
Habitat: *Breeding:* marshes, ponds, lakes and rivers. *In migration* and *winter:* open water of lakes, large ponds and rivers.
Nesting: in a tree cavity, but will use a

nest box; often close to water, but occasionally quite far from it; cavity is lined with wood chips and down; female incubates 6–10 blue green eggs for 28–32 days; 2 females may each lay a clutch in the same nest if cavities are in short supply.
Feeding: dives for crustaceans, mollusks and aquatic insect larvae; may also eat tubers, leeches, frogs and small fish.
Voice: *Male:* courtship calls are a nasal *peent* and a hoarse *kraaagh. Female:* a harsh croak.
Similar Species: *Barrow's Goldeneye* (p. 339): male has large, white, crescent-shaped "cheek" patch and purplish head; female has more orange on bill and more steeply sloped forehead.
Selected Sites: Erie Marsh Preserve; Pointe Mouillee SGA; St. Clair Flats WA; Fish Point SGA; Maple River SGA; Thorn L.; Allegan SGA; Muskegon Wastewater System; Dead Stream Flooding; Whitefish Point; Little Bay de Noc.

HOODED MERGANSER

Lophodytes cucullatus

Extremely attractive and exceptionally shy, the Hooded Merganser is one of the most sought-after ducks from a birder's perspective, and most of the attention is directed toward the handsome male. Much of the time the male Hooded Merganser's crest is held flat, but in moments of arousal or agitation he quickly unfolds his brilliant crest to attract a mate or to signal approaching danger. The drake displays his full range of colors and athletic abilities in elaborate, late-winter courtship displays and chases. • Nationally, Hoodies attain their greatest density in summer in the Great Lakes region, wherever woodlands occur near waterways. • All mergansers have thin bills with small, toothlike serrations to help the birds keep a firm grasp on slippery prey. The smallest of the mergansers, Hoodies have a more diverse diet than their larger relatives. They add crustaceans, insects and even acorns to the usual diet of fish. • Unusually, female Hooded Mergansers have been known to share incubation of eggs with female Wood Ducks and goldeneyes.

ID: slim body; crested head; dark, thin, pointed bill. *Male:* black head and back; bold white crest is outlined in black; white breast with 2 black slashes; rusty sides. *Female:* dusky brown body; shaggy, reddish brown crest. *In flight:* small, white wing patches.
Size: *L* 16–18 in; *W* 24 in.
Status: common migrant from mid-March to mid-November; uncommon breeder; rare winter resident.
Habitat: forest-edged ponds, wetlands, lakes and rivers.
Nesting: usually in a tree cavity 15–40 ft above the ground; may also use a nest box; cavity is lined with leaves, grass and down; female incubates 10–12 spherical, white eggs for 29–33 days; some females may lay

their eggs in other birds' nests, including the nests of other species.
Feeding: very diverse diet; dives for small fish, caddisfly and dragonfly larvae, snails, amphibians and crayfish.
Voice: low grunts and croaks. *Male:* frog-like *crrrrooo* in courtship display. *Female:* generally quiet; occasionally a harsh *gak* or a croaking *croo-croo-crook.*
Similar Species: *Bufflehead* (p. 76): male lacks black crest outline and black shoulder and breast slashes. *Red-breasted Merganser* (p. 80) and *Common Merganser* (p. 79): females have much longer, orange bill and gray back. *Other diving ducks* (pp. 66–81): females lack crest.
Selected Sites: Thorn L.; Waterloo SRA; Baker Sanctuary; Maple River SGA; Allegan SGA; Sleepy Hollow SP; Shiawassee Flats NWR; Arcadia Lake Marsh; Grass Lake Flooding; Betchler Lakes; Sylvania Recreation Area; Seney NWR.

COMMON MERGANSER

Mergus merganser

Straining like a jumbo jet in takeoff, the Common Merganser runs along the surface of the water, beating its wings until it gains sufficient speed to become airborne. Once up and away, this great duck flies arrow-straight, low over the water, making broad sweeping turns to follow the meanderings of rivers and lake shorelines. • The Common Merganser is highly social, and often gathers in large groups over winter and during migration. In winter, any source of open water with a fish-filled shoal may support good numbers of these skilled divers. • In Michigan, Common Mergansers breed among forest-edged waterways wherever there are cool, clear and unpolluted lakes and rivers. Common Mergansers are cavity nesters but will also nest on the ground in areas with good fishing and an absence of suitable cavities, such as the shores of the Great Lakes. • The Common Merganser is the most widespread and abundant merganser in North America. It also occurs in Europe and Asia, where it is called the "Goosander."

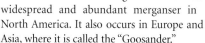

ID: large, elongated body. *Male:* glossy, green head without crest; blood red bill and feet; white body plumage; black stripe on back; dark eyes. *Female:* rusty neck and crested head; clean white "chin" and breast; orange bill; gray body; orangish eyes. *In flight:* shallow wingbeats; body is compressed and arrowlike.
Size: *L* 22–27 in; *W* 34 in.
Status: common migrant and winter resident from late September to late April; uncommon breeder.
Habitat: large rivers and deep lakes.
Nesting: often in a tree cavity 15–20 ft above the ground; occasionally on the ground, under a bush or log, on a cliff ledge or in a large nest box; usually not far from water; female incubates 8–11 pale buff eggs for 30–35 days.

Feeding: dives to depths of 30 ft for small fish, usually whitefish, trout, suckers, perch and minnows; young eat aquatic invertebrates and insects before switching to small fish.
Voice: *Male:* harsh *uig-a*, like a guitar twang. *Female:* harsh *karr karr*.
Similar Species: *Red-breasted Merganser* (p. 80): male has shaggy green crest and spotted, red breast; female lacks cleanly defined white throat. *Mallard* (p. 61): male has chestnut brown breast and yellow bill. *Common Goldeneye* (p. 77): male has white "cheek" patch and stubby, dark bill. *Common Loon* (p. 34): dark bill; white-spotted back.
Selected Sites: Pointe Mouillee SGA; Detroit R.; Anchor Bay; St. Clair Flats WA; St. Clair R.; Sault Ste. Marie; Whitefish Point; Muskegon Wastewater System; Arcadia L.; Grand Traverse Bay; Little Bay de Noc; Shiawassee Flats NWR.

RED-BREASTED MERGANSER

Mergus serrator

Its glossy, slicked-back crest and wild red eyes give the Red-breasted Merganser the disheveled, wave-bashed look of an adrenalized windsurfer. This species was formerly called "Sawbill" and "Sea-Robin," and it's a good thing that bird names are now standardized—who knows what we would be calling this punk-haired bird today. • Each spring and fall, the shores of the lower Great Lakes host huge congregations of Red-breasted Mergansers. During peak migration, thousands of these birds may congregate along inshore waters to rest and refuel. Unlike the other two merganser species, Red-breasts prefer to nest on the ground. This bird's lack of dependence on trees enables it to nest where related cavity-nesting species cannot. • Shortly after their mates have begun incubating, males fly off to join large offshore rafts for the duration of summer. During this time, a brief molt makes the males largely indistinguishable from their female counterparts. • Red-breasts will sometimes fish cooperatively, funneling fishes for easier capture.

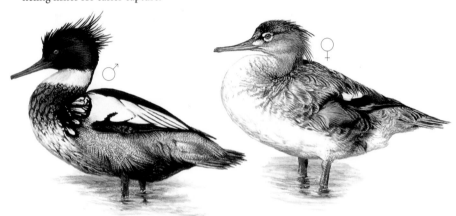

ID: large, elongated body; red eyes; thin, serrated, orange bill; shaggy, slicked-back head crest. *Male:* green head; light rusty breast spotted with black; white "collar"; gray sides; black-and-white shoulders. *Female:* gray brown overall; reddish head; white "chin," foreneck and breast. *In flight:* male has large, white wing patch crossed by 2 narrow, black bars; female has 1 dark bar separating white speculum from white upperwing patch.
Size: *L* 19–26 in; *W* 30 in.
Status: common migrant from April to May and from October to November; uncommon breeder and winter resident.
Habitat: lakes and large rivers, especially those with rocky shorelines and islands.

Nesting: usually on a rocky island or shoreline; on the ground, well concealed under bushes, driftwood or in dense vegetation; female lines a hollow with plant material and down; female incubates 7–10 olive buff eggs for 29–35 days.
Feeding: dives underwater for small fish; also eats aquatic invertebrates, fish eggs and crustaceans.
Voice: generally quiet. *Male:* catlike *yeow* during courtship and feeding. *Female:* harsh *kho-kha*.
Similar Species: *Common Merganser* (p. 79): male has clean white breast and blood red bill and lacks head crest; female's rusty foreneck contrasts with white "chin" and breast.
Selected Sites: Erie Marsh Preserve; Lake St. Clair; St. Clair R.; Sault Ste. Marie; Muskegon Wastewater System; Whitefish Point; Nayanquing Point WA.

RUDDY DUCK

Oxyura jamaicensis

The clown of the wetlands, the male Ruddy Duck displays energetic courtship behavior with comedic enthusiasm. The small male vigorously pumps his bright blue bill, almost touching his breast. The *plap, plap, plap-plap-plap* of the display increases in speed to its hilarious climax: a spasmodic jerk and sputter. • Female Ruddies commonly lay up to 10 eggs at a time—a remarkable feat considering that their eggs are bigger than those of a Mallard and that a Mallard is significantly larger than a Ruddy Duck. Females take part in an unusual practice, often dumping eggs in a communal "dummy" nest that may finally accumulate as many as 60 eggs that will receive no motherly care. • Some people might imagine birding paradise as a deep, lush green forest or a dense, marshy wetland, but few birders would visualize a local sewage lagoon. Birders searching for Ruddy Ducks, however, might find a sewage lagoon a desirable place to visit.

breeding

ID: large bill and head; short neck; long, stiff tail feathers (often held upward). *Breeding male:* white "cheek"; chestnut red body; blue bill; black tail and crown. *Female:* brown overall; dark "cheek" stripe; darker crown and back. *Nonbreeding male:* similar to female but with white "cheek."

Size: *L* 15–16 in.; *W* 18½ in.

Status: common migrant from April to May and from late September to mid-November; rare breeder and winter resident.

Habitat: *Breeding:* shallow marshes with dense emergent vegetation (such as cattails or bulrushes) and muddy bottoms. *In migration* and *winter:* sewage lagoons and lakes with open, shallow water.

Nesting: in cattails, bulrushes or other emergent vegetation; female suspends a woven platform nest over water; may use abandoned duck or coot nest, muskrat lodge or exposed log; female incubates 5–10 rough, whitish eggs for 23–26 days; occasional brood parasite.

Feeding: dives to the bottom of wetlands for seeds of pondweeds, sedges and bulrushes and for the leafy parts of aquatic plants; also eats a few aquatic invertebrates.

Voice: *Male: chuck-chuck-chuck-chur-r-r-r* during courtship display. *Female:* generally silent.

Similar Species: *Cinnamon Teal:* lacks white "cheek" and blue bill. *Other diving ducks* (pp. 66–81): females lack long, stiff tail and dark facial stripe.

Selected Sites: Erie Marsh Preserve; Pointe Mouillee SGA; St. Clair Flats WA; Thorn L.; Muskegon Wastewater System; Nayanquing Point WA; Maple River SGA; Whitefish Point; Little Bay de Noc.

OSPREY
Pandion haliaetus

The Osprey eats fish exclusively and is found near water. While hunting, an Osprey will survey waterways from the air—its white belly makes it hard for fish to see it hovering far above the water's surface. The Osprey's dark eye line blocks the glare from the water, enabling it to spot a slowly moving shadow or a flash of silver near the water's surface. Folding its wings, the Osprey hurls itself in a headfirst dive toward its target. An instant before striking the water, the bird rights itself and thrusts its feet forward to grasp its slippery prey, often striking the water with a tremendous splash. The Osprey's feet are specialized to prevent its catch from making a squirmy escape—two toes face forward, two face backward and the toes have sharp spines to help the Osprey clamp tightly onto the slipperiest of fish. • The Osprey is the only species in its family and is one of the most widely distributed birds in the world—it is found on every continent except Antarctica.

ID: dark brown upperparts; white underparts; dark eye line; yellow eyes; light crown. *Male:* all-white throat. *Female:* fine, dark "necklace." *In flight:* long wings are held in shallow "M"; dark "wrist" patches; brown-and-white banded tail.

Size: *L* 22–25 in; *W* 4½–6 ft.

Status: threatened; uncommon migrant from March to mid-October; uncommon breeder in northern two-thirds of the state.

Habitat: lakes and slowly flowing rivers and streams.

Nesting: on a treetop, usually near water; may also use a specially made platform, utility pole or tower up to 100 ft high; massive stick nest is reused over many years; pair incubates 2–4 yellowish eggs, spotted and blotched with reddish brown, for about 38 days; both adults feed the young, but the male hunts more.

Feeding: dramatic, feet-first dives into the water; fish, averaging 2 lbs, make up almost all of the diet.

Voice: series of melodious ascending whistles: *chewk-chewk-chewk;* also an often-heard *kip-kip-kip.*

Similar Species: *Bald Eagle* (p. 83): larger; holds its wings straighter while soaring; larger bill with yellow base; yellow legs; adult has clean white head and tail on otherwise dark body; lacks white underparts and dark "wrist" patches. *Rough-legged Hawk* (p. 92): smaller; hovers with wings in an open "V"; light phase has whitish wing linings and light tail band.

Selected Sites: Fletcher Pond; Dead Stream Flooding; Houghton L.; Sault Ste. Marie; Seney NWR; Whitefish Point; Isle Royale NP; Lake Erie Metropark.

BALD EAGLE
Haliaeetus leucocephalus

The Bald Eagle is a source of inspiration and wonder for anyone longing for a wilderness experience. Though it cannot compete with the Golden Eagle in strength of talon and character, legends persist that endow it with a mystical quality that is difficult to dispute. • Bald Eagles feed mostly on fish and scavenged carrion. Sometimes an eagle will steal food from an Osprey, resulting in a spectacular aerial chase. • Pairs perform dramatic aerial displays. The most impressive display involves the two birds flying to a great height, locking talons and then tumbling perilously toward the earth. The birds break off at the last second, just before crashing into the ground. • Bald Eagles do not mature until their fourth or fifth year, only then receiving their characteristic white head and tail plumage. • Bald Eagles generally mate for life. They renew their pair bonds each year by adding new sticks and branches to their massive nests, the largest of any North American bird.

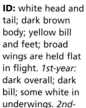

immature

ID: white head and tail; dark brown body; yellow bill and feet; broad wings are held flat in flight. *1st-year:* dark overall; dark bill; some white in underwings. *2nd-year:* dark "bib"; white in underwings. *3rd-year:* mostly white plumage; yellow at base of bill; yellow eyes. *4th-year:* light head with dark facial streak; variable pale and dark plumage; yellow bill; paler eyes. *In flight:* broad wings are held flat.
Size: *L* 30–43 in; *W* 5½–8 ft.
Status: threatened; uncommon migrant from March to April and from October to November; uncommon breeder; uncommon winter resident around ice-free waters.
Habitat: large lakes and rivers.
Nesting: usually in a tree bordering a lake or large river, but may be far from water; huge stick nest, up to 15 ft across, is often reused for many years; pair incubates 1–3 white eggs for 34–36 days; pair feeds the young.
Feeding: eats waterbirds, small mammals and fish captured at water's surface; frequently feeds on carrion; sometimes pirates fish from Ospreys.
Voice: thin, weak squeal or gull-like cackle: *kleek-kik-kik-kik* or *kah-kah-kah.*
Similar Species: adult is distinctive. *Golden Eagle* (p. 93): dark overall, except for golden nape; tail may appear faintly banded with white; immature has prominent white patch on wings and at base of tail. *Osprey* (p. 82): like a 4th-year Bald Eagle, but has dark "wrist" patches, dark bill, and M-shaped wings in flight.
Selected Sites: Lake Erie Metropark; Whitefish Point; Shiawassee Flats NWR; Seney NWR; Isle Royale NP; Hartwick Pines SP; Brockway Mountain Drive.

NORTHERN HARRIER

Circus cyaneus

The Northern Harrier may be the easiest raptor to identify on the wing because no other midsized bird routinely flies so close to the ground. It cruises low over fields, meadows and marshes, grazing the tops of long grasses and cattails, relying on sudden surprise attacks to capture its prey. Its owl-like, parabolic facial disc allows it to hunt easily by sound as well. • The Northern Harrier was once known as "Marsh Hawk" in North America, and it is still called "Hen Harrier" in Europe. Britain's Royal Air Force was so impressed by this bird's maneuverability that it named its Harrier aircraft after this hawk. • The courtship flight of the Northern Harrier is a spring event worth seeing. The pale-colored male climbs almost vertically and then stalls, sending himself into a reckless dive toward solid ground. At the last second he saves himself with a flight course that sends him skyward again. • In recent years, this bird has declined greatly in Michigan, owing to the loss of its wetland habitat.

ID: long wings and tail; white rump; black wing tips. *Male:* blue gray to silver gray upperparts; white underparts; indistinct tail bands, except for 1 dark subterminal band. *Female:* dark brown upperparts; streaky brown-and-buff underparts. *Immature:* rich reddish brown plumage; dark tail bands; streaked breast, sides and flanks.

Size: *L* 16–24 in; *W* 3½–4 ft.

Status: special concern; uncommon migrant from March to November; uncommon breeder; uncommon winter resident in the southern third of the state.

Habitat: open country, including fields, wet meadows, cattail marshes, bogs and croplands.

Nesting: on the ground, often on a slightly raised mound; usually in grass, cattails or tall vegetation; shallow depression or platform nest is lined with grass, sticks and cattails; female incubates 4–6 bluish white eggs for 30–32 days.

Feeding: hunts in low, rising and falling flights, often skimming the tops of vegetation; eats small mammals, birds, amphibians, reptiles and some invertebrates.

Voice: most vocal near the nest and during courtship, but generally quiet; high-pitched *ke-ke-ke-ke-ke-ke* near the nest.

Similar Species: *Rough-legged Hawk* (p. 92): broader wings; dark "wrist" patches; black tail with wide, white base; dark belly. *Red-tailed Hawk* (p. 91): lacks white rump and long, narrow tail.

Selected Sites: Lake Erie Metropark; St. Clair Flats WA; Erie Marsh Preserve; Maple River SGA; Allegan SGA; Baker Sanctuary; Brockway Mountain Drive.

SHARP-SHINNED HAWK

Accipiter striatus

After a successful hunt, the small Sharp-shinned Hawk usually perches on a favorite "plucking post," grasping its meal in its razor-sharp talons. These hawks prey almost exclusively on small birds, pursuing them in high-speed chases. • Most people never see a Sharpie nest, because the birds are very tight sitters. Disturb one, however, and you will feel the occupants' wrath. These birds are feisty defenders of their nest and young. • When delivering food to its nestlings, a male Sharp-shinned Hawk is cautious around his mate—she is typically one-third larger than he is and notoriously short-tempered. • Accipiters, named after their genus, are woodland hawks. Their short, rounded wings, long, rudderlike tails and flap-and-glide flight pattern give them the maneuverability necessary to negotiate a maze of forest foliage at high speed.

ID: short, rounded wings; long, straight, heavily barred, square-tipped tail; dark barring on pale underwings; blue gray back; red horizontal bars on underparts; red eyes. *Immature:* brown overall; dark eyes; vertical, brown streaking on breast and belly.
In flight: flap-and-glide flyer; very agile in wooded areas.
Size: *Male: L* 10–12 in; *W* 20–24 in. *Female: L* 12–14 in; *W* 24–28 in.
Status: common migrant from late March to mid-May and from August to early November; common breeder in northern Michigan; uncommon winter resident in the south.
Habitat: dense to semi-open forests and large woodlots; occasionally along rivers and in urban areas; favors bogs and dense, moist, coniferous forests for nesting.

Nesting: in a conifer; usually builds a new stick nest each year, but might remodel an abandoned crow nest; female incubates 4–5 brown-blotched, bluish white eggs for 34–35 days; male feeds the female during incubation.
Feeding: pursues small birds through forests; rarely takes small mammals, amphibians and insects.
Voice: silent except during breeding season, when an intense and often repeated *kik-kik-kik-kik* can be heard.
Similar Species: *Cooper's Hawk* (p. 86): larger; more rounded tail tip has broader terminal band; crown is darker than nape and back. *American Kestrel* (p. 94): long, pointed wings; 1 dark "tear streak" and 1 dark "sideburn"; typically seen in open country. *Merlin* (p. 95): pointed wings; rapid wingbeats; 1 dark "tear streak"; brown streaking on buff underparts; dark eyes.
Selected Sites: Lake Erie Metropark; Whitefish Point; Sleeper SP; Wilderness SP; Muskegon SP; J.W. Wells SP; Tawas Point SP; Nayanquing Point WA; St. Clair Flats WA; Brockway Mountain Drive; backyard feeders.

COOPER'S HAWK

Accipiter cooperii

Larger and heavier than the Sharp-shinned Hawk, the Cooper's Hawk glides silently along forest clearings, using surprise and speed to snatch its prey from midair. Females can seize and decapitate birds as large as Ruffed Grouse, which they sometimes pursue on the ground like overweight roadrunners. • These birds are now protected by law and the use of DDT has been banned throughout North America, with the result that the Cooper's Hawk is increasing in numbers and slowly recolonizing former habitats in the region. • Distinguishing the Cooper's Hawk from the Sharp-shinned Hawk is challenging. In flight, the Cooper's has a shallower, stiffer-winged flight, while the Sharpie has deeper wingbeats with more bending in the wings. Sharp-shins have a square tail, while the Cooper's tail is more rounded. As well, the Cooper's Hawk can be seen perching on fence posts, poles and tree branches, whereas the Sharp-shin perches almost exclusively on tree branches.

ID: short, rounded wings; long, straight, heavily barred, rounded tail; dark barring on pale undertail and underwings; squarish head; blue gray back; red horizontal barring on underparts; red eyes; white terminal tail band. *Immature:* brown overall; dark eyes; vertical brown streaks on breast and belly. *In flight:* flap-and-glide flyer.
Size: *Male: L* 15–17 in; *W* 27–32 in. *Female: L* 17–19 in; *W* 32–37 in.
Status: special concern; common migrant from mid-March to mid-April and from late September to late October; uncommon breeder; uncommon winter resident in the south.
Habitat: mixed woodlands, riparian woodlands and urban woodlots.
Nesting: nest of sticks and twigs is built 20–65 ft above the ground in the crotch of a deciduous or coniferous tree; often near a stream or pond; might reuse an abandoned crow nest; female incubates 3–5 bluish white eggs for 34–36 days; male feeds the female during incubation.
Feeding: pursues prey in flights through forests; eats mostly songbirds but occasionally takes squirrels and chipmunks; uses "plucking post" or nest for eating.
Voice: fast, woodpecker-like *cac-cac-cac-cac.*
Similar Species: *Sharp-shinned Hawk* (p. 85): smaller; less rounded tail tip; thinner terminal tail band. *American Kestrel* (p. 94): smaller; long, pointed wings; 1 dark "tear streak" and 1 dark "sideburn"; typically seen in open country. *Merlin* (p. 95): smaller; pointed wings; rapid wingbeats; 1 dark "tear streak"; brown streaking on buff underparts; dark eyes.
Selected Sites: Lake Erie Metropark; Whitefish Point; Sleeper SP; Wilderness SP; Muskegon SP; Tawas Point SP; Brockway Mountain Drive; backyard feeders.

NORTHERN GOSHAWK

Accipiter gentilis

The Northern Goshawk is an agile and powerful predator capable of negotiating lightning-fast turns through dense forest cover to overtake its prey. This raptor will prey on any animal it can overtake, dispatching its capture with powerful talons. This bird has even been known to chase quarry on foot should elusive prey disappear under the cover of dense thickets. • Goshawks are devoted parents that are equally ferocious when defending their nest sites. Unfortunate souls who wander too close to a goshawk nest may be assaulted by an almost deafening, squawking dive-bomb attack. • In the past, all three Accipiter species have been subjected to scorn and disapproval for their "bloodthirsty" habit of hunting songbirds. This type of thinking resulted in unwarranted persecution, which thankfully has largely been abandoned.

ID: rounded wings; long, banded tail with white terminal band; white "eyebrow"; dark crown; blue gray back; fine, gray, vertical streaking on pale breast and belly; gray barring on pale undertail and underwings; red eyes. *Immature:* brown overall; brown vertical streaking on whitish breast and belly; brown barring on pale undertail and underwings; yellow eyes.
Size: *Male: L* 21–23 in; *W* 3–3½ ft.
Female: L 23–25 in; *W* 3½–4 ft.
Status: special concern; rare to uncommon resident in the northern two-thirds of the state; rare to uncommon winter resident in the south.
Habitat: *Breeding:* mature coniferous, deciduous and mixed woodlands.
Nonbreeding: forest edges, semi-open parklands and farmlands.
Nesting: in deep woods; male builds a large, bulky, stick platform in the crotch

of a deciduous or coniferous tree, usually 25–80 ft above the ground; nest is often reused for several years; female incubates 2–4 bluish white eggs for 35–36 days; male feeds the female during incubation.
Feeding: low foraging flights through the forest; feeds primarily on grouse, rabbits and squirrels.
Voice: silent except during breeding season, when adult utters a loud, fast, shrill *kak-kak-kak-kak.*
Similar Species: *Cooper's Hawk* (p. 86) and *Sharp-shinned Hawk* (p. 85): smaller; reddish breast bars; lacks white "eyebrow" stripe; immatures are smaller and have yellow eyes, which become more orange with age. Buteo *hawks* (pp. 88–92): shorter tails; broader wings; gray or brown eyes. *Gyrfalcon* (p. 96): more pointed wings; dark eyes; often has dark "tear streak."
Selected Sites: Whitefish Point; Seney NWR; Isle Royale NP; Sylvania Recreation Area; Lake Erie Metropark; Muskegon SP; Brockway Mountain Drive.

RED-SHOULDERED HAWK

Buteo lineatus

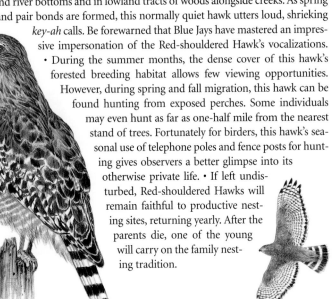

The Red-shouldered Hawk is a bird of wetter habitats than the closely related Broad-winged Hawk and Red-tailed Hawk. It nests in mature trees, usually around river bottoms and in lowland tracts of woods alongside creeks. As spring approaches and pair bonds are formed, this normally quiet hawk utters loud, shrieking *key-ah* calls. Be forewarned that Blue Jays have mastered an impressive impersonation of the Red-shouldered Hawk's vocalizations. • During the summer months, the dense cover of this hawk's forested breeding habitat allows few viewing opportunities. However, during spring and fall migration, this hawk can be found hunting from exposed perches. Some individuals may even hunt as far as one-half mile from the nearest stand of trees. Fortunately for birders, this hawk's seasonal use of telephone poles and fence posts for hunting gives observers a better glimpse into its otherwise private life. • If left undisturbed, Red-shouldered Hawks will remain faithful to productive nesting sites, returning yearly. After the parents die, one of the young will carry on the family nesting tradition.

ID: chestnut red shoulders on otherwise dark brown upperparts; reddish underwing linings; narrow, white bars on dark tail; barred, reddish breast and belly; reddish undertail coverts. *Immature:* large, brown "teardrop" streaks on white underparts; whitish undertail coverts. *In flight:* light and dark barring on underside of flight feathers and tail; white crescents or "windows" at base of primaries.

Size: *L* 19 in; *W* 3½ ft.

Status: threatened; uncommon migrant from mid-March to November; uncommon breeder in northern half of Lower Peninsula, rare elsewhere; rare winter resident in the south.

Habitat: mature deciduous and mixed forests, wooded riparian areas, swampy woodlands and large, mature woodlots.

Nesting: pair assembles a bulky nest of sticks and twigs, usually 15–80 ft above the ground in the crotch of a deciduous tree (prefers mature maple), ash and beech trees); nest is often reused; female incubates 2–4 darkly blotched, bluish white eggs for about 33 days; both adults raise the young.

Feeding: prey is usually detected from fence post, tree or telephone pole and caught in a swooping attack; may catch prey flushed by low flight; eats small mammals, birds, reptiles and amphibians.

Voice: repeated series of high *key-ah* notes.

Similar Species: *Broad-winged Hawk* (p. 89): lacks reddish shoulders; wings are broader, more whitish and dark-edged underneath; wide, white tail bands. *Red-tailed Hawk* (p. 91): lacks barring on tail and light "windows" at base of primaries.

Selected Sites: Lake Erie Metropark; Whitefish Point; Warren Woods Natural Area; Allegan SGA; Leelanau SP; Brockway Mountain Drive.

BROAD-WINGED HAWK

Buteo platypterus

The generally shy and secretive Broad-winged Hawk shuns the open fields and forest clearings favored by other buteos, such as the Red-tailed Hawk, to seclude itself in dense, often wet forests. In this habitat, its short, broad wings and highly flexible tail help it to maneuver in the heavy growth. • Most hunting is done from a high perch with a good view. After being flushed from its perch, the Broad-winged Hawk will return and resume its vigilant search for a meal. • At the end of the nesting season, "kettles" of buteos and other hawks spiral up from their forest retreats, testing thermals for the opportunity to head south. Broad-winged Hawks are often the most numerous species in these flocks. • Each fall, the mass exodus of Broad-wings in their migration to Central and South America offers birders a chance to enjoy an unforgettable experience. In good flight years, when cool temperatures, moderate northwest winds and sunny skies prevail, well over 30,000 Broad-wings can be observed in a single day at Lake Erie Metropark!

ID: broad, black and white tail bands; broad wings with pointed tips; heavily barred, rufous brown breast; dark brown upperparts. *Immature:* dark brown "teardrop" streaks on white breast, belly and sides; buff and dark brown tail bands. *In flight:* pale underwings are outlined with dark brown.

Size: *L* 14–19 in; *W* 32–39 in.

Status: uncommon migrant from April to May; common migrant from September to early October; common breeder in the north; uncommon breeder in the south.

Habitat: *Breeding:* dense mixed and deciduous forests and woodlots. *In migration:* escarpments and shorelines; also uses riparian and deciduous forests and woodland edges.

Nesting: usually in a deciduous tree, often near water; bulky stick nest is built in a crotch 20–40 ft above the ground; usually builds a new nest each year; mostly the female incubates 2–4 brown-spotted, whitish eggs for 28–31 days; both adults raise the young.

Feeding: swoops from a perch for small mammals, amphibians, insects and young birds; often seen hunting from roadside telephone poles in northern areas.

Voice: high-pitched, whistled *peeeo-wee-ee;* generally silent during migration.

Similar Species: *Other* buteo *hawks* (pp. 88–92): lack broad banding on tail and broad, dark-edged wings with pointed tips. Accipiter *hawks* (pp. 85–87): long, narrow tails with less distinct banding.

Selected Sites: Lake Erie Metropark; Sleeper SP; Muskegon SP; Whitefish Point; Brockway Mountain Drive; Barry Co. SGA; Island Lake SRA.

SWAINSON'S HAWK
Buteo swainsoni

This western Buteo rarely visits Michigan, but once you learn to look for relatively pointed wing tips, slightly uptilted wings and flight feathers that are darker than the wing lining, you may be able to identify this bird from as far away as you can see it. • Twice a year, Swainson's Hawks undertake long migratory journeys that may lead them as far south as the southern tip of South America and as far north as Alaska. Traveling up to 12,500 miles in a single year, the Swainson's Hawk is second only to the arctic-breeding Peregrine Falcon for long-distance travel among birds of prey. The massive "kettles" of Swainson's Hawks migrating through Central America have been likened to the legendary flocks of Passenger Pigeons that were said to blacken the sky. Unfortunately, many of these hawks are killed by the incautious use of insecticides in Argentina, reminding us that the conservation of migratory species requires international cooperation. • This hawk bears the name of Englishman William Swainson, an early 19th-century illustrator of natural history.

light morph

light morph

ID: long wings with pointed tips; narrowly banded tail; dark flight feathers. *Dark morph:* dark overall; brown wing linings blend with flight feathers. *Light morph:* dark "bib"; white belly; white wing linings contrast with dark flight feathers. *In flight:* holds wings in shallow "V."
Size: *L* 19–22 in; *W* 4½ ft.
Status: rare migrant from mid-April to May and from September to October; found mainly in the northern part of the state.
Habitat: open fields, grasslands, sagebrush and agricultural areas.

Nesting: does not nest in Michigan.
Feeding: dives for voles, mice and ground squirrels; also eats snakes, small birds and large insects, such as grasshoppers and crickets.
Voice: typical hawk call, *keeeaar,* is higher pitched than a Red-tail's.
Similar Species: *Red-tailed Hawk* (p. 91): more rounded wing tips; holds wings flat in flight. *Other* buteo *hawks* (pp. 88–92): flight feathers are paler than wing lining. *Golden Eagle* (p. 93): much larger; golden nape; massive bill.
Selected Sites: Whitefish Point; Brockway Mountain Drive, Lake Erie Metropark.

RED-TAILED HAWK

Buteo jamaicensis

The Red-tailed Hawk is the most commonly seen hawk in Michigan. It is conspicuous year-round, particularly near agricultural lands. An afternoon drive through the country will reveal resident Red-tails perching on exposed tree limbs, fence posts or utility poles overlooking open fields and roadsides. • During their spring courtship, excited Red-tailed Hawks dive at each other, sometimes locking talons and tumbling through the air together before breaking off to avoid crashing to the ground. • The Red-tailed Hawk's impressive piercing call is often paired with the image of an eagle in TV commercials and movies. • This hawk's tail does not obtain its brick red coloration until the bird matures into a breeding adult.

ID: red tail; dark upperparts with some white highlights; dark brown band of streaks across belly. *Immature:* extremely variable; lacks red tail; generally darker; band of streaks on belly. *In flight:* fan-shaped tail; white or occasionally tawny brown underside and underwing linings; dark leading edge on underside of wing; light underwing flight feathers with faint barring.
Size: *Male: L* 18–23 in; *W* 4–5 ft. *Female: L* 20–25 in; *W* 4–5 ft.
Status: common migrant; common to abundant breeder.
Habitat: open country with some trees; also roadsides, fields, woodlots, hedgerows, mixed forests and moist woodlands.
Nesting: in woodlands adjacent to open habitat; usually in a deciduous tree; rarely on a cliff or in a conifer; bulky stick nest is usually added to each year; pair incubates 2–4 brown-blotched, whitish eggs for

28–35 days; male brings food to the female and young.
Feeding: scans for food while perched or soaring; drops to capture prey; rarely stalks prey on foot; eats voles, mice, rabbits, chipmunks, birds, amphibians and reptiles; rarely takes large insects.
Voice: powerful, descending scream: *keeearrrr.*
Similar Species: *Rough-legged Hawk* (p. 92): white tail base; dark "wrist" patches on underwings; broad, dark, terminal tail band. *Broad-winged Hawk* (p. 89): broadly banded tail; broader wings with pointed tips; lacks dark "belt." *Red-shouldered Hawk* (p. 88): reddish wing linings and underparts; reddish shoulders. *Swainson's Hawk* (p. 90): all-dark back; more pointed wing tips; dark flight feathers and pale wing linings in flight; holds wings in shallow "V."
Selected Sites: Lake Erie Metropark; Brockway Mountain Drive; Whitefish Point; Sleeper SP; Muskegon SP; Waterloo SRA; Allegan SGA.

ROUGH-LEGGED HAWK
Buteo lagopus

Population levels of Rough-legged Hawks in their arctic breeding grounds change in relation to fluctuating densities of voles and northern lemmings. When lemming and vole numbers are high, Rough-legs can produce up to seven young, resulting in many sightings here in Michigan during the winter months. In lean years a pair is fortunate to raise a single chick, and sightings here are subsequently more rare. • While hunting, the Rough-legged Hawk often "wind-hovers" to scan the ground below, flapping to maintain a stationary position while facing upwind—a hunting technique that serves as an excellent long distance identification tool for birders. This hawk's habit of hovering is necessary because its open-country habitat often lacks high perches, though these birds will use fence posts and telephone poles when available. • Rough-legged Hawks show great variety in coloration, ranging from a whitish light morph with dark patterning to dark-morph birds that are almost entirely dark with distinctive whitish areas. • The name *lagopus*, meaning "hare's foot," refers to this bird's distinctive feathered legs, which are an adaptation for survival in cold climates.

light morph

immature

ID: white tail base with 1 wide, dark subterminal band; dark brown upper-parts; light flight feathers; legs are feathered to toes. *Dark morph:* dark wing linings, head and underparts. *Light morph:* wide, dark abdominal "belt"; dark streaks on breast and head; dark "wrist" patches; light underwing linings. *Immature:* lighter streaking on breast; bold belly band; buff leg feathers. *In flight:* most show dark "wrist" patches; frequently hovers.

Size: *L* 19–24 in; *W* 4–4½ ft.

Status: uncommon to common migrant and winter resident from October to May.

Habitat: fields, meadows, open bogs and agricultural croplands.

Nesting: does not nest in Michigan.

Feeding: soars and hovers while searching for prey; primarily eats small rodents; occasionally eats birds, amphibians and large insects.

Voice: alarm call is a catlike *kee-eer,* usually dropping at the end.

Similar Species: *Other* buteo *hawks* (pp. 88–91): rarely hover; lack dark "wrist" patches and white tail base. *Northern Harrier* (p. 84): facial disc; lacks dark "wrist" patches and dark belly band; longer, thinner tail lacks broad, dark subterminal band.

Selected Sites: Whitefish Point; Brockway Mountain Drive; Lake Erie Metropark; Muskegon Wastewater System; Maple River SGA.

GOLDEN EAGLE

Aquila chrysaetos

For many centuries, the Golden Eagle has embodied the wonder and wildness of the North American landscape. Unfortunately, with the advent of widespread human development and intensive agricultural practices, this noble bird became the victim of a lengthy persecution. Perceived as a threat to livestock, bounties were offered, encouraging the shooting and poisoning of this regal bird. Today, the Golden Eagle is protected under the Migratory Bird Act. • The Golden Eagle is actually more closely related to the buteos than it is to the Bald Eagle. • Unlike the Bald Eagle, the Golden Eagle is an active, impressive predator, taking prey as large as foxes, cranes and geese. The Golden Eagle can soar high above mountain passes for hours, sometimes stooping at great speeds—150 to 200 miles per hour—for prey or for fun. • The Golden Eagle is a western bird, associated with mountainous areas and is therefore a rare treat for Michigan birders. Previously thought to be nonmigratory, its migration route along the Rocky Mountains was discovered in 1992. • Few people ever forget the sight of a Golden Eagle soaring overhead—the average wingspan of an adult exceeds 6 feet!

immature

ID: very large; brown overall with golden tint to neck and head; brown eyes; dark bill; brown tail has grayish white bands; yellow feet; fully feathered legs. *Immature:* white tail base; white patch at base of underwing primary feathers. *In flight:* relatively short neck; long tail; long, large, rectangular wings.
Size: *L* 30–40 in; *W* 6½–7½ ft.
Status: rare migrant from April to May and from September to November; rare winter resident.
Habitat: *In migration:* along escarpments and lake shorelines. *Winter:* semi-open woodlands and fields.

Nesting: does not nest in Michigan.
Feeding: swoops on prey from a soaring flight; eats hares, grouse, rodents, foxes and occasionally young ungulates; often eats carrion.
Voice: generally quiet; rarely a short bark.
Similar Species: *Bald Eagle* (p. 83): longer neck; shorter tail; immature lacks distinct, white underwing patches and tail base. *Turkey Vulture* (p. 50): naked, pink head; pale flight feathers; dark wing linings. *Dark-morph Rough-legged Hawk* (p. 92): pale flight feathers; white tail base.
Selected Sites: Whitefish Point; Lake Erie Metropark; Brockway Mountain Drive; Allegan SGA; Thorn L.; Pointe Mouillee SGA; Great Lakes shorelines.

VAGRANT

AMERICAN KESTREL
Falco sparverius

The American Kestrel is the smallest and most common of our falcons. It hunts small rodents in open areas, and a kestrel perched on a telephone wire or fence post along an open field is a familiar sight throughout Michigan in summer, and even year-round. • Studies have shown that the Eurasian Kestrel can detect ultraviolet reflections from rodent urine on the ground. It is not known if the American Kestrel has this same ability, but it is frequently seen hovering above the ground while looking for small ground-dwelling prey. • A helpful identification tip when viewing this bird from afar—the American Kestrel repeatedly lifts its tail while perched to scout below for prey. • The American Kestrel's diminutive size allows it to nest in tree cavities; these excellent locations help protect defenseless young kestrels from hungry predators. • Old field guides and old-time birders refer to the American Kestrel as "Sparrow Hawk," and its scientific name *sparverius* means "pertaining to a sparrow."

ID: 2 distinctive facial stripes. *Male:* rusty back; blue gray wings; blue gray crown with rusty "cap"; lightly spotted underparts. *Female:* rusty back, wings and breast streaking. *In flight:* frequently hovers; long, rusty tail; buoyant, indirect flight style.
Size: *L* 7½–8 in; *W* 20–24 in.
Status: common migrant and breeder from April to September in northern part of state; common year-round in southern part of state.
Habitat: open fields, riparian woodlands, woodlots, forest edges, bogs, roadside ditches, grassy highway medians, grasslands and croplands.
Nesting: in a tree cavity (usually in an abandoned woodpecker or flicker cavity);

may use a nest box; mostly the female incubates 4–6 white to pale brown eggs, spotted with brown and gray, for 29–30 days; both adults raise the young.
Feeding: swoops from a perch (a tree, fenceline, post, road sign or powerline) or from hovering flight; eats mostly insects and some small rodents, birds, reptiles and amphibians.
Voice: loud, often repeated, shrill *killy-killy-killy* when excited; female's voice is lower pitched.
Similar Species: *Merlin* (p. 95): only 1 facial stripe; less colorful; does not hover; flight is more powerful and direct. *Sharp-shinned Hawk* (p. 85): short, rounded wings; reddish barring on underparts; lacks facial stripes; flap-and-glide flight.
Selected Sites: widespread along fields, woodlots and roadsides statewide.

MERLIN

Falco columbarius

Like all its falcon relatives, the main weapons of the Merlin are speed, surprise and sharp, daggerlike talons. This small falcon's sleek body, long, narrow tail and pointed wings increase its aerodynamic efficiency for high-speed songbird pursuits. Horned Larks and Cedar Waxwings are famous for trying to outfly the Merlin, which results in prey and pursuer circling to great heights. • Most Merlins migrate to Central and South America each fall, but a few overwinter in Michigan, capitalizing on the abundance of Cedar Waxwings, European Starlings and House Sparrows. • Medieval falconers termed the Merlin "the lady's hawk," and Catherine the Great and Mary Queen of Scots were among the enthusiasts who would pitch Merlin and Sky Lark *(Alauda arvensis)* into matches of aerial prowess. • The Merlin was formerly known as "Pigeon Hawk," and its scientific name *columbarius* comes from the Latin for "pigeon," which it somewhat resembles in flight.

ID: banded tail; heavily streaked underparts; 1 indistinct facial stripe; long, narrow wings and tail. *Male:* blue gray back and crown; rufous leg feathers. *Female:* brown back and crown. *In flight:* very rapid, shallow wingbeats.
Size: *L* 10–12 in; *W* 23–26 in.
Status: threatened; uncommon migrant from mid-March to mid-October; rare breeder in northern part of state.
Habitat: *Breeding:* open and second-growth, mixed and coniferous forests and plantations adjacent to open hunting grounds. *In migration:* open fields and lakeshores.
Nesting: in a coniferous or deciduous tree; usually reuses an abandoned raptor, crow, jay or squirrel nest; mostly the female incubates 4–5 whitish eggs, marked with reddish brown, for 28–32 days; male feeds the female away from the nest; both adults raise the young.

Feeding: overtakes smaller birds in flight; also eats rodents and large insects, such as grasshoppers and dragonflies; may also take bats.
Voice: loud, noisy, cackling cry: *kek-kek-kek-kek-kek* or *ki-ki-ki-ki;* calls in flight or while perched, often around the nest.
Similar Species: *American Kestrel* (p. 94): 2 facial stripes; more colorful; less direct flight style; often hovers. *Peregrine Falcon* (p. 97): larger; well-marked, dark "helmet"; pale, unmarked upper breast; black flecking on light underparts. *Sharp-shinned Hawk* (p. 85) and *Cooper's Hawk* (p. 86): short, rounded wings; reddish barring on breast and belly. *Rock Dove* (p. 163): broader wings in flight; shorter tail; often glides with wings held in a "V."
Selected Sites: Whitefish Point; Isle Royale NP; Brockway Mountain Drive; Seney NWR; Thunder Bay; Muskegon SP; Copper Harbor; Lake Erie Metropark.

GYRFALCON
Falco rusticolus

Every year, as the days get shorter and snow begins to fall, birders of our region anxiously await the return of the world's largest falcon. Rarely do Gyrfalcons leave the Hudson Bay Lowlands of Canada and the northern arctic tundra, but even a brief glimpse of a Gyrfalcon is enough to revive any birder who may have a bad case of the winter blues. • Watching a Gyrfalcon in flight is like watching an expertly piloted fighter plane. Cruising at slow speed, it looks for potential targets and then reacts with lightning swiftness. Unlike the Peregrine Falcon, the Gyrfalcon rarely swoops down from above with its wings closed—it prefers to outfly its prey, often launching a surprise attack from below. Soaring over open country, the Gyrfalcon treats almost any bird it encounters as a potential meal. When a duck is the unlucky target, its only possible escape might be to plunge into the water headfirst.

gray morph

gray morph

ID: long tail extends beyond wing tips when bird is perched; tail may be barred or unbarred. *Gray morph:* dark gray upperparts; streaking on white underparts. *Brown morph:* dark brown upperparts; streaking on white underparts. *White morph:* pure white head, breast and rump; white back and wings have dark flecking and barring. *Immature:* darker and more heavily streaked than adult; gray (rather than yellow) feet and cere.
Size: *Male: L* 20–22 in; *W* 4 ft. *Female: L* 22–25 in; *W* 4½ ft.
Status: rare winter visitor from October to April.
Habitat: open and semi-open areas, including fields and open wetlands where prey concentrate.

Nesting: does not nest in Michigan.
Feeding: locates prey from an elevated perch or by flying low over the ground; takes prey in midair or chases it down; eats mostly birds, especially waterfowl and shorebirds; takes Rock Doves in southern areas; also takes small mammals.
Voice: loud, harsh *kak-kak-kak*.
Similar Species: *Peregrine Falcon* (p. 97): prominent, dark "helmet"; shorter tail; unstreaked upper breast and throat. *Northern Goshawk* (p. 87): may be similar to gray morph; prominent, white "eyebrow"; dark "cap"; rounded wings in flight; grayer underparts with finer streaking; unstreaked, white undertail coverts; eyes are red (adult) or pale yellow (immature).
Selected Sites: Sault Ste. Marie waterfront; Muskegon Wastewater System; St. Joseph waterfront; Pointe Mouillee SGA.

PEREGRINE FALCON
Falco peregrinus

No bird elicits more admiration than a hunting Peregrine Falcon in full flight, and nothing causes more panic in a tightly packed flock of ducks or shorebirds. Every twist and turn the flock makes is matched by the falcon until it finds a weaker or less-experienced bird. Diving at speeds of up to 220 miles per hour, the Peregrine clenches its feet and then strikes its prey with a lethal blow that often sends both falcon and prey tumbling. • The Peregrine Falcon's awesome speed and hunting skills were little defense against the pesticide DDT. The chemical caused contaminated birds to lay eggs with thin shells, which broke when the adults incubated the eggs. This bird was completely eradicated east of the Mississippi River by 1964. DDT was banned in North America in 1972 and, in 1975, the Eastern Peregrine Recovery Program was created and has successfully reintroduced the Peregrine Falcon in the eastern U.S. • Peregrine Falcons are a cosmopolitan species, nesting on every continent except Antarctica.

immature

ID: blue gray back; prominent, dark "helmet"; light underparts with dark, fine spotting and flecking. *Immature:* brown where adult is blue gray; heavier breast streaks; gray (rather than yellow) feet and cere. *In flight:* pointed wings; long, narrow, dark-banded tail.

Size: *Male: L* 15–17 in; *W* 3–3½ ft. *Female: L* 17–19 in; *W* 3½–4 ft.

Status: endangered; reintroduced; rare to uncommon migrant from mid-March to mid-April and from mid-September to mid-October; very rare breeder.

Habitat: lakeshores, river valleys, river mouths, urban areas and open fields.

Nesting: usually on a rocky cliff or cutbank; may use a skyscraper ledge; no material is added, but nest is littered with prey remains, leaves and grass; nest sites are often reused; mostly the female incubates 3–4 creamy to buff eggs, heavily blotched with reddish brown, for 32–34 days.

Feeding: high-speed, diving stoops; strikes birds with clenched feet in midair; takes primarily pigeons, waterfowl, shorebirds, flickers and larger songbirds; rarely eats small mammals or carrion; prey is consumed on a nearby perch.

Voice: loud, harsh, continuous *cack-cack-cack-cack-cack* near the nest site.

Similar Species: *Gyrfalcon* (p. 96): larger; lacks dark "helmet"; longer tail; seen only in winter. *Merlin* (p. 95): smaller; lacks prominent, dark "helmet"; heavily streaked breast and belly.

Selected Sites: Lansing; Detroit; Grand Rapids; Holland; Monroe; Pictured Rocks; Whitefish Point; Lake Erie Metropark; Isle Royale NP; Muskegon SP.

RING-NECKED PHEASANT
Phasianus colchicus

A native of Asia, the spectacular Ring-necked Pheasant was introduced to Michigan in 1895 as a gamebird for hunters. Unfortunately, cold, snowy winters are a problem for this bird. Unlike native grouse, the Ring-necked Pheasant does not have feathered legs and feet to insulate it through the winter months, and it cannot survive on native plants alone. The availability of grain and corn crops, as well as hedgerows and sheltering woodlots, has allowed this pheasant to survive in southern Michigan. • Birders hear this bird more often than they see it, and the male's loud *ka-squawk* call is recognizable near farms, woodlots and brushy suburban parks. • Ring-necked Pheasants are not very strong long-distance fliers, but are swift runners and are able to fly in explosive bursts over small open areas to escape predators.

ID: large gamebird; long, barred tail; unfeathered legs. *Male:* green head; naked, red face patch; white "collar"; bronze underparts. *Female:* mottled brown overall; light underparts.
Size: *Male: L* 30–36 in; *W* 31 in. *Female: L* 20–26 in; *W* 31 in.
Status: locally common year-round resident.
Habitat: *Breeding:* grasslands, grassy ditches, hayfields and grassy or weedy fields, fencelines, crop margins and woodlot margins. *Nonbreeding:* grain and corn fields in fall; woodlots, cattail marshes and shrubby areas close to soybean or corn fields in winter.

Nesting: on the ground, among grass or sparse vegetation or next to a log or other natural debris; in a slight depression lined with grass and leaves; female incubates 10–12 olive buff eggs for 23–28 days; male takes no part in parental duties.
Feeding: *Summer:* gleans the ground and vegetation for weed seeds, grains and insects. *Winter:* eats mostly seeds, corn kernels and buds.
Voice: *Male:* loud, raspy, roosterlike crowing: *ka-squawk;* whirring of wings, mostly just before sunrise.
Similar Species: male is distinctive. *Ruffed Grouse* (p. 99): generally smaller; shorter tail than female pheasant.
Selected Sites: fields, woodlots, croplands and grassy fencerows in the southern third of the state.

RUFFED GROUSE

Bonasa umbellus

I t always seems to happen without warning: a mysterious drumbeat echoes through the forest and your body reverberates as if you've been caught in the shockwave of a mild earthquake. Actually, what you are feeling are the sounds of a "drumming" Ruffed Grouse. Every spring, and occasionally in fall, the male Ruffed Grouse proclaims his territory. He struts along a fallen log with his tail fanned and his neck feathers ruffed, periodically beating the air with accelerating wingstrokes. • The Ruffed Grouse is the most common and widespread grouse in Michigan, inhabiting a wide variety of woodland habitats ranging from small deciduous woodlots and suburban riparian woodlands to vast expanses of mixedwood and boreal forest. • Populations of Ruffed Grouse seem to fluctuate over a 10-year cycle. Many predators such as the Northern Goshawk rely on this bird as a food source and show population fluctuations that closely follow those of the Ruffed Grouse. • During winter, scales grow out along the sides of this bird's feet, giving the Ruffed Grouse temporary "snowshoes."

ID: small head crest; mottled, gray brown overall; black feathers on sides of lower neck (visible when fluffed out in courtship displays); gray- or reddish-barred tail has broad, dark, subterminal band and white tip. *Female:* incomplete subterminal tail band.
Size: *L* 15–19 in; *W* 22 in.
Status: year-round resident; common in northern Michigan; uncommon to rare in southern Michigan.
Habitat: deciduous and mixed forests and riparian woodlands; in many areas favors young, second-growth stands with birch and poplar.
Nesting: in a shallow depression among leaf litter; often beside boulders, under a log or at the base of a tree; female incubates 9–12 buff-colored eggs for 23–25 days.
Feeding: gleans from the ground and vegetation; omnivorous diet includes seeds, buds, flowers, berries, catkins, leaves, insects, spiders and snails; may take small frogs.
Voice: *Male:* uses his wings to produce a hollow, drumming courtship sound of accelerating, deep booms. *Female:* clucks and "hisses" around her chicks.
Similar Species: *Spruce Grouse* (p. 100): dark tail lacks barring and white tip; lacks head crest; male has red eye combs. *Sharp-tailed Grouse* (p. 101): lacks fan-shaped tail and black feathers on lower neck.
Selected Sites: Allegan SGA; Yankee Springs SRA; Sleeping Bear Dunes National Lakeshore; Pictured Rocks National Lakeshore; state and national forests in the northern part of the state.

SPRUCE GROUSE

Falcipennis canadensis

The secretive, forest-dwelling Spruce Grouse trusts its cryptic plumage to conceal it from view in its dark, damp, year-round home. The Northern Goshawk is its most common predator, but the Spruce Grouse must also be wary of many mammalian carnivores. Despite its many predators, this grouse often allows people to approach within a few feet, which is the reason it is often called "Fool Hen." Most of the time, however, its camouflage seems to work and many Spruce Grouse probably escape our detection. • The Spruce Grouse spends most of its time in upland black spruce stands and young jack pine forests searching for seasonally available food, such as blueberries, flowers, black spruce buds, moss spore capsules and insects. • Spruce Grouse are most conspicuous in late April and early May, when females issue their vehement calls and strutting males magically appear in open areas along trails, roads and campgrounds. The Spruce Grouse's deep call is nearly undetectable to the human ear, but displaying males attract attention as they transform from their usual dull camouflage to become red-eyebrowed, puff-necked, fan-tailed splendors.

ID: black, unbarred tail with chestnut tip; mottled gray, brown and black overall; feathered legs. *Male:* red eye combs; black throat, neck and breast; white-tipped under-tail, lower neck and belly feathers. *Female:* barred, mottled underparts.

Size: *L* 13–16 in; *W* 22 in.

Status: special concern; uncommon, local, year-round resident in northern part of state.

Habitat: conifer-dominated forest; prefers jack pine forest; sometimes disperses into deciduous forests.

Nesting: on the forest floor; in a well-hidden, shallow scrape lined with a few grasses and needles; female incubates 4–7 buff eggs, blotched and spotted with brown and chestnut, for up to 21 days.

Feeding: live buds and needles of spruce, pine and fir trees; also eats berries, seeds and a few insects in summer.

Voice: very low, guttural *krrrk krrrk krrrk.*

Similar Species: *Ruffed Grouse* (p. 99): crested head; tail has broad, dark, subterminal band and white tip; lacks black throat and breast. *Sharp-tailed Grouse* (p. 101): thinner, sharper tail; white throat; yellow eye combs.

Selected Sites: eastern Upper Peninsula; Yellow Dog Plains west of Marquette; Baraga Jack Pine Plains near Baraga; Lower Peninsula in Crawford, Oscoda and Ogemaw counties.

SHARP-TAILED GROUSE

Tympanuchus phasianellus

During the last weeks of April and into the first few weeks of May, male Sharp-tailed Grouse gather at traditional dancing grounds, known as "leks," to perform courtship dances. With their wings drooping at their sides, their long, thin tails pointed skyward and their purplish pink air sacs fully inflated, males furiously pummel the ground with their feet, vigorously cooing and cackling for a crowd of prospective mates. Each male has a small stage within the larger, circular lek, and the inner, central position features the most virile dancers. • Like other grouse, Sharp-tail numbers rise and fall dramatically over time. In years of high abundance, large numbers of Sharp-tails move great distances, often colonizing new areas of suitable habitat. Unlike some of their relatives, they do not require native grasslands and are able to capitalize on new habitats created by forest clearing practices. • The term "lek" is derived from the Swedish word for "play."

ID: mottled brown-and-black upper-parts, neck and breast; dark crescents on white belly; white undertail coverts and outer tail feathers; long central tail feathers; yellow eye combs; white throat; feathered legs. *Male:* purplish pink air sacs on neck are inflated during courtship display.
Size: *L* 15–20 in; *W* 25 in.
Status: special concern; uncommon year-round resident in northern part of state.
Habitat: grasslands, abandoned pastures and fields, grassy meadows, shrubby areas and burned or logged forest clearings.
Nesting: on the ground; occasionally under cover; in a depression lined with grass and leaves; female incubates 10–14 buff-colored eggs for 23–24 days.

Feeding: gleans the ground, trees and shrubs for buds, seeds, flowers, green shoots and berries; also eats insects when available.
Voice: rarely heard outside of courtship events: male gives a mournful, cooing call and a cackling call on the lek just before sunrise.
Similar Species: *Ruffed Grouse* (p. 99): slight crest; broad, fan-shaped tail with broad, dark subterminal band; black patches on neck. *Ring-necked Pheasant* (p. 98): female has longer tail and unfeathered legs; paler markings on underparts. *Spruce Grouse* (p. 100): black, fan-shaped tail; black or mottled throat; male has red eye combs.
Selected Sites: Sault Ste. Marie area; sparsely distributed across entire peninsula in state and national forests; Grayling and Fletcher areas.

WILD TURKEY

Meleagris gallopavo

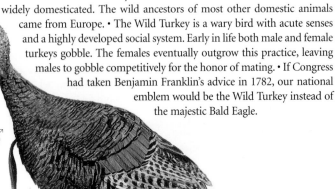

The Wild Turkey was once very common throughout southern Michigan, but during the 20th century, habitat loss and overharvesting took a toll on this bird. Today, efforts at restoration have reestablished the Wild Turkey nearly statewide. • Although turkeys prefer to feed on the ground and travel by foot—they can run faster than 19 miles per hour—they are able to fly short distances and they roost in trees at night. • This charismatic bird is the only native North American animal that has been widely domesticated. The wild ancestors of most other domestic animals came from Europe. • The Wild Turkey is a wary bird with acute senses and a highly developed social system. Early in life both male and female turkeys gobble. The females eventually outgrow this practice, leaving males to gobble competitively for the honor of mating. • If Congress had taken Benjamin Franklin's advice in 1782, our national emblem would be the Wild Turkey instead of the majestic Bald Eagle.

ID: naked, blue red head; dark, glossy, iridescent body plumage; barred, copper-colored tail; largely unfeathered legs. *Male:* long central breast tassel; colorful head and body; red wattles. *Female:* smaller; blue gray head; less iridescent body.

Size: *Male:* L 3–3½ ft; W 5½ ft. *Female:* L 3 ft; W 4 ft.

Status: common to uncommon year-round resident; locally common in Upper Peninsula.

Habitat: deciduous, mixed and riparian woodlands; occasionally eats waste grain and corn in late fall and winter.

Nesting: in a woodland or at a field edge; in a depression on the ground under thick cover; nest is lined with grass and leaves; female incubates 10–12 brown-speckled, pale buff eggs for up to 28 days.

Feeding: in fields near protective woods; forages on the ground for seeds, fruits, bulbs and sedges; also eats insects, especially beetles and grasshoppers; may take small amphibians.

Voice: wide array of sounds; courting male gobbles loudly; alarm call is a loud *pert;* gathering call is a *cluck;* contact call is a loud *keouk-keouk-keouk.*

Similar Species: all other grouse and grouselike birds are much smaller. *Ring-necked Pheasant* (p. 98): feathered head and neck; long, narrow tail.

Selected Sites: state and national parks; state game and recreation areas; lightly wooded agricultural areas in the southern half of the Lower Peninsula.

NORTHERN BOBWHITE

Colinus virginianus

Throughout fall and winter, Northern Bobwhites typically travel in large family groups called "coveys," collectively seeking out sources of food and huddling together during cold nights. When they huddle, members of the covey all face outward, enabling the group to detect danger from any direction. With the arrival of summer, breeding pairs break away from their coveys to perform elaborate courtship rituals in preparation for another nesting season. • The male's characteristic, whistled *bob-white* call, usually issued in spring, is often the only evidence of this bird's presence among the dense, tangled vegetation of its rural, woodland home. • Bobwhites benefit from habitat disturbance, using the early successional habitats created by fire, agriculture and forestry. • The Northern Bobwhite is the only native quail in eastern North America.

ID: mottled brown, buff and black upperparts; white crescents and spots edged in black on chestnut brown sides and upper breast; short tail. *Male:* white throat; broad, white "eyebrow." *Female:* buff throat and "eyebrow." *Immature:* smaller and duller overall; lacks black on underparts.
Size: *L* 10 in; *W* 13 in.
Status: uncommon year-round resident in southern half of Michigan.
Habitat: farmlands, open woodlands, woodland edges, grassy fencelines, roadside ditches and brushy, open country.

Nesting: in a shallow depression on the ground, often concealed by surrounding vegetation or a woven, partial dome; nest is lined with grass and leaves; pair incubates 12–16 white to pale buff eggs for 22–24 days.
Feeding: eats seasonally available seeds, berries, leaves, roots and nuts; also takes insects and other invertebrates.
Voice: whistled *hoy* is given year-round. *Male:* a whistled, rising *bob-white* in spring and summer.
Similar Species: *Ruffed Grouse* (p. 99): lacks conspicuous throat patch and broad "eyebrow"; long, fan-shaped tail has broad, dark subterminal band; black patches on sides of neck.
Selected Sites: agricultural areas.

YELLOW RAIL

Coturnicops noveboracensis

The Yellow Rail might be the most challenging breeding bird to find in Michigan. Not only is it quite rare and very cryptic, but it is most active at night, when most naturalists are dreaming of birds behind closed eyelids. Under a blanket of darkness, this secretive bird slips quietly through tall sedges, grasses and cattails, more like a small mammal than a bird, picking food from the ground and searching for snails and earthworms. By day, the shy Yellow Rail hides behind a cover of dense, marshy vegetation. This bird is more often heard than seen, and your best chance of encountering one in Michigan is at the Seney National Wildlife Refuge, where fluctuating water levels create its preferred habitat. Only in spring does the Yellow Rail reveal its presence by issuing its distinctive, repetitive "ticking" calls. • With their laterally compressed bodies, rails are masters at slipping through tightly packed stands of marsh vegetation. Their large feet, which distribute the birds' weight to help them rest atop thin mats of floating plant material, add to their strange appearance. • The rail may have gotten its name from the fact that it looks "as thin as a rail."

ID: short, pale bill; black and tawny stripes on upperparts (black stripes have fine, white barring); broad, dark line through eye; white throat and belly. *Immature:* darker overall; pattern on upperparts extends onto breast, sides and flanks. *In flight:* white trailing edge on inner wing.

Size: *L* 6½–7½ in; *W* 11 in.

Status: threatened; very rare migrant from mid-April to May and from September to October; very rare breeder.

Habitat: sedge marshes and wet sedge meadows.

Nesting: on the ground or low over water, hidden by overhanging plants; shallow cup nest is made of grass or sedges; female incubates 8–10 buff-colored eggs, speckled with reddish brown, for up to 18 days.

Feeding: picks food from the ground and aquatic vegetation; eats mostly snails, aquatic insects, spiders and possibly earthworms; occasionally eats seeds.

Voice: like 2 small stones clicking together: *tik, tik, tik-tik-tik.*

Similar Species: *Sora* (p. 106): lacks stripes on back and white patches on wings; breeding birds have black face and throat and bright yellow bill; distinctly different call. *Virginia Rail* (p. 105): long, reddish bill; rusty breast; gray face; lacks stripes on back and white patches on wings.

Selected Sites: Seney NWR; Houghton Lake WA; Munuscong Bay.

VIRGINIA RAIL
Rallus limicola

The best way to meet a Virginia Rail is to sit alongside a wetland marsh in spring, clap your hands three or four times to imitate this bird's *kidick* calls and wait patiently. If you are lucky, a Virginia Rail will reveal itself for a brief instant, but on most occasions you will only hear this elusive bird. • When pursued by an intruder or predator, a rail will almost always attempt to scurry away through dense, concealing vegetation, rather than risk exposure in a getaway flight. Rails are very narrow birds that have modified feather tips and flexible vertebrae, which allow them to squeeze through the narrow confines of their marshy homes. • The Virginia Rail and its relative the Sora are often found living in the same marshes. The secret of their successful coexistence is in their microhabitat preferences and distinct diets. The Virginia Rail typically favors dry shoresides of marshes and feeds on invertebrates, while the Sora prefers waterfront property and eats plants and seeds.

ID: long, down-curved, reddish bill; gray face; rusty breast; barred flanks; chestnut brown wing patch; very short tail. *Immature:* much darker overall; light bill.

Size: *L* 9–11 in; *W* 13 in.

Status: common migrant from mid-April to mid-September; fairly common breeder.

Habitat: wetlands, especially cattail and bulrush marshes.

Nesting: concealed in emergent vegetation, usually suspended just over the water; loose basket nest is made of coarse grass, cattail stems or sedges; pair incubates 5–13 spotted, pale buff eggs for up to 20 days.

Feeding: probes into soft substrates and gleans vegetation for invertebrates, such as beetles, snails, spiders, earthworms, insect larvae and nymphs; also eats some pondweeds and seeds.

Voice: call is an often-repeated, telegraph-like *kidick, kidick;* also "oinks" and croaks.

Similar Species: *King Rail* (p. 339): much larger; dark legs; lacks reddish bill and gray face; immature is mostly pale gray. *Sora* (p. 106): short, yellow bill; black face and throat. *Yellow Rail* (p. 104): short, pale yellowish bill; black-and-tawny stripes on back; white trailing edges of wings are seen in flight.

Selected Sites: St. Clair Flats WA; Fish Point SGA; Nayanquing Point WA; Tobico Marsh WA; Allegan SGA; Muskegon Wastewater System.

SORA

Porzana carolina

Two ascending whistles followed by a strange, descending whinny abruptly announce the presence of the often undetectable Sora. The Sora is the most common and widespread rail in North America, and like most rails is seldom seen by birders. Its elusive habits and preference for dense marshlands force most would-be observers to settle for a quick look at this small bird. On occasion, it has been known to parade around, unconcerned with onlookers, while it searches the shallows for food. • The Sora has two main calls: a clear, whistled *coo-wee* that is easy to imitate and a strange, descending whinny. • Even though its feet are not webbed or lobed, the Sora swims quite well over short distances. Though it appears to be a weak and reluctant flyer, the Sora migrates hundreds of miles each year between its breeding and wintering wetlands. • The species name *carolina* means "of Carolina" and this bird is also known as "Carolina Rail."

breeding

ID: short, yellow bill; black face, throat and fore-neck; gray neck and breast; long wings and tail; long, greenish legs. *Immature:* no black on face; buffier with paler underparts; more greenish bill.

Size: *L* 8–10 in; *W* 14 in.

Status: common migrant from mid-April to September; common breeder.

Habitat: wetlands with abundant emergent cattails, bulrushes, sedges and grasses.

Nesting: usually over water, but occasionally in a wet meadow under concealing vegetation; well-built basket nest is made of grass and aquatic vegetation; pair incubates 10–12 buff or olive buff, darkly speckled eggs for 18–20 days.

Feeding: gleans and probes for seeds, plants, aquatic insects and mollusks.

Voice: usual call is a clear, 2-note *coo-wee;* alarm call is a sharp *keek;* courtship song begins *or-Ah or-Ah,* descending quickly in a series of maniacal *weee-weee-weee* notes.

Similar Species: *Virginia Rail* (p. 105) and *King Rail* (p. 340): larger; long, downcurved bill; chestnut brown wing patch; rufous breast. *Yellow Rail* (p. 104): streaked back; tawny upperparts; white throat; white trailing edges of wings are seen in flight.

Selected Sites: Metrobeach Metropark; Tawas Point SP; Tobico Marsh WA; Haehnle Sanctuary; Rose Lake WA; Allegan SGA; Seney NWR.

COMMON MOORHEN
Gallinula chloropus

The Common Moorhen is a curious-looking creature that appears to have been assembled from bits and pieces left over from other birds: it has the bill of a chicken, the body of a duck and the long legs and large feet of a small heron. As it strolls around a wetland, its head bobs back and forth in synchrony with its legs, producing a comical, chugging stride. • Unlike most other members of the rail family, the Common Moorhen is quite comfortable feeding in open areas. • For moorhens, the responsibilities of parenthood do not end when their eggs have hatched—parents feed and shelter their young until they are capable of feeding themselves and flying on their own. • Although the Common Moorhen looks similar to its close relative, the American Coot, its delicate manner and elusive tendencies easily separate it from the loud and gregarious coot. • The scientific name *chloropus* is Greek for "green foot."

breeding

ID: reddish forehead shield; yellow-tipped bill; gray black body; white streak on sides and flanks; long, greenish yellow legs. *Breeding:* brighter bill and forehead shield. *Immature:* paler plumage; duller legs and bill; white throat.
Size: *L* 12–15 in; *W* 21 in.
Status: special concern; common migrant in southern half of Lower Peninsula from late April to late September; common local breeder.
Habitat: freshwater marshes, ponds, lakes and sewage lagoons.
Nesting: pair builds a platform nest or a wide, shallow cup of bulrushes, cattails and reeds in shallow water or along a shoreline; often built with a ramp leading to the water; pair incubates 8–11 buff-colored, spotted or blotched eggs for 19–22 days.
Feeding: eats mostly aquatic vegetation, berries, fruits, tadpoles, insects, snails, worms and spiders; may take carrion and eggs.
Voice: various sounds include chicken-like clucks, screams, squeaks and a loud *cup;* courting males give a harsh *ticket-ticket-ticket.*
Similar Species: *American Coot* (p. 108): white bill and forehead shield; lacks white streak on flanks.
Selected Sites: Erie Marsh Preserve; Pointe Mouillee SGA; Metrobeach Metropark; St. Clair Flats WA; Nayanquing Point WA; Allegan SGA.

AMERICAN COOT
Fulica americana

The American Coot is truly an all-terrain bird: in its quest for food it dives and dabbles like a duck, grazes confidently on land and swims about skillfully with its lobed feet. • American Coots squabble constantly during the breeding season, not just among themselves, but also with any waterbird that has the audacity to intrude upon their waterfront property. These odd birds can often be seen scooting across the surface of the water, charging rivals with flailing, splashing wings in an attempt to intimidate. Outside the breeding season, coots gather amicably together in large groups. During spring and fall, thousands congregate at a few select staging sites in our region. These numerous waterfowl are easy to spot because of their pendulous head movements while swimming. • The American Coot is colloquially known as "Mud Hen," and many people mistakenly believe that the American Coot is a species of duck.

ID: gray black overall; white, chicken-like bill with dark ring around tip; reddish spot on white forehead shield; long, greenish yellow legs; lobed toes; red eyes. *Immature:* lighter body color; darker bill and legs; lacks prominent forehead shield.

Size: *L* 13–16 in; *W* 24 in.

Status: common migrant from March to mid-November; common breeder in southern part of state.

Habitat: shallow marshes, ponds and wetlands with open water and emergent vegetation; also sewage lagoons.

Nesting: in emergent vegetation; pair builds a floating nest of cattails and grass; pair incubates 6–11 brown-spotted, buffy white eggs for 21–25 days.

Feeding: gleans the water's surface; sometimes dives, tips up or even grazes on land; eats aquatic vegetation, insects, snails, crayfish, worms, tadpoles and fish; may steal food from ducks.

Voice: calls frequently in summer, day and night: *kuk-kuk-kuk-kuk-kuk;* also grunts.

Similar Species: *Ducks* (pp. 57–81): all lack chickenlike, white bill and uniformly black body. *Grebes* (pp. 35–38): lack white forehead shield and all-dark plumage. *Common Moorhen* (p. 107): reddish forehead shield; yellow-tipped bill; white streak on flanks.

Selected Sites: Erie Marsh Preserve; Pointe Mouillee SGA; St. Clair Flats WA; Fish Point SGA; Shiawassee Flats NWR; Allegan SGA.

SANDHILL CRANE
Grus canadensis

Deep, resonant, rattling calls announce the approach of a flock of migrating Sandhill Cranes long before they pass overhead. The coiling of their trachea adds harmonies to the notes in Sandhill Crane calls, allowing them to call louder and farther. At first glance, the large, V-shaped flocks look very similar to flocks of Canada Geese, but cranes circle upward on thermal rises, then slowly soar downward until they find another rise, continuing this pattern all the way to their nesting sites. Migrating flocks of Sandhills consist mainly of mated pairs and close family members. • Cranes mate for life, reinforcing pair bonds each spring with an elaborate courtship dance. It has often been equated with human dancing—a seemingly strange comparison until you see the ritual firsthand. • Sandhill Cranes are sensitive nesters, so they prefer to raise their young in areas that are isolated from human disturbance.

ID: very large, gray bird with long neck and legs; naked, red crown; long, straight bill; plumage is often stained rusty red from iron oxides in the water.
Immature: lacks red crown; reddish brown plumage may appear patchy. *In flight:* extends neck and legs; often glides, soars and circles.
Size: *L* 3½–4 ft; *W* 6–7 ft.
Status: common migrant in March and November; locally uncommon breeder.
Habitat: *Breeding:* isolated, open marshes, fens and bogs surrounded by forests or shrubs. *In migration:* agricultural fields and shorelines.

Nesting: on a large mound of aquatic vegetation in water or along a shoreline; pair incubates 2 brown-splotched, olive buff eggs for 29–32 days; egg hatching is staggered; young fly at about 50 days.
Feeding: probes and gleans the ground for insects, soft-bodied invertebrates, waste grain, shoots and tubers; frequently eats small vertebrates.
Voice: loud, resonant, rattling *gu-rrroo gu-rrroo gurrroo.*
Similar Species: *Great Blue Heron* (p. 43): lacks red forehead patch; neck is folded back over shoulders in flight. *Whooping Crane:* all-white plumage; black flight feathers.
Selected Sites: Waterloo SRA; Haehnle Sanctuary; Baker Sanctuary; Maple River SGA; Whitefish Point; Seney NWR.

BLACK-BELLIED PLOVER
Pluvialis squatarola

During the last days of May, flocks of Black-bellied Plovers in black-and-white breeding plumage stand out against the drab soil of plowed fields. Small groups of these arctic breeders pass through our region for a brief period in spring and for a longer period in fall. From time to time, large flocks of hundreds of birds can be seen, but such occurrences are considered rare. The end of the fall passage is the best time to see these birds, with the adults in their worn-out breeding plumage appearing first, followed by the plain gray, immature birds. • Black-bellied Plovers forage for small invertebrates with a robinlike run-and-stop technique, frequently pausing to lift their heads for a reassuring scan of their surroundings. • Most plovers have three toes, but the Black-belly has a fourth toe higher on its leg, like most sandpipers. The largest North American plover, the Black-belly brings a haunting, whistled flight call to springtime.

nonbreeding

breeding

ID: short, black bill; long, black legs. *Breeding:* black face, breast, belly and flanks; white under-tail coverts; white stripe leads from crown down "collar," neck and sides of breast; mottled, black-and-white back. *Nonbreeding:* mottled, gray brown upperparts; lightly streaked, pale underparts. *In flight:* black "wing pits"; whitish rump; white wing linings.
Size: *L* 10½–13 in; *W* 29 in.
Status: uncommon migrant from mid-April to early June and from August to mid-November.

Habitat: plowed fields, sod farms, meadows, lakeshores and mudflats along the edges of reservoirs, marshes and sewage lagoons.
Nesting: does not nest in Michigan.
Feeding: run-and-stop foraging technique; eats insects, mollusks and crustaceans.
Voice: rich, plaintive, 3-syllable whistle: *pee-oo-ee.*
Similar Species: *American Golden-Plover* (p. 111): gold-mottled upperparts; black undertail coverts in breeding plumage; lacks black "wing pits."
Selected Sites: New Buffalo waterfront; St. Joseph waterfront; Muskegon Wastewater System; Muskegon SP; Pointe Mouillee SGA.

AMERICAN GOLDEN-PLOVER
Pluvialis dominica

A mere 150 years ago, the American Golden-Plover population was among the largest of any bird in the world, but in the late 1800s, market gunners mercilessly culled the great flocks in both spring and fall—a single day's shooting often yielded tens of thousands of birds. Populations have recovered somewhat, but they will likely never return to their former numbers. • Because they migrate through central North America, few Golden-Plovers are found here, though occasionally a large flock of 100 or more may be seen. • Although this bird is boldly marked, the white stripe down its side disrupts the vision of a predator, confusing the hunter as to where the bird's head or tail is. The cryptic coloration of speckles on the top of the body blends well with the golden, mottled earth of its arctic breeding grounds. • The Eskimo Curlew *(Numenius borealis)*, now possibly extinct, once migrated with the American Golden-Plover between the Canadian Arctic and South America. If the Eskimo Curlew does still exist, it may be found traveling alongside the American Golden-Plover.

breeding

nonbreeding

ID: straight, black bill; long, black legs. *Breeding:* black face and underparts, including undertail coverts; S-shaped, white stripe from forehead down to shoulders; dark upperparts are speckled with gold and white. *Nonbreeding:* broad, pale "eyebrow"; dark streaking on pale neck and underparts; much less gold on upperparts. *In flight:* gray "wing pits."
Size: *L* 10–11 in; *W* 26 in.
Status: uncommon migrant from mid-April to early June and from August to mid-November.

Habitat: cultivated fields, sod farms, meadows, lakeshores and mudflats along the edges of reservoirs, marshes and sewage lagoons.
Nesting: does not nest in Michigan.
Feeding: run-and-stop foraging technique; snatches insects, mollusks and crustaceans; also takes seeds and berries.
Voice: soft, melodious whistle: *quee, quee-dle.*
Similar Species: *Black-bellied Plover* (p. 110): white undertail coverts; whitish crown; lacks gold speckling on upperparts; conspicuous, black "wing pits" in flight.
Selected Sites: Shiawassee Flats NWR; Whitefish Point; New Buffalo and St. Joseph waterfronts; Muskegon Wastewater System.

SEMIPALMATED PLOVER
Charadrius semipalmatus

On the way to their arctic breeding grounds, small flocks of Semipalmated Plovers commonly touch down on our shorelines. Watch for them in late May and early June, but keep your eyes peeled because they are only around for a short time. If these birds seem to be in a hurry, they are! There is tremendous pressure for these long-distance migrants to begin breeding before the end of the short northern summer. After nesting, the adults will leave the breeding grounds as early as July to enjoy a prolonged, leisurely migration to the coastlines of the southern U.S., Central America or South America. The young begin their journey as soon as they are strong enough to fly. • The scientific name *semipalmatus* means "half-webbed" and refers to the slight webbing between the toes of this plover. The webbing is thought to give the bird's feet more surface area when it is walking on soft substrates.

breeding

breeding

ID: dark brown back; white breast with 1 black, horizontal band; long, orange legs; stubby, orange, black-tipped bill; white patch above bill; white throat and "collar"; brown head; black band across forehead; small, white "eyebrow." *Immature:* dark legs and bill; brown banding.
Size: *L* 7 in; *W* 19 in.
Status: common migrant from May to early June and from late July to late October.

Habitat: sandy beaches, lakeshores, river edges and mudflats.
Nesting: does not nest in Michigan.
Feeding: usually on shorelines and beaches; run-and-stop foraging technique; eats crustaceans, worms and insects.
Voice: crisp, high-pitched, 2-part, rising whistle: *tu-wee.*
Similar Species: *Killdeer* (p. 114): larger; 2 black bands across breast. *Piping Plover* (p. 113): lacks dark band through eyes; much lighter upperparts; narrower breast band is incomplete in females and most males.
Selected Sites: New Buffalo and St. Joseph waterfronts; Muskegon Wastewater System; Muskegon SP; Nayanquing Point WA.

PIPING PLOVER

Charadrius melodus

A master of illusion, the Piping Plover is hardly noticeable when it settles on shorelines and beaches. Its pale, sand-colored plumage is the perfect camouflage against a sandy beach. As well, the dark bands across its forehead and neckline resemble scattered pebbles or strips of washed-up vegetation. This plover's cryptic plumage, unfortunately, has done little to protect it from wetland drainage, increased predation and disturbance by humans. The recreational use of beaches during summer, and an increase in human-tolerant predators, such as gulls, raccoons and skunks, has impeded this plover's ability to reproduce successfully. Once common here, the Piping Plover is now an endangered species. It is estimated that only 42 pairs breed in Michigan, mostly along sandy, northern Great Lakes shorelines. • On beaches with wave action, these birds often employ a foot-trembling strategy to entice invertebrates to the surface. • If threatened, Piping Plover chicks typically take to the water and swim away, whereas adults rarely swim at all.

♂

breeding

ID: pale, sandy upperparts; white underparts; orange legs. *Breeding:* black-tipped, orange bill; black forehead band; black "necklace" (sometimes incomplete, especially on females). *Nonbreeding:* no breast or forehead band; all-black bill.
Size: *L* 7 in.; *W* 19 in.
Status: endangered; very rare migrant and locally rare breeder from late April to November.
Habitat: sandy beaches and open lakeshores.

Nesting: on bare sand along an open shoreline; in a shallow scrape sometimes lined with pebbles and tiny shells; pair incubates 4 pale buff eggs, blotched with dark brown and black, for 26–28 days.
Feeding: run-and-stop foraging technique; eats worms and insects; almost all its food is taken from the ground.
Voice: clear, whistled melody: *peep peep peep-lo.*
Similar Species: *Semipalmated Plover* (p. 112): dark band over eye; much darker upperparts. *Killdeer* (p. 114): larger; 2 breast bands; much darker upperparts.
Selected Sites: Grand Marais; Vermilion; North Manitou I.; South Manitou I.; Thunder Bay; Ludington SP; Wilderness SP.

113

KILLDEER

Charadrius vociferus

The ubiquitous Killdeer is often the first shorebird a birder learns to identify. Its boisterous calls rarely fail to catch the attention of people passing through its wide variety of nesting environments. The Killdeer's preference for open fields, gravel driveways, beach edges, golf courses and abandoned industrial areas has allowed it to thrive throughout our rural and suburban landscapes. • If you happen to wander too close to a Killdeer nest, the parent will try to lure you away by issuing loud alarm calls and feigning a broken wing. Most predators take the bait and are led far enough away for the parent to suddenly recover from its injury and fly off, sounding its piercing calls. Similar distraction displays are widespread phenomena in the bird world, but in our region, the Kildeer's broken wing act is by far the gold medal winner. • The scientific name *vociferus* aptly describes this vocal bird, but double-check all calls in spring, when the Killdeer is often imitated by frisky European Starlings.

ID: long, dark yellow legs; white upperparts with 2 black breast bands; brown back; white underparts; brown head; white "eyebrow"; white face patch above bill; black forehead band; rufous rump; tail projects beyond wing tips. *Immature:* downy; only 1 breast band.

Size: *L* 9–11 in; *W* 24 in.

Status: common to abundant migrant from mid-March to late October; common breeder.

Habitat: open ground, fields, lakeshores, sandy beaches, mudflats, gravel streambeds, wet meadows and grasslands.

Nesting: on open ground; in a shallow, usually unlined, depression; pair incubates 4 darkly spotted and blotched, pale buff eggs for 24–28 days; occasionally raises 2 broods.

Feeding: run-and-stop foraging technique; eats mostly insects; also takes spiders, snails, earthworms and crayfish.

Voice: loud, distinctive *kill-dee kill-dee kill-deer* and variations, including *deer-deer*.

Similar Species: *Semipalmated Plover* (p. 112): smaller; only 1 breast band. *Piping Plover* (p. 113): smaller; lighter upperparts; 1 breast band.

Selected Sites: extremely widespread; open areas and disturbed sites throughout the state.

AMERICAN AVOCET
Recurvirostra americana

An American Avocet in full breeding plumage is a strikingly elegant bird, with its long, peachy red neck accentuating the length of its slender bill and stiltlike legs. Often by August, their peach-colored "hoods" have been replaced by more subdued winter grays, which these birds will wear for the greater part of the year. It is the only avocet in the world that undergoes a yearly color change. • The American Avocet's upcurved bill looks bent out of shape, but is actually ideal for efficiently skimming aquatic vegetation and invertebrates off the surface of shallow water. Avocets will walk rapidly or run about in fairly deep water, swinging their bills from side to side along the muddy bottom. At other times, they use their webbed feet to swim and feed by tipping up like dabbling ducks. • If an American Avocet is disturbed while standing in its one-legged resting position, it will take off, switch legs in midair, and land on the rested leg.

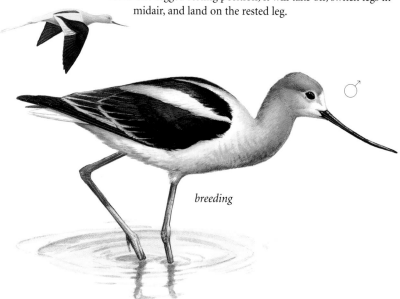

breeding

ID: long, upturned, black bill; long, pale blue legs; black wings with wide, white patches; white underparts; female's bill more upturned and shorter than male's. *Breeding:* peachy red head, neck and breast. *Nonbreeding:* gray head, neck and breast. *In flight:* a "winged stick"; long, skinny legs and neck; black-and-white wings.
Size: *L* 17–18 in; *W* 31 in.
Status: rare to uncommon migrant in May and from August to October.

Habitat: lakeshores, alkaline wetlands and exposed mudflats.
Nesting: does not nest in Michigan.
Feeding: sweeps its bill from side to side along the water's surface, picking up minute crustaceans, aquatic insects and occasionally seeds; male sweeps lower in the water than female; occasionally swims and tips up like a duck.
Voice: harsh, shrill *plee-eek plee-eek.*
Similar Species: *Willet* (p. 119): grayish overall; straight bill.
Selected Sites: Erie Marsh Preserve; Pointe Mouillee SGA; Tawas Point SP; Muskegon Wastewater System; Metrobeach Metropark; Saugatuck SP; Grand Mere SP.

GREATER YELLOWLEGS

Tringa melanoleuca

The Greater Yellowlegs is the more solitary of the two yellowlegs species, but it can be seen in small flocks during migration. It is one of the birds that performs the role of lookout among mixed flocks of shorebirds. At the first sign of danger, these large sandpipers bob their heads and call incessantly. If forced to, the Greater Yellowlegs will usually retreat into deeper water, becoming airborne only as a last resort. • During migration, many shorebirds, including the Greater Yellowlegs, often stand or hop around beachflats on one leg. These stubborn "one-leggers" may be mistaken for crippled individuals, but this stance may be an adaptation that conserves body heat. Despite its long bill, the Greater Yellowlegs does not probe for its food, but instead picks it off the water's surface or swings its bill from side to side in the water like an avocet. This sidesweeping behavior may be a clue that you are looking at a Greater Yellowlegs and not its Lesser relative, which uses this technique far less often.

nonbreeding

nonbreeding

ID: long, bright yellow legs; slightly upturned, dark bill is noticeably longer than head width. *Breeding:* brown black back and upperwing; fine, dense, dark streaking on head and neck; dark barring on breast often extends onto belly; subtle, dark eye line; light lores. *Nonbreeding:* gray overall; fine streaks on breast.
Size: *L* 13–15 in; *W* 28 in.
Status: common migrant from May to early June and from August to mid-October.
Habitat: almost all wetlands, including lakeshores, marshes, flooded fields and river shorelines.

Nesting: does not nest in Michigan.
Feeding: usually wades in water over its knees; sometimes sweeps its bill from side to side; primarily eats aquatic invertebrates, but will also eat small fish; occasionally snatches prey from the water's surface.
Voice: quick, whistled series of *tew-tew-tew,* usually 3 notes.
Similar Species: *Lesser Yellowlegs* (p. 117): smaller; straight bill is not noticeably longer than width of head; call is generally a pair of higher notes: *tew-tew.* *Willet* (p. 119): black-and-white wings; heavier, straighter bill; dark, greenish legs.
Selected Sites: Erie Marsh Preserve; Pointe Mouillee SGA; Metrobeach Metropark; Fish Point SGA; Sleepy Hollow SP; Maple River SGA.

LESSER YELLOWLEGS

Tringa flavipes

With a series of continuous, rapid-fire *tew-tew* calls, Lesser Yellowlegs streak across the surface of wetlands and lakeshores. Visits by yellowlegs are relatively brief in spring, but the fall migration period is lengthy, and these birds can be seen from mid-July to mid-October. • Many birders find it a challenge to separate Lesser Yellowlegs and Greater Yellowlegs in the field. With practice, you will notice that the Lesser's bill is finer, straighter and not noticeably longer than the width of its head. The Lesser appears to have longer legs and wings, making it seem slimmer and taller than the Greater, and is also more commonly seen in flocks. If your sight proves inadequate, open your ears: the Lesser Yellowlegs gives a pair of *peeps*, while the Greater gives three. If you are still puzzled at the bird's identity, simply write "yellowlegs spp." in your field notes and try again next time. • The scientific name *flavipes* is derived from Latin words meaning "yellow foot."

ID: bright yellow legs; all-dark bill is not noticeably longer than width of head; brown black back and upperwing; fine, dense, dark streaking on head, neck and breast; lacks barring on belly; subtle, dark eye line; light lores.
Size: *L* 10–11 in; *W* 24 in.
Status: common migrant from May to early June and from August to mid-October.
Habitat: shorelines of lakes, rivers, marshes and ponds.
Nesting: does not nest in Michigan.

Feeding: snatches prey from the water's surface; frequently wades in shallow water; primarily eats aquatic invertebrates, but also takes small fish and tadpoles.
Voice: typically a high-pitched pair of *tew* notes.
Similar Species: *Greater Yellowlegs* (p. 116): larger; bill slightly upturned and noticeably longer than width of head; *tew* call is usually given in a series of 3 notes. *Solitary Sandpiper* (p. 118): white eye ring; greenish legs. *Willet* (p. 119): much bulkier; black-and-white wings; heavier bill; dark, greenish legs.
Selected Sites: Erie Marsh Preserve; Pointe Mouillee SGA; Metrobeach Metropark; Fish Point SGA; Sleepy Hollow SP; Maple River SGA.

SOLITARY SANDPIPER

Tringa solitaria

True to its name, the Solitary Sandpiper is usually seen alone, bobbing its body like a spirited dancer as it forages for insects along our wetlands. Every so often, a lucky observer may happen upon a small group of these birds during spring or fall. • A favorite foraging method of the Solitary Sandpiper is to wade in shallow water, slowly advancing and vibrating the leading foot, thus stirring the bottom sufficiently to disturb prey. In this way it captures aquatic insects and their larvae, including water boatmen and small crustaceans. • Shorebirds lay very large eggs and incubate them for comparatively long periods of time. Once sandpiper chicks break out of their eggs, they are ready to run, hide and feed on their own. Highly developed hatchlings, known as precocial young, are immediately able to fend for themselves in a dangerous world.

ID: white eye ring; short, green legs; dark, yellowish bill with black tip; spotted, gray brown back; white lores; fine white streaks on gray brown head, neck and breast; dark upper tail feathers with black-and-white barring on sides. *In flight:* dark underwings.
Size: *L* 7½–9 in; *W* 22 in.
Status: common migrant from May to early June and from August to mid-October.
Habitat: wet meadows, sewage lagoons, muddy ponds, sedge wetlands, beaver ponds and wooded streams.
Nesting: does not nest in Michigan.

Feeding: stalks shorelines, picking up aquatic invertebrates, such as water boatmen and damselfly nymphs; also gleans for terrestrial invertebrates; occasionally stirs the water with its foot to spook out prey.
Voice: high, thin *peet-wheet* or *wheat wheat wheat.*
Similar Species: *Lesser Yellowlegs* (p. 117): no eye ring; longer, bright yellow legs. *Spotted Sandpiper* (p. 120): incomplete eye ring; spotted breast in breeding plumage; black-tipped, orange bill. *Other sandpipers* (pp. 116–39): black bills and legs; no white eye ring.
Selected Sites: Erie Marsh Preserve; Pointe Mouillee SGA; Metrobeach Metropark; Lake Erie Metropark; Fish Point SGA; Sleepy Hollow SP.

WILLET

Catoptrophorus semipalmatus

When it is grounded, the Willet cuts a rather dull figure. The moment it takes flight or displays, however, its black-and-white wings add sudden color while it calls out a loud, rhythmic *will-will willet, will-will-willet!* The bright, bold flashes of the Willet's wings may alert other shorebirds to imminent danger. If you look closely, you may notice that the white markings across the Willet's wingspan form a rough "W" as it flies away. • Willets are loud, social, easily identified birds—a nice change when dealing with sandpipers—but, unfortunately, very few are seen in Michigan. Most Willet sightings occur when the birds are foraging among large, mixed flocks of shorebirds along the shores of the lower Great Lakes, especially in southwestern Michigan.

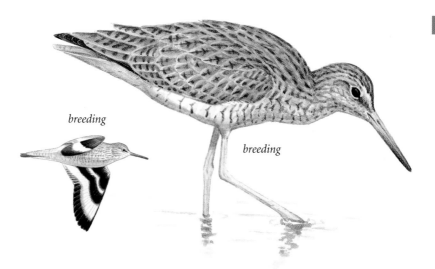

breeding

breeding

ID: plump; heavy, straight, black bill; light throat and belly. *Breeding:* dark steaking and barring overall. *In flight:* black-and-white wing pattern.
Size: *L* 14–16 in; *W* 26 in.
Status: rare migrant from late April to May and from July to September.
Habitat: wet fields and shorelines of marshes, lakes and ponds.
Nesting: does not nest in Michigan.
Feeding: feeds by probing muddy areas; also gleans the ground for insects; occasionally eats shoots and seeds.

Voice: loud, rolling *will-will willet, will-will-willet.*
Similar Species: *Marbled Godwit* (p. 124) and *Hudsonian Godwit* (p. 123): much longer, pinkish yellow bill with dark, slightly upturned tip; larger body; lack black-and-white wing pattern. *Greater Yellowlegs* (p. 116): long, yellow legs; slightly upturned bill; lacks black-and-white wing pattern.
Selected Sites: Nayanquing Point WA; Tawas Point SP; New Buffalo and St. Joseph waterfronts; Muskegon Wastewater System; Arcadia Lake Marsh; Warren Dunes SP; Pointe Mouillee SGA; Grand Mere SP; Holland SP; Lake Erie Metropark; Erie Marsh Preserve; Whitefish Point.

SPOTTED SANDPIPER

Actitis macularia

This diminutive shorebird is a widespread breeder here—during summer it is the most frequently encountered sandpiper throughout much of Michigan. • It wasn't until 1972 that the unexpected truth about the Spotted Sandpiper's breeding activities were realized. The female Spotted Sandpiper defends a territory and mates with more than one male in a single breeding season, leaving the male to tend the nest and eggs. This unusual nesting behavior, known as polyandry, is found in about one percent of all bird species. • Even though its breast spots are not noticeable from a distance, the Spotted Sandpiper's stiff-winged, quivering flight pattern and tendency to burst from the shore are easily recognizable. This bird is also known for its continuous "teetering" behavior as it forages. • The scientific name *macularia* is Latin for "spot," referring to the spots on this bird's underparts in breeding plumage.

nonbreeding

breeding

ID: teeters almost continuously. *Breeding:* white underparts heavily spotted with black; yellow orange legs; black-tipped, yellow orange bill; white "eyebrow."
Nonbreeding and *immature:* pure white breast, foreneck and throat; brown bill; dull yellow legs. *In flight:* flies close to the water's surface with very rapid, shallow wingbeats; white upperwing stripe.
Size: *L* 7–8 in; *W* 15 in.
Status: common migrant from late April to late September; common breeder.
Habitat: shorelines, gravel beaches, ponds, marshes, alluvial wetlands, rivers, streams, swamps and sewage lagoons; occasionally seen in cultivated fields.

Nesting: usually near water; often under overhanging vegetation among logs or under bushes; in a shallow depression lined with grass; almost exclusively the male incubates 4 creamy buff, heavily blotched and spotted eggs and raises the young.
Feeding: picks and gleans along shorelines for terrestrial and aquatic invertebrates; also snatches flying insects from the air.
Voice: sharp, crisp *eat-wheat, eat-wheat, wheat-wheat-wheat-wheat.*
Similar Species: *Solitary Sandpiper* (p. 118): complete eye ring; lacks spotting on breast; yellowish bill with dark tip. *Other sandpipers* (pp. 116–39): black bills and legs; lack spotting on breast.
Selected Sites: river banks, marshes, lakeshores, sewage ponds, mudflats, farm fields and wetlands; Erie Marsh Preserve.

UPLAND SANDPIPER

Bartramia longicauda

I n spring, Upland Sandpipers are sometimes seen perched atop fence posts, then flying high, emitting shrill "wolf-whistle" calls. Excited males will even launch into the air to perform courtship flight displays, combining song with shallow, fluttering wingbeats. At the height of the breeding season, however, these large-eyed, inland shorebirds are rarely seen, remaining hidden in the tall grass of abandoned fields and ungrazed pastures. • For an American birder who is accustomed to meeting the Upland Sandpiper in our grassy fields and meadows, meeting the same bird during a holiday in the grasslands of Argentina could be quite a shock. Twice each year, these wide-ranging shorebirds make the incredible journey between Michigan and South America without jet propulsion or inflight movies. • During the late 1800s, high market demand for this bird's meat led to severe overharvesting and catastrophic declines in its population over much of North America. Its numbers have since improved in our region, but recent declines in grassland habitats again threaten its welfare.

ID: small head; long, streaked neck; large, dark eyes; yellow legs; mottled, brownish upperparts; lightly streaked breast, sides and flanks; white belly and undertail coverts; bill is about same length as head.

Size: *L* 11–12½ in; *W* 26 in.

Status: locally uncommon migrant and breeder from early May to early September, mainly in the Lower Peninsula.

Habitat: hayfields, ungrazed pastures, grassy meadows, abandoned fields, natural grasslands and airports.

Nesting: in dense grass or along a wetland; in a depression, usually with grass arching over the top; pair incubates 4 pale to pinkish buff eggs, lightly spotted with reddish brown, for 22–27 days; both adults tend the young.

Feeding: gleans the ground for insects, especially grasshoppers and beetles.

Voice: courtship song is an airy, whistled *whip-whee-ee you;* alarm call is *quip-ip-ip.*

Similar Species: *Willet* (p. 119): longer, heavier bill; dark greenish legs; black-and-white wings in flight. *Buff-breasted Sandpiper* (p. 137): shorter neck; larger head; daintier bill; lacks streaking on "cheek" and foreneck. *Pectoral Sandpiper* (p. 133): streaking on breast ends abruptly; smaller eyes; shorter neck; usually seen in larger numbers.

Selected Sites: Allegan SGA; Muskegon Wastewater System; Port Huron SGA; grasslands in northern cut-over lands and meadows.

WHIMBREL

Numenius phaeopus

Whimbrels often travel in long lines and "V" formations, calling with four short whistles and sailing for short periods on set wings. Michigan birders are most likely to see Whimbrels during migration, as the birds pass along the shores of the Great Lakes. Whimbrels travel in flocks, so expect to see either sizeable groups of them or none at all. • It is impossible to talk about the Whimbrel without mentioning the Eskimo Curlew *(N. borealis)*. Both of these birds suffered devastating losses to their populations during the commercial hunts of the late 1800s. While the Whimbrel population slowly recovered, the Eskimo Curlew seemed to vanish into thin air—the last confirmed sighting of this bird was in 1963. Encouraging reports from South American wintering grounds in 1993 offer a glimmer of hope that a few still remain. • *Numenius,* from the Greek for "new moon," refers to the curved shape of this bird's bill.

ID: long, down-curved bill; striped crown; dark eye line; mottled brown body; long legs. *In flight:* dark underwings.
Size: *L* 18 in; *W* 32 in.

Status: rare migrant from May to early June and from August to mid-September.
Habitat: mudflats, sandy beaches, farmlands, grassy lakeshores, airports and flooded agricultural fields.
Nesting: does not nest in Michigan.
Feeding: probes and pecks for invertebrates in mud or vegetation; also eats berries in fall.

Voice: incoming flocks can be heard uttering a distinctive and easily imitated, rippling *bibibibibibibi* long before they come into sight.
Similar Species: *Upland Sandpiper* (p. 121): smaller; straight bill; lacks head markings; yellowish legs. *Willet* (p. 119): straight bill; plain, unmarked crown; gray color; prominent, white wing stripe along back. *Eskimo Curlew:* unbarrred primaries; pale cinnamon wing linings; shorter, slightly straighter bill; darker upperparts; thought to be extinct.
Selected Sites: Pointe Mouillee SGA; Fish Point SGA; Tawas Point SP; Whitefish Point; Muskegon Wastewater System; Pere Marquette SP.

HUDSONIAN GODWIT
Limosa haemastica

Each fall, a great number of Hudsonian Godwits gather on the shores of Hudson Bay in Canada and then embark on a nonstop journey to southern South America. This migration marathon means that these godwits are not often seen at typical stopover sites in Michigan. Their voyage is fueled solely by fat reserves that are built up on these birds' north-coast staging grounds before departure. Fortunately, not all godwits fly directly south in early fall, so birders who are scouting the shores of the Great Lakes—even as late as November—may be able to enjoy their presence. • For most of the year, Hudsonian Godwits can be seen probing sandy depths for worms, mollusks and crustaceans, sometimes with their bills buried up to their eyes! Female godwits and curlews consistently outcompete males in their ability to probe deeply into the sands because of the females' longer beaks. • The Hudsonian Godwit is smaller than the Marbled Godwit, and has distinct, black underwings that are easily seen in flight.

breeding ♂

breeding

ID: long, yellow orange bill with dark, slightly upturned tip; white rump; black tail; long, blue black legs. *Breeding:* heavily barred, chestnut red underparts; dark grayish upperparts; male is more brightly colored. *Nonbreeding:* grayish upperparts; whitish underparts may show a few short, black bars. *Immature:* dark, gray brown upperparts; pale underparts. *In flight:* white rump; black "wing pits" and wing linings.
Size: *L* 14–15½ in; *W* 29 in.
Status: rare migrant from late April to early June and from late July to early November.
Habitat: flooded fields, marshes, mudflats and lakeshores.

Nesting: does not nest in Michigan.
Feeding: probes deeply into water or mud; walks into deeper water than most shorebirds but rarely swims; eats mollusks, crustaceans, insects and other invertebrates; also picks earthworms from plowed fields.
Voice: usually quiet in migration; sometimes a sharp, rising *god-WIT!*
Similar Species: *Marbled Godwit* (p. 124): larger; mottled brown overall; lacks white rump. *Greater Yellowlegs* (p. 116): shorter, all-dark bill; bright yellow legs; lacks white rump. *Long-billed Dowitcher* (p. 139) and *Short-billed Dowitcher* (p. 138): smaller; straight, all-dark bills; yellow green legs; mottled, rust brown upperparts in breeding plumage.
Selected Sites: Erie Marsh Preserve; Fish Point SGA; Whitefish Point; Allegan SGA; Nayanquing Point WA; Pointe Mouillee SGA.

MARBLED GODWIT

Limosa fedoa

The Marbled Godwit's bill looks long enough to reach buried prey, but this bird doesn't seem content with its reach. It is frequently seen with its head submerged beneath the water or with its face pressed into a mudflat. These deep probings seem to pay off for this large, resourceful shorebird, and a godwit looks genuinely pleased with a freshly extracted meal and a face covered in mud. • Unlike Hudsonian Godwits, which undertake long migrations from the Arctic to South America, Marbled Godwits migrate relatively short distances to coastal wintering areas in the southern U.S. and Central America. Still, sightings of Marbled Godwits are rare in Michigan. • The genus name *Limosa*, meaning "muddy," refers to this bird's preference for muddy foraging habitats.

breeding

breeding

ID: long, yellow orange bill with dark, slightly upturned tip; long neck and legs; mottled, buff brown plumage is darkest on upperparts; long, black blue legs. *In flight:* cinnamon wing linings.
Size: *L* 16–20 in; *W* 30 in.
Status: rare migrant from mid-April to mid-June and from early August to mid-November.
Habitat: flooded fields, wet meadows, marshes, mudflats and lakeshores.
Nesting: does not nest in Michigan.
Feeding: probes deeply in soft substrates for worms, insect larvae, crustaceans and mollusks; picks insects from grass; may also eat the tubers and seeds of aquatic vegetation.
Voice: loud, ducklike, 2-syllable squawks: *co-rect co-rect* or *god-wit god-wit.*
Similar Species: *Hudsonian Godwit* (p. 123): smaller; chestnut red neck and underparts; white rump. *Greater Yellowlegs* (p. 116): shorter, all-dark bill; bright yellow legs. *Long-billed Dowitcher* (p. 139) and *Short-billed Dowitcher* (p. 138): smaller; straight, all-dark bills; white rump wedge; yellow green legs.
Selected Sites: Erie Marsh Preserve; Pointe Mouillee SGA; Whitefish Point; Saginaw Bay marshes; Nayanquing Point WA; New Buffalo and St. Joseph waterfronts.

RUDDY TURNSTONE

Arenaria interpres

During late May and early June, small flocks of boldly patterned Ruddy Turnstones settle on blacktop fields and along the shores of the Great Lakes to mingle and forage among the more populous shorebird migrants. These birds' painted faces and eye-catching, black-and-red backs set them apart from the multitudes of little brown-and-white sandpipers. • Ruddy Turnstones are truly long-distance migrants. Individuals that nest along the shores of Canada's Arctic routinely fly to South America or western Europe to avoid frosty winters. • The name "turnstone" is appropriate for this bird, which uses its bill to flip over pebbles, shells and washed-up vegetation to expose hidden invertebrates. Its short, stubby, slightly upturned bill is an ideal utensil for this unusual foraging style. The Ruddy Turnstone has a varied diet that may occasionally include the eggs of other birds.

nonbreeding

breeding

ID: white belly; black "bib" curves up to shoulder; stout, black, slightly upturned bill; orange red legs. *Breeding:* ruddy upperparts (female is slightly paler); white face; black "collar"; dark, streaky crown. *Nonbreeding:* brownish upperparts and face.
Size: *L* 9½ in; *W* 21 in.
Status: uncommon migrant from late April to mid-June and from late July to early November.
Habitat: shores of lakes, reservoirs, marshes and sewage lagoons; also in cultivated fields.

Nesting: does not nest in Michigan.
Feeding: probes under and flips rocks, weeds and shells for food items; picks, digs and probes for invertebrates from the soil or mud; also eats berries, seeds, spiders and carrion.
Voice: low, repeated contact notes; also a sharp *cut-a-cut* alarm call.
Similar Species: *Other sandpipers* (pp. 116–39): all lack the Ruddy Turnstone's bold patterning and flashy wing markings in flight. *Plovers* (pp. 110–13): equally bold plumage but in significantly different patterns.
Selected Sites: Pointe Mouillee SGA; Whitefish Point; Tawas Point SP; Shiawassee Flats NWR; Ludington SP; Muskegon Wastewater System; New Buffalo and St. Joseph waterfronts.

RED KNOT
Calidris canutus

Small flocks of Red Knots appear for a brief period, usually around the last week of May. Never abundant in Michigan, these tubby, red-bellied knots are distinguished from the masses of migrating plovers and sandpipers by their bright rufous spring plumage. • During the breeding season, their red plumage serves to attract mates and camouflage the birds against the sea of grasses and colorful wildflowers on their arctic nesting grounds. • In fall and winter, drab, gray-and-white Red Knots are difficult to distinguish from other migrating and overwintering shorebirds and blend in perfectly with the open sandy beaches that they inhabit at this time of year. • The Red Knot is another migratory champion, flying up to 19,000 miles in a single year. Some of these birds fly from their breeding grounds to winter on the southern tip of South America, while others migrate to western Europe.

nonbreeding

breeding

ID: chunky, round body; greenish legs. *Breeding:* rusty face, breast and underparts; brown, black and buff upperparts. *Nonbreeding:* pale gray upperparts; white underparts with some faint streaking on upper breast; faint barring on rump. *Immature:* buffy wash on breast; scaly-looking back. *In flight:* white wing stripe.
Size: *L* 10½ in; *W* 23 in.
Status: uncommon migrant from late May to early June and from early August to early November.
Habitat: lakeshores, marshes and plowed fields.
Nesting: does not nest in Michigan.

Feeding: gleans shorelines for insects, crustaceans and mollusks; probes soft substrates, creating lines of small holes.
Voice: melodious, soft *ker ek* in flight.
Similar Species: *Long-billed Dowitcher* (p. 139) and *Short-billed Dowitcher* (p. 138): much longer bills; barring under tail and on flanks; white "V" on rump and tail and on trailing edge of wings. *Buff-breasted Sandpiper* (p. 137): light buff in color; finer, shorter bill; dark flecking on sides. *Other peeps* (pp. 127–36): smaller; most have black legs; only Sanderling (p. 127) and Curlew Sandpiper (p. 339) show reddish coloration on undersides in breeding plumage.
Selected Sites: Pointe Mouillee SGA; Tawas Point SP; Whitefish Point; Lake Erie Metropark; Muskegon Wastewater System; Shiawassee Flats NWR.

SANDERLING

Calidris alba

A spring or fall stroll along the shores of the Great Lakes is often punctuated by the sight of tiny Sanderlings running and playing in the waves. Their well-known habit of chasing waves has a simple purpose: to snatch washed-up aquatic invertebrates before the next wave rolls onto shore. Sprinting along the beach while foraging, Sanderlings move so fast on their dark legs that they appear to be gliding across the sand. With the lack of crashing waves and coastal surf in Michigan, Sanderlings practice on calmer shores. Here, they often resort to unenthusiastic probes into wet soil, with a preference for sandy, rather than muddy, substrates. • When resting, Sanderlings often tuck one leg up to preserve body heat. • This sandpiper is one of the world's most widespread birds. It breeds across the Arctic in Alaska, Canada and Russia, and it spends winter running up and down sandy shorelines in North America, South America, Asia, Africa and Australia.

The Sanderling is classified as a sandpiper but has many characteristics of a plover: three toes, a smaller body and the run-and-snatch behavior.

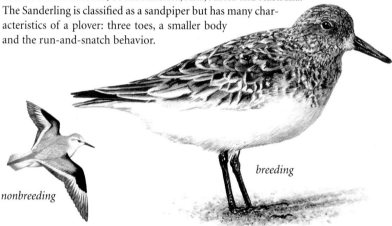

breeding

nonbreeding

ID: straight, black bill; black legs; white underparts; striking white wing bar; pale rump. *Breeding:* dark spotting or mottling on rufous head and breast.
Nonbreeding: pale gray upperparts; black shoulder patch (often concealed).
Size: *L* 7–8½ in; *W* 17 in.
Status: fairly common migrant from early May to mid-June and from late July to mid-October; a few may remain through summer and into early winter.
Habitat: shores of lakes, marshes and reservoirs.
Nesting: does not nest in Michigan.

Feeding: gleans shorelines for insects, crustaceans and mollusks; probes repeatedly, creating a line of small holes in the sand.
Voice: flight call is a sharp *kip*.
Similar Species: *Least Sandpiper* (p. 130): smaller and darker; yellowish legs; lacks rufous breast in breeding plumage. *Dunlin* (p. 135): larger and darker; slightly downcurved bill. *Red Knot* (p. 126): larger; gray-barred, whitish rump; breeding adult has unstreaked, reddish belly. *Western Sandpiper* (p. 129) and *Semipalmated Sandpiper* (p. 128): lack rufous breast in breeding plumage; sandy upperparts in nonbreeding plumage.
Selected Sites: Tawas Point SP; Whitefish Point; Pointe Mouillee SGA; Muskegon Wastewater System; Metrobeach Metropark; Shiawassee Flats NWR.

SEMIPALMATED SANDPIPER
Calidris pusilla

The small, plain Semipalmated Sandpiper can be difficult to identify among the swarms of similar-looking *Calidris* sandpipers that appear along the shores of the southern Great Lakes each spring. Known collectively as "peeps" because of the similarity in their high-pitched calls, these strikingly similar "miniatures," which include the Semipalmated, Least, Western, White-rumped and Baird's sandpipers, can make shorebird identification either a complete nightmare or an uplifting challenge. • Each spring, large numbers of Semipalmated Sandpipers touch down on our shorelines, pecking and probing in mechanized fury to replenish their body fat for the remainder of their long journey. Semipalmated Sandpipers fly almost the entire length of the Americas during migration, so their staging sites must provide ample food sources. Highly efficient, these birds raise up to four young in just a few weeks of arctic summer, then fly 2000 nonstop miles over water back to their wintering grounds.

nonbreeding

breeding

ID: short, straight, black bill; black legs. *Breeding:* mottled upperparts; slight tinge of rufous on ear patch, crown and scapulars; faint streaks on upper breast and flanks. *Nonbreeding:* white "eyebrow"; gray brown upperparts; white underparts with light brown wash on sides of upper breast. *In flight:* narrow, white wing stripe; black line through white rump.
Size: *L* 5½–7 in; *W* 14 in.
Status: common migrant from late April to mid-June and from mid-July to early October.
Habitat: mudflats and the shores of ponds and lakes.

Nesting: does not nest in Michigan.
Feeding: probes soft substrates and gleans for aquatic insects and crustaceans.
Voice: flight call is a harsh *cherk;* sometimes a longer *chirrup* or a chittering alarm call.
Similar Species: *Least Sandpiper* (p. 130): yellowish legs; darker upperparts. *Western Sandpiper* (p. 129): longer, slightly downcurved bill; bright rufous wash on crown and ear patch. *Sanderling* (p. 127): pale gray upperparts and blackish trailing edge on flight feathers in nonbreeding plumage. *White-rumped Sandpiper* (p. 131): larger; white rump; folded wings extend beyond tail. *Baird's Sandpiper* (p. 132): larger; longer bill; folded wings extend beyond tail.
Selected Sites: Lake Erie Metropark; Whitefish Point; Nayanquing Point WA; Muskegon Wastewater System; Shiawassee Flats NWR.

WESTERN SANDPIPER

Calidris mauri

Most Western Sandpipers are seen only along the Pacific Coast, but some adventurous individuals traverse the continent, often flying through Michigan on their way to the Atlantic for the winter. • Many identification guides will tell you to look for this bird's downcurved bill, and on paper this seems like a sensible plan. In the field, however, as angles and lighting change, the bills of "peeps" can look downcurved one moment, straight the next, and anything in between when double-checked. It is a good idea to spend some time getting to know the peeps before trying to identity them. The Western Sandpiper can be easily confused with other peeps, in particular the Semipalmated Sandpiper. • To track down the rare Western Sandpiper, try calling local birding hotlines to find out the locations of the most recent local sightings. Unless you are a particularly keen birder, there's no reason why you shouldn't let more experienced birders do most of the work for you!

nonbreeding

breeding

ID: black, slightly downcurved bill; black legs. *Breeding:* rufous crown, ear patch and scapulars; V-shaped streaking on upper breast and flanks; light underparts. *Nonbreeding:* white "eyebrow"; gray brown upperparts; white underparts; streaky, light brown wash on upper breast. *In flight:* narrow, white wing stripe; black line through white rump.
Size: L 6–7 in; W 14 in.
Status: rare migrant in May and from July to October.
Habitat: pond edges, lakeshores and mudflats.
Nesting: does not nest in Michigan.
Feeding: gleans and probes mud and shallow water; occasionally submerges its head; primarily eats aquatic insects, worms and crustaceans.

Voice: flight call is a high-pitched *cheep.*
Similar Species: *Semipalmated Sandpiper* (p. 128): shorter, straight bill; less rufous on crown, ear patch and scapulars. *Least Sandpiper* (p. 130): smaller; yellowish legs; darker breast wash in all plumages; lacks rufous patches. *White-rumped Sandpiper* (p. 131): larger; white rump; folded wings extend beyond tail; lacks rufous wing patches. *Baird's Sandpiper* (p. 132): larger; folded wings extend beyond tail; lacks rufous patches. *Dunlin* (p. 135): larger; black belly in breeding plumage; longer bill is thicker at base and droops at tip; grayer, unstreaked back in nonbreeding plumage. *Sanderling* (p. 127): nonbreeding plumage shows pale gray upperparts, blackish trailing edge on flight feathers and bold, white upperwing stripe in flight.
Selected Sites: Pointe Mouillee SGA; Ludington SP; Whitefish Point.

LEAST SANDPIPER
Calidris minutilla

The Least Sandpiper is the smallest North American shorebird, but its size does not deter it from performing migratory feats. Like most other "peeps," the Least Sandpiper migrates almost the entire length of the globe twice each year, from the Arctic to the southern tip of South America and back. • Arctic summers are incredibly short, so shorebirds must maximize their breeding efforts. Least Sandpipers lay large eggs relative to those of other sandpipers, and the entire clutch might weigh over half the weight of the female! The young hatch in an advanced state of development, getting an early start on preparations for the fall migration. These tiny shorebirds begin moving south as early as the first week of July, so they are some of the first fall migrants to arrive in Michigan. • Although light-colored legs are a good field mark for this species, bad lighting or mud can confuse matters. Dark mud can make the legs look dark, while light-colored mud can make other species' dark legs look light. • The scientific name *minutilla* is Latin for "very small"—apt for the littlest sandpiper.

breeding

ID: black bill; yellowish legs; dark, mottled back. *Breeding:* buff brown breast, head and nape; light breast streaking; prominent white "V" on back. *Non-breeding:* more gray brown overall. *Immature:* similar to adult, but with faintly streaked breast.
Size: *L* 5–6½ in; *W* 13 in.
Status: common migrant from mid-April to early June and from early July to October.
Habitat: sandy beaches, lakeshores, ditches, sewage lagoons, mudflats and wetland edges.

Nesting: does not nest in Michigan.
Feeding: probes or pecks for insects, crustaceans, small mollusks and occasionally seeds.
Voice: high-pitched *kreee*.
Similar Species: *Semipalmated Sandpiper* (p. 128): black legs; lighter upperparts; rufous tinge on crown, ear patch and scapulars. *Western Sandpiper* (p. 129): slightly larger; black legs; lighter breast wash in all plumages; rufous patches on crown, ear and scapulars in breeding plumage. *Other peeps* (pp. 126–36): all are larger; dark legs.
Selected Sites: Nayanquing Point WA; Pointe Mouillee SGA; Shiawassee Flats NWR; Whitefish Point; Tawas Point SP; New Buffalo and St. Joseph waterfronts.

WHITE-RUMPED SANDPIPER

Calidris fuscicollis

Just as a die-hard shorebird watcher is about to go into a peep-induced stupor, small brownish heads emerge from hiding, back feathers are ruffled, wings are stretched and, almost without warning, the birds take flight and flash pure white rumps. There is no doubt that the beautiful White-rumped Sandpiper has been identified. • This sandpiper's white rump may serve the same purpose as the tail of a white-tailed deer—to alert other birds when danger threatens. • When flocks of White-rumps and other sandpipers take to the air, they often defecate in unison. This spontaneous evacuation might benefit the birds by reducing their weight for takeoff. Flocks of White-rumped Sandpipers have also been known to collectively rush at a predator and then suddenly scatter in its face. • Like many sandpipers, White-rumps are accomplished long-distance migrants, often flying for stretches of 60 hours nonstop. • The scientific name *fuscicollis* means "brown neck," a characteristic this bird shares with many of its close relatives.

breeding

breeding

ID: black legs; black bill, about as long as head width. *Breeding:* brown-mottled upperparts; dark streaking on breast, sides and flanks. *In flight:* white rump; dark tail; indistinct wing bar.
Size: *L* 7–8 in; *W* 17 in.
Status: uncommon migrant from late May to mid-June and from mid-August to early November.
Habitat: shores of lakes, marshes, sewage lagoons and reservoirs; flooded and cultivated fields.

Nesting: does not nest in Michigan.
Feeding: gleans the ground and shorelines for insects, crustaceans and mollusks.
Voice: flight call is a characteristic, squeal-like *tzeet,* higher than any other peep.
Similar Species: *Other peeps* (pp. 126–36): all have dark line through rump. *Baird's Sandpiper* (p. 132): lacks clean white rump; breast streaking does not extend onto flanks. *Stilt Sandpiper* (p. 136) and *Curlew Sandpiper* (p. 339): much longer legs trail beyond tail in flight.
Selected Sites: Nayanquing Point WA; Shiawassee Flats NWR; Whitefish Point; Maple River SGA; Metrobeach Metropark; Muskegon Wastewater System; Tawas Point SP; Pointe Mouillee SGA.

BAIRD'S SANDPIPER
Calidris bairdii

The Baird's Sandpiper is one of the most difficult sandpipers to identify correctly. One clue is that while it often migrates with other sandpipers, upon landing it leaves them and feeds alone. • Like their *Calidris* relatives, these modest-looking shorebirds have extraordinary migratory habits—they fly from South America to the Arctic and back each year. • Baird's Sandpipers remain on their northern breeding grounds for only a short time. Soon after the chicks hatch and are able to fend for themselves, the adults flock together to begin their southward migration. After a few weeks of accumulating fat reserves, the young gather in a second wave of southbound migrants. • Spencer Fullerton Baird, an early director of the Smithsonian Institute, organized several natural history expeditions across North America. In the 19th century, Elliott Coues named this bird in recognition of Baird's efforts.

breeding

nonbreeding

ID: black legs and bill; faint, buff brown breast speckling; folded wings extend beyond tail. *Breeding:* large, black, diamondlike patterns on back and wing coverts.
Size: *L* 7–7½ in; *W* 17 in.
Status: rare migrant from mid-May; uncommon from July to mid-October.
Habitat: sandy beaches, mudflats and wetland edges.
Nesting: does not nest in Michigan.
Feeding: gleans aquatic invertebrates, especially larval flies; also eats beetles and grasshoppers; rarely probes.

Voice: soft, rolling *kriit kriit*.
Similar Species: "scaly" back is distinctive. *White-rumped Sandpiper* (p. 131): clean white rump; breast streaking extends onto flanks. *Pectoral Sandpiper* (p. 133): dark breast ends abruptly at edge of white belly. *Least Sandpiper* (p. 130): smaller; yellowish legs. *Western Sandpiper* (p. 129) and *Sanderling* (p. 127): lack streaked, gray buff breast. *Semipalmated Sandpiper* (p. 128): smaller; shorter bill; lacks streaked breast in nonbreeding plumage.
Selected Sites: Whitefish Point; Tawas Point SP; Muskegon Wastewater System; Pointe Mouillee SGA.

PECTORAL SANDPIPER

Calidris melanotos

This widespread traveler has been observed in every state and province in North America during its epic annual migrations. In spring and fall, Pectoral Sandpipers are conspicuous along the shores of the lower Great Lakes and in wet, grassy fields, often in large flocks of over 1000 birds. Peak numbers occur from late August to late October. • Unlike most sandpipers, the Pectoral exhibits sexual dimorphism—the female is only two-thirds the size of the male. • The name "pectoral" refers to the location of the male's prominent air sacs. When displaying on their arctic breeding grounds, the male will inflate these air sacs, causing his feathers to rise. Males also emit a hollow hooting sound during displays that has been likened to the sound of a foghorn. • If threatened, flocks of Pectorals suddenly launch into the air and converge into a single, swirling mass. • Pectoral Sandpipers are sometimes referred to as "Grass Snipes" because of their preference for wet meadows and grassy marshes.

ID: brown breast streaks end abruptly at edge of white belly; white under-tail coverts; black bill has slightly down-curved tip; long, yellow legs; mottled upperparts; may have faintly rusty, dark crown and back; folded wings extend beyond tail. *Immature:* less spotting on breast; broader, white feather edges on back form 2 white "V"s.
Size: *L* 9 in; *W* 18 in (female is noticeably smaller).
Status: common migrant from mid-April to early May and from late July to mid-November.

Habitat: lakeshores, marshes, mudflats and flooded fields or pastures.
Nesting: does not nest in Michigan.
Feeding: probes and pecks for small insects; eats mainly flies, but also takes beetles and some grasshoppers; may eat small mollusks, amphipods, berries, seeds, moss, algae and some plant material.
Voice: sharp, short, low *krrick krrick.*
Similar Species: *Other peeps* (pp. 126–36): all lack well-defined, dark "bib" and yellow legs.
Selected Sites: Erie Metropark; Tawas Point SP; Pointe Mouillee SGA; Shiawassee Flats NWR; Maple River SGA; Metrobeach Metropark.

PURPLE SANDPIPER
Calidris maritima

The Purple Sandpiper is chunky and has no flashy colors or ringing calls to applaud. However, you have to admire it for choosing to live on the edge. Unlike most shorebirds, which prefer shallow marshy areas, sand beaches or mudflats, Purple Sandpipers forage perilously close to crashing waves along rocky headlands, piers and breakwaters. These birds expertly navigate their way across rugged, slippery rocks while foraging for crustaceans, mollusks and insect larvae. In fact, they are rarely seen associated with any beach that is not near a rocky area. • Purple Sandpipers winter along the Atlantic Coast and breed in high arctic coastal regions, so few grace our shores each year. No other shorebird winters as far north along the Atlantic Coast as the Purple Sandpiper. • The name "purple" was given to this sandpiper for the purplish iridescence that is occasionally observed on its shoulders. *Maritima* is Latin for "belonging to the sea."

nonbreeding

ID: long, slightly drooping, black-tipped bill with yellow orange base; yellow orange legs; dull streaking on breast and flanks. *Breeding:* streaked neck; buff crown with dark streaks; dark back feathers with tawny to rusty brown edges. *Nonbreeding:* unstreaked, gray head, neck and upper breast form a "hood"; gray-spotted white belly.
Size: *L* 9 in; *W* 17 in.
Status: rare migrant from mid-May to early June and from mid-October to February.

Habitat: sandy beaches, rocky shorelines, piers and breakwaters.
Nesting: does not nest in Michigan.
Feeding: food is found visually and is snatched while moving over rocks and sand; eats mostly mollusks, insects, crustaceans and other invertebrates; also eats a variety of plant material.
Voice: call is a soft *prrt-prrt*.
Similar Species: *Other peeps* (pp. 126–36): all lack bicolored bill, yellow orange legs and unstreaked, gray "hood" in nonbreeding plumage.
Selected Sites: western Lake Michigan waterfronts—New Buffalo, South Haven, Muskegon, Ludington, Frankfort; Whitefish Point.

DUNLIN

Calidris alpina

Outside the breeding season, Dunlins form dynamic, synchronous flocks. These tight flocks are generally more exclusive than other shorebird troupes and rarely include other species. Sometimes hundreds of these birds are seen flying wing tip to wing tip. Unlike many of their shorebird relatives, Dunlins overwinter in North America, mostly in coastal areas—few ever cross the equator. They gather in flocks that can number in the tens of thousands. • Dunlins are fairly distinctive in their breeding attire: their black bellies and legs make them look as though they have been wading belly-deep in puddles of ink. • This bird was originally called "Dunling," meaning "little dark one," but with the passage of time, the "g" was dropped. It was also known as "Red-backed Sandpiper" because of its rufous back in breeding plumage.

nonbreeding

breeding

ID: slightly down-curved, black bill; black legs. *Breeding:* black belly; streaked, white neck and underparts; rufous wings, back and crown. *Nonbreeding:* pale gray underparts; brownish gray upperparts; light brown streaking on breast and nape. *In flight:* white wing stripe.

Size: *L* 7½–9 in; *W* 17 in.

Status: common migrant from mid-April to late June and from mid-July to November.

Habitat: mudflats and the shores of ponds, marshes and lakes.

Nesting: does not nest in Michigan.

Feeding: gleans and probes mudflats for aquatic crustaceans, worms, mollusks and insects.

Voice: flight call is a grating *cheezp* or *treezp*.

Similar Species: black belly in breeding plumage is distinctive. *Western Sandpiper* (p. 129) and *Semipalmated Sandpiper* (p. 128): smaller; nonbreeding plumage is browner overall; bill tips are less downcurved. *Least Sandpiper* (p. 130): smaller; darker upperparts; yellowish legs. *Sanderling* (p. 127): paler; straight bill; usually seen running in the surf.

Selected Sites: Pointe Mouillee SGA; Whitefish Point; Tawas Point SP; Nayanquing Point WA; Muskegon Wastewater System.

STILT SANDPIPER
Calidris himantopus

With the silhouette of a small Lesser Yellowlegs and the foraging behavior of dowitchers—two birds with which the Stilt Sandpiper often associates—this bird is easily overlooked by most birders. Named for its relatively long legs, this shorebird prefers to feed in shallow water, where it digs like a dowitcher, often dunking its head completely underwater. Because its bill is shorter than a dowitcher's, however, it has to lean farther forward than its larger cousin—a characteristic that can aid in identification. Moving on tall, stiltlike legs, this sandpiper will also wade into deep water up to its breast in search of a meal. • The omnivorous Stilt Sandpiper eats everything from insects to roots and seeds. To snag freshwater shrimp, insect larvae or tiny minnows from just below the water's surface, the Stilt may occasionally sweep its bill from side to side like an American Avocet. • Unlike many of their *Calidris* relatives, Stilt Sandpipers never gather in large flocks. At most, you may see a gathering of 50 or so Stilts between mid-August and the end of September.

breeding

ID: long, greenish legs; long bill droops slightly at tip. *Breeding:* chestnut red ear patch; white "eyebrow"; striped crown; streaked neck; barred underparts. *Nonbreeding:* less conspicuous white "eyebrow"; dirty white neck and breast; white belly; dark brownish gray upperparts. *In flight:* white rump; legs trail behind tail; no wing stripe.
Size: *L* 8–9 in; *W* 18 in.
Status: uncommon migrant from late July to late October; rare migrant in May.
Habitat: shores of lakes, reservoirs and marshes.

Nesting: does not nest in Michigan.
Feeding: probes deeply in shallow water; eats mostly invertebrates; occasionally picks insects from the water's surface or the ground; also eats seeds, roots and leaves.
Voice: simple, sharp *querp* or *kirr* in flight; clearer *whu*.
Similar Species: *Greater Yellowlegs* (p. 116) and *Lesser Yellowlegs* (p. 117): yellow legs; straight bills; lack red ear patch. *Curlew Sandpiper* (p. 339): bill has more obvious curve; black legs; paler gray upperparts in nonbreeding plumage. *Dunlin* (p. 135): shorter, black legs; dark rump; whitish wing bar.
Selected Sites: Muskegon Wastewater System; Pointe Mouillee SGA; Metrobeach Metropark; Shiawassee Flats NWR.

BUFF-BREASTED SANDPIPER

Tryngites subruficollis

Shy in behavior and humble in appearance, the Buff-breasted Sandpiper is a rare visitor to Michigan. • The Buff-breast prefers drier habitats than most other sandpipers. When feeding, this subtly colored bird stands motionless, blending beautifully into a backdrop of cultivated fields, mudflats or managed sod farms. Only when it catches sight of moving prey does it become visible, making a short, forward sprint to snatch a fresh meal. • Most Buff-breasted Sandpipers migrate through the center of the continent, so the individuals that we see here are mainly dispersing juveniles heading south in fall. These sandpipers regularly mingle with flocks of foraging Black-bellied Plovers and American Golden-Plovers.

ID: buffy, unpatterned face and foreneck; large, dark eyes; very thin, straight, black bill; buff underparts; small spots on crown, nape, breast, sides and flanks; "scaly" look to back and upperwings; yellow legs. *In flight:* pure white underwings; no wing stripe.

Size: *L* 7½–8 in; *W* 18 in.

Status: rare migrant from mid-May to mid-June and from mid-August to late September.

Habitat: shores of lakes, reservoirs and marshes; also sod farms and cultivated and flooded fields.

Nesting: does not nest in Michigan.

Feeding: gleans the ground and shorelines for insects, spiders and small crustaceans; may eat seeds.

Voice: usually silent; calls include *chup* or *tick* notes; *preet* flight call.

Similar Species: *Upland Sandpiper* (p. 121): bolder streaking on breast; longer neck; smaller head; larger bill; streaking on "cheek" and foreneck.

Selected Sites: Pointe Mouillee SGA; Tawas Point SP; Shiawassee Flats NWR; Nayanquing Point WA.

137

SHORT-BILLED DOWITCHER
Limnodromus griseus

T hese plump shorebirds are seen in good numbers on our mudflats, marshes and beaches during spring migration, but the largest concentrations usually occur during the protracted fall migration, which begins as early as mid-July. • Dowitchers tend to be stockier than most shorebirds, and they generally avoid venturing into deep water. While foraging along shorelines, these birds use their bills to "stitch" up and down into the mud with a rhythm like a sewing machine. This drilling motion liquefies the mud or sand, allowing the dowitchers to reach their hidden prey. This behavior is fascinating to watch and it is also helpful for long-range field identification. • The best way to distinguish between Short-billed Dowitchers and the very similar Long-billed Dowitchers is by their flight calls or by listening to them feeding— Long-bills chatter softly while feeding; Short-bills feed silently.

breeding

ID: straight, long, dark bill; white "eyebrow"; chunky body; yellow green legs. *Breeding:* white belly; dark spots or bars on reddish buff neck and upper breast; prominent dark barring on white sides and flanks. *Nonbreeding:* dirty gray upperparts; dirty white underparts. *In flight:* white wedge on rump and lower back.
Size: *L* 11–12 in; *W* 19 in.
Status: uncommon migrant from mid-May to early June and from mid-July to early October.
Habitat: shores of lakes, reservoirs and marshes.
Nesting: does not nest in Michigan.
Feeding: wades in shallow water or on mud, probing deeply into the substrate with a rapid up-down bill motion; eats aquatic invertebrates, including insects, mollusks, crustaceans and worms; may feed on seeds, aquatic plants and grasses.
Voice: generally silent; flight call is a mellow, repeated *tututu, toodulu* or *toodu.*
Similar Species: *Long-billed Dowitcher* (p. 139): black-and-white barring on red flanks in breeding plumage; very little white on belly; dark spotting on neck and upper breast; alarm call is a high-pitched *keek. Red Knot* (p. 126): much shorter bill; unmarked, red breast in breeding plumage; nonbreeding birds lack barring on tail and white wedge on back in flight. *Wilson's Snipe* (p. 140): heavy streaking on neck and breast; bicolored bill; pale median stripe on crown; shorter legs. *American Woodcock* (p. 141): unmarked, buff underparts; yellow bill; light-colored bars on black crown and nape.
Selected Sites: Shiawassee Flats NWR; Nayanquing Point WA; Pointe Mouillee SGA; Muskegon Wastewater System; Metrobeach Metropark.

LONG-BILLED DOWITCHER
Limnodromus scolopaceus

Each spring and fall, mudflats and marshes host small numbers of enthusiastic Long-billed Dowitchers. These chunky, sword-billed shorebirds diligently forage up and down through shallow water and mud in a quest for invertebrate sustenance. A diet of insects, freshwater shrimp, mussels, clams and snails provides migrating Long-bills with plenty of fuel for flight and essential calcium for bone and egg development. • Dowitchers have shorter wings than most shorebirds that migrate long distances. These shorter wings make it more practical for dowitchers to take flight from shallow water, where a series of hops helps them to become airborne. • Mixed flocks of shorebirds demonstrate a variety of foraging styles: some species probe deeply, while others pick at the water's surface or glean the shorelines. It is thought that large numbers of shorebird species are able to coexist because of their different foraging styles and specialized diets.

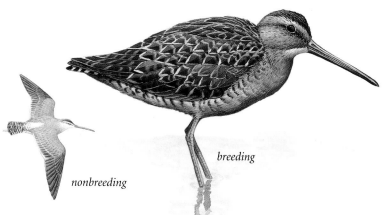

breeding

nonbreeding

ID: very long, straight, dark bill; dark eye line; white "eyebrow"; chunky body; yellow green legs. *Breeding:* black-and-white barring on reddish underparts; some white on belly; dark, mottled upperparts. *Nonbreeding:* gray overall; dirty white underparts. *In flight:* white wedge on rump and lower back.
Size: *L* 11–12½ in; *W* 19 in.
Status: rare migrant in May and from July to November.
Habitat: lakeshores, shallow marshes and mudflats.
Nesting: does not nest in Michigan.
Feeding: probes in shallow water and mudflats with a repeated up-down bill motion; frequently plunges its head under-

water; eats shrimps, snails, worms, larval flies and other soft-bodied invertebrates.
Voice: alarm call is a loud, high-pitched *keek,* occasionally given in series.
Similar Species: *Short-billed Dowitcher* (p. 138): white sides, flanks and belly; more spots than bars on reddish sides and flanks; brighter feather edges on upperparts; call is a lower-pitched *toodu* or *tututu. Red Knot* (p. 126): much shorter bill; unmarked, red breast in breeding plumage; nonbreeding birds lack barring on tail and white wedge on back in flight. *Wilson's Snipe* (p. 140): shorter legs; heavy streaking on neck and breast; bicolored bill; pale median stripe on crown. *American Woodcock* (p. 141): unmarked, buff underparts; yellow bill; light-colored bars on black crown and nape.
Selected Sites: Pointe Mouillee SGA; Shiawassee Flats NWR.

WILSON'S SNIPE
Gallinago delicata

Visit almost any open wetland in spring or early summer and you will hear the eerie, hollow, winnowing sound of courting male Wilson's Snipes. Their specialized outer tail feathers vibrate rapidly in the air as they perform daring, headfirst dives high above their marshland habitat. Snipes can be heard displaying, day or night during spring. • Outside the courtship season, this well-camouflaged bird enters its shy and secretive mode, remaining concealed in vegetation. Only when an intruder approaches too closely will a snipe flush from cover, performing a series of aerial zigzags—an evasive maneuver designed to confuse predators. Because of this habit, hunters who were skilled enough to shoot a snipe came to be known as "snipers," a term later adopted by the military. • The snipe's eyes are placed far back on its head, allowing the bird to see both forward and backward. • This bird used to be named "Common Snipe."

ID: long, sturdy, bicolored bill; relatively short legs; heavily striped head, back, neck and breast; dark eye stripe; dark barring on sides and flanks; unmarked white belly. *In flight:* quick zigzags on take off.
Size: *L* 10½–11½ in; *W* 18 in.
Status: common migrant from March to mid-November; common breeder.
Habitat: cattail and bulrush marshes, sedge meadows, poorly drained floodplains, bogs and fens; willow and red osier dogwood tangles.
Nesting: usually in dry grass, often under vegetation; nest is made of grass, moss and leaves; female incubates 4 olive buff to brown eggs, marked with dark brown, for 18–20 days; both parents raise the young, often splitting the brood.

Feeding: probes soft substrates for larvae, earthworms and other soft-bodied invertebrates; also eats mollusks, crustaceans, spiders, small amphibians and some seeds.
Voice: eerie, accelerating courtship song is produced in flight: *woo-woo-woo-woo-woo-woo;* often sings *wheat wheat wheat* from an elevated perch; alarm call is a nasal *scaip.*
Similar Species: *Short-billed Dowitcher* (p. 138) and *Long-billed Dowitcher* (p. 139): lack heavy striping on head, back, neck and breast; longer legs; all-dark bills; usually seen in flocks. *Marbled Godwit* (p. 124): much larger; slightly upturned bill; much longer legs. *American Woodcock* (p. 141): unmarked, buff underparts; yellowish bill; light-colored bars on black crown and nape.
Selected Sites: Maple River SGA; Erie Marsh Preserve; Whitefish Point; Shiawassee Flats NWR; Pointe Mouillee SGA.

AMERICAN WOODCOCK

Scolopax minor

The American Woodcock's behavior usually mirrors its cryptic and inconspicuous attire. This denizen of moist woodlands and damp thickets normally goes about its business in a quiet and reclusive manner, but during courtship the male woodcock reveals his true character. Just before dawn or just after sunset, he struts provocatively in an open woodland clearing or a brushy, abandoned field while calling out a series of loud *peeent* notes. He then launches into the air, twittering upward in a circular flight display until, with wings partly folded, he plummets to the ground in the zigzag pattern of a falling leaf, chirping at every turn. At the end of this stunning "sky dance," he lands precisely where he started. • The secretive American Woodcock has endured many changes to its traditional nesting grounds. The clearing of forests and draining of woodland swamps has degraded and eliminated large tracts of woodcock habitat, resulting in a decline in this bird's populations.

ID: very long, sturdy bill; very short legs; large head; short neck; chunky body; large, dark eyes; unmarked, buff underparts; light-colored bars on black crown and nape. *In flight:* rounded wings; makes a twittering sound when flushed from cover.
Size: *L* 11 in; *W* 18 in.
Status: common migrant from March to early November; common breeder.
Habitat: moist woodlands and brushy thickets adjacent to grassy clearings or abandoned fields.
Nesting: on the ground in woods or in an overgrown field; female digs a scrape and lines it with dead leaves and other debris; female incubates 4 pinkish buff eggs,

blotched with brown and gray, for 20–22 days; female tends the young.
Feeding: probes in soft, moist or wet soil for earthworms and insect larvae; also takes spiders, snails, millipedes and some plant material, including seeds, sedges and grasses.
Voice: nasal *peent;* during courtship dance male produces high-pitched, twittering, whistling sounds.
Similar Species: *Wilson's Snipe* (p. 140): heavily striped head, back, neck and breast; dark barring on sides and flanks. *Long-billed Dowitcher* (p. 139) and *Short-billed Dowitcher* (p. 138): all-dark bill; longer legs; lack light-colored barring on dark crown and nape; usually seen in flocks.
Selected Sites: Waterloo SRA; Sarett Nature Center; Fort Custer SRA; Allegan SGA; Lapeer SGA; Chippewa Nature Center; Yankee Springs SRA.

WILSON'S PHALAROPE
Phalaropus tricolor

Of the three North American phalarope species, the Wilson's Phalarope is the only one that breeds in Michigan and also the only one that does not feed at sea in winter. It is the most numerous phalarope seen in the state during migration. • Phalaropes are among the most colorful and unusual shorebirds. They practice an uncommon mating strategy known as polyandry: each female mates with several males and often produces a clutch of eggs with each mate. After laying a clutch, the female usually abandons her mate, leaving him to incubate the eggs and tend the precocial young. This reversal of gender roles includes a reversal of plumage characteristics—the female is more brightly colored than her male counterpart. Even John James Audubon was fooled by the these reversals: he mislabeled the male and female birds in all of his phalarope illustrations. • Most phalaropes have lobed, or individually webbed, feet for swimming in the shallows of wetlands, but the Wilson's Phalarope is more terrestrial than its relatives and lacks this characteristic.

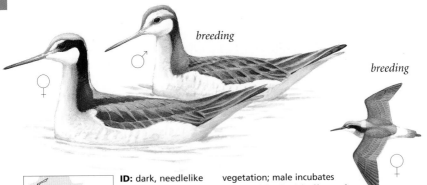

breeding

breeding

ID: dark, needlelike bill; white "eyebrow," throat and nape; light underparts; black legs. *Breeding female:* very sharp colors; gray "cap"; chestnut brown sides of neck; black eye line extends down side of neck and onto back. *Breeding male:* duller overall; dark "cap." *Nonbreeding:* all-gray upperparts; white "eyebrow" and gray eye line; white underparts; dark yellowish or greenish legs.

Size: *L* 9–9½ in; *W* 17 in.

Status: special concern; uncommon migrant from mid-April to mid-June and from mid-July to October; rare breeder.

Habitat: *Breeding:* cattail marshes and grass or sedge margins of sewage lagoons. *In migration:* lakeshores, marshes and sewage lagoons.

Nesting: often near water; well concealed in a depression lined with grass and other vegetation; male incubates 4 brown-blotched, buff eggs for 18–27 days; male rears the young.

Feeding: whirls in tight circles in shallow or deep water to stir up prey, then picks aquatic insects, worms and small crustaceans from the water's surface or just below it; on land makes short jabs to pick up invertebrates.

Voice: deep, grunting *work work* or *wu wu wu*, usually given on the breeding grounds.

Similar Species: *Red-necked Phalarope* (p. 143): rufous stripe down side of neck in breeding plumage; dark nape and line behind eye in nonbreeding plumage. *Red Phalarope* (p. 340): all-reddish neck, breast and underparts in breeding plumage; dark nape and broad, dark line behind eye in nonbreeding plumage; rarely seen inland. *Lesser Yellowlegs* (p. 117): larger; yellow legs; streaked neck; mottled upperparts.

Selected Sites: Maple River SGA; Nayanquing Point WA; Shiawassee Flats NWR; Wilderness SP; Pointe Mouillee SGA; Muskegon Wastewater System.

RED-NECKED PHALAROPE

Phalaropus lobatus

A birdwatching pilgrimage to a local sewage lagoon may not be your idea of an aesthetically pleasing birding experience, but these areas are often the best places to meet many species of birds, including the Red-necked Phalarope. • Most Red-necked Phalaropes migrate to and from their arctic wintering grounds via the Atlantic Coast, but every year small flocks of these tiny shorebirds take the inland route through Michigan. • When foraging on the water with other shorebirds, phalaropes can usually be singled out by their unusual behavior—they spin and whirl about in tight circles, stirring up tiny crustaceans, mollusks and other aquatic invertebrates. As prey funnels toward the water's surface, these birds daintily pluck at them with their needlelike bills. • "Phalarope" is the Greek word for "coot's foot." Like coots and grebes, Red-necked Phalaropes have individually webbed, or "lobed," toes, a feature that makes them proficient swimmers.

breeding

breeding

ID: thin, black bill; long, dark gray legs. *Breeding female:* chestnut brown stripe on neck and throat; white "chin"; blue black head; incomplete, white eye ring; white belly; 2 rusty buff stripes on each upperwing. *Breeding male:* white "eyebrow"; less intense colors than female. *Nonbreeding:* white underparts; black "cap"; broad, dark band from eye to ear; whitish stripes on blue gray upperparts.
Size: *L* 7 in; *W* 15 in.
Status: rare migrant from mid-April to early June and from late June to mid-November.
Habitat: open water bodies, including ponds, lakes, marshes and sewage lagoons.

Nesting: does not nest in Michigan.
Feeding: whirls in tight circles in shallow or deep water to stir up prey, then picks insects, mollusks and small crustaceans from the water's surface; on land makes short jabs to pick up invertebrates.
Voice: often noisy in migration; soft *krit krit krit*.
Similar Species: *Wilson's Phalarope* (p. 142): female has gray "cap" and black eye line extending down side of neck and onto back in breeding plumage. *Red Phalarope* (p. 340): all-red neck, breast and underparts in breeding plumage; lacks white stripes on upperwing in nonbreeding plumage.
Selected Sites: Muskegon Wastewater System; Pointe Mouillee SGA; Shiawassee Flats NWR; Nayanquing Point WA; Whitefish Point.

POMARINE JAEGER

Stercorarius pomarinus

Pomarine Jaegers are powerful, swift predators and notorious "pirates" of the vast, open oceans. Jaegers spend most of their lives in the air, occasionally resting on the ocean's surface, only seeking the solid footing of land during the nesting season. • Fall and early winter appear to be the best seasons for observing the small number of Pomarine Jaegers that make regular appearances in Michigan. Keen fall birders patrolling piers or beaches along the Great Lakes shorelines probably have the best chance of meeting a migrant Pomarine. • Most novice birders differentiate the three jaeger species based on the shape and length of their central tail feathers. This would seem to be an easy task, but this comparison only applies to adult jaegers. Knowing the subtleties of plumage, wingbeat rhythm and wing breadth is most important in making an accurate identification. It may take many years of detailed field observation and the study of museum specimens to accurately identify these birds in the field, only to find that many fall migrants cannot be reliably identified at all!

light morph

ID: long, twisted, central tail feathers; black "cap." *Dark morph:* dark body except for white in wing. *Light morph:* dark, mottled breast band, sides and flanks; dark vent. *Immature:* central tail feathers extend just past tail; white at base of upperwing primaries; variable, dark barring on underwings and underparts; lacks black "cap." *In flight:* wings are wide at base of body; white flash at base of underwing primaries; powerful, steady wingbeats.
Size: *L* 20–23 in; *W* 4 ft.
Status: rare migrant in spring and from late August to early January.
Habitat: shorelines of the Great Lakes.
Nesting: does not nest in Michigan.

Feeding: snatches fish from the water's surface while in flight; chases down small birds; pirates food from gulls; may scavenge at landfills.
Voice: generally silent; may give a sharp *which-yew,* a squealing *weak-weak* or a squeaky, whistled note during migration.
Similar Species: *Parasitic Jaeger* (p. 145): long, thin, pointed tail; lacks mottled sides and flanks; very little white on upperwing primaries; short, sharp tail streamers; immature and subadult have barred underparts. *Long-tailed Jaeger* (p. 340): very long, thin, pointed tail; very little white on upperwing primaries; lacks white on base of underwing primaries, very dark vent and dark, mottled breast band, sides and flanks; juvenile has stubby, spoon-shaped tail streamers and solid, dark markings on throat and upper breast.
Selected Sites: Great Lakes shorelines; frequently seen offshore, but no specific sites.

PARASITIC JAEGER

Stercorarius parasiticus

Although "jaeger" means "hunter" in German, "parasitic" more aptly describes this bird's foraging tactics. "Kleptoparasitism" is the scientific term for this jaeger's pirating ways, and these birds are truly relentless. Parasitic Jaegers will harass and intimidate terns and gulls until the victims regurgitate their partially digested meals. As soon as the food is ejected, these aerial pirates snatch it out of midair or pick it from the water's surface in a swooping dive. Less than 25 percent of these encounters are successful, and many Parasitic Jaegers are content to find their own food. • Jaegers, the most numerous predatory birds in the Arctic, fill the same niche over ocean waters and arctic tundra as hawks do over land. • On their arctic breeding grounds, adults defend their eggs and young aggressively. Both adults will attack approaching danger in stooping, parabolic dives or aggressive, blazing pursuits. In such scenarios, the intruders are forced into a rapid retreat, often assessing how many feathers or how much hair has been lost! • The Parasitic Jaeger is the most abundant jaeger in the world and the most commonly seen in our region.

breeding

ID: long, dark, pointed wings; slightly longer, pointed central tail feathers; brown upperparts; dark "cap"; light underwing tips. *Dark morph:* all-brown underparts and "collar." *Light morph:* white underparts; white to cream-colored "collar"; light brown neck band. *Immature:* barred underparts; central tail feather extends just past tail.
Size: *L* 15–20 in; *W* 3 ft.
Status: rare migrant from early May to early June and from August to mid-November.
Habitat: shorelines of the Great Lakes.

Nesting: does not nest in Michigan.
Feeding: pirates, scavenges and hunts for food; eats fish, eggs, large insects and small birds and mammals; often pirates food from other birds; may scavenge at landfills.
Voice: generally silent; may make shrill calls in migration.
Similar Species: *Pomarine Jaeger* (p. 144): shorter, blunt, twisted central tail feathers; dark, mottled sides and flanks; white on upperwing primaries. *Long-tailed Jaeger* (p. 340): much smaller; much longer, pointed central tail feathers; lacks dark neck band.
Selected Sites: Whitefish Point; Pointe Mouillee SGA; Pere Marquette SP; New Buffalo waterfront; Muskegon SP; Lake Erie shoreline.

145

LAUGHING GULL

Larus atricilla

The black-hooded Laughing Gull's beautiful plumage and lilting laugh are readily accepted by humans today, but life has not always been so easy for this bird. In the late 19th century, high commercial demand for egg collections and feathers for use in women's headresses resulted in the extirpation of this gull as a breeding species in many parts of its Atlantic Coast range. Today, East Coast populations are gradually assuming their former abundance, and the Laughing Gull now wanders into the southern Lake Michigan region. Although this gull may appear in any month of the year in our state, May, June, August and September support the most sightings. • The Laughing Gull's breeding range is primarily along the Atlantic and Gulf coasts of North America and in the Caribbean. It winters in Mexico and Central and South America. • While the laughing call explains this bird's common name, the Latin name *atricilla* refers to a black band present only on the tails of immature birds.

breeding

ID: *Breeding:* black head; broken, white eye ring; red bill. *Nonbreeding:* white head with some pale gray bands; black bill. *3rd-year:* white neck and underparts; dark gray back; black-tipped wings; black legs. *Immature:* variable plumage; brown to gray and white overall; broad, black subterminal tail band.

Size: *L* 15–17 in; *W* 3 ft.

Status: very rare migrant from March to October.

Habitat: shorelines of lakes and rivers, landfills and open water.

Nesting: does not nest in Michigan.

Feeding: omnivorous; gleans insects, small mollusks, crustaceans, spiders and small fish from the ground or water while flying, wading, walking or swimming; may steal food from other birds; may eat the eggs and nestlings of other birds; often scavenges at landfills.

Voice: loud, high-pitched, laughing call: *ha-ha-ha-ha-ha-ha.*

Similar Species: *Franklin's Gull* (p. 147): smaller overall; red legs; shorter, slimmer bill; nonbreeding adult has black "mask." *Black-headed Gull* and *Bonaparte's Gull* (p. 149): orange or reddish legs; slimmer bill (Bonaparte's has black bill); lighter mantle; white wedge on upper leading edge of wing; black "hood" on breeding adult does not extend over nape; white head with black head spot in nonbreeding plumage. *Little Gull* (p. 148): much smaller; paler mantle; reddish legs; dainty, black bill; no eye ring; lacks black wing tips.

Selected Sites: New Buffalo waterfront; Metrobeach Metropark; Whitefish Point.

FRANKLIN'S GULL

Larus pipixcan

Franklin's Gulls drift into Michigan from their prairie stronghold on a rare but regular basis. While making semi-annual tours through our area, individuals or small flocks are usually seen intermingled with large groups of Bonaparte's Gulls and other gull relatives. Most Franklin's Gulls are seen in May and early June and from late August to early November, although keen birders occasionally detect a few strays in summer and winter. • The Franklin's Gull is not a typical "seagull." A large part of its life is spent inland, and on its traditional nesting territory on the prairies, it is affectionately known as "Prairie Dove." It has a dovelike profile and often follows tractors across agricultural fields, snatching up insects from the tractor's path in much the same way its cousins follow fishing boats. • The Franklin's Gull is one of only two gull species that migrate long distances between breeding and wintering grounds—the majority of Franklin's Gulls winter along the Pacific coast of Peru and Chile. • This gull was named for Sir John Franklin, the British navigator and explorer who led four expeditions to the Canadian Arctic in the 19th century.

breeding

ID: dark gray mantle; broken, white eye ring; white underparts. *Breeding:* black head; orange red bill and legs; breast might have pinkish tinge. *Nonbreeding:* white head; dark patch on side of head. *In flight:* black crescent on white wing tips.
Size: *L* 13–15 in; *W* 3 ft.
Status: very rare migrant from late April to early June and from mid-August to late November.
Habitat: agricultural fields, marshlands, river and lake shorelines, rivermouths and landfills.
Nesting: does not nest in Michigan.
Feeding: very opportunistic; gleans agricultural fields and meadows for grasshoppers and insects; often catches dragonflies, mayflies and other flying invertebrates in midair; also eats small fish and some crustaceans.

Voice: mewing, shrill *weeeh-ah weeeh-ah* while feeding and in migration.
Similar Species: *Bonaparte's Gull* (p. 149): black bill; conspicuous white wedge on forewing. *Little Gull* (p. 148): much smaller; paler mantle; lacks black crescent on wing tips; breeding adult lacks broken, white eye ring and white nape; nonbreeding adult lacks black "mask." *Black-headed Gull:* paler mantle; conspicuous, white wedge on forewing; breeding adult has much more white on back of head; nonbreeding adult lacks black face "mask." *Sabine's Gull* (p. 157): large black, white and gray triangles on upperwing; dark, yellow-tipped bill. *Laughing Gull* (p. 146): larger; black legs; longer, heavier bill; nonbreeding adult lacks black "mask."
Selected Sites: Whitefish Point; St. Clair Flats WA; New Buffalo, St. Joseph and South Haven waterfronts; Muskegon Wastewater System; Shiawassee Flats NWR; Tawas Point SP.

147

LITTLE GULL
Larus minutus

This common Eurasian bird was first identified in North America around 1820 as a specimen collected on the first Franklin expedition. It was considered an exceptionally rare vagrant until 1962, when the first documented nest in the New World was discovered in Ontario, Canada. • Little Gull nest sites never remain in a given location for more than a few years, and these birds are often found in established Black Tern colonies. In North America, Little Gulls nest primarily in the Great Lakes region—although at only one location in Michigan. • Look for the Little Gull's dark underwings when it is in flight. This field mark makes it quite conspicuous among the masses of white-underwinged Bonaparte's Gulls, with which it usually mingles. • The Little Gull, true to its name, is the smallest of all gulls. Its Latin name *minutus* means "very small."

breeding

ID: white neck, rump, tail and underparts; gray back and wings; orange red legs. *Breeding:* black head; dark red bill. *Nonbreeding:* black bill; dark ear spot and "cap." *Immature:* pinkish legs; brown and black on wings and tail. *In flight:* white wing tips and trailing edge of wing; dark underwings.

Size: *L* 10–11 in; *W* 24 in.

Status: rare migrant from late March to early May; very rare breeder.

Habitat: freshwater marshes, ponds and beaches.

Nesting: on the ground near water; pair lines a shallow depression with vegetation or builds a raised mound on a wet site; pair incubates 1–5 olive to buff eggs, marked with brown and gray, for 23–25 days.

Feeding: gleans insects from the ground or from the water's surface while flying, wading, walking or floating; may also take small mollusks, fish, crustaceans, marine worms and spiders.

Voice: repeated *kay-ee* and a low *kek-kek-kek.*

Similar Species: *Bonaparte's Gull* (p. 149): black-tipped primary feathers; breeding adult has broken, white eye ring, larger, black bill and white nape; nonbreeding adult has white "cap." *Black-headed Gull:* black-tipped primary feathers; breeding adult has broken, white eye ring, larger bill and white nape; nonbreeding adult has white "cap" and red bill. *Franklin's Gull* (p. 147): larger; black wing tips; darker mantle; breeding adult has broken, white eye ring, white nape and brighter red bill; nonbreeding adult has black face "mask." *Laughing Gull* (p. 146): larger; black wing tips; darker mantle; black legs; breeding adult has broken, white eye ring and much larger bill. *Sabine's Gull* (p. 157): black fore-wing wedge; black legs; yellow-tipped bill.

Selected Sites: Pointe Mouillee SGA; Thorn L.; Tawas Point SP; New Buffalo, St. Joseph, Grand Haven and Muskegon waterfronts.

BONAPARTE'S GULL

Larus philadelphia

M any people feel great disdain for gulls, but they might change their minds when they meet the Bonaparte's Gull. This graceful, reserved gull is nothing like its contentious, aggressive relatives. Delicate in plumage and behavior, this small gull avoids landfills, preferring to dine on insects caught in midair or plucked from the water's surface. It sometimes tips up like a dabbling duck to catch small invertebrates in the shallows. Only when a flock of Bonaparte's spies a school of fish or an intruder do these birds raise their soft, scratchy voices in excitement. • In years when mild winter weather prevails, many of these gulls may remain in Michigan, flying about for hours on end, wheeling and flashing their pale wings. During cold winters, most Bonaparte's Gulls move south to the Atlantic Coast by December. • This gull was named after Charles-Lucien Bonaparte, a nephew of Napoleon and a naturalist who made significant contributions to the study of ornithology in the 1800s.

breeding

ID: black bill; gray mantle; white underparts. *Breeding:* black head; white eye ring; orange legs. *Nonbreeding:* white head; dark ear patch. *In flight:* white forewing wedge; black wing tips.
Size: *L* 11½–14 in; *W* 33 in.
Status: common migrant from March to early June and from late July to November.
Habitat: large lakes, rivers and marshes.
Nesting: does not nest in Michigan.
Feeding: dabbles and tips up for aquatic invertebrates, small fish and tadpoles; gleans the ground for terrestrial invertebrates; also captures insects in the air.

Voice: scratchy, soft *ear ear* while feeding.
Similar Species: *Franklin's Gull* (p. 147): larger; lacks white upper forewing wedge; breeding adult has orange bill; nonbreeding adult has black "mask." *Little Gull* (p. 148): smaller; daintier bill; adult has white wing tips; black "hood" of breeding adult lacks white eye ring and extends over nape; nonbreeding adult has white "cap." *Black-headed Gull:* larger overall; larger, red bill; dark underwing primaries; more red than orange on legs; breeding adult has brownish "hood." *Sabine's Gull* (p. 157): large black, white and gray triangles on upperwings; dark, yellow-tipped bill.
Selected Sites: Whitefish Point; Erie Marsh Preserve; Pointe Mouillee SGA; Muskegon Wastewater System; Tawas Point SP; St. Clair R.

RING-BILLED GULL

Larus delawarensis

The Ring-billed Gull's numbers have greatly increased in recent years, and its tolerance for humans has made it a part of our everyday lives—a connection that often involves Ring-bills scavenging our litter or fouling the windshields of our automobiles! • In the early 1900s, some naturalists were unsure if Ring-bills were even nesting in Michigan, although others felt certain there were small colonies nesting here. By 1940, there was no mistaking the estimated 20,000 breeding Ring-bills in Michigan, and in the mid-1960s the approximately 100,000 birds were impossible to miss. Some people feel that Ring-billed Gulls have become pests—many parks, beaches, golf courses and even fast-food parking lots are inundated with marauding gulls looking for food handouts. Few species, however, have fared as well as the Ring-billed Gull in the face of human development, which, in itself, is something to appreciate.

breeding

ID: white head; yellow bill and legs; black ring around bill tip; pale gray mantle; yellow eyes; white underparts. *Immature:* gray back; brown wings and breast. *In flight:* black wing tips with a few white spots.
Size: *L* 18–20 in; *W* 4 ft.
Status: common to abundant migrant; locally abundant breeder; frequent winter resident around southern L. Michigan and L. Erie.
Habitat: *Breeding:* sparsely vegetated islands, open beaches, breakwaters and dredge-spoil areas. *In migration* and *winter:* lakes, rivers, landfills, golf courses, fields and parks.
Nesting: colonial; in a shallow scrape on the ground lined with plants, debris, grass and sticks; pair incubates 2–4 brown-blotched, gray to olive eggs for 23–28 days.

Feeding: gleans the ground for human food waste, spiders, insects, rodents, earthworms, grubs and some waste grain; scavenges for carrion; surface-tips for aquatic invertebrates and fish.
Voice: high-pitched *kakakaka-akakaka;* also a low, laughing *yook-yook-yook.*
Similar Species: *California Gull* (p. 340): much larger; no bill ring; black and red spots near tip of lower mandible; dark eyes. *Herring* (p. 151), *Thayer's* (p. 152), *Glaucous* (p. 155), *Iceland* (p. 153) and *Slaty-backed gulls:* larger; pinkish legs; red spot near tip of lower mandible; lack bill ring. *Mew Gull:* less black on wing tips; dark eyes; darker mantle; lacks bill ring. *Lesser Black-backed Gull* (p. 154): larger; much darker mantle; much less white on wing tips; lacks bill ring.
Selected Sites: Great Lakes shores; Lake St. Clair; St. Clair R.; St. Mary's R.; large inland lakes; landfills; supermarket parking lots.

HERRING GULL

Larus argentatus

Although Herring Gulls are as adept as their smaller Ring-billed relatives at scrounging handouts on the beach, they are more likely to be found in wilderness areas than urban settings. Settling on lakes and large rivers where Ring-billed Gulls would never be found, Herring Gulls nest comfortably in large colonies, or a pair may choose a nest site miles from any other gulls. • Herring Gulls are skilled hunters, but they are also opportunistic birds that scavenge at landfills and in fast-food restaurant parking lots. Their foraging habits might seem unsanitary, but these birds have thrived by adopting the task of finishing off leftovers. In some areas, increasing Herring Gull populations have meant decreasing tern numbers owing to this gull's fondness for tern eggs and nestlings. • Like many gulls, Herring Gulls have a small red spot on the lower mandible that serves as a target for nestling young. When a downy chick pecks at the lower mandible, the parent recognizes the cue and regurgitates its meal.

breeding

ID: large gull; yellow bill; red spot on lower mandible; light eyes; light gray mantle; pink legs. *Breeding:* white head; white underparts. *Nonbreeding:* white head and nape are washed with brown. *Immature:* mottled brown overall. *In flight:* white-spotted, black wing tips.
Size: *L* 23–26 in; *W* 4 ft.
Status: abundant migrant, breeder and winter resident.
Habitat: large lakes, wetlands, rivers, landfills and urban areas.
Nesting: singly or colonially; often nests with other gulls and cormorants; on an open beach or island; on the ground in a shallow scrape lined with plants and sticks;

pair incubates 3 darkly blotched, olive to buff eggs for 31–32 days.
Feeding: surface-tips for aquatic invertebrates and fish; gleans the ground for insects and worms; scavenges dead fish and human food waste; eats other birds' eggs and young.
Voice: loud, buglelike *kleew-kleew;* also an alarmed *kak-kak-kak.*
Similar Species: *California Gull* (p. 340): smaller; dark eyes; yellowish legs; black-and-red spot on lower mandible. *Ring-billed Gull* (p. 150): smaller; black bill ring; yellow legs. *Thayer's* (p. 152), *Glaucous* (p. 155) and *Iceland* (p. 153) *gulls:* paler mantle; all lack black on wings. *Lesser Black-backed Gull* (p. 154) and *Slaty-backed Gull:* much darker mantle.
Selected Sites: Great Lakes shores; Lake St. Clair; St. Clair R.; St. Mary's R.; large inland lakes; landfills; supermarket parking lots.

THAYER'S GULL

Larus thayeri

Thayer's Gulls are rare throughout our region, and because many of these visitors are immature birds, the identification of which is beyond the scope of this book, it is often only the most experienced birders who recognize them. These gulls are most often sighted traveling inconspicuously among large flocks of Ring-billed Gulls and Herring Gulls during winter. • The Thayer's Gull is part of a group of recently evolved gulls that have similar traits and could potentially still interbreed. It was once considered a subspecies of the very similar-looking Herring Gull, and some ornithologists dispute the decision to grant the Thayer's full species status. Still other ornithologists believe that the Thayer's Gull is a subspecies of the Iceland Gull. • John Eliot Thayer was a Boston philanthropist who assembled a large collection of birds, as well as a comprehensive ornithological library. He also provided financial backing for a number of natural history expeditions.

nonbreeding

ID: white-spotted, dark gray wing tips; dark eyes; yellow bill has red spot at tip of lower mandible; pink legs. *Breeding:* clean white head, neck and upper breast. *Nonbreeding:* brown-flecked head, neck and upper breast. *Immature:* variable, mottled white-and-brown plumage; 1st-year has black bill; 2nd-year has black ring around dusky bill.
Size: *L* 22–25 in; *W* 4½ ft.
Status: rare winter resident from October to May.
Habitat: landfills and open water on large lakes and rivers.
Nesting: does not nest in Michigan.

Feeding: gleans from the water's surface while in flight; eats small fish, crustaceans, mollusks, carrion and human food waste.
Voice: various raucous and laughing calls are given, much like the Herring Gull's *kak-kak-kak*.
Similar Species: *Herring Gull* (p. 151): black wing tips; light eyes; darker mantle. *Iceland Gull* (p. 153): light eyes; more white than dark gray on wing tips. *Glaucous Gull* (p. 155): larger; longer, heavier bill; light eyes; pure white wing tips; lighter pink legs. *Ring-billed Gull* (p. 150): smaller; dark ring on yellow bill; yellow legs. *Lesser Black-backed Gull* (p. 154): darker mantle; black wing tips; yellow feet.
Selected Sites: Muskegon Wastewater System; New Buffalo waterfront; Ottawa Co. lakeshore; Metrobeach Metropark; Whitefish Point.

ICELAND GULL

Larus glaucoides

L ike its close relatives the Thayer's Gull and the Glaucous Gull, the pale Iceland Gull can be seen each winter in small numbers, usually among larger flocks of more common wintering gulls. This graceful glider spends much of its time searching for schools of fish over icy, open waters. When fishing proves unrewarding, this opportunistic gull has no qualms about digging through a landfill in search of food. Human onlookers might think that the Iceland Gull's dirty brown head and breast streaking are a result of its filthy scavenging habits, but in truth, these are the natural markings of its nonbreeding plumage. • The Iceland Gull appears in two well-recognized forms in our region, though one is more common than the other. More common is the "Kumlein's" form, which has gray on its wing tips in flight. On Baffin Island in Canada, the Kumlein's subspecies interbreeds with the Thayer's Gull, producing fertile hybrids that are also seen here occasionally. The other form is the "True" Iceland Gull, which nests in Greenland but occasionally appears in North America.

*nonbreeding
"Kumlein's"*

ID: *Breeding:* relatively short, yellow bill has red spot on lower mandible; rounded head; yellow eyes; dark eye ring; white wing tips with some dark gray; pink legs; white underparts; pale gray mantle. *Nonbreeding:* brown-streaked head and breast. *Immature:* dark eyes; black bill; various plumages with varying amounts of gray on upperparts and brown flecking over entire body.
Size: *L* 22 in; *W* 4½ ft.
Status: rare winter visitor from October to May.
Habitat: landfills and open water on large lakes and rivers.

Nesting: does not nest in Michigan.
Feeding: eats mostly fish; may also take crustaceans, mollusks, carrion and seeds; scavenges at landfills.
Voice: high, screechy calls.
Similar Species: *Herring Gull* (p. 151): black wing tips; darker mantle. *Thayer's Gull* (p. 152): more dark gray than white on wing tips; dark eyes. *Glaucous Gull* (p. 155): larger; longer, heavier bill; pure white wing tips. *Ring-billed Gull* (p. 150): smaller; dark ring on yellow bill; yellow legs. *Lesser Black-backed Gull* (p. 154): darker mantle; black wing tips; yellow feet.
Selected Sites: Muskegon Wastewater System; Lake Erie Metropark; Ottawa Co. and Mason Co. lakeshores; New Buffalo lakeshore; Whitefish Point.

LESSER BLACK-BACKED GULL

Larus fuscus

E quipped with long wings for long-distance flights, small numbers of Lesser Black-backed Gulls leave their familiar European and Icelandic surroundings each fall to make their way to North America. Most of these gulls settle along the Atlantic Coast during winter, but a few make their way into our region. In recent years, Lesser Black-backed sightings have increased in Michigan, so it is possible that this Eurasian species will soon colonize North America. Birders are advised to keep a close eye on Great Lakes shores and landfills—the most likely locations to find Lesser Black-backed Gulls. • The Lesser Black-backed Gull is most similar to the Herring Gull and the Great Black-backed Gull, but the Herring Gull lacks the Lesser's dark wings, the Great Black-backed is considerably larger, and neither sports the pink legs of the Lesser. Some Lesser Black-backed Gulls have already been found paired with Herring Gulls, which indicates that we may see even more puzzling hybrids in the future.

breeding

ID: *Breeding:* dark gray mantle; mostly black wing tips; yellow bill has red spot on lower mandible; yellow eyes; yellow legs; white head and underparts. *Nonbreeding:* brown-streaked head and neck. *Immature:* eyes may be dark or light; black bill or pale bill with black tip; various plumages with varying amounts of gray on upperparts and brown flecking over entire body.
Size: *L* 21 in; *W* 4½ ft.
Status: rare winter visitor from September to May.
Habitat: landfills and open water on large lakes and rivers.

Nesting: does not nest in Michigan.
Feeding: eats mostly fish, aquatic invertebrates, small rodents, seeds, carrion and human food waste; scavenges at landfills.
Voice: screechy call is like a lower-pitched version of the Herring Gull's call.
Similar Species: *Herring Gull* (p. 151): lighter mantle; pink legs. *Thayer's* (p. 152), *Glaucous* (p. 155) and *Iceland* (p. 153) *gulls:* pale gray mantle; white or gray wing tips; pink legs. *Ring-billed Gull* (p. 150): smaller; dark ring on yellow bill; paler mantle. *Slaty-backed Gull:* larger; more white on trailing edge of wing; pink legs. *Great Black-backed Gull* (p. 156): much larger; black mantle; pale pinkish legs.
Selected Sites: Muskegon Wastewater System; Grand Mere SP; Pointe Mouillee SGA; Bay City SRA; Lake Erie Metropark.

GLAUCOUS GULL

Larus hyperboreus

The Glaucous Gull's white underparts and pale gray mantle camouflage it against the cloud-filled winter skies as it scans the open waters of the Great Lakes. Its pale plumage also helps birders to distinguish its ghostly figure from other, more numerous, overwintering gull species. • Glaucous Gulls have traditionally fished for their meals or stolen food from smaller gulls. More recently, many wintering birds have traded the rigors of hunting for the job of defending plots of garbage at various landfills. • In summer, while other gulls are strolling along local beaches or hanging out in fast-food restaurant parking lots, the Glaucous Gull is far away in the arctic wilderness. The scientific name *hyperboreus* means "of the far north."

nonbreeding

ID: *Breeding:* relatively long, heavy, yellow bill has red spot on lower mandible; pure white wing tips; flattened crown profile; yellow eyes; pink legs; white underparts; very pale gray mantle. *Nonbreeding:* brown-streaked head, neck and breast. *Immature:* dark eyes; pale, black-tipped bill; various plumages have varying amounts of brown flecking on body.
Size: *L* 27 in; *W* 5 ft.
Status: rare winter visitor from mid-November to May.

Habitat: landfills; open water on large lakes and rivers.
Nesting: does not nest in Michigan.
Feeding: predator, pirate and scavenger; eats mostly fish, crustaceans, mollusks and some seeds; feeds on carrion and at landfills.
Voice: high, screechy *kak-kak-kak* calls are similar to Herring Gull's.
Similar Species: *Thayer's Gull* (p. 152) and *Iceland Gull* (p. 153): smaller; slightly darker mantle; gray on wing tips. *Herring Gull* (p. 151): slightly smaller; black wing tips; much darker mantle. *Great Black-backed Gull* (p. 156): darker in all plumages.
Selected Sites: Whitefish Point; Tawas Point SP; Muskegon Wastewater System; St. Joseph and New Buffalo waterfronts.

GREAT BLACK-BACKED GULL

Larus marinus

The Great Black-backed Gull's commanding size and bold, aggressive disposition enable it to dominate other gulls, ensuring that it has first dibs at food, whether it is fresh fish or a meal from a landfill. No other gull species, with the exception of the Glaucous Gull, is equipped to dispute ownership with this domineering gull. • In recent years, Great Black-backed Gulls have chosen the Great Lakes region as a new nesting area. Although they prefer to nest in colonies throughout most of their range, nesting efforts along Lake Huron have been limited to isolated pairs. In fall and winter, good numbers of Great Black-backs can be found at landfills and areas of open water in southeastern Michigan. • Like many other North American gulls, the Great Black-backed Gull is a "four-year gull," which means it goes through various plumage stages until its fourth winter, when it develops its refined adult plumage. Most immature gulls have dark streaking, spotting or mottling, which allows them to blend into their surroundings and avoid detection by predators.

breeding

ID: very large gull; all white except for gray underwings and black mantle; pale pinkish legs; light-colored eyes; large, yellow bill has red spot on lower mandible.
Immature: variable plumage; mottled gray brown, white and black; black bill or pale, black-tipped bill.
Size: *L* 30 in; *W* 5½ ft.
Status: uncommon winter visitor from August to mid-May; very rare breeder.
Habitat: landfills and open water on large lakes and rivers.
Nesting: in isolated pairs on beaches; pair builds a mound of vegetation and debris

on the ground, often near rocks; pair incubates 2–3 brown-blotched, olive to buff eggs for 27–28 days.
Feeding: opportunistic feeder; finds food by flying, swimming or walking; eats fish, eggs, birds, small mammals, berries, carrion, mollusks, crustaceans, insects and other invertebrates, as well as human food waste; scavenges at landfills.
Voice: a harsh *kyow*.
Similar Species: *All other gulls* (pp. 146–158): smaller; most lack black mantle.
Selected Sites: Berrien Co. and Ottawa Co. lakeshores; Whitefish Point; Tawas Point SP; Nayanquing Point WA; Pointe Mouillee SGA; Warren Dunes SP; Alpena waterfront.

SABINE'S GULL

Xema sabini

It is unfortunate that only a few people in Michigan will ever see this attractive, ternlike gull—the Sabine's Gull is a truly stunning bird. A rarity in our state, this gull can best be observed in fall, when small numbers trickle southward from the Arctic on their way to South Africa and other wintering sites. • The Sabine's Gull shares the same size, shape and head color pattern as the common, black-headed gulls of the genus *Larus*. Like the terns of the genus *Sterna*, the Sabine's Gull features a buoyant, dipping flight pattern and a forked tail. • Sabine's Gulls feed while in flight, gently dipping down to the water's surface to snatch up prey without landing. • Sir Edward Sabine was a distinguished military man whose primary interests were astronomy and terrestrial magnetism. He joined an expedition to explore the Arctic in 1819, and it was off the west coast of Greenland that he collected a specimen of the gull that was to be named in his honor.

nonbreeding

ID: yellow-tipped, black bill; dark gray mantle; black feet. *Breeding:* dark slate gray "hood" is trimmed with black. *Nonbreeding:* white head; dark gray nape. *In flight:* 3-toned wing, gray at base, then white, then black at tip; shallowly forked tail.
Size: *L* 13–14 in; *W* 33 in.
Status: very rare migrant from late August to early December.
Habitat: lakes and large rivers.

Nesting: does not nest in Michigan.
Feeding: gleans the water's surface while swimming or flying; eats mostly insects, fish and crustaceans.
Voice: ternlike *kee-kee;* not frequently heard in migration.
Similar Species: *Bonaparte's* (p. 149), *Franklin's* (p. 147), *Laughing* (p. 146) and *Black-headed gulls:* all lack boldly patterned wing tips, forked tail and yellow-tipped bill.
Selected Sites: Whitefish Point; Muskegon Wastewater System; Port Huron; Great Lakes shores.

BLACK-LEGGED KITTIWAKE

Rissa tridactyla

The Black-legged Kittiwake is more closely associated with the marine environment than any other North American gull. For this reason, few birders watching from the comfort of Michigan's shores will ever see this small, graceful gull. Most of the small numbers of Black-legged Kittiwakes that move through the state migrate well offshore over the open waters of Lake Huron. Even during the most violent storms, these birds remain in open water, floating among massive freshwater swells that are likely reminiscent of their saltwater homes. Because they spend most of their lives in saltwater environments, Black-legged Kittiwakes have evolved glands above their eyes that enable them to extract and secrete excess salt from the water—a feature that is of little use on the Great Lakes. • Unlike the majority of gulls in Michigan, the Black-legged Kittiwake makes its living by fishing rather than by foraging in landfills or near fast-food restaurants.

breeding

nonbreeding

ID: *Breeding:* black legs; gray mantle; white underparts; white head; yellow bill. *Nonbreeding:* gray nape; dark gray smudge behind eye. *Immature:* black bill; black "half collar"; dark ear patch. *In flight:* solid black, triangular wing tips; immature has black "M" on upper forewing from wing tip to wing tip and black terminal tail band.
Size: *L* 16–18 in; *W* 3 ft.
Status: very rare migrant and winter resident from mid-August to January.
Habitat: open water on large lakes and rivers.

Nesting: does not nest in Michigan.
Feeding: dips to water's surface to snatch prey; gleans the water's surface or plunges underwater while swimming; prefers small fish; also takes crustaceans, insects and mollusks.
Voice: calls are *kittewake* and *kekekek*.
Similar Species: *Franklin's* (p. 147), *Laughing* (p. 146), *Bonaparte's* (p. 149), *Black-headed* and *Little* (p. 148) *gulls:* all lack combination of black legs, yellow bill, gray nape and solid black, triangular wing tips. *Sabine's Gull* (p. 157): immature has gray brown wash on sides and head and lacks dark "M" on wings and mantle.
Selected Sites: Whitefish Point; Port Huron; Pere Marquette SP; New Buffalo waterfront; Great Lakes shorelines.

CASPIAN TERN

Sterna caspia

I n size and habits, the mighty Caspian Tern bridges the gulf between the smaller terns and the larger, raucous gulls. It is the largest tern in North America, and its wingbeats are slower and more gull-like than those of most other terns—a trait that can lead birders to confuse it with a gull. But this tern's distinctive, heavy, red orange bill and forked tail usually give away its identity. • Caspian Terns are often seen together with gulls on shoreline sandbars and mudflats during migration or during the breeding season, when they nest in colonies on exposed islands and protected beaches. • The sight of a Caspian Tern foraging for small, schooling fish is impressive. Flying high over open waters, this tern hovers, then suddenly folds its wings and plunges headfirst toward its target. • The Caspian Tern is strictly a migrant and breeder in our region, retreating to the Gulf of Mexico for the winter. • This species was first collected from the Caspian Sea, hence its name. Caspian Terns are found nesting the world over, in Eurasia, Africa and even Australia.

breeding

ID: black "cap"; heavy, red orange bill has faint black tip; light gray mantle; black legs; shallowly forked tail; white underparts; long, frosty, pointed wings; dark gray on underside of outer primaries. *Nonbreeding:* black "cap" is streaked with white.
Size: *L* 19–23 in; *W* 4–4½ ft.
Status: threatened; fairly common migrant and local breeder from April to mid-September.
Habitat: *Breeding:* usually on islands in the northern Great Lakes. *In migration:* wetlands and shorelines of large lakes and rivers.

Nesting: in a shallow scrape on bare sand, lightly vegetated soil or gravel; nest is sparsely lined with vegetation, rocks or twigs; pair incubates 1–3 pale buff eggs, spotted with brown or black, for 20–22 days.
Feeding: hovers over water and plunges headfirst after small fish, tadpoles and aquatic invertebrates; also feeds by swimming and gleaning at the water's surface.
Voice: low, harsh *ca-arr;* loud *kraa-uh.*
Similar Species: *Common* (p. 160), *Arctic* (p. 341) and *Forster's* (p. 161) *terns:* much smaller; daintier bills; lack dark underwing patch.
Selected Sites: Pointe Mouillee SGA; Tawas Point SP; Whitefish Point; New Buffalo waterfront; Alpena waterfront; Muskegon SP; Saugatuck SP.

COMMON TERN
Sterna hirundo

Common Terns patrol the shorelines of lakes and rivers during spring and fall and settle in large nesting colonies over the summer months, usually on islands. Both males and females perform aerial courtship dances, and for most pairs the nesting season commences when the female accepts her suitor's gracious fish offerings. • Tern colonies are noisy and chaotic, and are often associated with even noisier gull colonies. The most successful colonies seem to be the larger ones, which can number well into the thousands. Should an intruder approach a tern nest, the parent will dive repeatedly, often defecating on the offender. Needless to say, it is best to keep a respectful distance from nesting terns, and from all nesting birds, for that matter. • Terns are effortless fliers, as well as being some of the most impressive long-distance migrants. Once, a Common Tern banded in Great Britain was recovered in Australia.

breeding

ID: *Breeding:* black "cap"; thin, red, black-tipped bill; red legs; white rump; white tail with gray outer edges; white underparts. *Nonbreeding:* black nape; lacks black "cap." *In flight:* shallowly forked tail; long, pointed wings; dark gray wedge near lighter gray upperwing tips.
Size: *L* 13–16 in; *W* 30 in.
Status: threatened; common migrant and local breeder from April to mid-December.
Habitat: *Breeding:* natural and human-made islands, breakwaters and beaches. *In migration:* large lakes, open wetlands and slowly moving rivers.
Nesting: primarily colonial; usually on an island with nonvegetated, open areas; in a small scrape lined sparsely with pebbles,

vegetation or shells; pair incubates 1–3 variably marked eggs for up to 27 days.
Feeding: hovers over the water and plunges headfirst after small fish and aquatic invertebrates.
Voice: high-pitched, drawn-out *keee-are;* most commonly heard at colonies but also in foraging flights.
Similar Species: *Forster's Tern* (p. 161): gray tail with white outer edges; upper primaries have silvery look; broad, black eye band in nonbreeding plumage. *Arctic Tern* (p. 341): all-red bill; deeply forked tail; upper primaries lack dark gray wedge; grayer underparts; rare in migration. *Caspian Tern* (p. 159): much larger overall; much heavier, red orange bill; dark primary underwing patch.
Selected Sites: Pointe Mouilllee SGA; Tawas Point SP; Whitefish Point; Lake Erie Metropark; Alpena waterfront; Portage Point Marsh; St. Joseph and New Buffalo waterfronts; Great Lakes shorelines.

FORSTER'S TERN

Sterna forsteri

The Forster's Tern so closely resembles the Common Tern that the two often seem indistinguishable to the eyes of many observers. It is usually not until these terns acquire their distinct fall plumages that birders begin to note the Forster's presence. • Most terns are known for their extraordinary ability to catch fish in dramatic headfirst dives, but the Forster's excels at gracefully snatching flying insects in midair. • The Forster's Tern has an exclusively North American breeding distribution, but it bears the name of a man who never visited this continent: German naturalist Johann Reinhold Forster. Forster, who lived and worked in England, and who accompanied Captain Cook on his 1772 voyage around the world, examined tern specimens sent from Hudson Bay, Canada. He was the first to recognize this bird as a distinct species. Taxonomist Thomas Nuttall agreed, and in 1832, he named the species "Forster's Tern" in his *Manual of Ornithology.*

breeding

ID: *Breeding:* black "cap" and nape; thin, orange, black-tipped bill; orange legs; light gray mantle; pure white underparts; white rump; gray tail with white outer edges. *Nonbreeding:* lacks black "cap"; black band through eyes. *In flight:* forked, gray tail; long, pointed wings.
Size: *L* 14–16 in; *W* 31 in.
Status: special concern; uncommon migrant from mid-April to early June and from July to mid-October; rare breeder.
Habitat: *Breeding:* cattail marshes. *In migration:* lakes and marshes.
Nesting: colonial; in a cattail marsh, atop floating vegetation; occasionally on a muskrat lodge or an old grebe nest; pair

incubates 3 brown-marked, buff to olive eggs for 23–25 days.
Feeding: hovers above the water and plunges headfirst after small fish and aquatic invertebrates; catches flying insects and snatches prey from the water's surface.
Voice: flight call is a nasal, short *keer keer;* also a grating *tzaap.*
Similar Species: *Common Tern* (p. 160): darker red bill and legs; mostly white tail; gray wash on underparts; dark wedge near tip of primaries. *Arctic Tern* (p. 341): lacks black-tipped bill; short, red legs; gray underparts; white tail with gray outer edges. *Caspian Tern* (p. 159): much larger overall; much heavier, red orange bill.
Selected Sites: Lake Erie Metropark; Whitefish Point; Keweenaw Bay; Nayanquing Point WA; Pointe Mouillee SGA; New Buffalo and St. Joseph waterfronts; St. Clair Flats WA.

BLACK TERN

Chlidonias niger

Wheeling about in foraging flights, Black Terns pick small minnows from the water's surface or catch flying insects in midair. Black Terns have dominion over the winds and these acrobats slice through the sky with grace even in a stiff wind. When these terns leave our region in August and September, they head for the warmer climates of Central and South America. • Black Terns are finicky nesters and refuse to return to nesting areas that show even slight changes in water level or in the density of emergent vegetation. This selectiveness, coupled with the degradation of marshes across North America, has contributed to a significant decline in populations of this bird over recent decades. Commitment to restoring and protecting valuable wetland habitats will eventually help this bird to reclaim its once prominent place in Michigan. • In order to spell this tern's genus name correctly, one must misspell *chelidonias*, the Greek word for "swallow." This bird is named for its swallowlike, darting flight as it pursues insects.

breeding

ID: *Breeding:* black head and underparts; gray back, tail and wings; white undertail coverts; black bill; reddish black legs. *Nonbreeding:* white underparts and forehead; molting fall birds may be mottled with brown. *In flight:* long, pointed wings; shallowly forked tail.
Size: *L* 9–10 in; *W* 24 in.
Status: special concern; uncommon migrant and breeder from mid-April to mid-September.
Habitat: shallow, freshwater cattail marshes, wetlands, lake edges and sewage ponds with emergent vegetation.

Nesting: loosely colonial; flimsy nest of dead plant material is built on floating vegetation, a muddy mound or a muskrat house; pair incubates 3 darkly blotched, olive to pale buff eggs for 21–22 days.
Feeding: snatches insects from the air, tall grass and the water's surface; also eats small fish.
Voice: greeting call is a shrill, metallic *kik-kik-kik-kik-kik;* typical alarm call is *kreea.*
Similar Species: *Other terns* (pp. 159-61): all are light in color, not dark.
Selected Sites: Haehnle Sanctuary; Keweenaw Bay; Whitefish Point; Kensington Metropark; Nayanquing Point WA; Houghton L.; Pointe Mouillee SGA; Muskegon Wastewater System; Baker Sanctuary; Metrobeach Metropark.

ROCK DOVE
Columba livia

I ntroduced to North America in the early 17th century, Rock Doves have settled wherever cities, towns and farms are found. Rock Doves are commonly referred to as "pigeons," and, indeed, there is no technical difference between doves and pigeons. Most birds seem content to nest on buildings or farmhouses, but "wilder" members of this species can occasionally be seen nesting on tall cliffs, usually along lakeshores. • It is believed that Rock Doves were domesticated from Eurasian birds as a source of meat in about 4500 BC. Since their domestication, Rock Doves have been used as message couriers (both Caesar and Napoleon used them), scientific subjects and even as pets. Much of our understanding of bird migration, endocrinology and sensory perception derives from experiments involving Rock Doves. • All members of the pigeon family including doves feed "milk" to their young. Because birds lack mammary glands, it is not true milk, but a nutritious liquid produced by glands in the bird's crop. The chicks insert their bills down the adult's throat to eat the thick, protein-rich fluid. • No other "wild" bird varies as much in coloration—a result of semi-domestication and extensive inbreeding over time.

ID: color is highly variable (iridescent blue gray, red, white or tan); usually has white rump and orange feet; dark-tipped tail. *In flight:* holds wings in deep "V" while gliding.
Size: *L* 12–13 in; *W* 28 in.
Status: abundant year-round resident.
Habitat: urban areas, railroad yards and agricultural areas; high cliffs provide a more natural habitat for some.
Nesting: on a ledge in a barn or on a cliff, bridge, building or tower; flimsy nest is built from sticks, grass and assorted vegetation; pair incubates 2 eggs for 16–19 days; pair feeds the young "pigeon milk"; may raise broods year-round.
Feeding: gleans the ground for waste grain, seeds and fruits; occasionally eats insects.
Voice: soft, cooing *coorrr-coorrr-coorrr.*
Similar Species: *Mourning Dove* (p. 164): smaller; slimmer; pale brown plumage; long tail and wings. *Merlin* (p. 95): not as heavy bodied; longer tail; does not hold wings in a "V"; wings do not clap on takeoff.
Selected Sites: statewide in urban and rural areas.

MOURNING DOVE

Zenaida macroura

The soft cooing of the Mourning Dove that filters through our broken woodlands, farmlands and suburban parks and gardens is often confused with the muted sounds of a hooting owl. Yet when birders track down the source of these calls, they usually discover one or two doves perched upon a fence, tree branch or utility wire. • The Mourning Dove is one of the most abundant and widespread native birds in North America and one of the most popular game birds. This species has benefited from human-induced changes to the landscape and its numbers and distribution have increased since the continent was settled. It is encountered in both rural and urban habitats, but avoids heavily forested areas. • Despite its fragile look, the Mourning Dove is a swift, direct flier whose wings often whistle as it cuts through the air at high speed. When this bird bursts into flight, its wings clap above and below its body. • This bird's common name reflects its sad, cooing song. The scientific name *Zenaida* honors Zenaïde, Princess of Naples and the wife of Charles-Lucien Bonaparte, who was a naturalist and the nephew of the French emperor.

ID: buffy, gray brown plumage; small head; long, white-trimmed, tapering tail; sleek body; dark, shiny patch below ear; dull red legs; dark bill; pale rosy underparts; black spots on upperwing.

Size: *L* 11–13 in; *W* 18 in.

Status: very common year-round resident; less frequent in northern Michigan.

Habitat: open and riparian woodlands, woodlots, forest edges, agricultural and suburban areas and open parks; has benefited from human-induced habitat change.

Nesting: in the fork of a shrub or tree, occasionally on the ground; female builds a fragile, shallow platform nest from twigs supplied by the male; pair incubates 2 white eggs for 14 days; young are fed "pigeon milk."

Feeding: gleans the ground and vegetation for seeds; visits feeders.

Voice: mournful, soft, slow *oh-woe-woe-woe.*

Similar Species: *Rock Dove* (p. 163): stockier; white rump; shorter tail; iridescent neck. *Yellow-billed Cuckoo* (p. 166) and *Black-billed Cuckoo* (p. 165): curved bill; long tail with broad, rounded tip; brown upperparts; white underparts.

Selected Sites: suburban and agricultural areas statewide.

BLACK-BILLED CUCKOO

Coccyzus erythropthalmus

Shrubby field edges, hedgerows, tangled riparian thickets and abandoned, overgrown fields provide the elusive Black-billed Cuckoo with its preferred nesting haunts. Despite not being particularly rare in Michigan, it remains an enigma to many would-be observers. Arriving in late May, this cuckoo quietly hops, flits and skulks through low, dense, deciduous vegetation in its ultra-secret search for sustenance. Only when vegetation is in full bloom will males issue their loud, long, irregular calls, advertising to females that it is time to nest. After a brief courtship, newly joined Black-billed Cuckoo pairs construct a makeshift nest, incubate the eggs and raise their young, after which they promptly return to their covert lives. • The Black-billed Cuckoo is one of few birds that thrive on hairy caterpillars, particularly tent caterpillars. There is even evidence to suggest that populations of this bird increase when a caterpillar infestation occurs. • This cuckoo is reluctant to fly more than a short distance during nesting, but it will migrate as far as northwestern South America to avoid the North American winter.

ID: brown upperparts; white underparts; long, white-spotted undertail; dark, downcurved bill; reddish eye ring. *Juvenile:* buff eye ring; may have buff tinge on throat and undertail coverts.
Size: *L* 11–13 in; *W* 18 in.
Status: fairly common migrant and breeder from mid-May to mid-September.
Habitat: dense second-growth woodlands, shrubby areas and thickets; often in tangled riparian areas and abandoned farmlands with low deciduous vegetation and adjacent open areas.
Nesting: in a shrub or small deciduous tree; flimsy nest of twigs is lined with grass and other vegetation; occasionally lays

eggs in other birds' nests; pair incubates 2–5 blue green, occasionally mottled, eggs for 10–14 days.
Feeding: gleans hairy caterpillars from leaves, branches and trunks; also eats other insects and berries.
Voice: fast, repeated *cu-cu-cu* or *cu-cu-cu-cu-cu;* also a series of *ca, cow* and *coo* notes.
Similar Species: *Yellow-billed Cuckoo* (p. 166): yellow bill; rufous tinge to primaries; larger, more prominent, white undertail spots; lacks red eye ring. *Mourning Dove* (p. 164): short, straight bill; pointed, triangular tail; buffy, gray brown plumage; black spots on upperwing.
Selected Sites: Rouge River Bird Observatory; Port Huron SGA; Waterloo SRA; Chippewa Nature Center; Kalamazoo Nature Center; Traverse City Nature Education Reserve; Colonial Point Forest.

YELLOW-BILLED CUCKOO

Coccyzus americanus

Most of the time, the Yellow-billed Cuckoo skillfully negotiates its tangled home within impenetrable, deciduous undergrowth in silence, relying on obscurity for survival. Then, for a short period during nesting, the male cuckoo tempts fate by issuing a barrage of loud, rhythmic courtship calls. Some people have suggested that the cuckoo has a propensity for calling on dark, cloudy days in late spring and early summer. It is even called "Rain Crow" in some parts of its North American range. • In addition to consuming large quantities of hairy caterpillars, Yellow-billed Cuckoos feast on wild berries, young frogs and newts, small bird eggs and a variety of insects, including beetles, grasshoppers and cicadas. • Though some Yellow-billed Cuckoos may lay eggs in the unattended nests of neighboring Black-billed Cuckoos, neither of these cuckoos is considered to be a "brood parasite." • Some Yellow-billed Cuckoos migrate as far south as Argentina for the winter.

ID: olive brown upperparts; white underparts; down-curved bill with black upper mandible and yellow lower mandible; yellow eye ring; long tail with large white spots on underside; rufous tinge on primaries.

Size: *L* 11–13 in; *W* 18 in.

Status: common migrant and breeder from early May to late September; less common in Upper Peninsula.

Habitat: semi-open deciduous habitats; dense tangles and thickets at the edges of orchards, urban parks, agricultural fields and roadways; sometimes woodlots.

Nesting: on a horizontal branch in a deciduous shrub or small tree, within 7 ft of the ground; builds a flimsy platform of twigs lined with roots and grass; pair incubates 3–4 pale bluish green eggs for 9–11 days.

Feeding: gleans insect larvae, especially hairy caterpillars, from deciduous vegetation; also eats berries, small fruits, small amphibians and occasionally the eggs of small birds.

Voice: long series of deep, hollow *kuks,* slowing near the end: *kuk-kuk-kuk-kuk kuk kop kow kowlp kowlp.*

Similar Species: *Black-billed Cuckoo* (p. 165): all-black bill; lacks rufous tinge on primaries; less prominent, white undertail spots; red rather than yellow eye ring; juveniles have buff eye ring and may have buff wash on throat and undertail coverts. *Mourning Dove* (p. 164): short, straight bill; pointed, triangular tail; buffy gray brown plumage; black spots on upperwing.

Selected Sites: Rose Lake WA; Lost Nation SGA; Kalamazoo Nature Center; Warren Woods Natural Area; Allegan SGA; Chippewa Nature Center.

EASTERN SCREECH-OWL

Otus asio

The diminutive Eastern Screech-Owl is a year-round resident of deciduous woodlands, but its presence is rarely detected. Most screech-owls sleep away the daylight hours snuggled safely inside a tree cavity or an artificial nest box. • An encounter with a Screech-Owl is usually the result of a sound cue—the noise of mobbing hordes of chickadees or squawking gangs of Blue Jays can alert you to an owl's presence during daylight hours. Smaller birds that mob a screech-owl during the day often do so after losing a family member during the night. More commonly, you will find this owl by listening for the male's eerie, "horse-whinny" courtship calls and loud, spooky trills at night. • Despite its small size, the Eastern Screech-Owl is an adaptable hunter. It has a varied diet that ranges from insects, small rodents, earthworms and fish to birds larger than itself. • Unique among the owls found in our region, Eastern Screech-Owls are polychromatic: they show red or gray color morphs. The red birds are less common because they are less able to withstand Michigan's cold winters. Mixed-color pairs may produce young that are an intermediate, buffy brown.

gray morph

ID: short "ear" tufts; reddish or grayish overall; dark breast streaking; yellow eyes; pale grayish bill.
Size: *L* 8–9 in; *W* 20–22 in.
Status: common year-round resident in Lower Peninsula.
Habitat: mature deciduous forests, open deciduous and riparian woodlands, orchards and shade trees with natural cavities.
Nesting: in a natural cavity or artificial nest box; no lining is added; female incubates 4–5 white eggs for about 26 days; male brings food to the female during incubation.

Feeding: feeds at dusk and at night; takes small mammals, earthworms, fish, birds and insects, including moths in flight.
Voice: horselike "whinny" that rises and falls.
Similar Species: *Northern Saw-whet Owl* (p. 176): lacks "ear" tufts; long, reddish streaks on white underparts. *Long-eared Owl* (p. 173): much longer, slimmer body; longer, closer-set "ear" tufts; rusty facial disc; grayish, brown-and-white body. *Great Horned Owl* (p. 168): much larger; lacks vertical breast streaks.
Selected Sites: Warren Woods Natural Area; Allegan SGA; Kalamazoo Nature Center; Waterloo SRA; Indian Springs Metropark.

GREAT HORNED OWL

Bubo virginianus

The familiar *hoo-hoo-hoooo hoo-hoo* that resounds through campgrounds, suburban parks and farmyards is the call of the adaptable and superbly camouflaged Great Horned Owl. This formidable, primarily nocturnal hunter uses its acute hearing and powerful vision to hunt a wide variety of prey. Almost any small creature that moves is fair game for the Great Horned Owl. This bird apparently has a poorly developed sense of smell, which might explain why it is the only consistent predator of skunks. • Great Horned Owls often begin their courtship as early as January, at which time their hooting calls make them quite conspicuous. By February and March, females are already incubating their eggs, and by the time the last migratory birds have moved into our region, Great Horned owlets have already fledged. • The large eyes of an owl are fixed in place, so to look up, down or to the side, the bird must move its entire head. As an adaptation to this situation, an owl can swivel its neck 180 degrees to either side and 90 degrees up and down!

ID: yellow eyes; tall "ear" tufts set wide apart on head; fine, horizontal barring on breast; facial disc outlined in black and is often rusty orange in color; white "chin"; heavily mottled gray, brown and black upperparts; overall plumage varies from light gray to dark brown.

Size: *L* 18–25 in; *W* 3–5 ft.

Status: fairly common year-round resident.

Habitat: fragmented forests, agricultural areas, woodlots, meadows, riparian woodlands, wooded suburban parks and the wooded edges of landfills and town dumps.

Nesting: in the abandoned stick nest of another bird; may also nest on a cliff; adds little or no material to the nest; mostly the female incubates the 2–3 dull whitish eggs for 28–35 days.

Feeding: mostly nocturnal, but also hunts at dusk or by day in winter; usually swoops from a perch; eats small mammals, birds, snakes, amphibians and even fish.

Voice: call during the breeding season is 4–6 deep hoots: *hoo-hoo-hoooo hoo-hoo* or *eat-my-food, I'll-eat-you;* male also gives higher-pitched hoots.

Similar Species: *Long-eared Owl* (p. 173): smaller; thinner; vertical breast streaks; "ear" tufts are close together. *Eastern Screech-Owl* (p. 167): much smaller; vertical breast streaks. *Great Gray* (p. 172), *Short-eared* (p. 174) and *Barred* (p. 171) *owls:* no "ear" tufts.

Selected Sites: fragmented or open woodlands with an adjacent open area.

SNOWY OWL
Nyctea scandiaca

When the mercury drops and the landscape hardens in winter's icy grip, ghostly white Snowy Owls appear on fence posts, utility poles, fields and lakeshores throughout the region. Motorists and landowners with an eye for Snowies can often find them, even though these birds blend in perfectly against almost any flat, snow-covered landscape. Snow cover is not a prerequisite for a Snowy Owl visit—many of these birds perch conspicuously on earth-tone fields in snowless portions of our region each winter. • Feathered to the toes, a Snowy Owl can remain active at cold temperatures that often send other owls to the woods for shelter. • As Snowy Owls age, their plumage becomes lighter in color—older males are often pure white. • Snowy Owls are yearly visitors to Michigan, but their numbers can fluctuate quite dramatically. When lemming and vole populations crash in the Arctic, large numbers of Snowy Owls venture south in search of food. • Snowy Owls are recognizable in the oldest prehistoric cave art and may have inspired the first bird painting.

ID: predominantly white; yellow eyes; black bill and talons; no "ear" tufts. *Male:* almost entirely white with very little dark flecking. *Female:* prominent dark barring or flecking on breast and upperparts. *Immature:* heavier barring than adult female.
Size: *L* 20–27 in; *W* 4½–6 ft (female is noticeably larger).
Status: irregularly uncommon to rare winter resident from late September to early April.

Habitat: open country, including croplands, meadows, airports and lakeshores; often perches on fence posts, buildings and utility poles.
Nesting: does not nest in Michigan.
Feeding: swoops from a perch, often punching through the snow to take mice, voles, grouse, hares, weasels and, rarely, songbirds and waterbirds.
Voice: quiet in winter.
Similar Species: no other owl in the region is largely white and lacks "ear" tufts.
Selected Sites: Whitefish Point; Nayanquing Point WA; Fish Point SGA; Sault Ste. Marie; Muskegon Wastewater System.

NORTHERN HAWK OWL

Surnia ulula

Like the Snowy Owl, the Northern Hawk Owl is an "irruptive" winter visitor to Michigan, meaning that it may be common in some winters and rare in others. When a "Hawk Owl year" comes around, be sure to make the most of the event—there may not be a repeat performance for a decade or more. • Northern Hawk Owls summer in the remote boreal forests of northern Canada, where the days are long, so they are comfortable hunting in daylight. They are by no means the only owls that hunt during the day, but they are the ones most likely to rest on exposed perches. • With its long, slender, hawk-like features, and its direct, accipiter-like flight pattern, it is easy to understand how the Northern Hawk Owl got its name. Yet no matter how much it behaves like a hawk, this bird is unquestionably an owl. There is no mistaking its facial disc, a distinctive feature of the owl family that allows these birds to use sound to locate their prey.

ID: long tail; no "ear" tufts; fine, horizontal barring on underparts; white facial disc is bordered with black; pale bill; yellow eyes; white-spotted forehead.

Size: *L* 15–17 in; *W* 31–35 in.

Status: irregularly uncommon to rare winter visitor in Upper Peninsula; very rare breeder (1 record).

Habitat: black spruce bogs, old burns and tree-bordered clearings.

Nesting: in an abandoned woodpecker cavity or on a broken treetop; adds no lining to the nest; female incubates 5–7 whitish eggs for 25–30 days.

Feeding: swoops from a perch; eats mostly voles, mice and birds; also eats some large insects in summer.

Voice: usually quiet; whistled breeding trill; call is an accipiter-like *kee-kee-kee*.

Similar Species: *Boreal* (p. 175), *Northern Saw-whet* (p. 176) and *Short-eared* (p. 174) *owls:* much shorter tails; vertical breast streaks.

Selected Sites: Whitefish Point; Sault Ste. Marie.

BARRED OWL
Strix varia

Each spring, the memorable sound of courting Barred Owls echoes through our forests: *Who cooks for you? Who cooks for you-all?* The escalating laughs, hoots and gargling howls reinforce the bond between pairs. At the height of courtship and when raising young, a pair of Barred Owls may continue their calls well into daylight hours, and they may hunt actively day and night. They also tend to be more vocal during early evening or early morning when the moon is full and the air is calm. • Barred Owls are usually most active between midnight and 4 AM, when the forest floor rustles with the movements of mice, voles and shrews. These owls have relatively weak talons, so they prey on smaller animals, such as voles. They may also take small birds and even smaller owls. • Barred Owls were once inhabitants of the moist, deciduous woodlands and swamps that covered our region, but their numbers have declined with the destruction of these habitats. In the absence of suitable tree hollows—their preferred nesting sites—Barred Owls may resort to abandoned stick nests or may even nest on the ground.

ID: dark eyes; horizontal barring around neck and upper breast; vertical streaking on belly; pale bill; no "ear" tufts; mottled, dark gray brown plumage.
Size: *L* 17–24 in; *W* 3½–4 ft.
Status: uncommon year-round resident.
Habitat: mature deciduous and mixedwood forests, especially in dense stands near swamps, streams and lakes.
Nesting: in a natural tree cavity, broken treetop or abandoned stick nest; adds very little material to the nest; female incubates 2–3 white eggs for 28–33 days; male feeds the female during incubation.
Feeding: nocturnal; swoops down on prey from a perch; eats mostly mice, voles and squirrels; also takes amphibians and small birds.
Voice: most characteristic of all the owls; loud, hooting, rhythmic, laughing call is heard mostly in spring but also throughout the year: *Who cooks for you? Who cooks for you all?*; frequently called "Old Eight-Hooter."
Similar Species: *Great Gray Owl* (p. 172): larger; yellow eyes; well-defined, ringed facial disc; black "chin" patch; lacks horizontal barring on upper breast. *Northern Hawk Owl* (p. 170): yellow eyes; finely barred underparts. *Great Horned Owl* (p. 168): "ear" tufts; light-colored eyes. *Short-eared Owl* (p. 174): yellow eyes; lacks horizontal barring on upper breast.
Selected Sites: Whitefish Point; Seney NWR; Rifle River SRA; Chippewa Nature Center; Allegan SGA; Rose Lake WA; Warren Woods Natural Area.

GREAT GRAY OWL

Strix nebulosa

With a face shaped like a satellite dish, the Great Gray Owl is able to detect and locate the quietest scurry on the forest floor. This owl can even detect the faint sounds of a tiny rodent moving around under 20 inches of snow. The Great Gray's facial discs funnel sound waves into its asymmetrically placed ears, enabling it, through triangulation, to pinpoint the precise location of its prey. • This regal owl is highly sought after by Michigan birders, but its rare status and secretive lifestyle keep it well hidden. Great Grays occasionally appear in northern Michigan, usually in years when small mammal populations in Canada have crashed. In such years, the owls that reach Michigan are starved, so they resort to hunting in daylight to feed themselves. • Even though the Great Gray Owl is the largest North American owl, it is mostly "fluff" and is outweighed by as much as 15 percent by both the Snowy Owl and the Great Horned Owl.

ID: gray brown overall; large, rounded head; no "ear" tufts; long tail; yellow eyes and bill; well-defined, ringed facial disc; black "chin" is bordered with white.

Size: *L* 24–33 in; *W* 4½–5 ft.

Status: irregular rare winter visitor in Upper Peninsula from November to May; very rare year-round resident in eastern Upper Peninsula (1 breeding record).

Habitat: forest clearings, open meadows, spruce or poplar stands adjacent to open fens, bogs or meadows.

Nesting: usually near a spruce bog; in an abanboned hawk, raven or eagle nest, occasionally atop a tall, broken stump; adds little nest material; female incubates 2–4 white eggs for 28–36 days; male feeds the female during incubation.

Feeding: listens and watches from a perch; swoops down to catch voles, mice, shrews, squirrels and hares.

Voice: slow, deep, almost inaudible, resonating series of hoots; also a series of widely spaced, low, rising *wooo* notes.

Similar Species: *Barred Owl* (p. 171): dark eyes; horizontal barring on upper breast. *Great Horned Owl* (p. 168): large "ear" tufts; dark bill. *Snowy Owl* (p. 169): mostly white. *Short-eared Owl* (p. 174): much smaller; black eye sockets; dark bill; black "wrist" crescents.

Selected Sites: Whitefish Point; Neebish I.; Sault Ste. Marie area.

LONG-EARED OWL

Asio otus

Long-eared Owls are widespread but scarce throughout much of Michigan and are easily overlooked because of their cryptic plumage and reclusive habits. Only at dusk do these owls emerge from their secret hideouts to prey upon the small creatures of the night. Long-eared Owls are most noticeable during the winter months, when they roost together in groups of 10 to 20 birds in woodlots, hedgerows or isolated tree groves. • The Long-eared Owl will either inflate or compress its feathers in response to certain situations. To scare off an intruder, the owl expands its air sacs, puffs its feathers and spreads its wings; to hide from an intruder, it flattens its feathers and compresses itself into a long, thin, vertical form. • All owls, as well as many other birds, such as herons, gulls, crows and hawks, regurgitate "pellets." A pellet consists of the indigestible parts of the bird's prey compressed into an elongated ball. The feathers, fur and bones that make up the pellets are fascinating to analyze because they reveal what the bird has eaten.

ID: long, relatively close-set "ear" tufts; slim body; vertical belly markings; rusty brown facial disc; mottled brown plumage; yellow eyes; white around bill.

Size: *L* 13–16 in; *W* 3–4 ft.

Status: threatened; rare to uncommon breeder; uncommon migrant and winter resident from September to May.

Habitat: *Breeding:* dense coniferous, mixed and riparian forests and areas with tall shrubs. *Winter:* woodlots, dense riparian woodlands, hedgerows and isolated tree groves in meadows, fields, cemeteries, farmyards and parks.

Nesting: often in an abandoned hawk or crow nest; female incubates 2–6 white eggs for 26–28 days; male feeds the female during incubation.

Feeding: nocturnal; flies low, pouncing on prey from the air; eats mostly voles and mice; occasionally takes shrews, moles, small rabbits, small birds and amphibians.

Voice: breeding call is a low, soft, ghostly *quoo-quoo;* alarm call is *weck-weck-weck;* also issues various shrieks, hisses, whistles, barks, hoots and dovelike coos.

Similar Species: *Great Horned Owl* (p. 168): much larger; "ear" tufts are set farther apart; stout body; rounder face. *Short-eared Owl* (p. 174): lacks long "ear" tufts; nests on the ground. *Eastern Screech-Owl* (p. 167): much shorter, stout body; shorter, wider-set "ear" tufts.

Selected Sites: Whitefish Point; small pine plantations in more southern areas of the state.

SHORT-EARED OWL

Asio flammeus

Like the Snowy Owl of the Arctic, the Short-eared Owl lacks conspicuous "ear" tufts and fills a niche in open country that has been left unoccupied by forest-dwelling owls. In Michigan, the Short-eared Owl occupies habitats such as wet meadows, marshes, fields and bogs. These owls can be difficult to locate, especially during the summer breeding season when females sit tightly on their ground nests. • In spring, pairs perform dramatic courtship dances. Courting pairs fly together, and the male claps his wings together on each downstroke as he periodically performs short dives. Short-eared Owls do not "hoot" like forest-dwelling owls, perhaps because visual displays are a more effective means of communication in open environments. • Short-eared Owl populations grow and decline over many years in response to dramatic fluctuations in prey availability. Cold weather and decreases in small mammal populations occasionally force large numbers of these owls, especially immature birds, to become temporary nomads, often sending them to areas well outside their usual breeding range.

ID: yellow eyes set in black sockets; heavy, vertical streaking on buff belly; straw-colored upperparts; short, inconspicuous "ear" tufts. *In flight:* dark "wrist" crescents; deep wingbeats; long wings.

Size: *L* 13–17 in; *W* 3–4 ft.

Status: endangered; uncommon migrant and winter resident from October to April; rare breeder from April to October.

Habitat: open areas, including grasslands, wet meadows, marshes, fields, airports and forest clearings.

Nesting: on wet ground in an open area; a slight depression is sparsely lined with grass; female incubates 4–7 white eggs for 24–37 days; male feeds the female during incubation.

Feeding: forages while flying low over marshes, wet meadows and tall vegetation; pounces on prey from the air; eats mostly voles and other small rodents; also takes insects, small birds and amphibians.

Voice: generally quiet; produces a soft *toot-toot-toot* during the breeding season; also squeals and barks like a small dog.

Similar Species: *Long-eared Owl* (p. 173) and *Great Horned Owl* (p. 168): long "ear" tufts; rarely hunt during the day. *Barred Owl* (p. 171): dark eyes; horizontal barring on upper breast; nocturnal hunter. *Great Gray Owl* (p. 172): much larger; yellow bill; lacks black eye sockets and dark "wrist" crescents. *Burrowing Owl:* exceptionally rare visitor to Michigan; much longer legs; shorter tail; shorter wings.

Selected Sites: Maple River SGA; Whitefish Point; Rudyard Flats near Sault Ste. Marie; Muskegon Wastewater System; Shiawassee Flats NWR.

BOREAL OWL
Aegolius funereus

Boreal Owls routinely rank in the top five of the most desired species to see according to birdwatcher surveys across North America. Boreal Owls are best seen from March to May, when they perch conspicuously on bare branches and call regularly during long northern nights. Look for them in the Upper Peninsula among old-growth coniferous and mixed forests. • This small owl is well adapted to snowy forest environments—it is remarkably proficient at locating and catching prey that lives beneath the snow. Much remains to be learned about the ecology and behavior of this bird because of its nocturnal habits and preference for remote, inaccessible habitats. • This approachable owl was named "Blind One" by native peoples, because it was easily captured by hand. The Boreal Owl is one of the most common forest-dwelling owls in Eurasia where it is known as "Tengmalm's Owl." • The size difference between sexes—females are larger—is more pronounced in Boreals than in any other owl species.

ID: small; rounded head; whitish face with dark border; white spots on black forehead; yellowish bill; vertical, rusty streaks on underparts; white-spotted, brown upperparts; black "eyebrow"; short tail. *Juvenile:* brown underparts; brown face with white between eyes.
Size: *L* 9–12 in; *W* 21–29 in.
Status: rare to casual spring and fall migrant and winter resident from October to May.
Habitat: mature coniferous and mixed forests.

Nesting: does not nest in Michigan.
Feeding: swoops down from a perch to take voles, mice, shrews, flying squirrels and insects; often plunges through the snow to catch prey in winter; may cache food.
Voice: rapid, accelerating, continuous whistle: *whew-whew-whew-whew-whew-whew;* easily imitated.
Similar Species: *Northern Saw-whet Owl* (p. 176): dark bill; white forehead streaking; lacks dark, vertical "eyebrow"; juvenile has reddish underparts. *Northern Hawk Owl* (p. 170): much longer tail; fine horizontal barring on underparts.
Selected Sites: Whitefish Point.

NORTHERN SAW-WHET OWL

Aegolius acadicus

The tiny Northern Saw-whet Owl is an opportunistic hunter, taking whatever it can, whenever it can. If temperatures are below freezing and prey is abundant, this small owl may choose to catch more than it can eat in a single sitting. The extra food is usually stored in trees, where it quickly freezes. When hunting efforts fail, the hungry Saw-whet will return to thaw out its frozen cache by "incubating" the food as if it were a clutch of eggs! • Saw-whets are usually heard more than they are seen, and from midwinter to early spring, their slow, whistled notes are surprisingly common. Some say the sound reminds them of the "bleeps" a large truck gives when backing up. Northern Saw-whet Owls are most conspicuous in October, when they can be seen or heard in considerable numbers at some sites. • "Owl prowls" during Christmas bird counts frequently concentrate much energy on Saw-whets. These owls can be found in parts of Michigan, but they are often frustratingly silent. • The scientific name *acadicus*, Latin for "from Acadia," refers to the region in Canada where this bird was first collected.

ID: small body; large, rounded head; light, unbordered facial disc; dark bill; vertical, rusty streaks on underparts; white-spotted, brown upperparts; white-streaked forehead; short tail. *Juvenile:* white patch between eyes; rich brown head and breast; buff brown belly.
Size: *L* 7–9 in; *W* 17–22 in.
Status: uncommon migrant from March to May and from September to November; rare breeder; frequent winter resident.
Habitat: pure and mixed coniferous and deciduous forests; wooded city parks and ravines.
Nesting: in an abandoned woodpecker cavity, natural hollow in a tree or nest box; female incubates 5–6 white eggs for 27–29 days; male feeds the female during incubation.
Feeding: swoops down on prey from a perch; may cache food; eats mostly mice and voles, also larger insects, songbirds, shrews, moles and occasionally amphibians.
Voice: whistled, evenly spaced notes repeated about 100 times per minute: *whew-whew-whew-whew;* continuous and easily imitated.
Similar Species: *Boreal Owl* (p. 175): light-colored bill; white spotting on black forehead; dark, vertical "eyebrow"; dark border to facial disc; juvenile has dark chocolate brown breast. *Northern Hawk Owl* (p. 170): much longer tail; fine, horizontal barring on underparts; white spotting on black forehead.
Selected Sites: Dearborn Environmental Study Area; Whitefish Point; Sarett Nature Center; Lake Erie Metropark.

COMMON NIGHTHAWK

Chordeiles minor

Each May and June, the male Common Nighthawk flies high above forest clearings and lakeshores, gaining elevation in preparation for the climax of his noisy aerial dance. From a great height, the male dives swiftly, thrusting his wings forward in a final braking action as he strains to pull out of the steep dive. This quick thrust of the wings produces a deep, hollow *vroom* that attracts female nighthawks. • Like other members of the nightjar family, the Common Nighthawk is adapted for catching insects in midair: its gaping mouth is surrounded by feather shafts that funnel insects into its mouth. • Nighthawks are generally less nocturnal than other nightjars, but they still spend most of the daylight hours resting on a tree limb or on the ground. These birds have very short legs and small feet, and sit along the length of a tree branch, rather than across the branch as do most perched birds.

ID: cryptic, mottled plumage; barred underparts. *Male:* white throat. *Female:* buff throat. *In flight:* bold, white "wrist" patches on long, pointed wings; shallowly forked, barred tail; erratic flight.
Size: *L* 8½–10 in; *W* 24 in.
Status: common migrant and breeder from May to September.
Habitat: *Breeding:* in forest openings as well as burns, bogs, rocky outcroppings, gravel rooftops and sometimes fields with sparse cover or bare patches. *In migration:* anywhere large numbers of flying insects can be found; usually roosts in trees, often near water.
Nesting: on bare ground; no nest is built; female incubates 2 well-camouflaged eggs

for about 19 days; both adults feed the young.
Feeding: primarily at dawn and dusk, but also at other times; catches insects in flight, often high in the air; may fly around street lights at night to catch prey attracted to the light; eats mosquitoes, blackflies, midges, beetles, flying ants, moths and other flying insects.
Voice: frequently repeated, nasal *peent peent;* also makes a deep, hollow *vroom* with its wings during courtship flight.
Similar Species: *Whip-poor-will* (p. 178) and *Chuck-will's-widow:* less common; found in forests; lack white "wrist" patches; shorter, rounder wings; rounded tails.
Selected Sites: Detroit R. and Sault Ste. Marie waterfronts; Whitefish Point; Warren Dunes SP; Rouge River Bird Observatory; Baraga Jack Pine Plains.

WHIP-POOR-WILL

Caprimulgus vociferus

This nocturnal hunter fills the late evening with calls of its own name: *whip-poor-will*. Although the Whip-poor-will is heard throughout many of the open woodlands in Michigan, this cryptic bird is rarely seen. Because of its camouflaged plumage, sleepy daytime habits and secretive nesting behavior, a hopeful observer must literally stumble upon a Whip-poor-will to see it. Only occasionally is this bird seen roosting on an exposed tree branch or alongside a quiet road. • The Whip-poor-will is one of three members of the nightjar, or "goatsucker," family found in the state. Birds in this family were named "Goatsuckers" during the days of Aristotle, because there was a widely believed superstition that they would suck milk from the udders of female goats, causing the goats to go blind! • Within days of hatching, young Whip-poor-wills scurry away from their nest in search of protective cover. For the first 20 days after hatching, the parents feed them regurgitated insects.

ID: mottled, brown gray overall with black flecking; reddish tinge on rounded wings; black throat; long, rounded tail. *Male:* white "necklace"; white outer tail feathers. *Female:* buff "necklace."

Size: *L* 9–10 in; *W* 16–20 in.

Status: uncommon migrant and breeder from April to early November; fairly common in the north; rare in the south.

Habitat: open deciduous and pine woodlands; often along forest edges.

Nesting: often along the edge of a clearing under herbaceous plant growth; on the ground in leaf or pine needle litter; no nest is built; female incubates 2 whitish eggs, blotched with brown and gray, for 19–20 days; both adults raise the young.

Feeding: catches large, night-flying insects in flight; eats mostly moths, beetles and mosquitoes; some grasshoppers are taken and swallowed whole.

Voice: loud, whistled *whip-poor-will,* with emphasis on the *will.*

Similar Species: *Chuck-will's-widow:* larger; pale brown to buff throat; whitish "necklace"; darker breast; more reddish overall; much less white on male's tail; different call. *Common Nighthawk* (p. 177): shallowly forked, barred tail; white patches on wings; male has white throat; female has buff throat; much more conspicuous behavior.

Selected Sites: Waterloo SRA; Pinckney SRA; Tuscola SGA; Allegan SGA; Warren Woods Natural Area; Fort Custer SRA; Chippewa Nature Center; Rogue River SGA.

CHIMNEY SWIFT

Chaetura pelagica

Chimney Swifts are the "frequent fliers" of the bird world—they feed, drink, bathe, collect nesting material and even mate while in flight! They spend much of their time scooping up flying insects high above urban neighborhoods, and only the business of nesting or resting keeps these birds off their wings. Chimney Swifts are most conspicuous as they forage on warm summer evenings and during fall migration, when huge flocks migrate south alongside large numbers of Common Nighthawks. • Declining Chimney Swift populations may be the result of a decrease in available tree cavities for nesting. Chimney Swifts got their name from their second choice for nest sites—brick chimneys. • The legs of Chimney Swifts are so weak and small that if one of these birds lands on the ground it may not be able to gain flight again. Swifts do have strong claws, though, which allow them to cling to vertical surfaces.

ID: brown overall; slim body and long, thin, pointed, crescent-shaped wings; squared tail. *In flight:* rapid wingbeats; boomerang-shaped profile; erratic flight pattern.

Size: *L* 4½–5½ in; *W* 12–13 in.

Status: common migrant and breeder from early May to mid-September.

Habitat: forages over cities and towns; roosts and nests in chimneys; may nest in tree cavities in more remote areas.

Nesting: often colonial; nests deep in the interior of a chimney or tree cavity, or in the attic of an abandoned building; pair uses saliva to attach a half-saucer nest of short, dead twigs to a vertical wall; pair incubates 4–5 white eggs for 19–21 days; both adults feed the young.

Feeding: flying insects are swallowed whole during continuous flight.

Voice: rapid, chattering call is given in flight: *chitter-chitter-chitter;* also gives a rapid series of *chip* notes.

Similar Species: *Swallows* (pp. 216–20): broader, shorter wings; smoother flight pattern; most have forked or notched tail.

Selected Sites: most cities and towns; near large brick chimneys.

179

RUBY-THROATED HUMMINGBIRD

Archilochus colubris

Ruby-throated Hummingbirds span the ecological gap between birds and bees—they feed on the sweet, energy-rich nectar that flowers provide and pollinate the flowers in the process. Many avid gardeners and birders have long understood this interdependence and cultivate native, nectar-producing plants in their yards to attract these delightful birds. Even nongardeners can attract hummingbirds by maintaining a clean sugarwater feeder in a safe location. • Weighing about as much as a nickel, a hummingbird is capable of briefly achieving speeds of up to 62 miles per hour. It is also among the few birds that are able to fly vertically and in reverse. In straight-ahead flight, hummingbirds beat their wings up to 80 times per second, and their hearts can beat up to 1200 times per minute! • Each year, Ruby-throated Hummingbirds migrate across the Gulf of Mexico—an incredible, nonstop journey of more than 500 miles. In order to accomplish this, these little birds first double their body mass by fattening up on insects and nectar before departing.

ID: tiny; long bill; iridescent, green back; light underparts; dark tail. *Male:* ruby red throat; black "chin." *Female* and *immature:* fine, dark throat streaking.

Size: *L* 3½–4 in; *W* 4½ in.

Status: common migrant and breeder from May to mid-September.

Habitat: open, mixed woodlands, wetlands, orchards, tree-lined meadows, flower gardens and backyards with trees and feeders.

Nesting: on a horizontal tree limb; tiny, deep cup nest of plant down and fibers is held together with spider silk; lichens and leaves are pasted on the exterior wall of the nest; female incubates 2 white eggs for 13–16 days; female feeds the young.

Feeding: uses its long bill and tongue to probe blooming flowers and sugar-sweetened water from feeders; also eats small insects and spiders.

Voice: most noticeable is the soft buzzing of the wings while in flight; also produces a loud *chick* and other high squeaks.

Similar Species: *Rufous Hummingbird* (p. 341): male has bright, reddish orange on flanks and back; female has red-spotted throat and reddish flanks.

Selected Sites: backyard sugarwater feeders, flower gardens and orchards.

BELTED KINGFISHER
Ceryle alcyon

The boisterous Belted Kingfisher closely monitors many of our lakes, rivers, streams, marshes and beaver ponds. Never far from water, this bird is often found uttering its distinctive, rattling call while perched on a bare branch that extends out over a productive pool. With a precise headfirst dive, the Kingfisher can catch fish at depths of up to 23 inches, or snag a frog immersed in only a few inches of water. The Kingfisher has even been observed diving into water to elude avian predators. • During the breeding season, a pair of kingfishers typically takes turns excavating the nest burrow. The birds use their bills to chip away at an exposed sandbank and then kick loose material out of the tunnel with their feet. The female kingfisher has the traditional female reproductive role for birds but is more colorful than her mate—she has an extra red band across her belly. • In Greek mythology, Alcyon (Halcyone), the daughter of the wind god, grieved so deeply for her drowned husband that the gods transformed them both into kingfishers.

ID: bluish upperparts; shaggy crest; blue gray breast band; white "collar"; long, straight bill; short legs; white underwings; small, white patch near eye. *Male:* no "belt." *Female:* rust-colored "belt" (may be incomplete).
Size: *L* 11–14 in; *W* 20 in.
Status: common breeder from April to October; rare in the south from November to March.
Habitat: rivers, large streams, lakes, marshes and beaver ponds, especially near exposed soil banks, gravel pits or bluffs.

Nesting: in a cavity at the end of an earth burrow, often up to 6 ft long, dug by the pair with their bills and claws; pair incubates 6–7 white eggs for 22–24 days; both adults feed the young.
Feeding: dives headfirst into water, either from a perch or from hovering flight; eats mostly small fish, aquatic invertebrates and tadpoles.
Voice: fast, repetitive, cackling rattle, a little like a teacup shaking on a saucer.
Similar Species: *Blue Jay* (p. 211): more intense blue color; smaller bill and head; behaves in a completely different fashion.
Selected Sites: along the shallower parts of almost any stream, pond or lake that supports fish.

RED-HEADED WOODPECKER

Melanerpes erythrocephalus

Closely related to the western Acorn Woodpecker, this bird of the East lives mostly in deciduous woodlands, in urban parks and in fields with open groves of large trees. Red-headed Woodpeckers were once common throughout their range, but their numbers have declined dramatically over the past century. Since the introduction of the European Starling, Red-headed Woodpeckers have been largely outcompeted for nesting cavities. As well, these birds are frequent traffic fatalities, often struck by vehicles when they dart from their perches and over roadways to catch flying insects. • When Alexander Wilson, the "father" of American ornithology, first arrived in North America, the Red-headed Woodpecker was one of the first birds to greet him. Inspired, Wilson wrote of this woodpecker: "His tricolored plumage, so striking…A gay and frolicsome disposition, diving and vociferating around the high dead limbs of some large tree, amusing the passenger with their gambols." • This bird's scientific name *erythrocephalus* means "red head" in Greek.

ID: bright red head, "chin," throat and "bib" with black border; black back, wings and tail; white breast, belly, rump, lower back and inner wing patches. *Juvenile:* brown head, back, wings and tail; slight brown streaking on white underparts.

Size: *L* 9–9½ in; *W* 17 in.

Status: locally common migrant and breeder from late April to early November; irregular in winter in southern Lower Peninsula.

Habitat: open deciduous woodlands (especially oak woodlands), urban parks, river edges and roadsides with groves of scattered trees.

Nesting: male excavates a nest cavity in a dead tree or limb; pair incubates 4–5 white eggs for 12–13 days; both adults feed the young.

Feeding: flycatches for insects; hammers dead and decaying wood for grubs; eats mostly insects, earthworms, spiders, nuts, berries, seeds and fruit; may also eat some young birds and eggs.

Voice: loud series of *kweer* or *kwrring* notes; occasionally a chattering *kerr-r-ruck;* also drums softly in short bursts.

Similar Species: adult is distinctive. *Red-bellied Woodpecker* (p. 183): whitish face and underparts; black-and-white barred back. *Yellow-bellied Sapsucker* (p. 184): large, white wing patch.

Selected Sites: Seven Ponds Nature Center; Indian Springs Metropark; Waterloo SRA; Fort Custer SRA; Sleepy Hollow SP; Yankee Springs SRA; Warren Woods Natural Area.

RED-BELLIED WOODPECKER
Melanerpes carolinus

The Red-bellied Woodpecker occupies the extreme limit of its North American range in this region, and although it is found year-round, its numbers fluctuate depending on the availability of habitat and winter conditions. In recent years, mild winter weather has enabled the Red-bellied Woodpecker to increase its numbers in Michigan. • These birds often issue noisy, rolling *churr* calls as they poke around wooded landscapes in search of seeds, fruit and a variety of insects. Unlike most woodpeckers, Red-bellies consume large amounts of plant material, seldom excavating wood for insects. When occupying an area together with Red-headed Woodpeckers, Red-bellies will nest in the trunk, below the foliage, and the Red-heads will nest in dead branches among the foliage. • The Red-bellied Woodpecker's namesake, its red belly, is only a small reddish area that is difficult to see in the field. • Studies of banded Red-bellied Woodpeckers have shown that these birds have a life span in the wild of more than 20 years.

ID: black-and-white-barred back; white patches on rump and topside base of primaries; reddish tinge on belly. *Female:* red nape. *Male:* red nape extends to forehead. *Juvenile:* dark gray crown; streaked breast.
Size: *L* 9–10½ in; *W* 16 in.
Status: fairly common year-round resident in southern two thirds of Lower Peninsula.
Habitat: mature deciduous woodlands; occasionally in wooded residential areas.
Nesting: in a cavity; female selects one of several nest sites excavated by the male; pair may use a natural cavity or the abandoned cavity of another woodpecker; pair incubates 4–5 white eggs for 12–14 days; both adults raise the young.
Feeding: forages in trees, on the ground or occasionally on the wing; eats mostly insects, seeds, nuts and fruit; may also eat tree sap, small amphibians, bird eggs or small fish.
Voice: call is a soft, rolling *churr;* drums in second-long bursts.
Similar Species: *Northern Flicker* (p. 188): yellow underwings; gray crown; brown back with dark barring; black "bib"; large, dark spots on underparts. *Red-headed Woodpecker* (p. 182): all-red head; unbarred, black back and wings; white patch on trailing edge of wing.
Selected Sites: Seven Ponds Nature Center; Indian Springs Metropark; Waterloo SRA; Lost Nation SGA; Sleepy Hollow SP; Yankee Springs SRA.

YELLOW-BELLIED SAPSUCKER

Sphyrapicus varius

Yellow-bellied Sapsuckers are conspicuous in May, when they perform their courting rituals throughout our woodlands. The drumming of sapsuckers—with its irregular rhythm reminiscent of Morse code—differs from that of other Michigan woodpeckers. • Lines of parallel, freshly drilled "wells" in tree bark are a sure sign that sapsuckers are nearby. A pair of sapsuckers might drill a number of sites within their forest territory. The wells fill with sweet, sticky sap that attracts insects; the sapsuckers then make their rounds, eating both the trapped bugs and the pooled sap. Sapsuckers do not actually suck sap—they lap it up with a tongue that resembles a paintbrush. • Other species such as hummingbirds, kinglets, warblers and waxwings benefit from the wells made by Yellow-bellied Sapsuckers, especially early in the season when flying insects, fruits and nectar are rare.

ID: black "bib"; red forecrown; black-and-white face, back, wings and tail; large, white wing patch; yellow wash on lower breast and belly. *Male:* red "chin." *Female:* white "chin." *Juvenile:* brownish overall, but with large, clearly defined wing patches.
Size: *L* 7–9 in; *W* 16 in.
Status: uncommon to common migrant from April to November; frequent breeder in Upper Peninsula and northern half of Lower Peninsula.
Habitat: deciduous and mixed forests, especially dry, second-growth woodlands.
Nesting: in a cavity; usually in a live poplar or birch tree with heart rot; often lines the cavity with wood chips; pair incubates 5–6 white eggs for 12–13 days.

Feeding: hammers trees for insects; drills "wells" in live trees to collect sap and trap insects; also flycatches for insects.
Voice: nasal, catlike *meow;* territorial and courtship hammering has a quality and rhythm similar to Morse code.
Similar Species: *Red-headed Woodpecker* (p. 182): juvenile lacks white patch on wing. *Downy Woodpecker* (p. 185) and *Hairy Woodpecker* (p. 186): red nape; white back; lack large, white wing patches and red forecrown. *Black-backed Woodpecker* (p. 187) and *Three-toed Woodpecker* (p. 341): yellow forecrown; predominantly black head; lack white wing patch.
Selected Sites: Dearborn Environmental Study Area; Seven Ponds Nature Center; Indian Springs Metropark; Rose Lake WA; Kalamazoo Nature Center; Chippewa Nature Center; Colonial Point Forest.

DOWNY WOODPECKER

Picoides pubescens

A regular patron of backyard suet feeders, the small and widely common Downy Woodpecker is often the first woodpecker a novice birder will identify with confidence. It is generally more approachable and tolerant of human activities than are most birds, and once you become familiar with its dainty appearance, it won't be long before you recognize it by its soft taps and brisk staccato calls. These encounters are not all free of confusion, however, because the closely related Hairy Woodpecker looks remarkably similar. • The Downy Woodpecker's small bill is extremely effective for poking into tiny crevices and extracting invertebrates and wood-boring grubs. • Like other members of the woodpecker family, the Downy has evolved a number of features that help to cushion the repeated shocks of a lifetime of hammering. These characteristics include a strong bill, strong neck muscles, a flexible, reinforced skull, and a brain that is tightly packed in its protective cranium. Another feature that Downies share with other woodpeckers is feathered nostrils, which serve to filter out the sawdust it produces when hammering.

ID: clear white belly and back; black wings have white bars; black eye line and crown; short, stubby bill; mostly black tail; black-spotted, white outer tail feathers.
Male: small, red patch on back of head.
Female: no red patch.
Size: *L* 6–7 in; *W* 12 in.
Status: common year-round resident.
Habitat: all wooded environments, especially deciduous and mixed forests and areas with tall, deciduous shrubs.
Nesting: pair excavates a cavity in a dying or decaying trunk or limb and lines it with wood chips; excavation takes more than 2 weeks; pair incubates 4–5 white eggs for 11–13 days; both adults feed the young.
Feeding: forages on trunks and branches, often in saplings and shrubs; attracted to suet feeders; chips and probes for insect eggs, cocoons, larvae and adults; also eats nuts and seeds.
Voice: long, unbroken trill; calls are a sharp *pik* or *ki-ki-ki* or whiny *queek queek;* drums more than the Hairy Woodpecker and at a higher pitch, usually on smaller trees and dead branches.
Similar Species: *Hairy Woodpecker* (p. 186): larger; bill is as long as head is wide; no spots on white outer tail feathers. *Yellow-bellied Sapsucker* (p. 184): large, white wing patch; red forecrown; lacks red nape and clean white back. *Black-backed Woodpecker* (p. 187) and *Three-toed Woodpecker* (p. 341): larger; yellow forecrown; predominantly black head; black barring on sides.
Selected Sites: almost any wooded area; suburban bird feeders.

185

HAIRY WOODPECKER

Picoides villosus

A second or third look is often required to confirm the identity of the Hairy Woodpecker, because to it is so similar in appearance to its smaller cousin, the Downy Woodpecker. A convenient way to learn to distinguish one bird from the other is by watching these woodpeckers at a backyard feeder. It is not uncommon to see both of these birds vying for food, and the Hairy Woodpecker is larger and more aggressive. • The secret to woodpeckers' feeding success is hidden in their skulls. Most woodpeckers have very long tongues—in some cases more than four times the length of the bill—made possible by twin structures that wrap around the perimeter of the skull. These structures store the tongue in much the same way that a measuring tape is stored in its case. Besides being long and maneuverable, the tip of the tongue is sticky with saliva and is finely barbed to help seize reluctant wood-boring insects. • Rather than singing during courtship, woodpeckers drum rhythmically on trees.

ID: white-spotted, black wings; pure white belly; black "cheek" and crown; bill is about as long as head is wide; black tail with unspotted, white outer feathers. *Male:* small, red patch on back of head. *Female:* no red patch.
Size: *L* 8–9½ in; *W* 15 in.
Status: common year-round resident.
Habitat: deciduous and mixed forests.
Nesting: pair excavates a nest site in a live or decaying tree trunk or limb; excavation takes more than 2 weeks; cavity is lined with wood chips; pair incubates 4–5 white eggs for 12–14 days; both adults feed the young.
Feeding: forages on tree trunks and branches; chips, hammers and probes bark for insects and their eggs, cocoons and larvae; also eats nuts, fruit and seeds; attracted to feeders with suet, especially in winter.
Voice: loud, sharp call: *peek peek;* long, unbroken trill: *keek-ik-ik-ik-ik-ik;* drums less regularly and at a lower pitch than the Downy Woodpecker, always on tree trunks and large branches.
Similar Species: *Downy Woodpecker* (p. 185): smaller; shorter bill; dark spots on white outer tail feathers. *Yellow-bellied Sapsucker* (p. 184): large, white wing patch; red forecrown; lacks red nape and clean white back. *Black-backed Woodpecker* (p. 187) and *Three-toed Woodpecker* (p. 341): yellow forecrown; predominantly black head; black barring on sides.
Selected Sites: almost any large woodland; suburban bird feeders.

186

BLACK-BACKED WOODPECKER

Picoides arcticus

The Black-backed Woodpecker is a regular resident in northern Michigan but is uncommonly recorded in the rest of the state. This generally quiet woodpecker prefers a secretive life in remote, uninhabited tracts of coniferous forest. Only during the brief courtship season does the male Black-backed Woodpecker advertise his presence by drumming on the top of a broken, standing dead tree or "snag."
• This reclusive bird is most active in recently burned forest patches where wood-boring beetles thrive under the charred bark of spruce, pine and fir trees. When it forages on blackened tree trunks, this bird's black-backed form can be difficult to spot, especially from a distance. • Large, irruptive invasions of Black-backed and Three-toed woodpeckers seem to occur at six- to eight-year intervals.
• The scientific name *arcticus* reflects this bird's largely northern distribution.

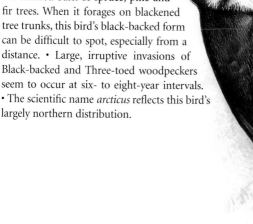

ID: solid black back; white underparts; black barring on sides; predominantly black head with white line below eye; black "mustache" stripe; 3 toes; black tail with pure white outer tail feathers. *Male:* yellow crown. *Female:* black crown.
Size: *L* 9–10 in; *W* 16 in.
Status: special concern; local, year-round irruptive resident in Upper Peninsula and north-central Lower Peninsula; rare breeder from late May to late June.
Habitat: coniferous forests, especially burned-over sites with many standing dead trees.
Nesting: excavates a cavity in a dead or dying conifer trunk or limb; excavation

takes up to 12 days; pair incubates 4 white eggs for 12–14 days; both adults feed the young.
Feeding: chisels away bark flakes to expose larval and adult wood-boring insects; may eat some nuts and fruits.
Voice: call is a low *kik;* drumming is a prolonged series of short bursts.
Similar Species: *Three-toed Woodpecker* (p. 341): white back with black, horizontal barring; black spots on white outer tail feathers. *Hairy Woodpecker* (p. 186): clean white back; lacks dark barring on sides. *Yellow-bellied Sapsucker* (p. 184): black-and-white back; large, white wing patch; red forecrown; black "bib"; yellow-tinged underparts.
Selected Sites: Whitefish Point; Seney NWR; Rapid River; Tahquamenon Falls SP; Mack L. area; any recently burned area.

187

NORTHERN FLICKER

Colaptes auratus

The Northern Flicker is the most common woodpecker in Michigan. Unlike most woodpeckers, this species spends much of its time on the ground, feeding mostly on ants. It appears almost robinlike as it hops about on ant hills and in grassy meadows, fields and along forest clearings. • Flickers are often seen bathing in dusty depressions. The dust particles absorb oils and bacteria that are harmful to the birds' feathers. To clean even more thoroughly, flickers will squish captured ants and then preen themselves with the remains: ants contain formic acid, which can kill small parasites on the flickers' skin and feathers. • Like many woodpeckers, the Northern Flicker has zygodactyl feet—each foot has two toes facing forward and two toes pointing backward—which allow the bird to move vertically up and down tree trunks. As well, stiff tail feathers help to prop up woodpeckers' bodies while they scale trees and excavate cavities.

ID: brown, barred back and wings; spotted, buff to whitish underparts; black "bib"; yellow underwings and undertail; white rump; long bill; brownish to buff face; gray crown. *Male:* black "mustache" stripe; red nape crescent. *Female:* no "mustache."

Size: *L* 12½–13 in; *W* 20 in.

Status: abundant migrant and breeder from April to late October; rare winter resident in southern Lower Peninsula.

Habitat: open deciduous, mixed and coniferous woodlands and forest edges, fields, meadows, beaver ponds and other wetlands.

Nesting: pair excavates a cavity in a dead or dying deciduous tree; either sex chooses the nest site; excavation takes about 2 weeks; may also use a nest box; cavity is lined with wood chips; pair incubates 5–8 white eggs for 11–16 days; both adults feed the young.

Feeding: forages on the ground for ants and other terrestrial insects; probes bark; also eats berries and nuts; occasionally flycatches.

Voice: loud, laughing, rapid *kick-kick-kick-kick-kick-kick; woika-woika-woika* issued during courtship.

Similar Species: *Red-bellied Woodpecker* (p. 183): black-and-white pattern on back; more red on head; dark underwings.

Selected Sites: almost any open woodland, woodlot or forest edge.

PILEATED WOODPECKER

Dryocopus pileatus

With its flaming red crest, swooping flight and maniacal call, this impressive, deep-forest dweller can stop hikers in their tracks. Using its powerful, dagger-shaped bill and stubborn determination, the Pileated Woodpecker chisels out uniquely shaped rectangular cavities in its unending search for grubs and ants. These cavities are often the first indication that a breeding pair is resident in an area. • Because they require large home territories, these magnificent birds are not encountered with much frequency. A pair of breeding Pileated Woodpeckers generally needs more than 100 acres of mature forest in which to settle. • As a primary cavity nester, the Pileated Woodpecker plays an important role in forest ecosystems. Other birds and even mammals depend on the activities of this woodpecker—ducks, small falcons, owls and even flying squirrels are frequent nesters in abandoned Pileated Woodpecker cavities. • Not surprisingly, a woodpecker's bill becomes shorter as the bird ages. In his historic painting of the Pileated Woodpecker, John J. Audubon correctly depicted the bills of the juveniles as slightly longer than those of the adults. • There is no real consensus on whether this bird's name is pronounced "pie-lee-ated" or "pill-ee-ated"—it's a matter of preference and good-natured debate.

ID: predominantly black; white wing linings; flaming red crest; yellow eyes; stout, dark bill; white stripe runs from bill to shoulder; white "chin." *Male:* red "mustache"; red crest (red extends from bill to nape). *Female:* no red "mustache"; red crest; gray brown forehead.
Size: *L* 16–19 in; *W* 29 in.
Status: rare to uncommon year-round resident; mainly in Upper Peninsula and northern half of Lower Peninsula.
Habitat: extensive tracts of mature deciduous, mixed or coniferous forests; some occur in riparian woodlands or woodlots in suburban and agricultural areas.

Nesting: pair excavates a cavity in a dead or dying tree trunk; excavation takes 3–6 weeks; cavity is lined with wood chips; pair incubates 4 white eggs for 15–18 days; both adults feed the young.
Feeding: often hammers the base of rotting trees, creating fist-sized or larger, rectangular holes; eats carpenter ants, wood-boring beetle larvae, berries and nuts.
Voice: loud, fast, laughing, rolling *woika-woika-woika-woika;* long series of *kuk* notes; loud resonant drumming.
Similar Species: *Other woodpeckers* (p. 182–88): much smaller. *American Crow* (p. 212) and *Common Raven* (p. 213): lack white underwings and flaming red crest.
Selected Sites: mature coniferous and deciduous woodlands in most state and national forests; state parks in Upper Peninsula and northern Lower Peninsula.

PASSERINES

Passerines are also commonly known as songbirds or perching birds. Although these terms are easier to comprehend, they are not as strictly accurate, because some passerines neither sing nor perch, and many nonpasserines do sing and perch. In a general sense, however, these terms represent passerines adequately: they are among the best singers, and they are typically seen perched on a branch or wire.

It is believed that passerines, which all belong to the order Passeriformes, make up the most recent evolutionary group of birds. Theirs is the most numerous of all orders, representing about 45 percent of the bird species in Michigan, and nearly three-fifths of all living birds worldwide.

Passerines are grouped together based on the sum total of many morphological and molecular similarities, including such things as the number of tail and flight feathers and reproductive characteristics. All passerines share the same foot shape: three toes

Eastern Meadowlark

face forward and one faces backward, and no passerines have webbed toes. Also, all passerines have a tendon that runs along the back side of the bird's knee and tightens when the bird perches, giving it a firm grip.

Some of our most common and easily identified birds are passerines, such as the Black-capped Chickadee, American Robin and House Sparrow, but the passerines also include some of the most challenging and frustrating birds to identify, until their distinct songs and calls are learned.

Baltimore Oriole

OLIVE-SIDED FLYCATCHER

Contopus cooperi

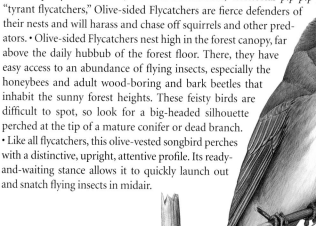

An early morning hike through a coniferous forest often reveals a most curious and incessant wild call: *quick-three-beers! quick-three-beers!* This interpretation of the male Olive-sided Flycatcher's courtship song may seem silly, but it is surprisingly accurate. Once nesting has begun, this flycatcher quickly changes its tune to an equally enthusiastic, but less memorable, territorial *pip-pip-pip*. Like other "tyrant flycatchers," Olive-sided Flycatchers are fierce defenders of their nests and will harass and chase off squirrels and other predators. • Olive-sided Flycatchers nest high in the forest canopy, far above the daily hubbub of the forest floor. There, they have easy access to an abundance of flying insects, especially the honeybees and adult wood-boring and bark beetles that inhabit the sunny forest heights. These feisty birds are difficult to spot, so look for a big-headed silhouette perched at the tip of a mature conifer or dead branch. • Like all flycatchers, this olive-vested songbird perches with a distinctive, upright, attentive profile. Its ready-and-waiting stance allows it to quickly launch out and snatch flying insects in midair.

ID: dark, olive gray "vest"; light throat and belly; olive gray to olive brown upperparts; white tufts on sides of rump; dark upper mandible; dull yellow orange base to lower mandible; inconspicuous eye ring.
Size: *L* 7–8 in; *W* 13 in.
Status: fairly common migrant from early May to early June and from mid-August to late September; frequent breeder in Upper Peninsula and northern Lower Peninsula.
Habitat: semi-open mixed and coniferous forests near water; prefers burned areas and wetlands.
Nesting: high in a conifer, usually on a horizontal branch far from the trunk; nest of twigs and plant fibers is bound with spider silk; female incubates 3 white to pinkish buff eggs, with dark spots concentrated at the larger end, for 14–17 days.
Feeding: flycatches insects from a perch.
Voice: *Male:* song is a chipper and lively *quick-three-beers!,* with the 2nd note highest in pitch; descending *pip-pip-pip* when excited.
Similar Species: *Eastern Wood-Pewee* (p. 192): smaller; lacks white rump tufts; gray breast; 2 faint wing bars. *Eastern Phoebe* (p. 198): lacks white rump tufts; all-dark bill; often wags tail. *Eastern Kingbird* (p. 201): lacks white rump tufts; all-dark bill; white-tipped tail.
Selected Sites: Indian Springs Metropark; Waterloo SRA; Warren Woods Natural Area; Chippewa Nature Center; Colonial Point Forest.

EASTERN WOOD-PEWEE

Contopus virens

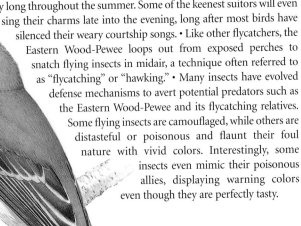

P erched on an exposed tree branch in a suburban park, woodlot edge or neighborhood yard, the male Eastern Wood-Pewee whistles his plaintive *pee-ah-wee pee-oh* all day long throughout the summer. Some of the keenest suitors will even sing their charms late into the evening, long after most birds have silenced their weary courtship songs. • Like other flycatchers, the Eastern Wood-Pewee loops out from exposed perches to snatch flying insects in midair, a technique often referred to as "flycatching" or "hawking." • Many insects have evolved defense mechanisms to avert potential predators such as the Eastern Wood-Pewee and its flycatching relatives. Some flying insects are camouflaged, while others are distasteful or poisonous and flaunt their foul nature with vivid colors. Interestingly, some insects even mimic their poisonous allies, displaying warning colors even though they are perfectly tasty.

ID: olive gray to olive brown upperparts; 2 narrow, white wing bars; whitish throat; gray breast and sides; whitish or pale yellow belly, flanks and undertail coverts; dark upper mandible; dull yellow orange base to lower mandible; no eye ring.
Size: *L* 6–6½ in; *W* 10 in.
Status: common migrant and breeder from mid-May to late September.
Habitat: open mixed and deciduous woodlands with a sparse understory, especially woodland openings and edges; rarely in open coniferous woodlands.
Nesting: on the fork of a horizontal deciduous branch, well away from the trunk; open cup of grass, plant fibers and lichen is bound with spider silk; female incubates

3 whitish eggs, with dark blotches concentrated at the larger end, for 12–13 days.
Feeding: flycatches insects from a perch; may also glean insects from foliage, especially while hovering.
Voice: *Male:* song is a clear, slow, plaintive *pee-ah-wee*, with the 2nd note lower, followed by a downslurred *pee-oh*, with or without intermittent pauses; also a *chip* call.
Similar Species: *Olive-sided Flycatcher* (p. 191): larger; white rump tufts; olive gray "vest"; lacks conspicuous, white wing bars. *Eastern Phoebe* (p. 198): lacks conspicuous, white wing bars; all-dark bill; often pumps its tail. *Eastern Kingbird* (p. 201): larger; white-tipped tail; brighter white underparts; all-dark bill. *Empidonax flycatchers* (pp. 193–97): smaller; more conspicuous wing bars; eye rings.
Selected Sites: open deciduous or mixed woodlands or woodlot edges.

YELLOW-BELLIED FLYCATCHER
Empidonax flaviventris

You can expect to find the reclusive Yellow-bellied Flycatcher deep within soggy, mosquito-infested bogs and fens in the Upper Peninsula. In late spring and early summer, the male spends much of his time singing plain, soft, liquidy *che-lek* songs and occasionally zipping out from inconspicuous perches to help reduce the insect population. Once nesting has begun, the male changes his tune to a slow, rising *per-wee* and focuses his attention on defending his nesting territory and supplying food to his growing young. • Michigan offers fine opportunities for birders to develop their *Empidonax* flycatcher identification skills—it boasts a large assemblage of these nearly indistinguishable flycatchers. The Yellow-bellied Flycatcher is the most elusive and secretive of this confusing genus. It does not habitually perch in the open but, in the breeding season, it distinguishes itself from other flycatchers by its yellow underparts and by nesting on the ground. Using a good pair of binoculars and paying close attention to fine details in plumage and voice should help you identify this flycatcher.

ID: olive green upperparts; 2 whitish wing bars; yellowish eye ring; white throat; yellow underparts; pale olive breast.
Size: *L* 5–6 in; *W* 8 in.

Status: fairly common migrant from mid-May to mid-June and from mid-August to mid-September; fairly common breeder in Upper Peninsula from May to August.
Habitat: coniferous bogs and fens and shady spruce and pine forests with a dense shrub understory.
Nesting: on the ground in dense sphagnum moss or among the upturned roots of a fallen tree; small cup nest of moss, rootlets and weeds is lined with grass, sedges and fine rootlets; female incubates 3–4 whitish eggs, lightly spotted with brown, for 12–14 days.
Feeding: flycatches for insects at low to middle levels of the forest; also gleans vegetation for larval and adult invertebrates while hovering.
Voice: *Male:* song is a soft *che-luck* or *che-lek* (2nd syllable is lower pitched); calls include a chipper *pe-wheep, preee, pur-wee* or *killik*.
Similar Species: *Acadian* (p. 194), *Willow* (p. 196), *Alder* (p. 195) and *Least* (p. 197) *flycatchers:* all lack extensive yellow wash from throat to belly; white eye rings; different songs; all but the Acadian have browner upperparts.
Selected Sites: Hiawatha National Forest; Ottawa National Forest; Porcupine Mountains Wilderness SP; Sylvania Recreation Area.

ACADIAN FLYCATCHER

Empidonax virescens

As most experienced birders will tell you, one of the keys to identifying a flycatcher is to listen for its distinctive song. The Acadian Flycatcher's signature song is a quick, forceful *peet-sa*. Unfortunately, this summer resident is rare and unlocalized in Michigan, so male singers feel little pressure to issue their hallmark song in defense of a breeding territory. • Learning to identify this bird is only half the fun. Its speedy, aerial courtship chases and the male's hovering flight displays are sights to behold—that is if you can survive the swarming hordes of bloodsucking mosquitoes deep within the swampy woodlands of the southern Lower Peninsula where this flycatcher is primarily found. • Maple and beech trees provide preferred nesting sites for the Acadian Flycatcher. The nest is built on a horizontal branch up to 20 feet above the ground, and can be quite conspicuous because loose material often dangles from the nest, giving it a sloppy appearance. • Flycatchers are members of the family Tyrannidae, or "Tyrant Flycatchers," so named because of their feisty, aggressive behavior.

ID: narrow, yellowish eye ring; 2 buff to yellowish wing bars; large bill has dark upper mandible and pinkish yellow lower mandible; white throat; faint olive yellow breast; yellow belly and undertail coverts; olive green upperparts; very long primaries.
Size: *L* 5½–6 in; *W* 9 in.
Status: uncommon migrant and breeder in southern Lower Peninsula from May to August.
Habitat: fairly mature deciduous woodlands, riparian woodlands and wooded swamps.
Nesting: low in a beech or maple tree, usually 6–13 ft above the ground; female builds a loose, sloppy-looking cup nest from bark strips, catkins, fine twigs and grasses held together with spider silk; female incubates 3 creamy white eggs,

lightly spotted with brown, for 13–15 days; both parents raise the young.
Feeding: forages primarily by hawking or by gleaning from foliage while hovering; takes insects and insect larvae including wasps, bees, spiders and ants; may also eat berries and small fruits.
Voice: song is a forceful *peet-sa;* call is a softer *peet;* may issue a loud, flickerlike *ti-ti-ti-ti-ti* during the breeding season.
Similar Species: *Alder Flycatcher* (p. 195): song is *fee-bee-o;* narrower, white eye ring is often inconspicuous; browner overall; smaller head relative to its body. *Willow Flycatcher* (p. 196): song is an explosive *fitz-bew;* browner overall; smaller head; very faint eye ring. *Least Flycatcher* (p. 197): song is a clear *che-bek;* prominent, white eye ring; rounded head; shorter wings. *Yellow-bellied Flycatcher* (p. 193): song is a liquid *che-lek;* yellow wash from throat to belly.
Selected Sites: Highland SRA; Rose L. WA; Pinckney SRA; Barry SGA; Allegan SGA; Warren Woods Natural Area.

ALDER FLYCATCHER

Empidonax alnorum

The nondescript Alder Flycatcher is well named because it is often found in alder and willow shrubs—a fact that can help in its identification. In Michigan, the Alder Flycatcher frequently competes against the Willow Flycatcher for control over dense, riparian alder and willow thickets. • The Alder Flycatcher is often indistinguishable from other *Empidonax* flycatchers until it opens its small, bicolored beak: with a hearty *fee-bee-o* or *free beer*, it reveals its identity. Once this aggressive bird has been spotted, its feisty behavior can often be observed without distraction as it drives away rivals and pursues flying insects. • Many birds have to learn their songs and calls, but Alder Flycatchers instinctively know the simple phrase of their species. Even if a young bird is isolated from the sounds of other Alder Flycatchers, it can produce a perfectly acceptable *fee-bee-o* when it matures. • The Willow Flycatcher is a close relative of the Alder Flycatcher, and until 1973 these two species were grouped together as a single species known as "Traill's Flycatcher."

ID: olive brown upperparts; 2 dull white to buff wing bars; faint, whitish eye ring; dark upper mandible; orange lower mandible; long tail; white throat; pale olive breast; pale yellowish belly.
Size: *L* 5½–6 in; *W* 8½ in.
Status: fairly common migrant and breeder from May to September.
Habitat: alder or willow thickets bordering lakes or streams.
Nesting: in a fork in a dense bush or shrub, usually less than 3 ft above the ground; small cup nest is loosely woven of grass and other plant materials; female incubates 3–4 white eggs, with dark spots concentrated around the larger end, for 12–14 days; both adults feed the young.

Feeding: flycatches from a perch for beetles, bees, wasps and other flying insects; also eats berries and occasionally seeds.
Voice: song is a snappy *free beer* or *fee-bee-o;* call is a *wheep* or *peep.*
Similar Species: *Eastern Wood-Pewee* (p. 192): larger; lacks eye ring and conspicuous wing bars. *Willow Flycatcher* (p. 196): song is an explosive *fitz-bew;* mostly found in drier areas. *Least Flycatcher* (p. 197): song is a clear *che-bek;* bolder white eye ring; greener upperparts; pale gray white underparts. *Acadian Flycatcher* (p. 194): song is a forceful *peet-sa;* yellowish eye ring; greener upperparts; yellower underparts. *Yellow-bellied Flycatcher* (p. 193): song is a liquid *che-lek;* yellowish eye ring; greener upperparts; yellower underparts.
Selected Sites: streams, lakes or other shorelines with dense willow or alder thickets.

WILLOW FLYCATCHER
Empidonax traillii

When warm spring winds flood our region with migrant songbirds, the characteristic, sneezy *fitz-bew* call of the Willow Flycatcher occasionally rises above the sounds of the crowd. Upon arriving in a suitable shrubby area of thick willows and tangled dogwood, male Willow Flycatchers swing energetically on advantageous perches to do vocal battle over preferred territory. Once the boundaries are drawn and the business of nesting begins, these flycatchers become shy, inconspicuous birds that prefer to remain out of sight. Only when an avian intruder violates an established boundary does the resident Willow Flycatcher aggressively reveal itself.
• After raising their young and fattening themselves up in late summer and early fall, Willow Flycatchers begin their journey to Central and South America.
• John James Audubon named this species after Thomas Stewart Traill, an Englishman who helped him to find a British publisher for his book *Ornithological Biography*.

ID: olive brown upperparts; 2 whitish wing bars; no eye ring; white throat; yellowish belly; pale olive breast.
Size: *L* 5½–6 in; *W* 8½ in.

Status: common migrant and breeder from May to September, mainly in southern Lower Peninsula.
Habitat: shrubby areas of hawthorn, apple, red-osier dogwood or willow on abandoned farmlands and in riparian corridors.
Nesting: in a fork or on a branch of a dense shrub, usually 3–7 ft above the ground; female builds an open cup nest with grass, bark strips and plant fibers and lines it with down; female incubates 3–4 whitish to pale buff eggs, with brown spots concentrated toward the larger end, for 12–15 days.

Feeding: flycatches insects and gleans them from vegetation, usually while hovering.
Voice: *Male:* song is a quick, sneezy *fitz-bew* that drops off at the end (repeated up to 30 times a minute); call is a quick *whit.*
Similar Species: *Eastern Wood-Pewee* (p. 192): larger; lacks eye ring and conspicuous wing bars. *Alder Flycatcher* (p. 195): song is *fee-bee-o;* usually found in wetter areas. *Least Flycatcher* (p. 197): song is a clear *che-bek;* bolder white eye ring; greener upperparts; pale gray white underparts. *Acadian Flycatcher* (p. 194): song is a forceful *peet-sa;* yellowish eye ring; greener upperparts; yellower underparts. *Yellow-bellied Flycatcher* (p. 193): song is a liquid *che-lek;* yellowish eye ring; greener upperparts; yellower underparts.
Selected Sites: Port Huron SGA; Indian Springs Metropark; Rose L. WA; Fort Custer SRA; Allegan SGA; Sarett Nature Center.

LEAST FLYCATCHER
Empidonax minimus

Even though it is not as colorful and glamorous as other birds, the Least Flycatcher is the most common and widespread *Empidonax* flycatcher in our region, and you should have no problem meeting one in most parts of Michigan. • This bird might not look like a bully, but the Least Flycatcher is one of the boldest and most pugnacious songbirds of our deciduous woodlands. During the nesting season, it is noisy and conspicuous, forcefully repeating its simple, two-part *che-bek* call throughout much of the day. Intense song battles normally eliminate the need for physical aggression, but feathers fly in fights that are occasionally required to settle disputes over territory and courtship privileges. • These birds often fall victim to nest parasitism by the Brown-headed Cowbird, whose hatched young often smother the much smaller Least Flycatcher nestlings. • *Empidonax* flycatchers are aptly named: the literal translation is "mosquito king" and refers to their insect-hunting prowess.

ID: olive brown upperparts; 2 white wing bars; bold, white eye ring; fairly long, narrow tail; mostly dark bill has yellow orange lower base; white throat; gray breast; gray white to yellowish belly and undertail coverts.

Size: *L* 4½–6 in; *W* 7¾ in.

Status: common migrant and breeder from May to September; somewhat more common breeder in northern areas.

Habitat: open deciduous or mixed woodlands; forest openings and edges; often in second-growth woodlands and occasionally near human habitation.

Nesting: in the crotch or fork of a small tree or shrub, often against the trunk; female builds a small cup nest of plant fibers and bark and lines it with fine grass, plant down and feathers; female incubates 4 creamy white eggs for 13–15 days; both adults feed the young.

Feeding: flycatches insects; gleans trees and shrubs for insects while hovering; may also eat some fruit and seeds.

Voice: *Male:* song is a constantly repeated, dry *che-bek che-bek.*

Similar Species: *Eastern Wood-Pewee* (p. 192): larger; lacks eye ring and conspicuous wing bars. *Alder Flycatcher* (p. 195): song is *fee-bee-o;* faint eye ring; different song; usually found in wetter areas. *Willow Flycatcher* (p. 196): song is an explosive *fitz-bew;* lacks eye ring; greener upperparts; yellower underparts. *Acadian Flycatcher* (p. 194) song is a forceful *peet-sa;* yellowish eye ring; greener upperparts; yellower underparts. *Yellow-bellied Flycatcher* (p. 193): song is a liquid *che-lek;* yellowish eye ring; greener upperparts; yellower underparts. *Ruby-crowned Kinglet* (p. 233): broken eye ring; much daintier bill; shorter tail.

Selected Sites: open deciduous or mixed woodlands.

197

EASTERN PHOEBE

Sayornis phoebe

Whether you are poking around your summer cottage, a campground picnic shelter or your backyard shed, there is a very good chance you will stumble upon an Eastern Phoebe family and its marvelous mud nest. The Eastern Phoebe's nest building and territorial defense is normally well underway by the time most other songbirds arrive in our region in mid-May. Once limited to nesting on natural cliffs and fallen riparian trees, this adaptive flycatcher has gradually found success in nesting on buildings and bridges, although it prefers sites near water. • Eastern Phoebes sometimes reuse their nest sites for many years and, too often, people unnecessarily destroy the phoebe's mud nests. Some people have caught on to the benefits of having phoebe tenants, because these birds can be effective at controlling pesky insects. • Some other birds pump their tails while perched, but few species can match the zest and frequency of the Eastern Phoebe's tail pumping.

breeding

ID: gray brown upperparts; white underparts with gray wash on breast and sides; belly may be washed with yellow in fall; no eye ring; no obvious wing bars; all-black bill; dark legs; frequently pumps its tail.

Size: L 6½–7 in; W 10½ in.

Status: common migrant and breeder from April to October.

Habitat: open deciduous woodlands, forest edges and clearings; usually near water.

Nesting: under the ledge of a building, picnic shelter, culvert, bridge, cliff or well; cup-shaped mud nest is lined with moss, grass, fur and feathers; female incubates 4–5 white eggs, often with a few reddish brown spots, for about 16 days; both adults feed the young.

Feeding: flycatches beetles, flies, wasps, grasshoppers, mayflies and other insects; occasionally plucks aquatic invertebrates and small fish from the water's surface.

Voice: *Male:* song is a hearty, snappy *fee-bee,* delivered frequently; call is a sharp *chip.*

Similar Species: *Eastern Wood-Pewee* (p. 192): smaller; pale wing bars; bicolored bill; does not pump its tail. *Olive-sided Flycatcher* (p. 191): dark "vest"; white, fluffy patches border rump. Empidonax *flycatchers* (pp. 193–97): most have eye ring and conspicuous wing bars. *Eastern Kingbird* (p. 201): white-tipped tail; black upperparts.

Selected Sites: barns, sheds and other buildings; also under bridges.

GREAT CRESTED FLYCATCHER

Myiarchus crinitus

The Great Crested Flycatcher's nesting habits are unusual for a flycatcher: it is a cavity nester, and although it prefers to nest in a natural tree cavity or abandoned woodpecker nest, it will occasionally use a nest box intended for a bluebird. Once in a while, the Great Crested Flycatcher will decorate the entrance of its nest with a shed snakeskin. The purpose of this practice is not fully understood, though it might make any would-be predators think twice! In some instances, this versatile bird has even been known to substitute translucent plastic wrap for genuine reptilian skin. The Great Crested Flycatcher prefers open or semi-open hardwood forests and is a common summer resident in Michigan. • Songbirds such as the Great Crested Flycatcher are often thought of as birds that fly south for the winter. In reality, it would be more correct to say that they fly north for the summer. This flycatcher, as well as many other migrants, are subtropical or tropical birds of Central and South America that visit our country only briefly to raise their young before returning home.

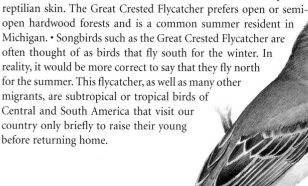

Size: *L* 8–9 in; *W* 13 in.

Status: common migrant and breeder from early May to mid-September.

Habitat: deciduous and mixed woodlands and forests, usually near openings or edges.

Nesting: in a tree cavity, nest box or other artificial cavity; nest is lined with grass, bark strips and feathers; may hang a shed

ID: bright yellow belly and undertail coverts; gray throat and upper breast; reddish brown tail; peaked, "crested" head; dark olive brown upperparts; heavy black bill.

snakeskin or plastic wrap from the entrance hole; female incubates 5 creamy white to pale buff eggs, marked with lavender, olive and brown, for 13–15 days.

Feeding: often in the upper branches of deciduous trees, where it flycatches for insects; may also glean caterpillars and occasionally fruit.

Voice: loud, whistled *wheep!* and a rolling *prrrrreet!*

Similar Species: *Yellow-bellied Flycatcher* (p. 193): much smaller; yellow throat; lacks reddish brown tail and large, all-black bill. *Western Kingbird* (p. 200): all-gray head, neck and breast; lacks head crest; darker tail with white outer margins.

Selected Sites: deciduous or mixed woodland openings.

WESTERN KINGBIRD

Tyrannus verticalis

More typical of the prairies, the Western Kingbird is a rare visitor to Michigan. Very few are reported here each year, most often in May and September in popular birding areas, such as Whitefish Point and Keweenaw Peninsula. • Western Kingbirds can be observed surveying for prey from fence posts, power lines or utility poles. When a kingbird spots an insect, it may chase it for up to 50 feet before a capture is made. • Once you have witnessed the kingbird's brave attacks against much larger birds, such as crows and hawks, it is easy to understand why this brawler was awarded the name "kingbird." Its scientific name *verticalis* refers to the bird's hidden, red crown patch, which is flared during courtship displays and while in combat with rivals. This red patch, however, is not a good identification mark because it is rarely visible outside the breeding season. • The tumbling, aerial courtship display of the Western Kingbird is a good indication that this bird might be breeding. The male twists and turns as he rises to heights of 65 feet above the ground, then he stalls as he tumbles, flips and twists his way back to earth. • On several occasions, Western Kingbirds have hybridized with Eastern Kingbirds.

ID: gray head and breast; yellow belly and undertail coverts; black tail; white edge on outer tail feathers; white "chin"; black bill; ashy gray upperparts; faint, dark gray "mask"; thin, orange red crown (rarely seen).

Size: *L* 8–9 in; *W* 15½ in.

Status: very rare migrant and irregular breeder from May to September; mainly in Upper Peninsula and western Lower Peninsula.

Habitat: open scrubland areas with scattered patches of brush or hedgerows; along the edges of open fields.

Nesting: in a deciduous tree near the trunk; bulky cup nest of grass, weeds and twigs is lined with fur, plant down and feathers; female incubates 3–5 whitish, heavily blotched eggs for 18–19 days.

Feeding: flycatches aerial insects, including bees, wasps, butterflies, moths, grasshoppers and flies; occasionally eats berries.

Voice: chatty, twittering *whit-ker-whit;* also a short *kit* or extended *kit-kit-keetle-dot.*

Similar Species: *Eastern Kingbird* (p. 201): black upperparts; white underparts; white-tipped tail. *Great Crested Flycatcher* (p. 199): slightly crested head; brownish upperparts; reddish brown tail; yellowish wing bars; lacks white edges to outer tail feathers.

Selected Sites: Whitefish Point; Keweenaw Peninsula; Muskegon SP; Kalamazoo area.

EASTERN KINGBIRD

Tyrannus tyrannus

When you think of a tyrant, images of an oppressive dictator or a large carnivorous dinosaur are much more likely to come to mind than images of a little bird. True as that might be, no one familiar with the pugnacity of the Eastern Kingbird is likely to refute its scientific name, *Tyrannus tyrannus*. This bird is a brawler, and it will fearlessly attack crows, hawks and even humans that pass through its territory. Intruders are often vigorously pursued, pecked and plucked for some distance until the kingbird is satisfied that there is no further threat. In contrast, its butterfly-like courtship flight, which is characterized by short, quivering wingbeats, reveals a gentler side of this bird. • Eastern Kingbirds are common and widespread in Michigan, so during a drive in the country it is likely you will spot at least one of these birds sitting on a fenceline or utility wire along a roadside. • Eastern Kingbirds rarely walk or hop on the ground—they prefer to fly, even for very short distances.

ID: dark gray to black upperparts; white underparts; white-tipped tail; black bill; small head crest; thin orange red crown (rarely seen); no eye ring; black legs.

Size: *L* 8½ in; *W* 15 in.

Status: common migrant and breeder from May to early September.

Habitat: rural fields with scattered trees or hedgerows, clearings in fragmented forests, open roadsides, burned areas and near human settlements.

Nesting: on a horizontal tree or shrub limb; also on a standing stump or an upturned tree root; pair builds a cup nest of weeds, twigs and grass and lines it with root fibers, fine grass and fur; female incubates 3–4 darkly blotched, white to pinkish white eggs for 14–18 days.

Feeding: flycatches aerial insects; infrequently eats berries.

Voice: call is a quick, loud, chattering *kit-kit-kitter-kitter;* also a buzzy *dzee-dzee-dzee.*

Similar Species: *Tree Swallow* (p. 216): iridescent, dark blue back; lacks white-tipped tail; more streamlined body; smaller bill. *Olive-sided Flycatcher* (p. 191): 2 white tufts border rump; lacks white-tipped tail and all-white underparts. *Eastern Wood-Pewee* (p. 192): smaller; bicolored bill; lacks white-tipped tail and all-white underparts.

Selected Sites: open rural areas.

LOGGERHEAD SHRIKE

Lanius ludovicianus

A shrike resembles a Northern Mockingbird in body shape and color, but the Loggerhead's method of hunting is very different. This predatory songbird has very acute vision, and it often perches atop trees and on wires to scan for small prey, which is caught in fast, direct flight or a swooping dive. • Males display their hunting prowess by impaling prey on thorns or barbed wire. This behavior may also serve as a means of storing excess food during times of plenty. In spring, you may see a variety of skewered creatures baking in the sun—reminiscent of the way some people used to display the carcasses of hawks, foxes and coyotes on farm fences. • Loggerhead Shrike populations have severely declined in Michigan and in many other parts of its North American range, earning this bird endangered species status. Habitat destruction is thought to be the main reason for the population decline. Another cause of Loggerhead mortality is encounters with motor vehicles: on their wintering grounds in the southern U.S., shrikes often become traffic fatalities when they fly low across roads to prey on insects attracted to the warm pavement.

ID: black tail and wings; gray crown and back; white underparts; black "mask" extends above hooked bill onto forehead. *In flight:* white wing patches; white-edged tail. *Juvenile:* brownish gray, barred upperparts.
Size: *L* 9 in; *W* 12 in.
Status: endangered; very rare migrant and breeder from March to September.
Habitat: grazed pastures and marginal and abandoned farmlands with scattered hawthorn shrubs, fence posts, barbed wire and nearby wetlands.
Nesting: low in the crotch of a shrub or small tree; thorny hawthorn shrubs are often preferred; bulky cup nest of twigs and grass is lined with animal hair, feathers, plant down and rootlets; female incubates 5–6 pale buff to grayish white eggs, with dark spots concentrated at the larger end, for 15–17 days.
Feeding: swoops down on prey from a perch or attacks in pursuit; takes mostly large insects; regularly eats small birds, rodents and shrews; also eats carrion, small snakes and amphibians.
Voice: *Male:* high-pitched, hiccupy *bird-ee bird-ee* in summer; infrequently a harsh *shack-shack* year-round.
Similar Species: *Northern Shrike* (p. 203): winter visitor; larger; fine barring on sides and breast; black "mask" does not extend above hooked bill; immature has unbarred, light brown upperparts and strongly, but finely, barred underparts. *Northern Mockingbird* (p. 245): slim bill; no "mask"; slimmer overall.
Selected Sites: Allegan SGA.

NORTHERN SHRIKE

Lanius excubitor

L ike many of our raptors, Northern Shrikes appear in our region each winter in unpredictable and highly variable numbers. During their winter visits, they are typically seen perched like hawks on exposed treetops, from which they survey open and semi-open hunting grounds. Winter feeding stations also tempt many shrikes to test their hunting skills on the feeding birds. • The adult Northern Shrike looks somewhat like a gray robin with the bill of a small hawk, and it specializes in catching and killing small birds and rodents. When this bird strikes a large target, it relies on its sharp, hooked beak to dispatch its quarry, although it may use its feet to help. Shrikes are the world's only true carnivorous songbirds and the greatest diversity of shrikes occurs in Africa and Eurasia. • The Northern Shrike's habit of impaling its kills on thorns and barbs has earned it the name "Butcher Bird," and in Europe, "Nine-Killer." *Lanius* is Latin for "butcher," and *excubitor* is Latin for "watchman" or "sentinel"—"watchful butcher" is an appropriate description of the Northern Shrike's foraging behavior.

ID: black tail and wings; pale gray upperparts; finely barred, light underparts; black "mask" does not extend above hooked bill. *In flight:* white wing patches; white-edged tail. *Immature:* faint "mask"; light brown upperparts; brown barring on underparts.

Size: *L* 10 in; *W* 14½ in.

Status: uncommon and erratic winter resident from October to April.

Habitat: open country, including fields, shrubby areas, forest clearings and roadsides.

Nesting: does not nest in Michigan.

Feeding: swoops down on prey from a perch or chases prey through the air; regularly eats small birds, shrews, rodents and large insects; may also take snakes and frogs; prey may be impaled on a thorn or barb for later consumption.

Voice: usually silent; infrequently gives a long grating laugh: *raa-raa-raa-raa.*

Similar Species: *Loggerhead Shrike* (p. 202): generally absent in winter; black "mask" extends above bill onto forehead; lacks barring on underparts; juvenile has barred underparts, crown and back. *Northern Mockingbird* (p. 245): slim bill; no "mask"; slimmer overall; paler wings and tail.

Selected Sites: Whitefish Point; Seney NWR; Jordan R. Valley; Muskegon Wastewater System; Chippewa Nature Center; Allegan SGA; Sleepy Hollow SP.

WHITE-EYED VIREO

Vireo griseus

Proclaiming its spring arrival, the White-eyed Vireo sings *chick-ticha-wheeyou, chick-ticha-wheeyou-chick* among vibrant early spring blossoms in local forests. Like most vireos, the White-eyed Vireo can be a challenge to spot as it sneaks through dense tangles of branches and foliage in search of insects. • Even more secretive than the bird itself is the location of its precious nest. Intricately woven from grass, twigs, bark, lichen, moss, plant down, leaves and the fibrous paper from a wasp nest, the nest of the White-eyed Vireo is hung between the forking branches of a tree or shrub. • White-eyed Vireos are renowned for their complex vocalizations. A single bird may have a repertoire of a dozen or more songs. This vireo is also an excellent vocal mimic and may incorporate the calls of other bird species in its own songs! • The White-eyed Vireo is a relatively new addition to Michigan's avifauna—its first confirmed breeding record here was reported in 1960.

ID: yellow "spectacles"; olive gray upperparts; white underparts with yellow sides and flanks; 2 whitish wing bars; dark wings and tail; pale eyes.

Size: *L* 5 in; *W* 7½ in.

Status: migrant and very rare breeder from April to October in extreme southern Lower Peninsula.

Habitat: dense, shrubby undergrowth and thickets in open, swampy, deciduous woodlands, overgrown fields, young second-growth woodlands, woodland clearings and along woodlot edges.

Nesting: in a deciduous shrub or small tree; cup nest hangs from a horizontal fork; pair incubates 4 lightly speckled, white eggs for 13–15 days; both adults feed the young.

Feeding: gleans insects from branches and foliage during very active foraging; often hovers while gleaning.

Voice: loud, snappy, 3–9-note song, usually beginning and ending with "chick": *chick-ticha-wheeyou, chick-ticha-wheeyou-chick!*

Similar Species: *Pine Warbler* (p. 266) and *Yellow-throated Vireo* (p. 205): yellow throat. *Blue-headed Vireo* (p. 206): white "spectacles"; dark eyes; yellow highlights on wings and tail.

Selected Sites: Lost Nation SGA; Hidden Lake Gardens; Grand Mere SP; Sarett Nature Center.

YELLOW-THROATED VIREO
Vireo flavifrons

The Yellow-throated Vireo, usually found in mature deciduous woodlands with little or no understory, particularly likes tall oaks and maples. Like its treetop neighbor the Cerulean Warbler, the Yellow-throated Vireo forages high above the forest floor, making it a difficult bird to observe. • An unmated male will sing tirelessly as he searches for nest sites, often placing a few pieces of nest material in several locations. When a female appears, the male dazzles her with his displays and leads her on a tour of potential nesting sites within his large territory. If a bond is established, they will mate and build an intricately woven, hanging nest in the forking branches of a deciduous tree. The male is a devoted helper, assisting the female to build the nest, incubate the eggs and rear the young. • The Yellow-throat is North America's most colorful vireo. It is the only vireo with a bright yellow throat and breast and white belly. The scientific name *flavifrons* means "yellow front."

ID: bright yellow "spectacles," "chin," throat and breast; olive upperparts, except for gray rump and dark wings and tail; 2 white wing bars; white belly and undertail coverts; bluish gray legs.

Size: *L* 5½ in; *W* 9½ in.

Status: uncommon migrant and breeder from May to mid-October in Lower Peninsula and southwestern Upper Peninsula.

Habitat: mature deciduous woodlands with minimal understory.

Nesting: pair builds a hanging cup nest in the fork of a horizontal, deciduous tree branch; pair incubates 4 creamy white to pinkish eggs, with dark spots toward the larger end, for 14–15 days; each parent takes on guardianship of half the fledged young.

Feeding: forages by inspecting branches and foliage in the upper canopy; eats mostly insects, but also feeds on seasonally available berries.

Voice: song is a slowly repeated series of hoarse phrases with long pauses in between: *ahweeo, eeoway, away;* calls include a throaty *heh heh heh.*

Similar Species: *Pine Warbler* (p. 266): olive yellow rump; thinner bill; faint, darkish streaking along sides; yellow belly; faint "spectacles." *White-eyed Vireo* (p. 204): white "chin" and throat; grayer head and back; white eyes. *Blue-headed Vireo* (p. 206): white "spectacles" and throat; yellow highlights on wings and tail.

Selected Sites: Ottawa Recreation Area; Allegan SGA; Yankee Springs SRA; Kalamazoo Nature Center; Fort Custer SRA.

BLUE-HEADED VIREO
Vireo solitarius

From the canopies of shady woodlands, the purposeful, liquid notes of the Blue-headed Vireo penetrate the dense foliage. This vireo prefers different habitat than many of its relatives—it is the only vireo to commonly occupy coniferous forests. • During courtship, male Blue-headed Vireos fluff out their yellowish flanks and bob ceremoniously to their prospective mates. When mating is complete and the eggs are in the nest, the parents become extremely quiet. Once the young hatch, however, Blue-headed parents will readily scold an intruder long before it gets close to the nest. Even so, Brown-headed Cowbirds manage to find temporarily vacated vireo nests in which to lay their eggs. As human development continues to fragment our forests, cowbirds pose an increasing threat to their Blue-headed hosts. • The distinctive "spectacles" that frame this bird's eyes provide a good field mark. They are among the boldest of the eye rings seen on our songbirds. • Until 1997, the now newly named Blue-headed, Cassin's *(V. cassinii)* and Plumbeous *(V. plumbeus)* vireos were lumped together as one species, the Solitary Vireo.

ID: white "spectacles"; blue gray head; 2 white wing bars; olive green upperparts; white underparts; yellow sides and flanks; yellow highlights on dark wings and tail; stout bill; dark legs.
Size: *L* 5–6 in; *W* 9½ in.
Status: fairly common migrant in May and from early September to mid-October; uncommon breeder from May to September in Upper Peninsula and northern and southwestern Lower Peninsula.
Habitat: remote, mixed coniferous-deciduous forests; also pure coniferous forests and pine plantations.
Nesting: in a horizontal fork in a coniferous tree or tall shrub; hanging, basketlike cup nest is made of grass, roots, plant down, spider silk and cocoons; pair incubates 3–5 whitish eggs, lightly spotted with black and brown, for 12–14 days.
Feeding: gleans branches for insects; frequently hovers to pluck insects from vegetation.
Voice: *Male:* slow, purposeful, slurred, robinlike notes with moderate pauses in between: *chu-wee, taweeto, toowip, cheerio, teeyay;* churr call.
Similar Species: *White-eyed Vireo* (p. 204): yellow "spectacles"; light-colored eyes. *Yellow-throated Vireo* (p. 205): yellow "spectacles" and throat.
Selected Sites: Whitefish Point; Ottawa National Forest; Van Riper SP; Colonial Point Forest; Allegan SGA; Kalamazoo Nature Center.

WARBLING VIREO
Vireo gilvus

The charming Warbling Vireo is a common summer resident of the sparsely wooded parts of Michigan. By early May, its wondrous voice fills many local parks and backyards. Because this vireo often settles close to urban areas, its bubbly, warbling songs should be familiar to most people. • The Warbling Vireo lacks splashy field marks and is only readily observed when it moves from one leaf-hidden stage to another. Searching treetops for this generally inconspicuous vireo may literally be a "pain in the neck," but the satisfaction of visually confirming its identity is exceptionally rewarding. • The hanging nests of vireos are usually much harder to find than the birds themselves. In winter, however, nests are revealed as they swing precariously from bare deciduous branches. • During their brief stay in our region, Warbling Vireos prefer old maples and cottonwoods as foraging and nesting sites.

breeding

ID: partial, dark eye line borders white "eyebrow"; no wing bars; olive gray upperparts; greenish flanks; white to pale gray underparts; gray crown; bluish gray legs.
Size: *L* 5–5½ in; *W* 8½ in.
Status: common migrant and breeder from May to early September.
Habitat: open deciduous woodlands; parks and gardens with deciduous trees.
Nesting: in a horizontal fork in a deciduous tree or shrub; hanging, basketlike cup nest is made of grass, roots, plant down, spider silk and a few feathers; pair incubates 4 darkly speckled, white eggs for 12–14 days.
Feeding: gleans foliage for insects; occasionally hovers to glean insects from vegetation.
Voice: *Male:* long, musical warble of slurred whistles.
Similar Species: *Philadelphia Vireo* (p. 208): yellow breast, sides and flanks; full, dark eye line borders white "eyebrow." *Red-eyed Vireo* (p. 209): black eye line extends to bill; blue gray crown; red eyes. *Tennessee Warbler* (p. 253): blue gray "cap" and nape; olive green back; slimmer bill. *Orange-crowned Warbler* (p. 254): yellow overall; slimmer bill.
Selected Sites: riparian woods, open woodland edges and well-wooded parks.

PHILADELPHIA VIREO

Vireo philadelphicus

Although many similar-looking birds sound quite different, the Philadelphia Vireo and Red-eyed Vireo are two species that sound very similar but are easy to tell apart once you locate them with your binoculars. However, managing to track down bluish green vireos among the rich green foliage where they prefer to forage is never easy. The fact that most forest songbirds are initially identified by voice means that the Philadelphia Vireo is often overlooked because its song is almost identical to that of the more abundant Red-eyed Vireo. • The Philadelphia Vireo nests in mixed boreal forests where it fills a niche left unoccupied by the strictly deciduous-dwelling Warbling Vireo. • This bird bears the name of the city in which the first scientific specimen of this species was collected. Philadelphia was the center of America's budding scientific community in the early 1800s, and much of the study of birds and other natural sciences originated in Pennsylvania.

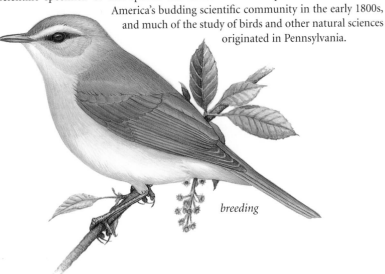

breeding

ID: gray "cap"; full, dark eye line borders bold, white "eyebrow"; dark olive green upperparts; pale yellow breast, sides and flanks; white belly (underparts may be completely yellow in fall); robust bill; pale eyes.

Size: *L* 4½–5 in; *W* 8 in.

Status: uncommon migrant in latter half of May and from late August to September; uncommon breeder from May to September in Upper Peninsula.

Habitat: woodlands with aspen and alder.

Nesting: high in a deciduous tree or low in a shrub; basketlike cup nest hangs from a horizontal fork; nest is made of grass, roots, plant down and spider silk; pair incubates 4 white eggs, darkly spotted on the larger end, for about 14 days.

Feeding: gleans vegetation for insects; frequently hovers to glean food from foliage.

Voice: *Male:* song is similar to that of the Red-eyed Vireo, but is usually slower, slightly higher pitched and not as variable: *Look-up way-up tree-top see-me.*

Similar Species: *Red-eyed Vireo* (p. 209): black-bordered, blue gray "cap"; red eyes; lacks yellow breast; song is very similar. *Warbling Vireo* (p. 207): partial, dark eye line (mostly behind eye); lacks yellow breast. *Tennessee Warbler* (p. 253): blue gray "cap" and nape; olive green back; slimmer bill; lacks yellow breast.

Selected Sites: Whitefish Point; Hiawatha National Forest; Ottawa National Forest; Porcupine Mountains Wilderness SP.

RED-EYED VIREO
Vireo olivaceus

The Red-eyed Vireo is the undisputed champion of vocal endurance in our region. In spring and early summer, males sing continuously through the day, carrying on long after most songbirds have curtailed their courtship melodies, usually five or six hours after sunrise. One particularly vigorous Red-eyed Vireo male holds the record for most songs delivered in a single day: approximately 22,000! • The Red-eyed Vireo adopts a particular stance when it hops up and along branches. It tends to be more hunched over than other songbirds and hops with its body diagonal to the direction of travel. • There is no firm agreement about the reason for this vireo's red eye color. Red eyes are very unusual among songbirds and tend to be more prevalent in non-passerines, such as accipiters, grebes and some herons. • This vireo is the most common and widespread vireo in Michigan, and its adaptive nature has enabled it to become part of many of our communities. Red-eyed Vireos sound a lot like American Robins, and beginning birders are often delighted to discover these nifty birds hiding behind a familiar song.

breeding

ID: dark eye line; white "eyebrow"; black-bordered, blue gray crown; olive "cheek"; olive green upper parts; white to pale gray underparts; may have yellow wash on sides, flanks and undertail coverts, especially in fall; no wing bars; red eyes (seen only at close range).
Size: *L* 6 in; *W* 10 in.
Status: very common migrant and breeder from early May to early October.
Habitat: deciduous woodlands with a shrubby understory.
Nesting: in a horizontal fork in a deciduous tree or shrub; hanging, basketlike cup nest is made of grass, roots, spider silk and cocoons; female incubates 4 white eggs,

darkly spotted at the larger end, for 11–14 days.
Feeding: gleans foliage for insects, especially caterpillars; often hovers; also eats berries.
Voice: call is a short, scolding *neeah. Male:* song is a continuous, variable, robinlike run of quick, short phrases with distinct pauses in between: *Look-up, way-up, tree-top, see-me, here-I-am!*
Similar Species: *Philadelphia Vireo* (p. 208): yellow breast; lacks black border to blue gray "cap"; song is very similar but slightly higher pitched. *Warbling Vireo* (p. 207): dusky eye line does not extend to bill; lacks black border on gray "cap." *Tennessee Warbler* (p. 253): blue gray "cap" and nape; olive green back; slimmer bill.
Selected Sites: deciduous woodlands or tree groves.

GRAY JAY

Perisoreus canadensis

Few other birds in Michigan rival the mischievous Gray Jay for curiosity and boldness. Attracted by any foreign sound or potential feeding opportunity, small family groups glide gently and unexpectedly out of spruce, pine and fir stands. Campgrounds and picnic areas are the most common places to find these mooching marauders. • Gray Jays lay their eggs and begin incubation as early as late February. Their nests are well insulated to conserve heat, and getting an early start on nesting means that young jays will learn how to forage efficiently and store food before the next cold season approaches. • In preparation for the winter months, Gray Jays often store food. Their specialized salivary glands coat the food with a sticky mucus that helps to preserve it. • Pairs have strong bonds, and after absences they seek each other out and touch or nibble bills. • This common bird has some interesting alternate names: "Whiskey Jack" is derived from the Algonquin name for this bird, *wis-kat-jon*; others affectionately call this bird "Camp Robber."

ID: fluffy, pale gray plumage; fairly long tail; white forehead, "cheek," throat and undertail coverts; dark gray nape and upperparts; light gray breast and belly; dark bill.
Immature: dark sooty gray overall; pale bill with dark tip.
Size: *L* 11–13 in; *W* 18 in.
Status: common to abundant year-round resident in Upper Peninsula.
Habitat: dense and open coniferous and mixed forests, bogs and fens; also picnic sites and campgrounds.
Nesting: on a branch in a coniferous tree; bulky, well-insulated nest is made of plant fibers, roots, moss, twigs, feathers and fur; female incubates 3–4 pale gray to greenish eggs, marked with brown, greenish or reddish dots, for 17–22 days.
Feeding: searches the ground and vegetation for insects, fruit, seeds, fungi, bird eggs and nestlings, carrion and berries; stores food items at scattered cache sites.
Voice: complex vocal repertoire includes a soft, whistled *quee-oo*, a chuckled *cla-cla-cla* and a *churr*; also imitates other birds.
Similar Species: *Northern Shrike* (p. 203) and *Loggerhead Shrike* (p. 202): black "mask"; black-and-white wings and tail; hooked bill. *Northern Mockingbird* (p. 245): darker wings and tail; white patch on wings; white outer tail feathers; longer, slimmer bill.
Selected Sites: Whitefish Point; Hiawatha National Forest; Ottawa National Forest; Porcupine Mountains Wilderness SP; Seney NWR; Sylvania Recreation Area.

BLUE JAY

Cyanocitta cristata

The large trees and bushy ornamental shrubs of our suburban neighborhoods and rural communities are perfect habitat for the adaptable Blue Jay. Common wherever there are fruit-bearing plants and backyard feeding stations that are maintained with a generous supply of sunflower seeds and peanuts, this jay is one of the most recognizable songbirds. Blue Jays can appear a bit "piggish" at the feeder but they are often only storing the food in caches strategically placed around the neighborhood. • The Blue Jay embodies all the admirable traits and aggressive qualities of the corvid family, which also includes the magpie, crow and raven. Beautiful, resourceful and vocally diverse, the Blue Jay occasionally raids nests and bullies other feeder occupants. • Whether on its own or gathered in a mob, the Blue Jay will rarely hesitate to drive away smaller birds, squirrels or even cats when threatened. It seems there is no predator, not even the Great Horned Owl, that is too formidable for this bird to cajole or harass.

ID: blue crest; black "necklace"; black eyeline; blue upperparts; white underparts; white bar and flecking on wings; dark bars and white corners on blue tail; black bill.

Size: *L* 11–12½ in; *W* 16 in.

Status: common to abundant migrant and breeder from March to November; uncommon to fairly common winter visitor from November to March.

Habitat: mixed deciduous forests, agricultural areas, scrubby fields and townsites.

Nesting: in the crotch of a tree or tall shrub; pair builds a bulky stick nest and incubates 4–5 greenish, buff or pale blue eggs, spotted with gray and brown, for 16–18 days.

Feeding: forages on the ground and among vegetation for nuts, berries, eggs, nestlings and birdseed; also eats insects and carrion.

Voice: noisy, screaming *jay-jay-jay;* nasal *queedle queedle queedle-queedle* sounds a little like a muted trumpet; often imitates sounds.

Similar Species: none.

Selected Sites: cities and towns, especially at bird feeders.

AMERICAN CROW
Corvus brachyrhynchos

American Crows are wary and intelligent birds that have flourished despite considerable human effort, over many generations, to reduce their numbers. These birds are ecological generalists, and much of their strength lies in their ability to adapt to a variety of habitats. • The American Crow is a common bird throughout much of Michigan in summer and a common winter resident in the southern Lower Peninsula. In fall, crows group together in flocks numbering in the hundreds or thousands. In some places, many thousands of crows may roost together on any given winter night. • Aggregations of crows are known as "murders." Crows are impressive mimics, able to whine like a dog, cry like a child, squawk like a hen, and laugh like a human. Some crows in captivity are able to repeat simple spoken words. • The American Crow's cumbersome-sounding scientific name *Corvus brachyrhynchos* is Latin for "raven with the small nose."

ID: all-black body; square-shaped tail; black bill and legs; slim, sleek head and throat.
Size: *L* 17–21 in; *W* 3 ft.
Status: abundant year-round resident; less numerous in northern Michigan in winter.
Habitat: urban areas, agricultural fields and other open areas with scattered woodlands; also among clearings, marshes, lakes and rivers in densely forested areas.
Nesting: in a coniferous or deciduous tree or on a utility pole; large stick-and-branch nest is lined with fur and soft plant materials; female incubates 4–6 gray green to blue green eggs, blotched with brown and gray, for about 18 days.
Feeding: very opportunistic; feeds on carrion, small vertebrates, other birds' eggs and nestlings, berries, seeds, invertebrates and human food waste; also visits bird feeders.
Voice: distinctive, far-carrying, repetitive *caw-caw-caw*.
Similar Species: *Common Raven* (p. 213): larger; wedge-shaped tail; shaggy throat; heavier bill.
Selected Sites: cities and towns; agricultural areas and forest clearings.

COMMON RAVEN

Corvus corax

Whether stealing food from a flock of gulls, harassing a soaring hawk in midair, dining from a roadside carcass or confidently strutting among campers at a park, the Common Raven is worthy of its reputation as a bold and clever bird. Glorified in native cultures across the Northern Hemisphere as a "trickster," the Common Raven does not act by instinct alone. From its complex vocalizations to its occasional playful bouts of sliding down a snowbank, this raucous bird exhibits behaviors that many people once thought of as exclusively human. • Ravens maintain loyal, lifelong pair bonds, and pairs endure everything from food scarcity and harsh weather to the raising of young. • Few birds occupy as large a natural range as the Common Raven. Distributed throughout the Northern Hemisphere, it is found along coastlines, in deserts, on mountaintops and even on the arctic tundra. Ravens once inhabited every corner of our region, but poisoning, trapping and shooting campaigns led to great declines in their population. • The Common Raven is the largest passerine, or perching bird.

ID: all-black plumage; heavy, black bill; wedge-shaped tail; shaggy throat; rounded wings.
Size: *L* 17–21 in; *W* 4 ft.
Status: uncommon to common year-round resident in the northern two thirds of the state; very rare winter resident from October to May in the south.
Habitat: coniferous and mixed forests and woodlands; also townsites, campgrounds and landfills.
Nesting: on a ledge, bluff or utility pole or in a tall coniferous tree; large stick-and-branch nest is lined with fur and soft plant materials; female incubates 4–6 greenish eggs, blotched with brown or olive, for 18–21 days.
Feeding: very opportunistic; some birds forage along roadways; feeds on carrion, small vertebrates, other birds' eggs and nestlings, berries, invertebrates and human food waste.
Voice: deep, guttural, far-carrying, repetitive *craww-craww* or *quork quork;* also many other vocalizations.
Similar Species: *American Crow* (p. 212): smaller; square-shaped tail; slim throat; slimmer bill; call is a higher-pitched *caw-caw-caw.*
Selected Sites: forests, woodlands and landfills in Upper Peninsula and northern half of Lower Peninsula.

HORNED LARK

Eremophila alpestris

The tinkling sounds of Horned Larks flying over pastures and fields are a sure sign that another spring has arrived. Horned Larks are among the earliest arrivals in our region, settling on the fields long before the snows are gone. • The male Horned Lark performs an elaborate song-flight courtship display. Flying and gliding in circles as high up as 800 feet, the male issues his sweet, tinkling song before he closes his wings and plummets in a dramatic, high-speed dive that he aborts at the last second to avoid hitting the ground. • These open-country inhabitants are most common in spring and fall migration and in early winter as they congregate in flocks on farm fields, beaches and airfields, often in the company of Snow Buntings and Lapland Longspurs. Horned Larks are commonly found along the shoulders of gravel roads, where they search for seeds. These birds are easy to see but often tough to identify because they fly off into the adjacent fields at the approach of any vehicle.

ID: *Male:* small black "horns" (rarely raised); black line under eye extends from bill to "cheek"; light yellow to white face; dull brown upperparts; black breast band; dark tail with white outer tail feathers; pale throat. *Female:* less distinctively patterned; duller plumage overall.
Size: *L* 7 in; *W* 12 in.
Status: common migrant and breeder from February to November in Lower Peninsula; scarce in Upper Peninsula.
Habitat: *Breeding:* open areas, including pastures, croplands, sparsely vegetated fields, weedy meadows and airfields. *In migration* and *winter:* croplands, fields and roadside ditches.

Nesting: on the ground; in a shallow scrape lined with grass, plant fibers and roots; female chooses the nest site and incubates 3–4 pale gray to greenish white eggs, blotched and spotted with brown, for 10–12 days.
Feeding: gleans the ground for seeds; feeds insects to its young during the breeding season.
Voice: call is a tinkling *tsee-titi* or *zoot;* flight song is a long series of tinkling, twittered whistles.
Similar Species: *Sparrows* (pp. 291–306), *Lapland Longspur* (p. 308) and *American Pipit* (p. 248): all lack distinctive facial pattern, "horns" and solid black breast band.
Selected Sites: roadsides, fields and pastures throughout Lower Peninsula and south-central Upper Peninsula.

PURPLE MARTIN

Progne subis

Purple Martins once nested in natural tree hollows and cliff crevices, but with today's modern martin "condo" complexes, these birds have all but abandoned natural nest sites. To be successful in attracting these large swallows to your backyard, make the complex with cavity openings that are the right size for Purple Martins and place the martin condo high on a pole in a large, open area, preferably near water. Remove any aggressive House Sparrows and European Starlings that may lay claim to the luxurious digs and drive away the rightful owners. The condo must be cleaned out and closed up each winter. If all goes well, a Purple Martin colony will return to your martin complex each spring. The result will be an endlessly entertaining summer spectacle as the martin adults spiral around the house in pursuit of flying insects, and the young birds perch clumsily at the opening of their apartment cavity. • The scientific name *Progne* refers to Procne, the daughter of the king of Athens who, according to Greek mythology, was transformed into a swallow.

ID: glossy, dark blue body; slightly forked tail; pointed wings; small bill. *Male:* dark underparts. *Female:* sooty gray underparts. **Size:** *L* 7–8 in; *W* 18 in.

Status: common migrant and local breeder from April to September.
Habitat: semi-open areas, often near water.
Nesting: communal; usually in a human-made, apartment-style birdhouse; also in a hollowed-out gourd; rarely in a tree cavity or cliff crevice; nest materials include feathers, grass, mud and vegetation; female incubates 4–5 white eggs for 15–18 days.

Feeding: mostly while in flight; usually eats flies, ants, bugs, dragonflies and mosquitoes; may also walk on the ground, taking insects and rarely berries.
Voice: rich, fluty, robinlike *pew-pew,* often heard in flight.
Similar Species: *European Starling* (p. 247): longer bill (yellow in summer); lacks forked tail. *Barn Swallow* (p. 220): deeply forked tail; buff orange to reddish brown throat; whitish to cinnamon underparts. *Tree Swallow* (p. 216): white underparts.
Selected Sites: martin houses in urban, rural and cottage-country backyards, usually near water; southern Lower Peninsula.

TREE SWALLOW

Tachycineta bicolor

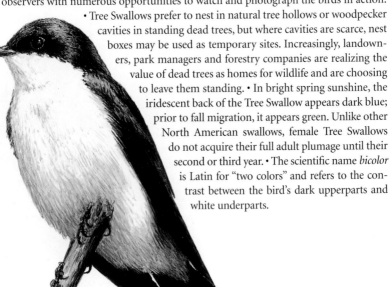

Tree Swallows, our most common summer swallows, are often seen perched beside their fence-post nest boxes. When conditions are favorable, these busy birds are known to return to their young 10 to 20 times per hour, providing observers with numerous opportunities to watch and photograph the birds in action. • Tree Swallows prefer to nest in natural tree hollows or woodpecker cavities in standing dead trees, but where cavities are scarce, nest boxes may be used as temporary sites. Increasingly, landowners, park managers and forestry companies are realizing the value of dead trees as homes for wildlife and are choosing to leave them standing. • In bright spring sunshine, the iridescent back of the Tree Swallow appears dark blue; prior to fall migration, it appears green. Unlike other North American swallows, female Tree Swallows do not acquire their full adult plumage until their second or third year. • The scientific name *bicolor* is Latin for "two colors" and refers to the contrast between the bird's dark upperparts and white underparts.

ID: iridescent, dark blue or green head and upperparts; white underparts; no white on "cheek"; dark rump; small bill; long, pointed wings; shallowly forked tail. *Female:* slightly duller. *Immature:* brown above; white below.
Size: *L* 5½ in; *W* 14½ in.
Status: common migrant and breeder from late March to mid-October.
Habitat: open areas, such as beaver ponds, marshes, lakeshores, field fencelines, townsites and open woodlands.
Nesting: in a tree cavity or nest box lined with weeds, grass and feathers; female incubates 4–6 white eggs for up to 19 days.

Feeding: catches flies, midges, mosquitoes, beetles and ants on the wing; also takes stoneflies, mayflies and caddisflies over water; may eat some berries and seeds.
Voice: alarm call is a metallic, buzzy *klweet. Male:* song is a liquid, chattering twitter.
Similar Species: *Purple Martin* (p. 215): female has sooty gray underparts; male is dark blue overall. *Eastern Kingbird* (p. 201): larger; white-tipped tail; longer bill; dark gray to blackish upperparts. *Bank Swallow* (p. 218) and *Northern Rough-winged Swallow* (p. 217): brown upperparts. *Barn Swallow* (p. 220): buff orange to reddish brown throat; deeply forked tail.
Selected Sites: agricultural areas, marshes, beaver ponds and lakeshores, especially in areas with nest boxes.

NORTHERN ROUGH-WINGED SWALLOW

Stelgidopteryx serripennis

The inconspicuous Northern Rough-winged Swallow typically nests in sandy banks along rivers and streams, enjoying its own private piece of waterfront. This swallow is usually seen in single pairs, but it doesn't mind joining a crowd, often gulping down insects in the company of other swallow species. Once in a while, a pair may nest among a large colony of Bank Swallows. In the wheeling flocks of feeding birds, the Northern Rough-winged Swallow is often completely overlooked among its similar-looking cousins. The Rough-wing is most likely to be feeding over water, picking off insects on or near the water's surface. • Unlike other Michigan swallows, male Northern Rough-wings have curved barbs along the outer edge of their primary wing feathers. The purpose of this saw-toothed edge remains a mystery, but it may be used to produce sound during courtship displays. The ornithologist who initially named this bird must have been very impressed with its wings: *Stelgidopteryx* means "scraper wing" and *serripennis* means "saw feather."

ID: brown upperparts; light, brownish gray underparts; small bill; dark "cheek"; pale throat; dark rump. *In flight:* long, pointed wings; notched tail.

Size: *L* 5½ in; *W* 14 in.

Status: common migrant and breeder from April to September.

Habitat: open and semi-open areas, including fields and open woodlands, usually near water; also gravel pits.

Nesting: occasionally in small colonies; pair excavates a long burrow in a steep, earthen bank; the end of the burrow is lined with leaves and dry grass; sometimes reuses a kingfisher burrow, rodent burrow or other land crevice; mostly the female incubates 4–8 white eggs for 12–16 days.

Feeding: catches flying insects on the wing; occasionally eats insects from the ground; drinks while flying.

Voice: generally quiet; occasionally a quick, short, squeaky *brrrtt*.

Similar Species: *Bank Swallow* (p. 218): dark breast band. *Tree Swallow* (p. 216): dark, iridescent bluish to greenish upperparts; clean white underparts. *Cliff Swallow* (p. 219): brown-and-blue upperparts; buff forehead and rump patch.

Selected Sites: rivers, lakes, marshes and open fields near water; Great Lakes shorelines.

BANK SWALLOW

Riparia riparia

A colony of Bank Swallows can be a constant flurry of activity as eager parents pop in and out of their earthen burrows with mouthfuls of insects for their insatiable young. The parents can quickly distinguish their own nestlings' demanding squeaks among the thousands of cries for food in the colony's bankside chambers. All this activity tends to attract attention, but few predators are able to catch these swift and agile birds. • Bank Swallows usually excavate their own nest burrows, first using their small bills and later digging with their feet. Most nestlings are safe from predators within their nest chamber, which is typically at the end of a burrow that is 2 to 3 feet in length. • In medieval Europe, it was believed that swallows spent winter in the mud at the bottom of swamps because they were not seen at that time of year. In those days, it was beyond imagination that these birds might fly south for the winter. • *Riparia* is from the Latin for "riverbank," which is a common nesting site for this bird.

ID: brown upperparts; light underparts; brown breast band; long, pointed wings; shallowly forked tail; white throat; gray brown crown; dark "cheek"; small legs.

Size: *L* 5¹/₂ in; *W* 13 in.

Status: common migrant and breeder from May to early September.

Habitat: steep banks, lakeshore bluffs and gravel pits.

Nesting: colonial; pair excavates or reuses a long burrow in a steep earthen bank; the end of the burrow is lined with grass, rootlets, weeds, straw and feathers; pair incubates 4–5 white eggs for 14–16 days.

Feeding: catches flying insects; drinks on the wing.

Voice: twittering chatter: *speed-zeet speed-zeet.*

Similar Species: *Northern Rough-winged Swallow* (p. 217): lacks dark, defined breast band. *Tree Swallow* (p. 216): dark, iridescent bluish to greenish upperparts; lacks dark breast band. *Cliff Swallow* (p. 219): brown-and-blue upperparts; buff forehead and rump; lacks dark breast band.

Selected Sites: Great Lakes shorelines; St. Mary's, St. Clair and Detroit rivers; gravel pits; rivers, lakes, marshes and open fields.

CLIFF SWALLOW

Petrochelidon pyrrhonota

I f the Cliff Swallow were to be renamed in the 20th century, it would probably be called "Bridge Swallow," because so many bridges over rivers in eastern North America have a colony living under them. If you stop to inspect the underside of a bridge, you may see hundreds of gourd-shaped mud nests stuck to the pillars and structural beams. Clouds of Cliff Swallows will often swirl up along either side of the roadway, dazzling passersby with their acrobatics and impressive numbers. • Master mud masons, Cliff Swallows roll mud into balls with their bills and press the pellets together to form their characteristic nests. Brooding parents peer out of the circular neck of the nest, their gleaming eyes watching the world go by. Their white forehead patch warns intruders that somebody is home. Cliff Swallows observe the feeding habitats of neighbors to find the best spots for foraging. • Cliff Swallows are brood parasites—females often lay one or more eggs in the temporarily vacant nests of neighboring Cliff Swallows. The owners of parasitized nests accept the foreign eggs and care for them as if they were their own.

ID: orangy rump; buff forehead; blue gray head and wings; rusty nape, "cheek" and throat; buff breast; white belly; spotted undertail coverts; nearly square tail.
Size: *L* 5½ in; *W* 13½ in.
Status: uncommon migrant and breeder from May to mid-September.
Habitat: steep banks, cliffs, bridges and buildings, often near watercourses.
Nesting: colonial; under a bridge or on a cliff or building; often under the eaves of a barn; pair builds a gourd-shaped mud nest with a small opening near the bottom; pair incubates 4–5 brown-spotted, white to pinkish eggs for 14–16 days.
Feeding: forages over water, fields and marshes; catches flying insects on the wing; occasionally eats berries; drinks on the wing.
Voice: twittering chatter: *churrr-churrr;* also an alarm call: *nyew.*
Similar Species: *Barn Swallow* (p. 220): deeply forked tail; dark rump; usually has rust-colored underparts and forehead.
Other swallows (pp. 216–19): lack buff forehead and rump patch.
Selected Sites: buildings and bridges in open country, usually near water.

BARN SWALLOW

Hirundo rustica

Although Barn Swallows do not occur in mass colonies, they are very familiar birds because they usually build their nests on human-made structures. Barn Swallows once nested on cliffs and in entrances to caves, but their cup-shaped mud nests are now found under house eaves, in barns and boathouses, under bridges or on any other structure that provides shelter. • Unfortunately, not everyone appreciates nesting Barn Swallows—the young can be very messy—and people often scrape barn swallow nests off buildings just as the nesting season begins. However, these graceful birds are natural pest controllers, and their close association with urban areas and tolerance for human activity affords us the wondrous opportunity to observe and study the normally secretive reproductive cycle of birds. • "Swallow tail" is a term used to describe something that is deeply forked. In Michigan, the Barn Swallow is the only swallow that displays this tail feature. • *Hirundo* is Latin for "swallow," while *rustica* refers to this bird's preference for rural habitats.

ID: long, deeply forked tail; rufous throat and forehead; blue black upperparts; rust- to buff-colored underparts; long, pointed wings.
Size: *L* 7 in; *W* 15 in.

Status: common to abundant migrant and breeder from April to September.
Habitat: open rural and urban areas where bridges, culverts and buildings are found near rivers, lakes, marshes or ponds.
Nesting: singly or in small, loose colonies; on a vertical or horizontal building structure under a suitable overhang, on a bridge or in a culvert; half or full cup nest is made of mud and grass or straw; pair incubates 4–7 white eggs, spotted with brown, for 13–17 days.
Feeding: catches flying insects on the wing.
Voice: continuous, twittering chatter: *zip-zip-zip;* also *kvick-kvick.*
Similar Species: *Cliff Swallow* (p. 219): squared tail; buff rump and forehead; pale underparts. *Purple Martin* (p. 215): shallowly forked tail; male is completely blue black; female has sooty gray underparts. *Tree Swallow* (p. 216): clean white underparts; notched tail.
Selected Sites: buildings near water that are not frequently disturbed.

BLACK-CAPPED CHICKADEE
Poecile atricapilla

In winter, when most birds retreat into a slower mode of living or escape to warmer climes, the spunky Black-capped Chickadee remains to remind us that winter can never keep a good bird down. Flocks of energetic Black-capped Chickadees can be seen year-round as they flit from tree to tree, scouring branches and shriveled leaves for insects and sometimes hanging upside down to catch the fleeing bugs. In winter, all other residents seem to fall into step with the lively, active chickadees, and in spring and fall, migrants rely on the local knowledge of Black-caps to find the best food areas. • Most songbirds, including the Black-capped Chickadee, have both songs and calls. The chickadee's *swee-tee* song is heard primarily during spring courtship, and its *chick-a-dee-dee-dee* call keeps flocks together and maintains contact among flock members. • The scientific name *atricapilla* is Latin for "black crown."

ID: black "cap" and "bib"; white "cheek"; gray back and wings; white underparts; light buff sides and flanks; dark legs; white edging on wing feathers.
Size: *L* 5–6 in; *W* 8 in.
Status: common year-round resident.
Habitat: deciduous and mixed forests and woodlands, riparian woodlands, wooded urban parks and backyards with bird feeders.
Nesting: excavates a cavity in a soft, rotting stump or tree; cavity is lined with fur, feathers, moss, grass and cocoons; will often use a birdhouse; female incubates 6–8 white eggs with fine, reddish brown dots for 12–13 days.

Feeding: gleans vegetation, branches and the ground for small insects and spiders; visits backyard feeders; also eats conifer seeds and invertebrate eggs.
Voice: call is a chipper, whistled *chick-a-dee-dee-dee;* song is a slow, whistled *swee-tee* or *fee-bee.*
Similar Species: *Boreal Chickadee* (p. 222): gray brown "cap," sides and flanks. *Blackpoll Warbler* (p. 271): breeding male has 2 white wing bars, dark streaking on white underparts, orangy legs and longer, paler bill. *Carolina Chickadee:* exceptionally rare vagrant; higher-pitched call; neater edge to black "bib"; lacks white edgings on wing feathers.
Selected Sites: bird feeders in wooded backyards; woodlots or riparian woodlands.

221

BOREAL CHICKADEE

Poecile hudsonicus

Birders generally love chickadees, and the Boreal Chickadee is especially sought after as the northern representative of this endearing family. As its name suggests, the Boreal Chickadee resides primarily in boreal forests. Unlike the more common and familiar Black-capped Chickadee, the Boreal Chickadee prefers the seclusion of coniferous forests and tends to be softer spoken. During the nesting season, the Boreal Chickadee is so quiet that you often never know it is there at all. • Chickadees burn so much energy that they must replenish their stores daily to survive winter—they have insufficient fat reserves to survive a prolonged stretch of cold weather. Chickadees store food in holes and on the undersides of branches where it will be easy to find once the snow falls. These birds gain important energy savings to withstand harsh Michigan winters by lowering their body temperatures at night by as much as 22° F. • The scientific name *hudsonicus* refers to the Hudson Bay region of Canada, the Boreal Chickadee's primary range.

ID: gray brown "cap," back, sides and flanks; black "bib"; whitish breast, belly and "cheek" patch; gray wings and tail.
Size: *L* 5–5½ in; *W* 8 in.

Status: uncommon local year-round resident in Upper Peninsula.
Habitat: spruce, fir and pine forests; occasionally in mixed coniferous forests with a small deciduous component.
Nesting: excavates a cavity in soft, rotting wood or uses a natural cavity or abandoned woodpecker nest in a conifer tree; female

lines the nest with fur, feathers, moss and grass; female incubates 5–8 white eggs, finely dotted with reddish brown, for 11–16 days.
Feeding: gleans vegetation, branches and infrequently the ground for spiders and small, tree-infesting insects (including their pupae and eggs); also eats conifer seeds.
Voice: soft, nasal, wheezy *scick-a day day day*, slower and wheezier than the Black-capped Chickadee.
Similar Species: *Black-capped Chickadee* (p. 221): black "cap"; buffy flanks; more grayish than brownish overall.
Selected Sites: Whitefish Point; Seney NWR; Hiawatha National Forest; Ottawa National Forest.

TUFTED TITMOUSE

Baeolophus bicolor

This bird's amusing feeding antics and its insatiable appetite keep curious observers entertained at bird feeders. Grasping an acorn or sunflower seed with its tiny feet, the dexterous Tufted Titmouse strikes its dainty bill repeatedly against the hard outer coating, exposing the inner core. • A breeding pair of Tufted Titmice will maintain their bond throughout the year, even when joining small, multispecies flocks for the cold winter months. The titmouse family bond is so strong that the young from one breeding season will often stay with their parents long enough to help them with nesting and feeding duties the following year. In late winter, mating pairs break from their flocks to search for nesting cavities and soft lining material. If you are fortunate enough to have titmice living in your area, you might be able to attract nesting pairs by setting out your own hair that has accumulated in a hairbrush. There is a good chance that these curious birds will gladly incorporate your offering into the construction of their nest, allowing you the pleasure of knowing you are helping to keep titmice eggs and young as snug as can be.

ID: gray crest and upperparts; black forehead; white underparts; buffy flanks.
Size: *L* 6–6½ in; *W* 10 in.
Status: year-round resident in Lower Peninsula; common in the south; rare and local in the north.
Habitat: deciduous woodlands, groves and suburban parks with large, mature trees.
Nesting: in a natural cavity or woodpecker cavity lined with soft vegetation and animal hair; female may be fed by the male from courtship to time of hatching; female incubates 5–6 finely dotted, white eggs for 12–14 days; both adults and occasionally a "helper" raise the young.
Feeding: forages on the ground and in trees, often hanging upside down like a chickadee; eats insects, supplemented with seeds, nuts and fruits; will eat seeds and suet from feeders.
Voice: noisy, scolding call, like that of a chickadee; song is a whistled *peter peter* or *peter peter peter*.
Similar Species: none.
Selected Sites: bird feeders in wooded backyards; almost any deciduous or riparian woodland.

RED-BREASTED NUTHATCH
Sitta canadensis

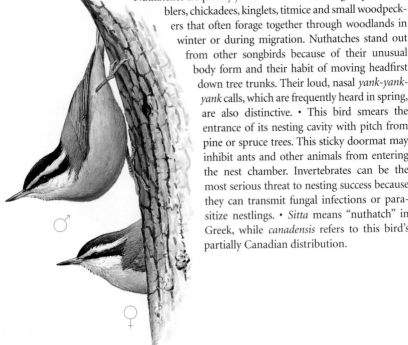

The Red-breasted Nuthatch looks a lot like a red rocket as it streaks toward a neighborhood bird feeder from the cover of a coniferous tree. The nuthatch ejects empty shells left behind by other birds and then selects its own meal before speeding off, never lingering longer than it takes to pick up a seed. • Red-breasted Nuthatches frequently join in on bird waves—groups of warblers, chickadees, kinglets, titmice and small woodpeckers that often forage together through woodlands in winter or during migration. Nuthatches stand out from other songbirds because of their unusual body form and their habit of moving headfirst down tree trunks. Their loud, nasal *yank-yank-yank* calls, which are frequently heard in spring, are also distinctive. • This bird smears the entrance of its nesting cavity with pitch from pine or spruce trees. This sticky doormat may inhibit ants and other animals from entering the nest chamber. Invertebrates can be the most serious threat to nesting success because they can transmit fungal infections or parasitize nestlings. • *Sitta* means "nuthatch" in Greek, while *canadensis* refers to this bird's partially Canadian distribution.

ID: rusty underparts; gray blue upperparts; white "eyebrow"; black eye line; black "cap"; straight bill; short tail; white "cheek." *Male:* deeper rust on breast; black crown. *Female:* light red wash on breast; dark gray crown.
Size: *L* 4½ in; *W* 8½ in.
Status: fairly common year-round resident in the north; irregularly frequent migrant and winter resident from September to May in the south.
Habitat: *Breeding:* spruce–fir and pine forests; pine plantations. *In migration and winter:* mixed woodlands, especially those near bird feeders.

Nesting: excavates a cavity or uses an abandoned woodpecker nest; usually smears the entrance with pitch; nest is made of bark shreds, grass and fur; female incubates 5–6 white eggs, spotted with reddish brown, for about 12 days.
Feeding: forages down trees while probing under loose bark for larval and adult invertebrates; eats pine and spruce seeds in winter; often seen at feeders.
Voice: call is a slow, continually repeated, nasal *eenk eenk eenk,* higher than the White-breasted Nuthatch; also a short *tsip.*
Similar Species: *White-breasted Nuthatch* (p. 225): larger; lacks black eye line and red underparts.
Selected Sites: backyard feeders; coniferous forests.

WHITE-BREASTED NUTHATCH
Sitta carolinensis

T o a novice birder, seeing a White-breasted Nuthatch calling repeatedly while clinging to the underside of a branch is an odd sight. Moving headfirst down a tree trunk, the White-breasted Nuthatch forages for invertebrates, sometimes pausing to survey its surroundings and occasionally issuing a noisy call. Unlike woodpeckers and creepers, nuthatches do not use their tails to brace themselves against tree trunks—nuthatches grasp the tree through foot power alone. • Nuthatches are presumably named for their habit of wedging seeds and nuts into crevices and hacking them open with their bills. • Although the White-breasted Nuthatch is a regular visitor to most backyard feeders, it only sticks around long enough to grab a seed and then dash off. Only an offering of suet can persuade this tiny bird to remain in a single spot for any length of time. • The scientific name *carolinensis* means "of Carolina"—the first White-breasted Nuthatch specimen was collected in South Carolina.

ID: white underparts; white face; gray blue back; rusty undertail coverts; short tail; straight bill; short legs. *Male:* black "cap." *Female:* dark gray "cap."
Size: *L* 5½–6 in; *W* 11 in.
Status: common year-round resident.
Habitat: mixedwood forests, woodlots and backyards.
Nesting: in a natural cavity or an abandoned woodpecker nest in a large deciduous tree; female lines the cavity with bark, grass, fur and feathers; female incubates 5–8 white eggs, spotted with reddish brown, for 12–14 days.
Feeding: forages down trees headfirst in search of larval and adult invertebrates; also eats nuts and seeds; regularly visits feeders.
Voice: song is a fast nasal *yank-hank yank-hank,* lower than the Red-breasted Nuthatch; calls include *ha-ha-ha ha-ha-ha, ank ank* and *ip.*
Similar Species: *Red-breasted Nuthatch* (p. 224): black eye line; rusty underparts. *Black-capped Chickadee* (p. 221): black "bib."
Selected Sites: backyard feeders; mixed woodlands.

225

BROWN CREEPER

Certhia americana

The cryptic Brown Creeper is never easy to find. Inhabiting old-growth forests for much of the year, it often goes unnoticed until a flake of bark suddenly takes the shape of a bird. If a creeper is frightened, it will freeze and flatten itself against a tree trunk, becoming even more difficult to see. • The Brown Creeper feeds by slowly spiraling up a tree trunk, searching for hidden invertebrates. When it reaches the upper branches, the creeper floats down to the base of a neighboring tree to begin another foraging ascent. Its long, stiff tail feathers prop it up against vertical tree trunks as it hitches its way skyward. • Like the call of the Golden-crowned Kinglet, the thin whistle of the Brown Creeper is so high pitched that many birders often fail to hear it. To increase the confusion, the creeper's song often takes on the boisterous, warbling quality of a wood-warbler song. • There are many species of creepers in Europe and Asia, but the Brown Creeper is the only member of its family found in North America.

ID: brown back with buffy white streaks; white "eyebrow"; white underparts; downcurved bill; long, pointed tail feathers; rusty rump.
Size: *L* 5–5½ in; *W* 7½ in.

Status: common migrant from early April to early May and from late September to late November; uncommon breeder from June to July in the north; rare winter resident.
Habitat: mature deciduous, coniferous and mixed forests and woodlands, especially in wet areas with large, dead trees; also found near bogs.
Nesting: under loose bark; nest of grass and conifer needles is woven together with spider silk; female incubates 5–6 whitish eggs, dotted with reddish brown, for 14–17 days.
Feeding: hops up tree trunks and large limbs, probing loose bark for adult and larval invertebrates.
Voice: song is a faint, high-pitched *trees-trees-trees see the trees;* call is a high *tseee.*
Similar Species: *Red-breasted Nuthatch* (p. 224) and *White-breasted Nuthatch* (p. 224): gray blue back; straight or slightly upturned bill. *Woodpeckers* (pp. 182–89): straight bills; lack brown back streaking.
Selected Sites: Dearborn Environmental Study Area; Holly SRA; Kensington Metropark; Waterloo SRA; Kalamazoo Nature Center; Warren Woods Natural Area; Allegan SGA; Whitefish Point.

CAROLINA WREN

Thryothorus ludovicianus

The energetic and cheerful Carolina Wren can be shy and retiring, often hiding deep inside dense shubbery. The best opportunity for viewing this large wren is when it sits on a conspicuous perch while unleashing its impressive song. Pairs perform lively "duets" at any time of day and in any season. The duet often begins with introductory chatter by the female, followed by innumerable ringing variations of *tea-kettle tea-kettle tea-kettle tea* from her mate. • In years of mild winter weather, Carolina Wren populations remain stable, but a winter of frigid temperatures with ice and snow can decimate an otherwise healthy population. Fortunately, the effects of such disasters are only temporary and populations recover within a few years. • Carolina Wrens readily nest in the brushy thickets of an overgrown backyard or in an obscure nook or crevice in a house or barn. If conditions are favorable, two broods may be raised in a single season.

ID: long, prominent, white "eyebrow"; rusty brown upperparts; rich, buff-colored underparts; white throat; slightly downcurved bill.
Size: *L* 5½ in; *W* 7½ in.

Status: rare year-round resident in the south.
Habitat: dense forest undergrowth, especially shrubby tangles and thickets.
Nesting: in a nest box or natural or artificial cavity; both adults fill the cavity with twigs and vegetation and line it with finer materials; nest cup may be domed and may include a snakeskin; female incubates 4–5 brown-blotched, white eggs for 12–16 days; both adults feed the young.

Feeding: usually forages in pairs on the ground and among vegetation; eats mostly insects and other invertebrates; also takes berries, fruits and seeds; will visit bird feeders for peanuts and suet.
Voice: loud, repetitious *tea-kettle tea-kettle tea-kettle* may be heard at any time of day or year; female often chatters while male sings.
Similar Species: *House Wren* (p. 228) and *Winter Wren* (p. 229): lack prominent, white "eyebrow." *Marsh Wren* (p. 231): black, triangular back patch is streaked with white; prefers marsh habitat. *Sedge Wren* (p. 230): dark crown and back are streaked with white; pale, indistinct "eyebrow."
Selected Sites: backyard suet feeders in urban areas; Pointe Mouillee SGA; Waterloo SRA; Lost Nation SGA; Baker Sanctuary; Warren Woods Natural Area.

HOUSE WREN
Troglodytes aedon

The House Wren's bubbly song and energetic demeanor make it a welcome addition to any neighborhood. A small cavity in a standing dead tree or a custom-made nest box is usually all it takes to attract this joyful bird to most backyards. Sometimes even an empty flowerpot or vacant drainpipe is deemed a suitable nest site, provided there is a local abundance of insect prey. Occasionally, you may find that your nest site offering is packed full of twigs and left abandoned without any nesting birds in sight. Male wrens often build numerous nests, which later serve as decoys or "dummy" nests. In such a case, you should just clean out the cavity and hope that another pair of wrens will find your real estate more appealing. • In Greek mythology, Zeus transformed Aedon, the queen of Thebes, into a nightingale. The wonderfully warbled song of the House Wren is somewhat similar to a nightingale's. • This bird is sometimes called "Jenny Wren."

ID: brown upperparts; fine, dark barring on upper wings and lower back; faint, pale "eyebrow" and eye ring; short, upraised tail is finely barred with black; whitish throat; whitish to buff underparts; faintly barred flanks.

Size: *L* 4¹/₂–5 in; *W* 6 in.

Status: common migrant and breeder from late April to October.

Habitat: thickets and shrubby openings in or at the edge of deciduous or mixed woodlands; often in shrubs and thickets near buildings.

Nesting: in a natural cavity or abandoned woodpecker nest; also in a nest box or other artificial cavity; nest of sticks and grass is lined with feathers, fur and other soft materials; female incubates 6–8 white eggs, heavily dotted with reddish brown, for 12–15 days.

Feeding: gleans the ground and vegetation for insects, especially beetles, caterpillars, grasshoppers and spiders.

Voice: song is a smooth, running, bubbly warble: *tsi-tsi-tsi-tsi oodle-oodle-oodle-oodle*, lasting about 2–3 seconds.

Similar Species: *Winter Wren* (p. 229): smaller; darker overall; much shorter, stubby tail; prominent, dark barring on flanks. *Sedge Wren* (p. 230): faint white streaking on dark crown and back.

Selected Sites: thick, rural hedgerows; shrubby fencelines; riparian thickets; shrubby, tangled fields or woodland edges.

WINTER WREN
Troglodytes troglodytes

Winter Wrens boldly announce their claims to patches of moist coniferous woodland, where they often make their homes in the green moss and gnarled upturned roots of decomposing tree trunks. • The song of the Winter Wren is distinguished by its explosive delivery, melodious, bubbly tone and extended duration. Few other singers in Michigan can sustain their songs for up to 10 music-packed seconds. When the Winter Wren is not singing or nesting, it skulks through the forest understory, quietly probing the myriad nooks and crannies for invertebrates. • While the female raises the young, the male wren brings food to the nest and defends the territory through song. At night, the male sleeps away from his family in an unfinished nest.

• Most of our Winter Wrens migrate south for winter, but a few choose to brave the colder months in southern Michigan. • *Troglodytes* is Greek for "creeping in holes" or "cave dweller." • The Winter Wren is the only North American wren that is also found across Europe and Asia, where it is a common garden bird known simply as a "Wren."

ID: very short, stubby, upraised tail; fine, pale buff "eyebrow"; dark brown upperparts; lighter brown underparts; prominent, dark barring on flanks.

Size: *L* 4 in; *W* 5½ in.

Status: uncommon migrant from April to early May and from October to early November; uncommon breeder from June to July in the north.

Habitat: *Breeding:* moist boreal forest, spruce bogs, cedar swamps and mixed forests dominated by mature pine and hemlock; often near water. *In migration:* woodland thickets.

Nesting: in an abandoned woodpecker cavity, in a natural cavity, under bark or upturned tree roots; bulky nest is made of twigs, moss, grass and fur; male frequently builds up to 4 "dummy" nests prior to egg laying; female incubates 5–7 white eggs,

dotted with reddish brown toward the larger end, for 14–16 days.

Feeding: forages on the ground and on trees for beetles, wood-boring insects and other invertebrates.

Voice: *Male:* song is a warbled, tinkling series of quick trills and twitters, often more than 8 seconds long; call is a sharp *chip-chip.*

Similar Species: *House Wren* (p. 228): tail is longer than leg; paler overall; less conspicuous barring on flanks. *Carolina Wren* (p. 227): much larger; long, bold, white "eyebrow"; long tail. *Marsh Wren* (p. 231): white streaking on black back; bold, white "eyebrow." *Sedge Wren* (p. 230): white streaking on black back and crown; longer tail; paler underparts.

Selected Sites: Waterloo SRA; Lost Nation SGA; Rose Lake WA; Kalamazoo Nature Center; Allegan SGA; Chippewa Nature Center; Seney NWR.

SEDGE WREN

Cistothorus platensis

Like most wrens, the Sedge Wren is secretive and difficult to observe. It is the least familiar of all our wrens because it keeps itself well concealed in dense stands of sedges and tall, wet grass. Sedge Wrens are also less loyal to specific sites than other wrens, and may totally disappear from an area after a few years for no apparent reason. • Sedge Wrens are feverish nest builders, and construction begins immediately after they settle on a nesting territory. Each energetic male may build several incomplete nests throughout his territory before the females arrive. The decoys or "dummy" nests are not wasted: they often serve as dormitories for young and adult birds later in the season. • The scientific name *platensis* refers to the Rio de la Plata in Argentina, where another isolated population of this wren is found. • This bird used to be known as "Short-billed Marsh Wren."

ID: short, narrow tail (often upraised); faint, pale "eyebrow"; dark crown and back are faintly streaked with white; barring on wing coverts; whitish underparts with buff orange sides, flanks and undertail coverts.

Size: *L* 4–4¹/₂ in; *W* 5¹/₂ in.

Status: rare and local migrant and breeder from May to September.

Habitat: wet sedge meadows, wet grassy fields, alfalfa hay fields, marshes, bogs and beaver ponds; often in abandoned, wet fields with low, shrubby willows and alders.

Nesting: usually less than 3 ft from the ground; well-built globe nest with a side entrance is woven from sedges and grasses; female incubates 4–8 unmarked, white eggs for about 14 days.

Feeding: forages low in dense vegetation, where it picks and probes for adult and larval insects and spiders; occasionally catches flying insects.

Voice: song is a few short, staccato notes followed by a rattling trill: *chap-chap-chap-chap, chap, churr-r-r-r-r-r;* call is a sharp *chat* or *chep.*

Similar Species: *Marsh Wren* (p. 231): broad, conspicuous white "eyebrow"; prominent white streaking on black back; unstreaked crown; prefers cattail marshes. *Winter Wren* (p. 229): darker overall; shorter, stubby tail; unstreaked crown. *House Wren* (p. 228): unstreaked, dark brown crown and back.

Selected Sites: Erie Marsh Preserve; Pointe Mouillee SGA; St. Clair Flats WA; Waterloo SRA; Allegan SGA; Dead Stream Flooding; Portage Point Marsh; Seney NWR; also lush hay fields.

MARSH WREN

Cistothorus palustris

Fueled by newly emerged aquatic insects, the Marsh Wren zips about in short bursts through tall stands of cattails and bulrushes. This expert hunter catches flying insects with lightning speed, but don't expect to see the Marsh Wren in action—it is a reclusive bird that prefers to remain hidden deep within its dense marshland habitat. A patient observer might be rewarded with a brief glimpse of a Marsh Wren, but it is more likely that this bird's distinctive song, reminiscent of an old-fashioned treadle sewing machine, will inform you of its presence. • The Marsh Wren occasionally destroys the nests and eggs of other Marsh Wrens and other marsh-nesting songbirds such as the Red-winged Blackbird. Other birds are usually prevented from doing the same, because the Marsh Wren's globe nest keeps the eggs well hidden, and several decoy nests help to divert predators from the real nest. • The scientific name *palustris* is Latin for "marsh." This bird was formerly known as "Long-billed Marsh Wren."

ID: white "chin" and belly; white to light brown upperparts; black triangle on upper back is streaked with white; bold, white "eyebrow"; unstreaked brown crown; long, thin, downcurved bill.

Size: *L* 5 in; *W* 6 in.

Status: special concern; locally common migrant and breeder from late April to October.

Habitat: large cattail and bulrush marshes interspersed with open water; occasionally in tall grass–sedge marshes.

Nesting: in a marsh among cattails or tall emergent vegetation; globelike nest is woven from cattails, bulrushes, weeds and grass and lined with cattail down; female incubates 4–6 white to pale brown eggs, heavily dotted with dark brown, for 12–16 days.

Feeding: gleans vegetation and flycatches for adult aquatic invertebrates, especially dragonflies and damselflies.

Voice: *Male:* rapid, rattling, staccato warble sounds like an old-fashioned treadle sewing machine; call is a harsh *chek*.

Similar Species: *Sedge Wren* (p. 230): smaller; streaked crown. *House Wren* (p. 228): faint "eyebrow"; black back lacks white streaking. *Carolina Wren* (p. 227): larger; buff underparts; black back lacks white streaking.

Selected Sites: Erie Marsh Preserve; Pointe Mouillee SGA; St. Clair Flats WA; Waterloo SRA; Allegan SGA; Dead Stream Flooding; Seney NWR; Portage Point Marsh.

GOLDEN-CROWNED KINGLET

Regulus satrapa

Golden-crowned Kinglets are best seen in spring and fall in most parts of Michigan. As they refuel on insects and berries, kinglets use tree branches as swings and trapezes, flashing their regal crowns and constantly flicking their tiny wings. During summer, these dainty forest sprites are often too busy to make an appearance for admiring observers. Not much larger than hummingbirds, Golden-crowned Kinglets can be difficult to spot as they flit and hover among coniferous treetops. • In winter, Golden-crowned Kinglets are commonly seen and heard among multispecies flocks that often include chickadees, Red-breasted Nuthatches and Brown Creepers. Golden-crowned Kinglets manage to survive cold winter temperatures by roosting together in groups or in empty squirrel nests. Like chickadees, these birds can lower their body temperatures at night to conserve energy. • The Golden-crowned Kinglet's extremely high-pitched call is very faint and is often lost in the slightest woodland breeze.

ID: olive back; darker wings and tail; light underparts; dark "cheek"; 2 white wing bars; black eye line; white "eyebrow"; crown has black border. *Male:* reddish orange crown. *Female:* yellow crown.
Size: *L* 4 in; *W* 7 in.
Status: common migrant from mid-March to early May and from September to mid-November; common breeder from April to September in the north; uncommon winter resident in Lower Peninsula from September to March.
Habitat: *Breeding:* mixed and pure mature coniferous forests, especially those dominated by spruce; also conifer plantations. *In migration* and *winter:* coniferous, deciduous and mixed forests and woodlands.

Nesting: usually in a spruce or conifer; hanging nest is made of moss, lichens, twigs and leaves; female incubates 8–9 whitish to pale buff eggs, spotted with gray and brown, for 14–15 days.
Feeding: gleans and hovers among the forest canopy for insects, berries and occasionally sap.
Voice: song is a faint, high-pitched, accelerating *tsee-tsee-tsee-tsee, why do you shilly-shally?;* call is a very high-pitched *tsee tsee tsee.*
Similar Species: *Ruby-crowned Kinglet* (p. 233): bold, broken, white eye ring; crown lacks black border. *Black-capped Chickadee* (p. 221) and *Boreal Chickadee* (p. 222): lack bright, colorful crown.
Selected Sites: Dearborn Environmental Study Area; Port Huron SGA; Indian Springs Metropark; Fenner Nature Center; Kalamazoo Nature Center; Chippewa Nature Center; Tawas Point SP; Whitefish Point.

RUBY-CROWNED KINGLET
Regulus calendula

The loud, rolling song of the Ruby-crowned Kinglet is a familiar tune that echoes through our coniferous forests in May and June. The male kinglet erects his brilliant, red crown and sings to impress prospective mates during courtship. Throughout most of the year, though, his crown remains hidden among dull gray feathers on the bird's head and is impossible to see even through binoculars.
• While in migration, Ruby-crowned Kinglets are regularly seen flitting among tree-tops, intermingling with a colorful assortment of warblers and vireos. This bird might be mistaken for an *Empidonax* flycatcher, but the kinglet's frequent hovering and energetic wing-flicking behavior set it apart from look-alikes. The wing flicking is thought to startle insects into movement, allowing the kinglet to spot them and pounce.

ID: bold, broken eye ring; 2 bold, white wing bars; olive green upperparts; dark wings and tail; whitish to yellowish underparts; short tail; flicks its wings. *Male:* small, red crown (usually hidden). *Female:* lacks red crown.
Size: *L* 4 in; *W* 7½ in.
Status: common migrant from mid-April to late May and from September to late October; common breeder in Upper Peninsula from June to August.
Habitat: mixed woodlands and pure coniferous forests, especially those dominated by spruce; often found near wet forest openings and edges.
Nesting: usually in a spruce or conifer; female builds a hanging nest made of moss, lichen, twigs and leaves and lines it with feathers, fur and plant down; female incubates 7–8 brown-spotted, whitish to pale buff eggs for 13–14 days.
Feeding: gleans and hovers for insects and spiders; also eats seeds and berries.
Voice: *Male:* song is an accelerating and rising *tea-tea-tea-tew-tew-tew look-at-Me, look-at-Me, look-at-Me.*
Similar Species: *Golden-crowned Kinglet* (p. 232): dark "cheek"; black border around crown; male has orange crown with yellow border; female has yellow crown. *Orange-crowned Warbler* (p. 254): no eye ring or wing bars. Empidonax *flycatchers* (pp. 193–97): complete eye ring or no eye ring at all; larger bill; longer tail; all lack red crown.
Selected Sites: Indian Springs Metropark; Waterloo SRA; Fort Custer SRA; Russ Forest; Warren Woods Natural Area; Chippewa Nature Center; Kalamazoo Nature Center; Tawas Point SP; J. W. Wells SP; Van Riper SP.

BLUE-GRAY GNATCATCHER
Polioptila caerulea

The fidgety Blue-gray Gnatcatcher is constantly on the move. This woodland inhabitant holds its tail upward like a wren and issues a quiet, banjolike twang as it flits restlessly from shrub to shrub, gleaning insects from branches and leaves. • Gnatcatcher pairs remain close once a bond is established, and both parents share the responsibilities of nest building, incubation and raising the young. As soon as the young gnatcatchers are ready to fly, they leave the nest for the cover of dense shrubby tangles along woodland edges. Like most songbirds, Blue-gray Gnatcatchers mature quickly and will fly as far as South America within months of hatching. • Although this bird undoubtedly eats gnats, this food item is only a small part of its insectivorous diet. • The scientific name *Polioptila* means "gray feather," while *caerulea* means "blue."

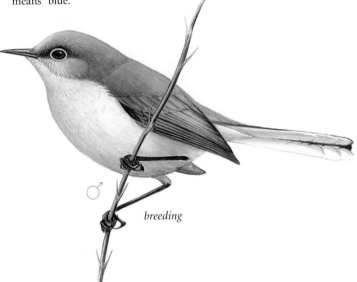

breeding

ID: blue gray upperparts; long tail; white eye ring; pale gray underparts; no wing bars; black uppertail with white outer tail feathers. *Breeding male:* darker upperparts; black border on side of forecrown.
Size: *L* 4½ in; *W* 6 in.
Status: uncommon migrant and breeder from mid-April to November in southern Lower Peninsula.
Habitat: deciduous woodlands along streams, ponds, lakes and swamps; also in orchards, shrubby tangles along woodland edges and oak savannas.

Nesting: on a branch, usually halfway to the trunk; cup nest is made of plant fibers and bark chips, decorated with lichens and lined with fine vegetation, hair and feathers; female incubates 3–5 pale bluish white eggs, dotted with reddish brown, for 11–15 days; male feeds female and young.
Feeding: gleans vegetation and flycatches for insects, spiders and other invertebrates.
Voice: *Male:* song is a faint, airy *puree;* call is a banjolike, high-pitched twang: *chee.*
Similar Species: *Golden-crowned Kinglet* (p. 232) and *Ruby-crowned Kinglet* (p. 233): olive green overall; short tail; wing bars.
Selected Sites: Dearborn Environmental Study Area; Stony Creek Metropark; Holly SRA; Lost Nation SGA; Kalamazoo Nature Center; Allegan SGA; Rose Lake WA.

EASTERN BLUEBIRD

Sialia sialis

Perhaps no other bird is as cherished and admired in rural areas as the lovely Eastern Bluebird. With the colors of the cool sky on its back and the warm setting sun on its breast, the male Eastern bluebird looks like a piece of pure sky come to life. • When House Sparrows and European Starlings were introduced to North America, Eastern Bluebirds were forced to compete with them for nest sites, and bluebird numbers began to decline. The creation of bluebird nest boxes has helped matters—these boxes exclude competing European Starlings because the entrances are too small for them but are perfect for bluebirds. The development of "bluebird trails" has allowed bluebird populations to recover gradually throughout Michigan. Nest boxes are mounted on fence posts along highways and rural roads, providing bluebirds with convenient nesting places. • Eastern Bluebirds are fond of fields, uncultivated farmlands and mature wood edges, but an elevated perch is necessary as a base from which to hunt insects.

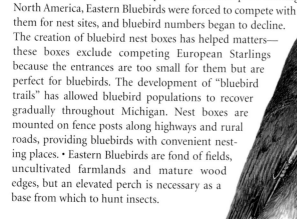

ID: chestnut red "chin," throat, breast and sides; white belly and undertail coverts; dark bill and legs. *Male:* deep blue upperparts. *Female:* thin, white eye ring; gray brown head and back are tinged with blue; blue wings and tail; paler chestnut on underparts.

Size: *L* 7 in; *W* 13 in.

Status: common migrant and breeder from March to October; rare winter resident in southern Lower Peninsula.

Habitat: cropland fencelines, meadows, fallow and abandoned fields, pastures, forest clearings and edges; also golf courses, large lawns and cemeteries.

Nesting: in an abandoned woodpecker cavity, natural cavity or nest box; female builds a cup nest of grass, weed stems and small twigs and lines it with finer materials; mostly the female incubates 4–5 pale blue eggs for 13–16 days.

Feeding: swoops from a perch to pursue flying insects; also forages on the ground for invertebrates.

Voice: song is a rich, warbling *turr, turr-lee, turr-lee;* call is a chittering *pew.*

Similar Species: *Mountain Bluebird:* lacks chestnut red underparts; very rare.

Selected Sites: Waterloo SRA; Rose Lake WA; Kalamazoo Nature Center; Yankee Springs SRA; Fort Custer SRA; Allegan SGA; Sarett Nature Center; Tawas Point SP.

TOWNSEND'S SOLITAIRE

Myadestes townsendi

Few birds characterize the mountain forests of the West better than the Townsend's Solitaire. Slim and graceful, this bird makes up for its plain plumage with remarkable bursts of sustained song. It is an inconspicuous bird, perching for minutes at a time at the top of a tall tree or snag, or on the upturned roots of a fallen tree. From its perch, it flutters out to catch insects in midair or follows them to the ground and grasps them with a soft pounce reminiscent of a bluebird. In flight, the warm, peachy wing linings of this beautiful bird shine like sunlight through a bedroom window. • During the winter months, Townsend's Solitaires defend feeding grounds of juniper berries and other fruit-bearing trees. Solitaires have the unusual habit of picking fruit off trees while in flight. • During the summer months, when away from Michigan, solitaires are true to their name and are rarely seen in groups.

ID: gray body; darker wings and tail; peach-colored wing patches (very evident in flight); white eye ring; white outer tail feathers; long tail. *Immature:* brown body is heavily spotted with buff; pale eye ring.

Size: *L* 8½ in; *W* 14½ in.

Status: very rare winter visitor from October to early April.

Habitat: woodland edges, especially in areas with fruit-bearing shrubs and trees.

Nesting: does not nest in Michigan.

Feeding: flycatches and gleans vegetation and the ground for invertebrates and berries; plucks berries from branches while in flight.

Voice: call is a harsh *piink. Male:* song is a long, bubbly warble.

Similar Species: *Gray Catbird* (p. 244): black "cap"; red undertail coverts. *Eastern Bluebird* (p. 235): female lacks peach-colored wing and tail patches and white outer tail feathers. *Mountain Bluebird:* female has a faint rusty breast.

Selected Sites: no consistent sites.

VEERY

Catharus fuscescens

Navigating its way across the forest floor, the Veery travels in short, springy hops, flipping leaves and scattering leaf litter in search of worms and grubs. This shy, well-camouflaged bird is always attuned to the sounds of wiggling prey or approaching danger. The Veery is the most terrestrial of the North American thrushes and is often difficult to find. Listen for it in spring and early summer when its fluty, cascading song is easily detected. • When startled by an intruder, the Veery either flushes or faces the threat with its faintly streaked, buffy breast exposed, hoping for concealment. • This bird's name is an imitation of its airy song. The scientific name *fuscescens* is from the Latin word for "dusky," in reference to the Veery's color. • These birds migrate to South America each winter, so there's a very good chance that the Veery pairs nesting in your local ravine might soon be traveling to the rainforests of the Amazon!

ID: reddish brown or tawny upperparts; very thin, grayish eye ring; faintly streaked, buff throat and upper breast; light underparts; gray flanks and face patch.

Size: *L* 6½–7½ in; *W* 12 in.

Status: fairly common migrant and breeder from May to September.

Habitat: cool, moist deciduous and mixed forests and woodlands with a dense understory of shrubs and ferns; often in disturbed woodlands. *In migration:* a variety of forested areas, parks and backyards.

Nesting: on the ground or in a shrub; female builds a bulky nest of leaves, weeds, bark strips and rootlets; female incubates 3–4 pale, greenish blue eggs for 10–15 days.

Feeding: gleans the ground and lower vegetation for invertebrates and berries.

Voice: *Male:* song is a fluty, descending *da-vee-ur, vee-ur, vee-ur, veer, veer, veer;* call is a high, whistled *feeyou.*

Similar Species: *Swainson's Thrush* (p. 239): bold eye ring; olive brown upperparts; darker spotting on throat and upper breast. *Hermit Thrush* (p. 240): reddish rump and tail; brownish back; bold eye ring; buff brown flanks; large, dark spots on throat and breast. *Gray-cheeked Thrush* (p. 238): gray brown upperparts; dark breast spots; brownish gray flanks.

Selected Sites: Indian Springs Metropark; Rose Lake WA; Russ Forest; Warren Woods Natural Area; Chippewa Nature Center; Kalamazoo Nature Center; Sarett Nature Center; Allegan SGA.

GRAY-CHEEKED THRUSH

Catharus minimus

Few people have ever heard of the Gray-cheeked Thrush, but keen birders find this inconspicuous bird a source of great interest. A champion migrant, this thrush winters as far south as Peru and regularly summers in the Arctic, farther north than any other North American thrush. Each spring the Gray-cheeked Thrush migrates through our region to the Hudson Bay Lowlands in Canada, where it nests among willows and stunted black spruce. Unfortunately, the inaccessibility of this remote northern region has prevented most birders and ornithologists from documenting more than a few nesting records for this elusive bird. • In migration, the Gray-cheeked Thrush travels primarily at night, so it is most often seen or heard rustling through shrub-covered leaf litter early in the morning. This bird will settle in almost any habitat while migrating, but it does not stay for long, rarely uttering more than a simple warning note during its brief refueling stops.

ID: gray brown upperparts; gray face; inconspicuous eye ring may not be visible; heavily spotted breast; pale underparts; brownish gray flanks; pink legs.

Size: *L* 7–8 in; *W* 13 in.

Status: uncommon migrant from late April to early June and from late August to late October.

Habitat: a variety of forested areas, parks and backyards.

Nesting: does not nest in Michigan.

Feeding: hops along the ground, picking up insects and other invertebrates; may also feed on berries during migration.

Voice: typically thrushlike in tone, ending with a clear, descending whistle: *wee-a, wee-o, wee-a, titi wheeee*; call is a downslurred *wee-o*.

Similar Species: *Swainson's Thrush* (p. 239): prominent eye ring; buff "cheek" and upper breast. *Hermit Thrush* (p. 240): reddish tail; olive brown upperparts; lacks gray "cheek." *Veery* (p. 237): reddish brown upperparts; very light breast streaking.

Selected Sites: Dearborn Environmental Study Area; Indian Springs Metropark; Waterloo SRA; Yankee Springs SRA; Kalamazoo Nature Center; Warren Woods Natural Area; Allegan SGA; Chippewa Nature Center.

SWAINSON'S THRUSH
Catharus ustulatus

The upward spiral of this thrush's song lifts the soul of any listener with each rising note. The Swainson's Thrush is an integral part of the morning chorus, and its inspiring song is also heard at dusk. In fact, this bird is routinely the last of the forest singers to be silenced by nightfall. • Most thrushes feed on the ground, but the Swainson's Thrush is also adept at gleaning food from the airy heights of trees, sometimes briefly hover-gleaning like a warbler or vireo. • On its breeding grounds in northern Michigan, the Swainson's Thrush is most often seen perched high in a treetop, cast in silhouette against the sky. In migration, this bird skulks low on the ground under shrubs and tangles, occasionally finding itself in backyards and neighborhood parks. A wary bird, this thrush does not allow many viewing opportunities, and it often gives a sharp warning call from some distance. • William Swainson was an English zoologist and illustrator in the early 19th century. His name also graces the Swainson's Hawk.

ID: gray brown upperparts; noticeable buff eye ring; buff wash on "cheek" and upper breast; spots arranged in streaks on throat and breast; white belly and undertail coverts; brownish gray flanks.
Size: *L* 7 in; *W* 12 in.
Status: common migrant from late April to early June and from mid-August to late October; common breeder from May to September in Upper Peninsula.
Habitat: edges and openings of coniferous and mixed boreal forests; prefers moist areas with spruce and fir. *In migration:* a variety of forested areas, parks and backyards.
Nesting: usually in a shrub or small tree; small cup nest is made of grass, moss, leaves, roots and lichen and is lined with

fur and soft fibers; female incubates 3–4 pale blue eggs, with brown spots toward the larger end, for 12–14 days.
Feeding: gleans vegetation and forages on the ground for invertebrates; also eats berries.
Voice: song is a slow, rolling, rising spiral: *Oh, Aurelia will-ya, will-ya will-yeee;* call is a sharp *wick.*
Similar Species: *Gray-cheeked Thrush* (p. 238): gray "cheek"; less or no buff wash on breast; lacks conspicuous eye ring. *Hermit Thrush* (p. 240): reddish tail and rump; grayish brown upperparts; darker breast spotting on whiter breast. *Veery* (p. 237): lacks bold eye ring; upperparts are more reddish; faint breast streaking.
Selected Sites: Dearborn Environmental Study Area; Indian Springs Metropark; Waterloo SRA; Rose Lake WA; Kalamazoo Nature Center; Allegan SGA; Chippewa Nature Center; Whitefish Point.

HERMIT THRUSH

Catharus guttatus

If the beauty of forest birds was gauged by sound rather than by appearance, there is no doubt the Hermit Thrush would be deemed one of the most beautiful birds in Michigan. On its nesting grounds, its song is a familiar theme, as much a part of the forest ecosystem as are the trees and wildflowers. Similar to the song of the Swainson's Thrush, the song of the Hermit Thrush is almost always preceded with a single questioning note, as if this bird's hermitlike behavior prompts it to ask if the coast is clear. • For the first two days after arriving in a male's territory, a female Hermit Thrush will be attacked and chased. If the female still remains after these two days the male gradually accepts her and the union is formed. • The Hermit Thrush is a ground nester, often hiding its cryptic cup nest in a natural hollow between raised, mossy hummocks under the low branches of a spruce or fir. The female incubates the eggs on her own while the male defends the territory. This means that there is less activity around the nest, which probably benefits the vulnerable eggs. • The scientific name *guttatus* is Latin for "spotted" or "speckled," in reference to this bird's breast.

ID: reddish brown tail and rump; grayish brown upperparts; black-spotted throat and breast; pale underparts; gray flanks; thin, whitish eye ring; thin bill; pink legs.

Size: *L* 7 in; *W* 11½ in.

Status: common migrant from April to mid-May and from mid-September to October; common breeder from May to September in northern half of Michigan.

Habitat: deciduous, mixed or coniferous woodlands; wet coniferous bogs bordered by trees.

Nesting: usually on the ground; occasionally in a small tree or shrub; female builds a bulky cup nest of grass, twigs, moss, ferns and bark strips; female incubates 4 pale blue to greenish blue eggs, sometimes with dark flecks, for 11–13 days.

Feeding: forages on the ground and gleans vegetation for insects and other invertebrates; also eats berries.

Voice: song is a series of beautiful flutelike notes, both rising and falling in pitch; a small questioning note may precede the song; calls include a faint *chuck* and a fluty *treee*.

Similar Species: *Swainson's Thrush* (p. 239): buff "cheek" and wash on breast; grayish brown back and tail. *Veery* (p. 237): lightly streaked upper breast; reddish brown upperparts and tail. *Gray-cheeked Thrush* (p. 238): gray "cheek"; lacks conspicuous eye ring. *Fox Sparrow* (p. 300): stockier build; conical bill; brown breast spots.

Selected Sites: Dearborn Environmental Study Area; Waterloo SRA; Fort Custer SRA; Allegan SGA; Fenner Nature Center; Chippewa Nature Center; Rose Lake WA; Whitefish Point.

WOOD THRUSH

Hylocichla mustelina

The loud, warbled notes of the Wood Thrush once resounded through our woodlands, but forest fragmentation and urban sprawl have eliminated much of this bird's nesting habitat. Broken forests and diminutive woodlots have allowed for the invasion of common, open-area predators and parasites, such as raccoons, skunks, crows, jays and cowbirds, which traditionally had little access to nests that were insulated deep within vast stands of hardwood forest. Many tracts of forest that have been urbanized or developed for agriculture now host families of American Robins rather than the once-prominent Wood Thrush. • The Wood Thrush's wintering grounds extend from southeastern Mexico down to Panama. It makes its way northward each spring, breeding primarily in the eastern U.S., from the Gulf Coast to southern Canada. • Naturalist and author Henry David Thoreau considered the Wood Thrush's song to be the most beautiful of avian sounds. The male Wood Thrush can even sing two notes at once!

ID: plump body; large, black spots on white breast, sides and flanks; bold white eye ring; streaked "cheeks"; rusty head and back; brown wings, rump and tail.

Size: *L* 8 in; *W* 13 in.

Status: uncommon migrant and breeder from mid-April to early November.

Habitat: moist, mature and preferably undisturbed deciduous woodlands and mixed forests.

Nesting: low in a fork of a deciduous tree; female builds a bulky cup nest of grass, twigs, moss, weeds, bark strips and mud and lines it with softer materials; female incubates 3–4 pale, greenish blue eggs for 13–14 days.

Feeding: forages on the ground and gleans vegetation for insects and other invertebrates; also eats berries.

Voice: *Male:* bell-like phrases of 3–5 notes, with each note at a different pitch and followed by a trill: *Will you live with me? Way up high in a tree, I'll come right down and...seeee!;* calls include a *pit pit* and *bweebeebeep.*

Similar Species: *Other thrushes* (pp. 238–43): smaller spots on underparts; most have colored wash on sides and flanks; all lack bold white eye ring and rusty "cap" and back.

Selected Sites: Indian Springs Metropark; Waterloo SRA; Lost Nation SGA; Russ Forest; Warren Woods Natural Area; Rose Lake WA; P. J. Hoffmaster SP; Allegan SGA.

241

AMERICAN ROBIN

Turdus migratorius

American Robins are widely recognized as harbingers of spring, often arriving in early March. These birds are widespread and abundant in many of our natural habitats, but they are familiar to most of us because they commonly inhabit residential lawns, gardens and parks. Robins may overwinter in southern Michigan, but sightings are not common because such birds tend to remain hidden. • A hunting robin may appear to be listening for prey, but it is actually looking for movements in the soil—it tilts its head because its eyes are placed on the sides of its head. • Robins are occasionally seen hunting with their bills stuffed full of earthworms and grubs, a sign that hungry young robins are somewhere close at hand. Young robins are easily distinguished from their parents by their disheveled appearance and heavily spotted underparts. • The American Robin was named by English colonists after the Robin (*Erithacus rubecula*) of their native land. Both birds look and behave similarly, even though they are only distantly related. The American Robin's closest European relative is, in fact, the Blackbird (*T. merula*), which is identical in all aspects except plumage.

ID: gray brown back; dark head; white throat streaked with black; white undertail coverts; incomplete, white eye ring; black-tipped, yellow bill. *Male:* deep brick red breast; black head. *Female:* dark gray head; light red orange breast. *Juvenile:* heavily spotted breast.
Size: *L* 10 in; *W* 17 in.
Status: abundant migrant and breeder from late March to early November; rare and irregular year-round resident in south.
Habitat: residential lawns and gardens, pastures, urban parks, broken forests, bogs and river shorelines.

Nesting: in a coniferous or deciduous tree or shrub; sturdy cup nest is built of grass, moss and loose bark and cemented with mud; female incubates 4 light blue eggs for 11–16 days; may raise up to 3 broods each year in some areas.
Feeding: forages on the ground and among vegetation for larval and adult insects, earthworms, other invertebrates and berries.
Voice: song is an evenly spaced warble: *cheerily cheer-up cheerio;* call is a rapid *tut-tut-tut.*
Similar Species: *Varied Thrush* (p. 243): black breast band; 2 orange wing bars.
Selected Sites: suburban lawns or gardens.

VARIED THRUSH

Ixoreus naevius

Varied Thrushes are rare in Michigan, so if you find one don't be surprised if fellow birders question your identification skills. Varied Thrushes are typically western birds, but a few invariably wander off course each fall and make their way into our region. There are one to three sightings reported in Michigan each year, usually at backyard feeders with nearby dense coniferous trees that provide shelter for this wayward wanderer. Berries, fruits, seeds, nuts, acorns and suet are some of the offerings that might encourage a lengthy visit from a Varied Thrush—provided that Blue Jays and other backyard regulars don't dominate the wealth of goodies. • While feeding, the Varied Thrush performs a "bunny hop," snatching up leaf litter with its bill, hopping backward and then tossing the leaf litter aside. The thrush then examines the bare ground for food before hopping forward and repeating the process.

ID: dark upperparts; orange "eyebrow"; orange throat and belly; 2 orange wing bars. *Male:* black breast band; blue black upperparts. *Female:* brown upperparts; faint breast band.

Size: L 9 in; W 16 in.

Status: rare winter resident from October to April.

Habitat: areas with dense coniferous cover near an active backyard feeding station.

Nesting: does not nest in Michigan.

Feeding: forages on the ground and among vegetation for insects, seeds and berries; takes a variety of foods at feeders, especially suet.

Voice: not vocal in Michigan.

Similar Species: *American Robin* (p. 242): lacks black breast band and orange "eyebrow," throat and wing bars.

Selected Sites: feeding stations in northern half of the state.

GRAY CATBIRD

Dumetella carolinensis

The Gray Catbird is most common in summer, when nesting pairs build their loose cup nest deep within impenetrable tangles of shrubs, brambles and thorny thickets. The Gray Catbird vigorously defends its nesting territory with such effective defense tactics that the nesting success of neighboring warblers and sparrows may increase as a result of this catbird's constant vigilance. Gray Catbirds are less prone to parasitism by Brown-headed Cowbirds because female catbirds are very loyal to their nests. Even if a cowbird sneaks past the watchful female catbird to deposit an egg in the nest, the mother catbird often recognizes the foreign egg and immediately ejects it. • True to its name, this bird's call sounds much like the scratchy mewing of a house cat. The Gray Catbird is a member of the mockingbird family, and its characteristic call and boisterous, hectic, mimicked phrases are often the only evidence of this bird's presence. • Near our homes, Gray Catbirds can often be seen at dawn, feeding on insects attracted to electric lights.

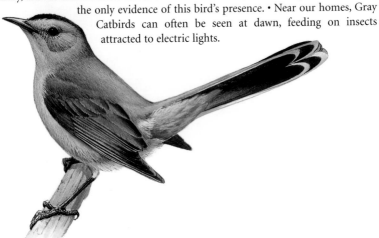

ID: dark gray overall; black "cap"; long tail may be dark gray to black; chestnut undertail coverts; black eyes, bill and legs.
Size: *L* 8½–9 in; *W* 11 in.

Status: common migrant and breeder from mid-May to October.
Habitat: dense thickets, brambles, shrubby or brushy areas and hedgerows, often near water.
Nesting: in a dense shrub or thicket; bulky cup nest is loosely built with twigs, leaves and grass and is lined with fine material; female incubates 4 greenish blue eggs for 12–15 days.
Feeding: forages on the ground and in vegetation for a wide variety of ants,

beetles, grasshoppers, caterpillars, moths and spiders; also eats berries and visits feeders.
Voice: calls include a catlike *meoow* and a harsh *check-check*; song is a variety of warbles, squeaks and mimicked phrases repeated only once and often interspersed with a *mew* call.
Similar Species: *Gray Jay* (p. 210), *Northern Mockingbird* (p. 245) and *Townsend's Solitaire* (p. 236): lack black "cap" and chestnut undertail coverts. *Brown Thrasher* (p. 246): rusty brown upperparts; streaked underparts; wing bars; repeats each song phrase twice.
Selected Sites: Dearborn Environmental Study Area; Stony Creek Metropark; Waterloo SRA; Fort Custer SRA; Kalamazoo Nature Center; Rose Lake WA; Yankee Springs SRA; Chippewa Nature Center.

NORTHERN MOCKINGBIRD
Mimus polyglottos

Northern Mockingbirds are slowly establishing themselves as year-round residents in Michigan. In winter, they rely heavily on wild and ornamental fruits, especially the bounty of nutritious rose hips. Generous offerings of suet, raisins and fruit at feeders can go a long way toward luring these and other birds into your yard. • The Northern Mockingbird's vocal repertoire is amazing—over 400 different song types have been attributed to this bird. It can imitate almost anything, from the vocalizations of other birds and animals to musical instruments. In fact, it replicates sounds so accurately that even computerized auditory analysis may be unable to detect the difference between the original source and the mockingbird's imitation. • The Northern Mockingbird's energetic territorial dance is delightful to watch, as males square off in what appears to be a swordless fencing duel. • The scientific name *polyglottos* is Greek for "many tongues" and refers to this bird's ability to mimic a wide variety of sounds.

ID: gray upperparts; dark wings; 2 thin, white wing bars; long, dark tail with white outer tail feathers; light gray underparts. *Juvenile:* paler overall; spotted breast. *In flight:* large white patch at base of black primaries.

Size: *L* 10 in; *W* 14 in.

Status: rare migrant and breeder from late April to late October in western Lower Peninsula; rare winter resident from October to March in southwestern Michigan.

Habitat: hedges, suburban gardens and orchard margins with an abundance of available fruit; hedgerows of multiflora roses are especially important in winter.

Nesting: often in a small shrub or small tree; cup nest is built with twigs, grass, fur and leaves; female incubates 3–4 brown-blotched, bluish gray to greenish eggs for 12–13 days.

Feeding: gleans vegetation and forages on the ground for beetles, ants, wasps and grasshoppers; also eats berries and wild fruit; visits feeders for suet and raisins.

Voice: song is a medley of mimicked phrases, with the phrases often repeated 3 times or more; calls include a harsh *chair* and *chewk*.

Similar Species: *Northern Shrike* (p. 203) and *Loggerhead Shrike* (p. 202): thicker, hooked bill; black mask; juveniles are stockier and less vocal. *Townsend's Solitaire* (p. 236): prominent eye ring; peach rather than white on wings. *Gray Catbird* (p. 244): gray overall; black "cap"; chestnut undertail coverts; lacks white outer tail feathers.

Selected Sites: western counties within 50 mi of L. Michigan.

BROWN THRASHER

Toxostoma rufum

Amid the various chirps and warbles that rise from woodland and lakefront edges in spring and early summer, the song of the male Brown Thrasher stands alone—its lengthy, complex chorus of twice-repeated phrases is truly unique. This thrasher has the most extensive vocal repertoire of any North American bird, and estimates indicate it is capable of up to 3000 distinctive combinations of various phrases. • Despite its relatively large size, the Brown Thrasher generally goes unnoticed in its shrubby domain. A typical sighting of this thrasher consists of nothing more than a flash of rufous as it zips from one tangle to another. • Because the Brown Thrasher nests on or close to the ground, its eggs and nestlings are particularly vulnerable to predation by snakes, weasels, skunks and other animals. Even though Brown Thrashers are aggressive, vigilant nest defenders, the parents' spirited defense, sometimes to the point of drawing blood, is not always enough to protect their progeny. • Unlike other notable singers, such as the Northern Mockingbird and the similarly shaped, shrub-dwelling Gray Catbird, the Brown Thrasher prefers to live well away from urban areas.

ID: reddish brown upperparts; pale underparts with heavy, brown spotting and streaking; long, slender, down-curved bill; yellow orange eyes; long, rufous tail; yellow legs; 2 white wing bars.

Size: *L* 11½ in; *W* 13 in.

Status: uncommon migrant and breeder from late April to October.

Habitat: dense shrubs and thickets, overgrown pastures (especially those with hawthorns), woodland edges and brushy areas; rarely close to human habitation.

Nesting: usually in a low shrub; often on the ground; cup nest made of grass, twigs and leaves is lined with fine vegetation; pair incubates 4 bluish white to pale blue eggs, dotted with reddish brown, for 11–14 days.

Feeding: gleans the ground and vegetation for larval and adult invertebrates; occasionally tosses leaves aside with its bill; also eats seeds and berries.

Voice: sings a large variety of phrases, with each phrase usually repeated twice: *dig-it dig-it, hoe-it hoe-it, pull-it-up pull-it-up;* calls include a loud crackling note, a harsh *shuck,* a soft *churr* and a whistled, 3-note *pit-cher-ee.*

Similar Species: *Hermit Thrush* (p. 240): shorter tail; gray brown back and crown; dark brown eyes; much shorter bill; lacks wing bars.

Selected Sites: protected brushy areas or farmland.

EUROPEAN STARLING
Sturnus vulgaris

The European Starling was introduced to North America in 1890 and 1891, when about 100 birds were released into New York's Central Park as part of the local Shakespeare society's plan to introduce all the birds mentioned in their favorite author's writings. The European Starling quickly established itself in the New York landscape, then spread rapidly across the continent, often at the expense of many native cavity-nesting birds, such as the Tree Swallow, Eastern Bluebird and Red-headed Woodpecker. Despite many concerted efforts to control or even eradicate this species, the European Starling will no doubt continue to assert its claim in the New World. The more than 200 million starlings in North America today are believed to have sprung from these first 100 birds.

• Courting European Starlings are infamous for their ability to reproduce the sounds of other birds such as Killdeers, Red-tailed Hawks, Soras and meadowlarks.

breeding

ID: short, squared tail; dark eyes. *Breeding:* blackish, iridescent plumage; yellow bill. *Nonbreeding:* black-ish wings; feather tips are heavily spotted with white and buff. *Juvenile:* gray brown plumage; brown bill. *In flight:* pointed, triangular wings.
Size: L 8½ in; W 16 in.
Status: abundant year-round resident.
Habitat: agricultural areas, townsites, woodland and forest edges, landfills and roadsides.
Nesting: in an abandoned woodpecker cavity, natural cavity, nest box or other arti-ficial cavity; nest is made of grass, twigs and straw; mostly the female incubates 4–6 bluish to greenish white eggs for 12–14 days.
Feeding: forages mostly on the ground; diverse diet includes many invertebrates, berries, seeds and human food waste.
Voice: variety of whistles, squeaks and gur-gles; imitates other birds.
Similar Species: *Rusty Blackbird* (p. 319): longer tail; black bill; lacks spotting; yellow eyes; rusty tinge on upperparts in fall. *Brewer's Blackbird* (p. 320): longer tail; black bill; lacks spotting; male has yellow eyes; female is brown overall. *Brown-headed Cowbird* (p. 322): lacks spotting; adult male has longer tail, shorter, dark bill and brown head; juvenile has streaked underparts, stout bill and longer tail.
Selected Sites: widespread in cities, towns and agricultural areas.

AMERICAN PIPIT

Anthus rubescens

Each fall, agricultural fields and open shorelines serve as refueling stations for large concentrations of migratory American Pipits. Flocks of pipits may go unnoticed to untrained eyes, because their dull brown-and-buff plumage blends into the landscape. But to keen observers, their plain attire, white outer tail feathers and habit of continuously wagging their tails makes them readily identifiable. The best indicator that pipits are near is their telltale, two-syllable call of *pip-it pip-it*, which is usually given in flight. • Although adults may already be paired upon arriving on their nesting grounds—a strategy that is thought to save valuable nesting time—a conspicuous courtship display helps each pair establish and defend the boundaries of their exclusive nesting territory. American Pipits nest in the Arctic, so few of us will ever have a chance to view this bird on its nesting grounds. • This bird was formerly known as "Water Pipit" (*A. spinoletta*).

breeding

ID: faintly streaked, gray brown upperparts; lightly streaked "necklace" on upper breast; streaked sides and flanks; dark legs; dark tail with white outer tail feathers; buff-colored underparts; slim bill and body.
Size: *L* 6–7 in; *W* 10½ in.
Status: uncommon fall migrant from September to early November; rare spring migrant from April to early June.

Habitat: agricultural fields, pastures and shores of wetlands, lakes and rivers.
Nesting: does not nest in Michigan.
Feeding: gleans the ground and vegetation for terrestrial and aquatic invertebrates and for seeds.
Voice: familiar flight call is *pip-it pip-it*. *Male:* harsh, sharp *tsip-tsip* or *chiwee*.
Similar Species: *Horned Lark* (p. 214): black "horns"; facial markings. *Sprague's Pipit:* lighter back with strong streaking; paler buff breast.
Selected Sites: Allegan SGA; Whitefish Point; Berrien Co.

BOHEMIAN WAXWING

Bombycilla garrulus

Descending upon mountain-ash and other ornamental plantings, great flocks of Bohemian Waxwings thrill us with their unpredictable appearances. Bohemian Waxwings nest in northern forests in Alaska and western Canada, and visit Michigan only during winter in search of food. Their faint, quavering whistles attract attentive naturalists who take pleasure in watching the birds descend on berry-filled trees. In most years, Bohemians are only seen in small groups, usually intermingled with overwintering flocks of similar-looking Cedar Waxwings. Their chestnut undertail coverts readily distinguish them from their Cedar Waxwing counterparts. • Waxwings get their name from the spots on their secondary feathers. These "waxy" spots are actually colorful enlargements of the feather shafts, whose pigments are derived from the birds' berry-filled diet. Juvenile birds have smaller pigment spots that will grow in size until the birds reach their adult plumage.

ID: gray and cinnamon crest; black "mask" and throat; soft brownish gray body; yellow terminal tail band; chestnut undertail coverts; small white, red and yellow markings on wings. *Juvenile:* gray brown upperparts; streaked underparts; pale throat; no "mask"; white wing patches.
Size: *L* 8 in; *W* 14 in.
Status: irregularly uncommon to absent winter resident statewide; uncommon winter resident in Upper Peninsula from October to March.

Habitat: natural and residential areas with wild berries and fruit.
Nesting: does not nest in Michigan.
Feeding: gleans vegetation for insects and wild fruit or catches flying insects on the wing; depends on berries and fruit in winter.
Voice: faint, high-pitched, quavering whistle.
Similar Species: *Cedar Waxwing* (p. 250): smaller; browner overall; slight yellow wash on belly; white undertail coverts; lacks yellow on wings.
Selected Sites: Whitefish Point; Seney NWR; Marquette; Grand Marais; Pictured Rocks National Lakeshore; Garden Peninsula; Porcupine Mountains Wilderness SP.

CEDAR WAXWING

Bombycilla cedrorum

Flocks of handsome Cedar Waxwings gorge on berries during late summer and fall. Waxwings have a remarkable ability to digest a wide variety of berries, some of which are inedible or even poisonous to humans. If the fruits have fermented, these birds will show definite signs of tipsiness. Native berry-producing trees and shrubs planted in your backyard can attract Cedar Waxwings and will often encourage them to nest in your area. • Cedar Waxwing pairs perform a wonderful courtship dance: the male first lands slightly away from the female, then tentatively hops toward her and offers her a berry. The female accepts the berry and hops away from the male, then she stops, hops back, and offers him the berry. This gentle ritual can last for several minutes. Cedar Waxwings are late nesters, which ensures that the berry crops will be ripe when nestlings are ready to be fed. • Practiced observers learn to recognize this bird by its high-pitched, trilling calls.

ID: cinnamon crest; brown upperparts; black "mask"; yellow wash on belly; gray rump; yellow terminal tail band; white undertail coverts; small red "drops" on wings. *Juvenile:* no "mask"; streaked underparts; gray brown body.
Size: *L* 7 in; *W* 12 in.
Status: common year-round resident.
Habitat: wooded residential parks and gardens, overgrown fields, forest edges, second-growth, riparian and open woodlands.
Nesting: in a coniferous or deciduous tree or shrub; cup nest of twigs, grass, moss and lichen is lined with fine grass; female incubates 3–5 pale gray to bluish gray eggs, with fine dark spotting, for 12–16 days.
Feeding: catches flying insects on the wing or gleans vegetation; also eats large amounts of berries and wild fruit, especially in fall and winter.
Voice: faint, high-pitched, trilled whistle: *tseee-tseee-tseee.*
Similar Species: *Bohemian Waxwing* (p. 249): larger; chestnut undertail coverts; small white, red and yellow markings on wings; juvenile has chestnut undertail coverts and white wing patches.
Selected Sites: wooded areas statewide.

BLUE-WINGED WARBLER
Vermivora pinus

During the mid-1800s, the Blue-winged Warbler began expanding its range eastward and northward from its home in the central midwestern U.S., finding new breeding territories among overgrown fields and pastures near abandoned human settlements. Eventually it came into contact with the Golden-winged Warbler, a bird with completely different looks but practically identical habitat requirements and breeding biology. Where both species share the same habitat, a distinctive, fertile hybrid known as the Brewster's Warbler may be produced. This hybrid tends to be more grayish overall, like the Golden-winged Warbler, but it retains the thin, black eye line and the touch of yellow on the breast from its Blue-winged parent. In rare instances when two of these hybrids are able to reproduce successfully, a second-generation hybrid known as the Lawrence's Warbler is produced. It is more yellowish overall, like the Blue-winged Warbler, but has the black "mask," "chin" and throat of the Golden-winged Warbler.

breeding

ID: bright yellow head and underparts, except for white to yellowish undertail coverts; olive yellow upperparts; bluish gray wings and tail; black eye line; thin, dark bill; 2 white wing bars; bold white tail spots on underside of tail.
Size: *L* 4½–5 in; *W* 7½ in.
Status: common migrant and breeder from early May to mid-September in southern Lower Peninsula.
Habitat: second-growth woodlands, willow swamps, shrubby, overgrown fields, pastures, woodland edges and woodland openings.
Nesting: on or near the ground, concealed by vegetation; female builds a narrow, inverted, cone-shaped nest of grass, leaves and bark strips and lines it with soft materials; female incubates 5 white eggs, with fine brown spots toward the larger end, for about 11 days.
Feeding: gleans insects and spiders from the lower branches of trees and shrubs.
Voice: buzzy, 2-note song: *beee-bzzz*.
Similar Species: *Prothonotary Warbler* (p. 275): lacks black eye line and white wing bars. *Pine Warbler* (p. 266): darker; white belly; faint streaking on sides and breast. *Yellow Warbler* (p. 257): yellow wings; lacks black eye line. *Prairie Warbler* (p. 268): black streaking on sides and flanks; darker wings.
Selected Sites: Port Huron SGA; Indian Springs Metropark; Pinckney SRA; Kalamazoo Nature Center; Warren Woods Natural Area; Allegan SGA; Rose Lake WA.

GOLDEN-WINGED WARBLER

Vermivora chrysoptera

Unlike people, who are able to build fences around their property, the male Golden-winged Warbler uses song to defend his nesting territory. If song fails to repel rival males, then body language and aggression calls warn intruders to stay away. When a male's claim is seriously challenged, a warning call, a raised crown and a spread tail may be employed. The last resort is to physically remove the competitor in a high-speed chase or a winged duel. • The battle to maintain breeding territory is not confined within the species—the Golden-winged Warbler may be losing ground to its colonizing relative the Blue-winged Warbler, which seems to be outcompeting the Golden-winged Warbler through hybridization. • Blue-winged and Golden-winged Warblers have very similar songs. The Blue-winged Warbler will sometimes sing the Golden-winged Warbler's primary song, which can make identification based on song very difficult.

♂ *breeding*

♀

ID: yellow forecrown and wing patch; dark "chin," throat and "mask" over eye are bordered by white; bluish gray upperparts and flanks; white undersides; white tail spots on underside of tail. *Female* and *immature:* duller overall with gray throat and mask.
Size: *L* 4½–5 in; *W* 7½ in.
Status: common migrant from May to early June and from August to September; common breeder from June to August in the north.
Habitat: moist shrubby fields, woodland edges and early-succession forest clearings.
Nesting: on the ground, concealed by vegetation; female builds an open cup nest of grasses, leaves and grapevine bark and lines it with softer materials; female incubates 5 pinkish to pale cream eggs, marked with brown and lilac, for about 11 days.
Feeding: gleans insects and spiders from tree and shrub canopies.
Voice: buzzy song begins with a higher note: *zee-bz-bz-bz;* call is a sweet *chip.*
Similar Species: *Yellow-rumped Warbler* (p. 262): white throat; dark breast patches; yellow sides. *Yellow-throated Warbler* (p. 265): lacks yellow crown; 2 white wing bars; yellow throat. *Black-throated Green Warbler* (p. 263): lacks dark "mask"; 2 white wing bars; black streaking on sides.
Selected Sites: Port Huron SGA; Holly SRA; Rose Lake WA; Gratiot–Saginaw SGA; P. J. Hoffmaster SP; Chippewa Nature Center.

TENNESSEE WARBLER

Vermivora peregrina

Tennessee Warblers lack the bold, bright features found on other warblers. Even so, they are difficult birds to miss because they have a loud, familiar song and are relatively common in Michigan. • Migrating Tennessee Warblers often sing their tunes and forage for insects high in the forest canopy. However, inclement weather and the need for food after a long flight can force these birds to lower levels in the forest. • Females build their nests on the ground and usually remain close to the forest floor when foraging. • Tennessee Warblers thrive during spruce budworm outbreaks. During times of plenty, these birds may produce more than seven young in a single brood. • Alexander Wilson discovered this bird along the Cumberland River in Tennessee and named it after that state. It is just a migrant in Tennessee, though, and breeds only in Canada, northern Michigan and north-eastern Minnesota. • Tennessee Warblers are easily confused with Warbling Vireos and Philadelphia Vireos.

breeding

ID: *Breeding male:* blue gray "cap"; olive green back, wings and tail edgings; white "eyebrow"; black eye line; clean white underparts; thin bill. *Breeding female:* yellow wash on breast and "eyebrow"; olive gray "cap." *Non-breeding:* olive yellow upperparts; yellow "eyebrow"; yellow underparts except for white undertail coverts; male may have white belly.
Size: *L* 4½–5 in; *W* 8 in.
Status: common migrant from May to early June and from mid-August to early October; rare breeder from June to July in Upper Peninsula.
Habitat: *Breeding:* coniferous or mixed mature forests and occasionally spruce bogs. *In migration:* woodlands or areas with tall shrubs.

Nesting: on the ground or on a raised hummock; female builds a small cup nest of grass, moss and roots and lines it with fur; female incubates 5–6 white eggs, marked with brown or purple, for 11–12 days.
Feeding: gleans foliage and buds for small insects, caterpillars and other invertebrates; also eats berries; occasionally visits suet feeders.
Voice: male's song is a loud, sharp, accelerating *ticka-ticka-ticka swit-swit-swit-swit chew-chew-chew-chew-chew;* call is a sweet *chip.*
Similar Species: *Warbling Vireo* (p. 207): stouter overall; thicker bill; much less green on upperparts. *Philadelphia Vireo* (p. 208): stouter overall; thicker bill; yellow breast and sides. *Orange-crowned Warbler* (p. 254): lacks white "eyebrow" and blue gray head.
Selected Sites: Indian Springs Metropark; Waterloo SRA; Kalamazoo Nature Center; Allegan SGA; Tawas Point SP; Whitefish Point; Wilderness SP.

ORANGE-CROWNED WARBLER

Vermivora celata

Don't be disappointed if you can't see the Orange-crowned Warbler's orange crown, because this bird's most distinguishing characteristic is its lack of field marks: wing bars, eye rings and color patches are all conspicuously absent. • The Orange-crowned Warbler is generally rare to uncommon in Michigan. When encountered, it usually appears as a blurred, olive yellow bundle flitting nervously among the leaves and branches of low shrubs. In addition, its drab, olive yellow appearance makes it frustratingly similar to females of other warbler species. • The Orange-crowned Warbler is often the most common species to capitalize on the sap wells drilled by Yellow-bellied Sapsuckers. • *Vermivora* is Latin for "worm eating," while *celata* is derived from the Latin word for "hidden," a reference to this bird's inconspicuous crown.

ID: olive yellow to olive gray body; faintly streaked underparts; bright yellow undertail coverts; thin, faint, dark eye line; bright yellow "eyebrow" and broken eye ring; thin bill; faint orange crown patch (rarely seen).

Size: *L* 5 in; *W* 7 in.

Status: uncommon migrant from late April to late May and from late August to late October.

Habitat: woodlands or areas with tall shrubs.

Nesting: does not nest in Michigan.

Feeding: gleans foliage for invertebrates, berries, nectar and sap; often hover-gleans.

Voice: *Male:* faint trill that breaks downward halfway through; call is a clear, sharp *chip*.

Similar Species: *Tennessee Warbler* (p. 253): blue gray head; dark eye line; bold white "eyebrow"; white underparts including undertail coverts. *Ruby-crowned Kinglet* (p. 233): broken white eye ring; white wing bars. *Wilson's Warbler* (p. 285): complete, bright yellow eye ring; brighter yellow underparts; pale legs; lacks breast streaks. *Yellow Warbler* (p. 257): brighter head and underparts; reddish breast streaks (faint or absent on female). *Common Yellowthroat* (p. 283): female has darker face and upperparts; lacks breast streaks.

Selected Sites: Stony Creek Metropark; Waterloo SRA; Fort Custer SRA; Allegan SGA; Chippewa Nature Center; Whitefish Point; Marquette.

NASHVILLE WARBLER

Vermivora ruficapilla

Nashville Warblers have an unusual distribution, with two widely separated summer populations: one eastern and the other western. These populations are believed to have been created thousands of years ago when a single core population was split apart during continental glaciation. • Nashville Warblers are common migrants and breeders in Michigan. They are best found in overgrown farmland and second-growth forest as they forage low in trees and thickets, often at the edge of a dry forest or burn area. • The Nashville Warbler's song is a thin, two-part trill, which is used infrequently if other competing Nashvilles are absent from the area. • This warbler was first described near Nashville, Tennessee, but it does not breed in that state. This misnomer is not an isolated incident: the Tennessee, Cape May and Connecticut warblers all bear names that misrepresent their breeding distributions.

ID: bold white eye ring; yellow green upperparts; yellow underparts; white between legs. *Male:* blue gray head; may show a small, chestnut red crown. *Female and immature:* duller overall; light eye ring; olive gray head; blue gray nape.
Size: L 4½–5 in; W 7½ in.
Status: common migrant from late April to May and from late August to mid-October; common breeder from June to August in the north.
Habitat: second-growth mixed woodlands are preferred; also wet coniferous forests, riparian woodlands, cedar-spruce swamps and moist, shrubby, abandoned fields.
Nesting: on the ground under a fern, sapling or shrubby cover; female builds a cup nest of grass, bark strips, ferns and moss and lines it with conifer needles, fur and fine grasses; female incubates 4–5 white eggs, with reddish brown spots toward the larger end, for 11–12 days.
Feeding: gleans foliage for insects, such as caterpillars, flies and aphids.
Voice: *Male:* song begins with a thin, high-pitched *see-it see-it see-it see-it,* followed by a trilling *ti-ti-ti-ti-ti;* call is a metallic *chink.*
Similar Species: *Common Yellowthroat* (p. 283) and *Wilson's Warbler* (p. 285): all-yellow underparts; females lack grayish head and bold white eye ring. *Connecticut Warbler* (p. 282) and *Mourning Warbler* (p. 281): yellow between legs; females have grayish to brownish "hood."
Selected Sites: Dearborn Environmental Study Area; Indian Springs Metropark; Waterloo SRA; Fort Custer SRA; P. J. Hoffmaster SP; Tawas Point SP; Whitefish Point; J. W. Wells SP.

NORTHERN PARULA

Parula americana

Young Northern Parulas spend the first few weeks of their lives enclosed in a fragile, socklike nest suspended from a tree branch. Once they have grown too large for the nest and their wing feathers are strong enough to allow for a short, awkward flight, the young leave their warm abode, dispersing among the surrounding trees and shrubs. As warm summer nights slip away to be replaced by cooler fall temperatures, newly fledged Northern Parulas migrate to the warmer climes of Central America, but mature birds winter in the U.S. • Nesting Northern Parulas are typically found in older forests where the lichens that they use in their nests have had a chance to mature. Males spend most of their time singing and foraging among the tops of tall coniferous spires. When the young are hatched, Parulas expand their foraging areas from just conifers to include deciduous trees, or from only deciduous trees to include understory shrubs, to obtain the extra food needed for the new family.

breeding

ID: blue gray upperparts; olive patch on back; 2 bold white wing bars; bold, white eye ring is broken by black eye line; yellow "chin," throat and breast; white belly and flanks. *Male:* 1 black and 1 orange breast band.

Size: L 4½ in; W 7 in.

Status: uncommon migrant from late April to late May and from early August to mid-October; uncommon breeder from June to August in the north.

Habitat: *Breeding:* moist coniferous forests, humid riparian woodlands and swampy deciduous woodlands, especially where lichens hang from branches. *In migration:* woodlands or areas with tall shrubs.

Nesting: usually in a conifer; female weaves a small hanging nest into hanging strands of tree lichens; may add lichens to a dense cluster of conifer boughs; pair incubates 4–5 brown-marked, whitish eggs for 12–14 days.

Feeding: forages for insects and other invertebrates by hovering, gleaning or hawking; feeds from the tips of branches and occasionally on the ground.

Voice: song is a rising, buzzy trill ending with an abrupt, lower-pitched *zip*.

Similar Species: *Cerulean Warbler* (p. 272): streaking on breast and sides; lacks white eye ring. *Blue-winged Warbler* (p. 251): yellow underparts. *Yellow-rumped Warbler* (p. 262): yellow rump and crown; lacks yellow throat. *Yellow-throated Warbler* (p. 265) and *Kirtland's Warbler* (p. 267): heavy black streaking along sides.

Selected Sites: Indian Springs Metropark; Waterloo SRA; Kalamazoo Nature Center; Allegan SGA; Wilderness SP; Whitefish Point; Garden Peninsula.

YELLOW WARBLER

Dendroica petechia

Yellow Warblers usually arrive here in early May in search of caterpillars, aphids, beetles and other invertebrates. Flitting from branch to branch among open woodland edges and riparian shrubs, these inquisitive birds seem to be in perpetual motion. • Yellow Warblers are among the most frequent victims of nest parasitism by Brown-headed Cowbirds. Unlike many birds, they can recognize the foreign eggs and many pairs will either abandon their nest or build another nest overtop the old eggs. Some persistent Yellow Warblers build over and over, creating bizarre, multilayered, high-rise nests. • During fall migration, silent, plain-looking Yellow Warblers and other similar-looking warblers can cause confusion for birders who have been lulled into a false sense of familiarity with these birds. Yellow Warblers are unique, however, in having yellow flashes on the sides of their tails. • Because of their bright yellow plumage, Yellow Warblers are often mistakenly called "Wild Canaries."

breeding

ID: bright yellow body; yellowish legs; black bill and eyes; bright yellow highlights on dark yellow olive tail and wings. *Breeding male:* red breast streaks. *Breeding female:* faint, red breast streaks.
Size: *L* 5 in; *W* 8 in.
Status: common migrant and breeder from May to August.
Habitat: moist, open woodlands with dense, low scrub; also shrubby meadows, willow tangles, shrubby fencerows and riparian woodlands; usually near water.
Nesting: in a fork in a deciduous tree or small shrub; female builds a compact cup nest of grass, weeds and shredded bark and lines it with plant down and fur;

female incubates 4–5 speckled or spotted, greenish white eggs for 11–12 days.
Feeding: gleans foliage and vegetation for invertebrates, especially caterpillars, inchworms, beetles, aphids and cankerworms; occasionally hover-gleans.
Voice: *Male:* song is a fast, frequently repeated *sweet-sweet-sweet summer sweet.*
Similar Species: *Orange-crowned Warbler* (p. 254): darker olive plumage overall; lacks reddish breast streaks. *American Goldfinch* (p. 333): black wings and tail; male often has black forehead. *Wilson's Warbler* (p. 285): shorter, darker tail; male has black "cap"; female has darker crown and upperparts. *Common Yellowthroat* (p. 283): darker face and upperparts; female lacks yellow highlights on wings.
Selected Sites: moist, open woodlands with dense shrubbery; also shrubby fencerows.

CHESTNUT-SIDED WARBLER

Dendroica pensylvanica

When colorful waves of warbler migrants flood across the landscape each May, the Chestnut-sided Warbler is consistently ranked among the most anticipated arrivals. The boldly patterned males never fail to dazzle onlookers as they flit about at eye level. • Chestnut-sided Warblers tend to favor early-succession forests, which have become abundant over the past century. Although clear-cut logging has had a negative impact on other warbler species, it has created suitable habitat for the Chestnut-sided Warbler in many parts of Michigan. A good indicator of this species' success is the fact that each spring you can easily see more Chestnut-sided Warblers in a single day than John J. Audubon saw in his entire life—he saw only one! • Although other warblers lose some of their brighter colors in fall yet still look familiar, the Chestnut-sided Warbler undergoes a complete transformation, looking more like a flycatcher or kinglet in its green-and-gray coat.

breeding

ID: *Breeding male:* chestnut brown sides; white underparts; yellow "cap"; black legs; yellowish wing bars; black "mask." *Breeding female:* similar to male; washed-out colors; dark streaking on yellow "cap." *Nonbreeding:* yellow green crown, nape and back; white eye ring; gray face and sides; white underparts. *Immature:* similar to nonbreeding adult, but has brighter yellow wing bars.

Size: *L* 5 in; *W* 8 in.

Status: common migrant in May and from mid-August to October; breeder from June to August, local in the south, increasingly abundant toward the north.

Habitat: shrubby, deciduous second-growth woodlands, abandoned fields and orchards; especially in areas that are regenerating after logging or fire.

Nesting: low in a shrub or sapling; small cup nest is made of bark strips, grass, roots and weed fibers and lined with fine grasses, plant down and fur; female incubates 4 brown-marked, whitish eggs for 11–12 days.

Feeding: gleans trees and shrubs at midlevel for insects.

Voice: loud, clear song: *so pleased, pleased, pleased to MEET-CHA!;* musical *chip* call.

Similar Species: *Bay-breasted Warbler* (p. 270): black face; dark chestnut hind-crown, upper breast and sides; buff belly and undertail coverts; white wing bars. *American Redstart* (p. 274): female has large, yellow patches on wings and tail; more grayish overall.

Selected Sites: Stony Creek Metropark; Pinckney SRA; Kalamazoo Nature Center; Gratiot–Saginaw SGA; P. J. Hoffmaster SP; Wilderness SP; Whitefish Point.

MAGNOLIA WARBLER

Dendroica magnolia

The Magnolia Warbler is widely regarded as one of the most beautiful wood warblers. Like a customized Cadillac, the Magnolia comes fully loaded with all the fancy features: bold "eyebrows," flashy wing bars and tail patches, an elegant "necklace," a bright yellow rump and breast and a dark "mask." It frequently forages along the lower branches of trees and among shrubs, allowing for reliable, close-up observations. • Male Magnolias flash their white wing and tail patches, snap bills, chase and use *chip* notes to discourage intruders, but competitive singing is used to settle the most intense disputes. • When spring cold fronts meet with flocks of migrant songbirds riding warm air across the Great Lakes, thousands of birds may be landbound. Magnolia Warblers and many other songbirds migrate at night. Unfortunately, many birds are killed each year when they collide with buildings, radio towers and tall smokestacks.

breeding

ID: *Breeding male:* yellow underparts with bold black streaks; black "mask"; white "eyebrow"; blue gray crown; dark upperparts; white wing bars often blend into larger patch. *Female* and *nonbreeding male:* duller overall; pale "mask"; 2 distinct white wing bars; streaked, olive back. *In flight:* yellow rump; white tail patches.
Size: L 4¹/₂–5 in; W 7¹/₂ in.
Status: common migrant throughout May and from early September to early October; breeder from June to August, common in Upper Peninsula, uncommon in northern Lower Peninsula.
Habitat: *Breeding:* open coniferous and mixed forests, mostly in natural openings and along edges, often near water; often prefers areas with short balsam fir and white spruce. *In migration:* woodlands or areas with tall shrubs.

Nesting: on a horizontal limb in a conifer; loose cup nest is made of grass, twigs and weeds and is lined with rootlets; female incubates 4 white eggs, marked with olive, brown, gray and lavender, for 11–13 days.
Feeding: gleans vegetation and buds; occasionally flycatches for beetles, flies, wasps, caterpillars and other insects; sometimes eats berries.
Voice: *Male:* song is a quick, rising *pretty pretty lady* or *wheata wheata wheet-zu;* call is a *clank.*
Similar Species: *Yellow-rumped Warbler* (p. 262): white throat; yellow hindcrown patch; white belly. *Cape May Warbler* (p. 260): chestnut "cheek" patch on yellow face; lacks white tail patches. *Prairie Warbler* (p. 268): dusky jaw stripe; faint, yellowish wing bars; immature lacks white tail patches.
Selected Sites: Holly SRA; Waterloo SRA; Fort Custer SRA; Warren Woods Natural Area; Allegan SGA; Chippewa Nature Center; Wilderness SP; Whitefish Point; Sylvania Recreation Area.

259

CAPE MAY WARBLER

Dendroica tigrina

Cape May Warblers require mature forests that are at least 50 years old for secure nesting habitat and an abundance of canopy-dwelling insects—in Michigan they nest mainly in mature spruce bogs. You may find yourself with "a pain in the neck" as you strain your head back for a glimpse of these warblers as they forage and sing at the very tops of tall trees. • Throughout most of their breeding range, these small birds are spruce budworm specialists. In years of budworm outbreaks, Cape Mays successfully fledge more young. In Michigan, harvesting of old-growth spruce adversely affects breeding populations of these warblers. • The Cape May's semi-tubular tongue is unique among wood-warblers and allows it to feed on nectar and fruit juices, both during migration and on its tropical wintering grounds. Named after Cape May, New Jersey, where the first scientific specimen was collected in 1811, this bird was not recorded there again for more than 100 years!

breeding

ID: dark streaking on yellow underparts; yellow side "collar"; dark olive green upperparts; yellow rump; clean white undertail coverts. *Breeding male:* chestnut "cheek" on yellow face; dark crown; large, white wing patch. *Female:* paler overall; 2 faint, thin, white wing bars; grayish "cheek" and crown.

Size: *L* 4½–5½ in; *W* 8 in.

Status: common migrant from early May to June and from mid-August to early October; breeder from June to August, uncommon in Upper Peninsula, rare in northern Lower Peninsula.

Habitat: mature coniferous and mixed forests, especially in dense old-growth stands of white spruce and balsam fir.

Nesting: near the top of a spruce or fir, often near the trunk; female builds a cup nest of moss, weeds and grass and lines it with feathers and fur; female incubates 6–7 whitish eggs, spotted with reddish brown, for about 12 days.

Feeding: gleans treetop branches and foliage for spruce budworms, flies, beetles, moths, wasps and other insects; occasionally hover-gleans.

Voice: song is a very high-pitched, weak *see see see see*; call is a very high-pitched *tsee*.

Similar Species: *Bay-breasted Warbler* (p. 270): male has black face and chestnut throat, upper breast and sides; 2 white wing bars; buff underparts lack black streaking. *Black-throated Green Warbler* (p. 263): black throat or upper breast or both; white lower breast and belly; lacks chestnut "cheek" patch; 2 white wing bars. *Magnolia Warbler* (p. 259): white tail patches; less streaking on underparts; lacks chestnut "cheek" patch and yellow side collar.

Selected Sites: Port Huron SGA; Waterloo SRA; P. J. Hoffmaster SP; Kalamazoo Nature Center; Gratiot-Saginaw SGA; Chippewa Nature Center; Wilderness SP; Whitefish Point.

BLACK-THROATED BLUE WARBLER

Dendroica caerulescens

Dark and handsome, the male Black-throated Blue Warbler is a treasured sight to the eyes of any bird enthusiast or casual admirer. The female looks nothing like her male counterpart, however, appearing more like a vireo or a plain-colored Tennessee Warbler. The males and females are so different in appearance that early naturalists, including John J. Audubon, initially thought that they were two different species. • When foraging, this warbler prefers to work methodically over a small area, snatching up insects from branches and foliage, and gleaning insects from the undersides of leaves. It is generally shy and inconspicuous, foraging secretly within the dense confines of low shrubs and saplings. • Typical of warblers, the Black-throated Blue female is able to construct a highly sophisticated nest within three to five days using cobwebs and saliva to glue strips of bark together. The inside of the nest is usually padded with shredded bark, moss, pine needles and any available mammal hair, such as skunk and human hair.

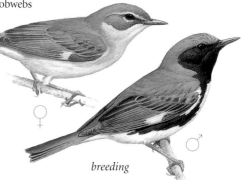

breeding

ID: *Male:* black face, throat, upper breast and sides; dark blue upperparts; clean white underparts and wing patch. *Female:* olive brown upperparts; unmarked buff underparts; faint white "eyebrow"; small, buff to whitish wing patch (may not be visible).

Size: *L* 5–5¹/₂ in; *W* 7¹/₂ in.

Status: common migrant from May to early June and from mid-August to late September; common breeder from June to July in northern Michigan.

Habitat: *Breeding:* upland deciduous and mixed forests of northern Michigan with a dense understory of deciduous saplings and shrubs; second-growth woodlands and brushy clearings. *In migration:* shrubby woodlands or areas with tall shrubs.

Nesting: in the fork of a dense shrub or sapling, usually within 3 ft of the ground; female builds an open cup nest of weeds,

bark strips and spider webs and lines it with moss, hair and pine needles; female incubates 4 creamy white eggs, blotched with reddish brown and gray toward the larger end, for 12–13 days.

Feeding: thoroughly gleans the understory for caterpillars, moths, spiders and other insects; occasionally eats berries and seeds; feeds less energetically than other wood-warblers.

Voice: song is a slow, wheezy *I am soo lay-zeee*, rising slowly throughout; call is a short *tip*.

Similar Species: male is distinctive. *Tennessee Warbler* (p. 253): lighter "cheek"; greener back; lacks white wing patch. *Philadelphia Vireo* (p. 208): stouter bill; lighter "cheek"; more yellowish white below; lacks white wing patch. *Cerulean Warbler* (p. 272): female has 2 white wing bars; broader, yellowish "eyebrow."

Selected Sites: Highland SRA; Kalamazoo Nature Center; Grand Mere SP; Yankee Springs SRA; Sleeping Bear Dunes National Lakeshore; Sylvania Recreation Area; Isle Royale NP.

YELLOW-RUMPED WARBLER

Dendroica coronata

The Yellow-rumped Warbler is the most abundant and widespread wood-warbler in North America. Your greatest chance of meeting it is each spring from late April to late May, though an occasional observation is made in southern Michigan during winter. The best time to look for this bird is during the first few hours after dawn, when most Yellow-rumps forage among streamside and lakeshore trees. • Two races of the Yellow-rumped Warbler, which were once considered separate species, occur in Michigan: the white-throated race, formerly called "Myrtle Warbler," and the very rarely seen yellow-throated western race, formerly called "Audubon's Warbler." • Adults are generally quiet when they have eggs or young to guard. When they are noisy and aggressive, it is a good sign that the young have left the nest. • The scientific name *coronata*, Latin for "crowned," refers to this bird's yellow crown.

♂

♀

breeding
"Myrtle Warbler"

ID: yellow fore-shoulder patches and rump; white underparts; dark "cheek"; faint white wing bars; thin "eyebrow." *Male:* yellow crown; blue gray upper-parts with black streaking; black "cheek," breast band and streaking along sides and flanks. *Female:* gray brown upperparts with dark streaking; dark streaking on breast, sides and flanks.

Size: *L* 5–6 in; *W* 9 in.

Status: common migrant from mid-April to May and from August to October; common breeder from June to July in northern Michigan; rare winter resident from November to March in southern Michigan.

Habitat: *Breeding:* coniferous and mixed forests; rarely in open deciduous woodlands. *In migration:* woodlands or shrubby areas.

Nesting: in the crotch or on a horizontal limb of a conifer; female builds a compact cup nest of grass, bark strips, moss, lichen and spider silk and lines it with feathers and fur; female incubates 4–5 creamy white eggs, marked with brown and gray, for about 12 days.

Feeding: hawks and hovers for beetles, flies, wasps, caterpillars, moths and other insects; also gleans vegetation; sometimes eats berries.

Voice: *Male:* song is a tinkling trill, often given in 2-note phrases that rise or fall at the end (there can be much variation among individuals); call is a sharp *chip* or *check*.

Similar Species: *Magnolia Warbler* (p. 259): yellow underparts; yellow throat; bold, white "eyebrow"; lacks yellow crown; white patches on tail. *Chestnut-sided Warbler* (p. 258): chestnut sides on other-wise clean white underparts; lacks yellow rump. *Cape May Warbler* (p. 260): heavily streaked yellow throat, breast and sides; lacks yellow crown. *Yellow-throated Warbler* (p. 265): yellow throat; bold, white "eyebrow," ear patch and wing bars; lacks yellow crown and rump.

Selected Sites: Holly SRA; Pinckney SRA; Warren Woods Natural Area; Rogue River SGA; Gratiot-Saginaw SGA; Leelanau SP.

BLACK-THROATED GREEN WARBLER

Dendroica virens

Before the first warm rays of dawn brighten the spires of our forests, male Black-throated Green Warblers offer up their distinctive *see-see-see SUZY!* tunes. On their breeding grounds, not only do males use song to defend their turf, but they also seem to thrive on chasing each other, and even other songbirds, from their territories. • In other parts of its range, the Black-throated Green Warbler is a denizen of old-growth coniferous forests; in Michigan, however, it also nests in mixed woodlands, pure deciduous forests and even conifer plantations. • When foraging among the forest canopy, males are highly conspicuous as they dart from branch to branch, chipping noisily as they go. Females often prefer to feed at lower levels among the foliage of tall shrubs and sapling trees. • Black-throated Green females will lay one egg every day for four to five days, and will not begin to brood the eggs until the last egg is laid.

breeding

ID: yellow face; may show a faint dusky "cheek" or eye line; black upper breast band; streaking along sides; olive crown, back and rump; dark wings and tail; 2 bold, white wing bars; white lower breast, belly and undertail coverts. *Male:* black throat. *Female:* yellow throat; thinner wing bars.
Size: *L* 4½–5 in; *W* 7½ in.
Status: common migrant from late April to May and from late August to early October; common breeder from June to August in the southwest along L. Michigan and in northern Michigan.
Habitat: *Breeding:* coniferous and mixed forests; also in some deciduous woodlands composed of beech, maple or birch; may inhabit cedar swamps, hemlock ravines and conifer plantations. *In migration:* woodlands or areas with tall shrubs.

Nesting: in a crotch or on a horizontal limb, usually in a conifer; compact cup nest of grass, weeds, twigs, bark, lichens and spider silk is lined with moss, fur, feathers and plant fibers; female incubates 4–5 creamy white to gray eggs, scrawled or spotted with reddish brown, for 12 days.
Feeding: gleans vegetation and buds for beetles, flies, wasps, caterpillars and other insects; sometimes takes berries; frequently hover-gleans.
Voice: fast *see-see-see SUZY!* or *zoo zee zoo zoo zee;* call is a fairly soft *tick.*
Similar Species: *Blackburnian Warbler* (p. 264): female has yellowish underparts and angular, dusky facial patch. *Cape May Warbler* (p. 260): heavily streaked yellow throat, breast and sides. *Pine Warbler* (p. 266): yellowish breast and upper belly; lacks black upper breast band.
Selected Sites: Stony Creek Metropark; Pinckney SRA; Russ Forest; Allegan SGA; Gratiot-Saginaw SGA; Whitefish Point; Garden Peninsula.

263

BLACKBURNIAN WARBLER

Dendroica fusca

High among towering coniferous spires lives the colorful Blackburnian Warbler, its fiery orange throat ablaze in spring. Widely regarded as one of the most beautiful warblers in Michigan, the Blackburnian Warbler stays hidden in the upper canopy for much of the summer. • Different species of wood-warblers are able to coexist through a partitioning of foraging niches and feeding strategies. This intricate partitioning reduces competition for food sources and avoids the exhaustion of particular resources. Some warblers inhabit high treetops, a few feed and nest along outer tree branches—some at high levels and some at lower levels—and others restrict themselves to inner branches and tree trunks.

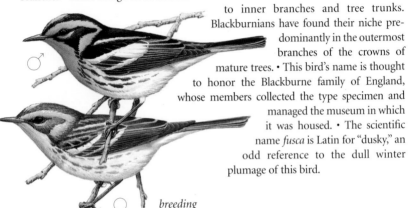

Blackburnians have found their niche predominantly in the outermost branches of the crowns of mature trees. • This bird's name is thought to honor the Blackburne family of England, whose members collected the type specimen and managed the museum in which it was housed. • The scientific name *fusca* is Latin for "dusky," an odd reference to the dull winter plumage of this bird.

breeding

ID: *Breeding male:* fiery reddish orange upper breast and throat; yellow orange head with angular, black "mask"; 2 broad, black crown stripes; blackish upperparts; large, white wing patch; yellowish to whitish underparts; dark streaking on sides and flanks; may show some white on outer tail feathers. *Female:* brown version of male; yellower upper breast and throat than male.
Size: L 4½–5½ in; W 8½ in.
Status: common migrant in May and from mid-August to mid-September; common breeder from June to August southwest along L. Michigan and in northern Michigan.
Habitat: *Breeding:* mature coniferous and mixed forests. *In migration:* woodlands or areas with tall shrubs.
Nesting: high in a mature conifer, often near a branch tip; female builds a cup nest

of bark, twigs and plant fibers and lines it with conifer needles, moss and fur; female incubates 3–5 white to greenish white eggs, blotched with reddish brown toward larger end, for about 13 days.
Feeding: forages on uppermost branches, gleaning budworms, flies, beetles and other invertebrates; occasionally hover-gleans.
Voice: song is a soft, faint, high-pitched *ptoo-too-too-too tititi zeee* or *see-me see-me see-me see-me;* call is a short *tick*.
Similar Species: *Yellow-throated Warbler* (p. 265): blue gray upperparts; white "eyebrow," ear patch and eye crescent; lacks orange throat. *Prairie Warbler* (p. 268): faint, yellowish wingbars; black facial stripes do not form a solid angular patch.
Selected Sites: Port Huron SGA; Allegan SGA; Sleeping Bear Dunes National Lakeshore; Whitefish Point; Tahquamenon Falls SP; Van Riper SP.

YELLOW-THROATED WARBLER

Dendroica dominica

The striking Yellow-throated Warbler is a breeding bird in the southeastern U.S., but a few pioneers have expanded their traditional range and migrated into riverine woodlands in southwestern Michigan. It's quite possible that global warming and efforts to encourage the regrowth of our southern deciduous forest might in time result in more Yellow-throated Warblers nesting in our state. Yellow-throats are fond of wet, lowland forests, and show a preference for the upper canopy. This warbler forages more like a creeper than a warbler, inserting its unusually long bill into cracks and crevices in bark. Yellow-throated Warblers often forage on the undersides of horizontal branches, and sometimes on the trunk, techniques also used by Black-and-white Warblers. • Fall and early winter can produce the odd wayward Yellow-throated Warbler at a backyard feeder.

breeding ♂

ID: yellow throat and upper breast; triangular, black face "mask"; black forehead; bold, white "eyebrow" and ear patch; white underparts with black streaking on sides; 2 white wing bars; bluish gray upperparts.

Size: *L* 5–5½ in; *W* 8 in.

Status: threatened; very rare migrant and breeder from early April to October along the southwestern border.

Habitat: primarily riparian woodlands with many tall sycamore trees; occasionally seen at backyard feeders in winter.

Nesting: high in a sycamore tree, often near a branch tip; female builds a cup nest of fine grasses, weed stems, plant down and caterpillar silk and lines it with sycamore down and feathers; female incubates 4 greenish white or gray white eggs, blotched and speckled with lavender, gray and wine red, for 12–13 days.

Feeding: primarily insectivorous; gleans insects from tree trunks and foliage by creeping along tree surfaces; often flycatches insects in midair; wintering birds may eat suet from feeders.

Voice: boisterous song is a series of downslurred whistles with a final rising note: *tee-ew tee-ew tee-ew tew-wee;* call is a loud *churp.*

Similar Species: *Magnolia Warbler* (p. 259): black "necklace"; yellow breast, belly and rump; lacks white ear patch. *Blackburnian Warbler* (p. 264): yellow orange to orange red throat, "eyebrow," ear patch and crown stripe; dark brown to blackish upperparts; often shows yellowish underparts. *Yellow-throated Vireo* (p. 205): lacks black and white on face and dark streaking on sides. *Kentucky Warbler* (p. 280): unmarked, all-yellow underparts; yellow "eyebrow"; lacks white ear patch and wing bars.

Selected Sites: Galien R. and its tributaries in and near Warren Woods Natural Area.

PINE WARBLER
Dendroica pinus

These unassuming birds are perfectly named because they are bound to majestic, sheltering pines. Pine Warblers are often difficult to find because they typically forage near the tops of very tall, mature pine trees. They are particularly attracted to stands of long-needled white pines and red pines, and tend to avoid pine trees with shorter needles. Occasionally, foraging Pine Warblers can be seen smeared with patches of sticky pine resin. • The Pine Warbler's modest appearance, which is very similar to that of a number of immature and fall-plumaged vireos and warblers, forces birders to obtain a good, long look before making a positive identification. This warbler is most often confused with the Bay-breasted Warbler or Blackpoll Warbler in drab fall plumage. • The Pine Warbler is peculiar among the wood-warblers in that both its breeding and wintering ranges are located almost entirely within Canada and the United States.

breeding

ID: *Male:* olive green head and back; dark grayish wings and tail; whitish to dusky wing bars; yellow throat and breast; faded, dark streaking or dusky wash on sides of breast; white undertail coverts and belly; faint dark line through eye; faint yellow, broken eye ring. *Female:* similar to male but duller, especially in fall. *Immature:* duller; brownish olive head and back; pale yellow (male) to creamy white (female) throat and breast; brown wash on flanks.
Size: *L* 5–5½ in; *W* 8½ in.
Status: uncommon migrant from mid-April to mid-May and from mid-August to mid-October; uncommon breeder from May to September.
Habitat: *Breeding:* open, mature pine woodlands and mature pine plantations. *In migration:* mixed and deciduous woodlands.
Nesting: toward the end of a pine limb; female builds a deep, open cup nest of twigs, bark, weeds, grasses, pine needles and spider webs and lines it with feathers;

pair incubates 3–5 whitish eggs, with brown specks toward the larger end, for about 10 days.
Feeding: gleans from the ground or foliage by climbing around trees and shrubs; may hang upside down on branch tips like a chickadee or titmouse; eats mostly insects, berries and seeds.
Voice: song is a short, musical trill; call note is a sweet *chip*.
Similar Species: *Prairie Warbler* (p. 268): distinctive, dark facial stripes; darker streaking on sides; yellowish wing bars. *Kirtland's Warbler* (p. 267): darker streaking on sides; broken, white eye ring; bluish gray upperparts. *Bay-breasted Warbler* (p. 270) and *Blackpoll Warbler* (p. 271): nonbreeding and immatures have dark streaking on head or back or both; long, thin, yellow "eyebrow." *Yellow-throated Vireo* (p. 205): bright yellow "spectacles"; gray rump; lacks streaking on sides.
Selected Sites: Allegan SGA; Port Huron SGA; Rifle River SRA; Seney NWR; Pictured Rocks National Lakeshore; Porcupine Mountains Wilderness SP.

KIRTLAND'S WARBLER

Dendroica kirtlandii

Those of us living in Michigan are lucky—our chances of spotting a Kirtland's Warbler are better here than anywhere else in the world. This very rare warbler is estimated to have a population of 2100 birds nesting almost exclusively in the jack pine forests of the Au Sable River drainage in Michigan. Furthermore, the forests need to be just the right age: the Kirtland's Warbler will only nest under trees that are 3 to 25 feet tall, which generally means that the forest must be 5 to 15 years old. • Because it is such a habitat specialist, this bird has likely always been relatively uncommon and local. However, fire suppression and Brown-headed Cowbird nest parasitism have placed added pressure on the Kirtland's Warbler. More recently, controlled forest burns and jack pine plantations that provide new low growth have helped to make breeding habitat more available. Lure trapping and removal of cowbirds have also helped the Kirtland's Warbler to make a small step toward population recovery. • The Kirtland's Warbler is equally selective of its winter habitat: pine forests in the Bahamas.

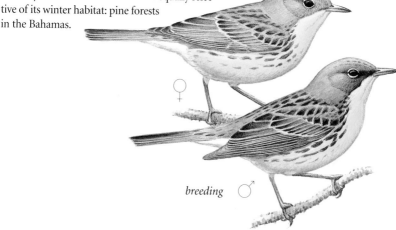

breeding ♂

ID: *Male:* blue gray upperparts; yellow underparts; black streaks on back, sides and flanks; whitish undertail coverts; bold, broken, white eye ring; black patch in front of eyes. *Female:* duller gray overall; lacks black face markings.

Size: *L* 6 in; *W* 8½ in.

Status: endangered; very rare migrant; very local breeder from early May to early September in north-central Lower Peninsula.

Habitat: young jack pine stands, primarily in the Au Sable River drainage.

Nesting: usually hidden in low vegetation; ground nest is built on sandy soil at the base of a small jack pine; female builds a compact cup nest from grass, sedge, pine needles, oak leaves and lines it with rootlets, hair and moss; female incubates 4–5 buff brown, spotted eggs for 13–15 days.

Feeding: gleans insects from the ground and from the lower parts of trees; also eats blueberries.

Voice: song is a loud, low-pitched *chip-chip-che-way-o* or *chip chip chip-chip-chip tew tew weet weet;* call is a low *chip.*

Similar Species: *Canada Warbler* (p. 286): yellow eye ring; black "necklace"; orange legs. *Magnolia Warbler* (p. 259): white streak behind eye; yellow rump.

Selected Sites: breeding areas closed to public entry. Conducted tours are provided by U.S. Fish and Wildlife Service from Grayling and by U.S. Forest Service from Mio, May 15 to July 15.

PRAIRIE WARBLER

Dendroica discolor

Open scrublands host the summer activities of the inappropriately named Prairie Warbler. This bird occupies early successional areas with such poor soil conditions that the vegetation remains short and scattered. • It is thought the Prairie Warbler was rare over much of its current breeding range in the early 1800s, before North America was widely colonized. As settlers cleared land, the Prairie Warbler gradually occupied what is now its current range. Because this bird uses early successional habitats, which change over time, its breeding locations change as well. A male Prairie Warbler may return each year to a favored nest site until the vegetation in that area grows too tall and dense, at which point he moves to a new area. Although Prairie Warblers are considered common in the southeastern states they are extremely uncommon in Michigan, both as migrants and as residents. • On their nesting territories, song wars occasionally result in physical fights between competing males. When the dust and feathers clear, the victor resumes his slow, graceful, butterfly-like courtship flight.

breeding

ID: *Male:* bright yellow face and underparts, except for white undertail coverts; dark "cheek" stripe and eye line; black streaking on sides; olive gray upperparts; inconspicuous chestnut streaks on back; 2 faint, yellowish wing bars. *Female* and *immature:* similar to male but duller in color.
Size: *L* 4½–5 in; *W* 7 in.
Status: endangered; rare migrant and very rare breeder from May to mid-September in Lower Peninsula.
Habitat: *Breeding:* dry, open scrubby sand dunes; young jack pine plains; shrubby, small tree, burned-over sites; young pine plantations with deciduous scrub. *In migration:* shrubby sites and young pine plantations.
Nesting: low in a shrub or small tree; female builds an open cup nest of soft vegetation and lines it with animal hair; female incubates 4 whitish eggs, with brown spots toward the larger end, for 11–14 days; both adults raise the young; small, loose nesting colonies may be formed.
Feeding: gleans, hover-gleans and occasionally hawks for prey; mainly insectivorous; will also eat berries and tree sap exposed by sapsuckers; caterpillars are a favored item for nestlings.
Voice: buzzy song is an ascending series of *zee* notes; call is sweet *chip.*
Similar Species: *Pine Warbler* (p. 266): lighter streaking on sides; whitish wing bars; lacks distinctive dark streaking on face. *Yellow-throated Warbler* (p. 265): white belly; bold, white wing bars, "eyebrow" and ear patch. *Kirtland's Warbler* (p. 267): immature female has brownish upperparts and pale white eye ring. *Baybreasted Warbler* (p. 270) and *Blackpoll Warbler* (p. 271): nonbreeding and immature birds have white bellies and wing bars, and lighter upperparts with dark streaking.
Selected Sites: Sleeping Bear Dunes National Lakeshore; Allegan SGA; Grand Mere SP.

PALM WARBLER

Dendroica palmarum

Considering this bird's subtropical wintering range, it may make sense to call it the Palm Warbler, even though it doesn't actually forage in palm trees. Based on its summer range, however, it could just as easily have been named the "Bog Warbler" because of its preference for northern bogs and fens of sphagnum moss and black spruce. Despite its name, the Palm Warbler nests farther north than all other wood-warblers except the Blackpoll Warbler. • The Palm Warbler is unusual in its preference for foraging on the ground or in low shrubs and vegetation. This warbler nests directly on the ground in a bog, usually below a young conifer. • Whether the Palm Warbler is hopping on the ground or perched momentarily on an elevated limb, it incessantly bobs its tail. This trait is a prominent field mark, particularly in fall, when its distinctive chestnut crown fades to olive brown.

breeding

ID: chestnut brown "cap" (may be inconspicuous in fall); yellow "eyebrow"; yellow throat and undertail coverts; yellow or white breast and belly; dark streaking on breast and sides; olive brown upperparts; may show dull, yellowish rump; frequently bobs its tail.

Size: *L* 4–5¹/₂ in; *W* 8 in.

Status: common migrant from late April to late May and from mid-August to mid-October; local breeder from late May to July mainly in Upper Peninsula.

Habitat: *Breeding:* along the edges of mature bogs with scattered black spruce; less frequently in openings of spruce-tamarack forests with sphagnum moss and shrubs; rarely jack pine plains. *In migration:* woodlands or areas with tall shrubs.

Nesting: on the ground or in a low shrub or stunted spruce; often on a sphagnum hummock concealed by grass; female builds a cup nest of grass, weeds and bark and lines it with feathers; female incubates 4–5 brown-marked, creamy white eggs for about 12 days.

Feeding: gleans the ground and vegetation for a wide variety of insects and berries while perched or hovering; occasionally hawks for insects; may take some seeds.

Voice: *Male:* song is a weak, buzzy trill with a quick finish; call is a sharp *sup* or *check*.

Similar Species: *Yellow-rumped Warbler* (p. 262): white wing bars, throat and undertail coverts; female has bright yellow rump, crown patch and foreshoulder patch. *Prairie Warbler* (p. 268): dark jaw stripe; darker eye line; lacks chestnut crown and dark streaking on breast. *Chipping Sparrow* (p. 292) and *American Tree Sparrow* (p. 291): stouter bodies; unstreaked, grayish underparts; lack yellow plumage. *Pine Warbler* (p. 266): faint, whitish wing bars; white undertail coverts; lacks chestnut "cap" and bold yellow "eyebrow."

Selected Sites: Kensington Metropark; Fenner Nature Center; Kalamazoo Nature Center; Kirtland Warbler Nesting Area; Seney NWR; Tahquamenon Falls SP.

BAY-BREASTED WARBLER

Dendroica castanea

Deep within stands of old-growth spruce and fir is where you will have to search to find the handsome Bay-breasted Warbler. It typically forages midway up a tree, often on the inner branches, so it's difficult to spot. • Bay-breasted Warblers are spruce budworm specialists, and their populations fluctuate from year to year along with the cyclical rise and fall of budworm numbers. Bay-breasted Warblers are invaluable when it comes to long-term suppression of budworm outbreaks, typically moving to where the larvae are most numerous. It is estimated that in outbreak years, one Bay-breasted Warbler can eat over 5000 budworms per acre through the breeding season. Although Bay-breasts are insectivorous on their breeding grounds, they switch to an almost all-fruit diet while they winter in Panama and Colombia.

breeding

ID: *Breeding male:* black face and "chin"; chestnut crown, throat, sides and flanks; creamy yellow belly, undertail coverts and patch on side of neck; 2 white wing bars. *Breeding female:* paler colors overall; dusky face; whitish to creamy underparts and neck patch; faint chestnut "cap"; rusty wash on sides and flanks. *Nonbreeding:* yellow olive head and back; dark streaking on crown and back; whiter underparts. *Immature:* resembles nonbreeding adult, but has less prominent streaking on upperparts; lacks chestnut sides and flanks.
Size: *L* 5–6 in; *W* 9 in.
Status: common migrant from mid-May to early June and from late August to mid-October; uncommon breeder from June to July in Upper Peninsula.
Habitat: *Breeding:* mature coniferous and mixed boreal forest; almost exclusively in stands of spruce and fir. *In migration:* woodlands or areas with tall shrubs.
Nesting: usually on a horizontal conifer branch; open cup nest is built of grass,

twigs, moss, roots and lichen and is lined with fine bark strips and fur; female incubates 4–5 whitish eggs, with dark marks toward the larger end, for about 13 days.
Feeding: usually forages at the midlevel of trees; gleans vegetation and branches for caterpillars and adult invertebrates; eats numerous spruce budworms when available.
Voice: song is an extremely high-pitched *seeee-seese-seese-seee;* call is a high *see.*
Similar Species: *Cape May Warbler* (p. 260): chestnut "cheek" on yellow face; dark streaking on mostly yellow underparts; lacks reddish flanks and crown. *Chestnut-sided Warbler* (p. 258): yellow crown; white "cheek" and underparts; fall birds have a white eye ring, unmarked whitish face and underparts and lack bold streaking on lime green upperparts. *Blackpoll Warbler* (p. 271): white undertail coverts; nonbreeding and immature birds have dark streaking on breast and sides and lack chestnut on sides and flanks.
Selected Sites: Indian Springs Metropark; Gratiot-Saginaw SGA; Fort Custer SRA; Rogue River SGA; Grand Marais; Keweenaw Bay shore woodlands.

BLACKPOLL WARBLER

Dendroica striata

The Blackpoll Warbler is the greatest warbler migrant: weighing less than a wet teabag, this bird is known to fly south over the Atlantic, leaving land at Cape Cod and flying for 88 nonstop hours until it reaches the northern coast of Venezuela. In such a trip, a Blackpoll Warbler will cover almost 1900 miles, and in a single year, it may fly up to 15,000 miles! In migration, the Blackpoll Warbler adjusts its flying altitude—sometimes flying at heights of 20,000 feet—to best use shifting prevailing winds to reach its destination. This bird is truly an international resident, so conservation of its habitat requires the efforts of several nations. • Blackpoll Warblers in fall plumage are easily confused with very similar-looking Bay-breasted Warblers. Most Blackpolls, however, migrate later in fall than their Bay-breasted counterparts. • This bird's scientific name *striata* means "striped" in Latin.

breeding

ID: 2 white wing bars; black streaking on underparts; white undertail coverts. *Breeding male:* black "cap" and "mustache" stripe; white "cheek"; black-streaked, olive gray upperparts; white underparts; orange legs. *Breeding female:* streaked, yellow olive head and back; white underparts; small, dark eye line; pale "eyebrow." *Nonbreeding:* olive yellow head, back, rump, breast and sides; yellow "eyebrow"; dark legs. *Immature:* paler streaking.
Size: *L* 5–5½ in; *W* 9 in.
Status: common migrant from mid-May to early June and from late August to early October.
Habitat: mixed woodlands.

Nesting: does not nest in Michigan.
Feeding: gleans buds, leaves and branches for aphids, mosquitoes, beetles, wasps, caterpillars and many other insects; often flycatches for insects.
Voice: song is an extremely high-pitched, uniform trill: *tsit tsit tsit;* call is a loud *chip.*
Similar Species: *Black-and-white Warbler* (p. 273): dark legs; black-and-white-striped crown; male has black "chin," throat and "cheek" patch. *Black-capped Chickadee* (p. 221): black "chin" and throat; lacks wing bars and black streaking on underparts. *Bay-breasted Warbler* (p. 270): chestnut sides and flanks; buff undertail coverts; nonbreeding and immatures lack dark streaking on underparts.
Selected Sites: Seven Ponds Nature Center; Rose Lake WA; Grand Mere SP; Sturgeon Point SP; Wilderness SP; Pictured Rocks National Lakeshore.

CERULEAN WARBLER

Dendroica cerulea

The Cerulean Warbler leads a mysterious life concealed high in the canopy of mature deciduous forests. The handsome blue-and-white male is particularly difficult to observe as he blends into the sunny summer sky while foraging among treetop foliage. Often the only evidence of a meeting with this largely unobservable canopy-dweller is the precious sound of the male's buzzy, trilling voice. • Only in the last few decades have ornithologists been able to document this bird's breeding behavior. Courtship, mating, nesting and the rearing of young all tend to take place high in the canopy, well out of sight of most casual observers. Cerulean Warblers also attack each other high in the canopy: flying aggressively toward one another they collide with an audible thud, then spiral together toward the ground. Females also fight, and an aggressive female may even knock her own mate off his perch in a similar manner.

breeding

ID: white undertail coverts and wing bars. *Male:* blue upperparts; white throat and underparts; black "necklace" and streaking on sides. *Female:* blue green crown, nape and back; dark eye line; yellow "eyebrow," throat and breast; pale streaking on sides. *Immature:* pale yellow underparts and "eyebrow"; yellowish to white wing bars; pale olive green upperparts.

Size: *L* 4¹⁄₂–5 in; *W* 7 in.

Status: special concern; uncommon migrant and breeder from early May to early September in southern Lower Peninsula.

Habitat: mature deciduous hardwood forests and extensive woodlands with a clear understory; particularly drawn to riparian stands.

Nesting: high on the end of a branch in a deciduous tree; female builds an open cup nest of bark strips, weeds, grass, lichen and spider silk and lines it with fur and moss; female incubates 3–5 brown-spotted, gray to creamy white eggs, for about 12–13 days.

Feeding: insects are gleaned from upper canopy foliage and branches; often hawks for insects.

Voice: song is a rapid, accelerating sequence of buzzy notes leading into a higher trilled note; call is a sharp *chip*.

Similar Species: *Black-throated Blue Warbler* (p. 261): male has black face, "chin" and throat; female has small, white wing patch; lacks wing bars. *Blackpoll Warbler* (p. 271) and *Bay-breasted Warbler* (p. 270): similar to female Cerulean but have more yellow than green on mantle. *Pine Warbler* (p. 266): browner; similar to female Cerulean but has more yellow on mantle.

Selected Sites: Port Huron SGA; Pinckney SRA; Warren Woods Natural Area; Allegan SGA; Rose Lake WA; Kalamazoo Nature Center; Lost Nation SGA.

BLACK-AND-WHITE WARBLER

Mniotilta varia

The foraging behavior of the Black-and-white Warbler stands in sharp contrast to that of most of its kin. Rather than dancing or flitting quickly between twig perches, Black-and-white Warblers behave like creepers and nuthatches—a distantly related group of birds. Birders with frayed nerves and tired eyes from watching flitty warblers will be refreshed by the sight of this bird as it methodically creeps up and down tree trunks, probing bark crevices. • Novice birders can easily identify this unique, two-tone warbler, which retains its standard plumage throughout its stay in our region. Even a trip to its wintering grounds will reveal this warbler in the same black-and-white outfit. A keen ear also helps to identify this forest-dweller: its gentle oscillating song—like a wheel in need of greasing—is easily recognized and remembered.

ID: black-and-white-striped crown; dark upperparts with white streaking; 2 white wing bars; white underparts with black streaking on sides, flanks and undertail coverts; black legs. *Male:* black "cheek" and throat. *Female:* gray "cheek"; white throat.
Size: *L* 4½–5½ in; *W* 8 in.
Status: common migrant from late April to May and from mid-August to early October; common breeder from late May to early July in northern Michigan.
Habitat: deciduous or mixed forests, often near water; also in cedar swamps and alder and willow thickets bordering muskeg and beaver ponds.
Nesting: usually on the ground next to a tree, log or large rock; in a shallow scrape, often among a pile of dead leaves; female builds a cup nest with grass, leaves, bark strips, rootlets and pine needles and lines it with fur and fine grasses; female incubates 5 creamy white eggs, with brown flecks toward the larger end, for 10–12 days.
Feeding: gleans insect eggs, larval insects, beetles, spiders and other invertebrates while creeping along tree trunks and branches.
Voice: series of high, thin, 2-syllable notes: *weetsee weetsee weetsee weetsee weetsee weetsee;* call is a sharp *pit* and a soft, high *seat.*
Similar Species: *Blackpoll Warbler* (p. 271): breeding male has solid black "cap" and clean white undertail coverts.
Selected Sites: Metrobeach Metropark; Waterloo SRA; Sarett Nature Center; Muskegon SP; Wilderness SP; Pictured Rocks National Lakeshore; Peninsula Point.

AMERICAN REDSTART

Setophaga ruticilla

American Redstarts are a consistent favorite among birders. These supercharged birds flit from branch to branch in dizzying pursuit of prey. Even when perched, their tails sway rhythmically back and forth. Few birds can rival a mature male redstart for his contrasting black-and-orange plumage and amusing behavior. • A common foraging technique used by the American Redstart is to flash its wings and tail patches to flush prey. If a concealed insect tries to flee, the redstart will give chase. The American Redstart behaves much the same way on its Central American wintering grounds, where it is known locally as *candelita*, meaning "little candle." • Although Redstarts are common here, their beautiful, trilly songs are so variable that identifying one is a challenge to birders of all levels.

ID: *Male:* black overall; red orange foreshoulder, wing and tail patches; white belly and undertail coverts. *Female:* olive brown upperparts; gray green head; yellow foreshoulder, wing and tail patches; clean white underparts.

Size: *L* 5 in; *W* 8 in.

Status: common migrant and breeder from early May to early October.

Habitat: shrubby woodland edges, open and semi-open deciduous and mixed forests with a regenerating deciduous understory of shrubs and saplings; often near water.

Nesting: in the fork of a shrub or sapling, usually 3–23 ft above the ground; female builds an open cup nest of plant down, bark shreds, grass and rootlets and lines it with feathers; female incubates 4 whitish eggs, marked with brown or gray, for 11–12 days.

Feeding: actively gleans foliage and hawks for insects and spiders on leaves, buds and branches; often hover-gleans.

Voice: male's song is a highly variable series of *tseet* or *zee* notes, often given at different pitches; call is a sharp, sweet *chip*.

Similar Species: none.

Selected Sites: Highland SRA; Waterloo SRA; Fort Custer SRA; Sarett Nature Center; Chippewa Nature Center; Leelanau SP; Van Riper SP.

PROTHONOTARY WARBLER

Protonotaria citrea

The Prothonotary Warbler is the only eastern wood-warbler to nest in cavities. Standing dead trees and stumps riddled with natural cavities and woodpecker excavations provide perfect nesting habitat for this bird, especially if the site is near stagnant, swampy water. Much of the Prothonotary's swampy habitat is inaccessible to most birders, but if you are in the right place at the right time, you might be lucky enough to come across this bird as it forages for insects along tree trunks and decaying logs, in low, tangled thickets and on debris floating on the water's surface. • Suitable Prothonotary Warbler nesting sites are so rare in Michigan that a breeding pair will often return to the same nest cavity year after year. The male can be very aggressive when defending his territory, and often resorts to combative aerial chases when songs and warning displays fail to intimidate an intruder. Unfortunately for neighboring birds, this scorn is unprejudiced—other cavity-nesting birds such as woodpeckers, wrens and bluebirds are often victims of this fury. • This bird acquired its unusual name because its plumage was thought to resemble the yellow hoods worn by prothonotaries, high-ranking clerics in the Catholic Church.

ID: large, dark eyes; long bill; unmarked, yellow head; yellow undersides except for white undertail coverts; olive green back; unmarked, bluish gray wings and tail.

Size: *L* 5½ in; *W* 8½ in.

Status: special concern; rare migrant and breeder from early May to August in southern Michigan.

Habitat: wooded deciduous swamps and riparian woodlands.

Nesting: cavities in standing dead trees, rotten stumps, birdhouses or abandoned woodpecker nests, from water level to 10 ft above the ground; often returns to the same nest site; mostly the male builds a cup nest of twigs, leaves, moss and plant down and lines it with soft plant material;

female incubates 4–6 brown-spotted, creamy to pinkish eggs for 12–14 days.

Feeding: forages for a variety of insects and small mollusks; gleans from vegetation; may hop on floating debris or creep along tree trunks.

Voice: *Male:* song is a loud, ringing series of *sweet* or *zweet* notes issued on a single pitch; flight song is *chewee chewee chee chee;* call is a brisk *tink.*

Similar Species: *Blue-winged Warbler* (p. 251): white wing bars; black eye line; yellowish white undertail coverts. *Yellow Warbler* (p. 257): dark wings and tail with yellow highlights; yellow undertail coverts; male has reddish streaking on breast. *Hooded Warbler* (p. 284): female has yellow undertail coverts and yellow olive upperparts.

Selected Sites: Holly SRA; Shiawassee Flats NWR; Maple River SGA; Allegan SGA; Sarett Nature Center; Warren Woods Natural Area; Muskegon SGA.

WORM-EATING WARBLER

Helmitheros vermivorus

People wishing to see this bird have a challenge ahead of them because the Worm-eating Warbler is rare here. To make things more difficult, this warbler's subdued colors allow it to blend in with the decomposing twigs, roots and leaves that litter the forest floor. Most of this bird's time is spent foraging for caterpillars, small terrestrial insects and spiders among dense undergrowth and dead leaves in deciduous forests. • The Worm-eating Warbler typically nests near water and on a slope, and it is one of a small group of eastern warblers that nest on the ground. The female becomes completely still if she is approached while on the nest, relying on her striped crown for concealment. • The Worm-eating Warbler is yet another trilling singer. Its trill is faster and more insectlike than the Chipping Sparrow's, and it seems louder in the middle of the trill and weaker at the beginning and end.

ID: black-and-buff-orange head stripes; brownish olive upperparts; rich buff orange breast; whitish undertail coverts. **Size:** *L* 5 in; *W* 8½ in.

Status: very rare migrant and breeder from late April to August in southwestern Michigan.
Habitat: steep, deciduous woodland slopes, ravines and swampy woodlands with shrubby understory cover.
Nesting: usually on a hillside or ravine bank, often near water; on the ground hidden under leaf litter; female builds a cup nest of decaying leaves and lines it with fine grass, moss stems and hair; female incubates 3–5 white eggs, speckled with reddish brown, for about 13 days.
Feeding: forages on the ground and in trees and shrubs; eats mostly small insects.
Voice: song is a faster, thinner version of the Chipping Sparrow's chipping trill; call is a buzzy *zeep-zeep*.
Similar Species: *Red-eyed Vireo* (p. 209): gray crown; white "eyebrow"; red eyes; yellow undertail coverts. *Louisiana Waterthrush* (p. 279) and *Northern Waterthrush* (p. 278): darker upperparts; bold white or yellowish "eyebrow"; dark streaking on white breast; lacks striped head.
Selected Sites: Grand Mere SP; Allegan SGA; Ottawa County sand dune forest; Kellogg Forest.

OVENBIRD

Seiurus aurocapillus

The Ovenbird's loud and joyous "ode to teachers" is a common sound that echoes through deciduous and mixed forests in spring. Unfortunately, pinpointing the exact location of this resonating call is not always easy. An Ovenbird will rarely expose itself, and even when it does, active searching and patience is necessary to get a good look at it. What may sound like one long-winded Ovenbird may actually be two neighboring males singing and responding on the heels of each other's song. • The name "Ovenbird" refers to this bird's unusual, dome-shaped ground nest. An incubating female nestled within her woven dome usually feels so secure that she will choose to sit tight rather than flee when approached. The nest is so well camouflaged that few people ever find one, even though nests are often located near hiking trails and bike paths. • Robert Frost was so moved by the Ovenbird's spring songs that he dedicated a poem to them entitled "Ovenbird."

ID: olive brown upperparts; white eye ring; heavy, dark streaking on white breast, sides and flanks; rufous crown has black border; pink legs; white undertail coverts; no wing bars.

Size: *L* 6 in; *W* 9½ in.

Status: common migrant and breeder from early May to October.

Habitat: *Breeding:* undisturbed, mature deciduous, mixed and coniferous forests with a closed canopy and very little understory; often in ravines and riparian areas. *In migration:* dense riparian shrubbery and thickets and a variety of woodlands.

Nesting: on the ground; female builds an oven-shaped, domed nest of grass, weeds, bark, twigs and dead leaves and lines it with animal hair; female incubates 4–5 white eggs, spotted with gray and brown, for 11–13 days.

Feeding: gleans the ground for worms, snails, insects and occasionally seeds.

Voice: loud, distinctive *tea-cher tea-cher Tea-CHER Tea-CHER,* increasing in speed and volume; night song is an elaborate series of bubbly, warbled notes, often ending in *teacher-teacher;* call is a brisk *chip, cheep* or *chock.*

Similar Species: *Northern Waterthrush* (p. 278) and *Louisiana Waterthrush* (p. 279): bold, yellowish or white "eyebrow"; darker upperparts; lacks rufous crown. *Thrushes* (pp. 237–43): all are larger and lack rufous crown outlined in black.

Selected Sites: Indian Springs Metropark; Waterloo SRA; Kalamazoo Nature Center; Chippewa Nature Center; Sleeping Bear Dunes National Lakeshore; Whitefish Point; Porcupine Mountains Wilderness SP.

NORTHERN WATERTHRUSH

Seiurus noveboracensis

Although this bird's long body looks "thrushlike," the Northern Waterthrush is actually a wood-warbler. • Birders who are not satisfied with simply hearing a Northern Waterthrush in its nesting territory must literally get their feet wet if they hope to see one. This bird skulks along the shores of deciduous swamps or coniferous bogs, and the fallen logs, shrubby tangles and soggy ground may discourage human visitors. During the relatively bug-free months in spring and fall, migrating Northern Waterthrushes typically appear among drier, upland forests or along lofty park trails and boardwalks. Backyards featuring a small garden pond may also attract migrating waterthrushes. • The voice of the Northern Waterthrush is loud and raucous for such a small bird, so it seems fitting that this bird was once known as the New York Warbler, in reference to the city so well known for its decibels. The scientific name *noveboracensis* means "of New York."

ID: pale yellowish to buff "eyebrow"; pale yellowish to buff underparts with dark streaking; finely spotted throat; olive brown upperparts; pinkish legs; frequently bobs its tail.

Size: *L* 5–6 in; *W* 9½ in.

Status: common migrant from late April to May and from mid-August to mid-September; common breeder from June to July in northern Michigan.

Habitat: wooded edges of swamps, lakes, beaver ponds, bogs and rivers; also in moist, wooded ravines and riparian thickets.

Nesting: on the ground, usually near water; female builds a cup nest made of moss, leaves, bark shreds, twigs and pine needles and lines it with moss, hair and rootlets; female incubates 4–5 whitish eggs, spotted and blotched with brown and purple gray, for about 13 days.

Feeding: gleans foliage and the ground for invertebrates, frequently tossing aside ground litter with its bill; may also take aquatic invertebrates and small fish from shallow water.

Voice: song is a loud, 3-part *sweet sweet sweet, swee wee wee, chew chew chew chew;* call is a brisk *chip* or *chuck*.

Similar Species: *Louisiana Waterthrush* (p. 279): broader, white "eyebrow"; unspotted, white throat; buff orange wash on flanks. *Ovenbird* (p. 277): rufous crown bordered by black stripes; white eye ring; unspotted throat; lacks pale "eyebrow."

Selected Sites: Indian Springs Metropark; Rose Lake WA; Fort Custer SRA; Leelanau SP; Tuscola SGA; Porcupine Mountains Wilderness SP; Whitefish Point.

LOUISIANA WATERTHRUSH

Seiurus motacilla

In Michigan, the Louisiana Waterthrush is often seen sallying along the shorelines of babbling streams and gently swirling pools in search of its next meal. This bird inhabits swamps and sluggish streams throughout much of its North American range, but where its range overlaps with the Northern Waterthrush it inhabits shorelines near fast-flowing water. Louisiana Waterthrushes have never been recorded in great numbers here, partly because little suitable habitat remains for them. • The Louisiana Waterthrush has a larger bill, pinker legs, whiter eye stripes and less streaking on its throat than the Northern Waterthrush. Both waterthrushes are easily identified by their habit of bobbing their heads and moving their tails up and down as they walk, but the Louisana Waterthrush bobs its tail more slowly and also tends to sway from side to side. This bird's scientific name *motacilla* is Latin for "wagtail."

ID: brownish upperparts; long bill; pink legs; white underparts with buff orange wash on flanks; long, dark streaks on breast and sides; bicolored, buff-and-white "eyebrow"; clean white throat.

Size: *L* 6 in; *W* 10 in.

Status: special concern; uncommon migrant and breeder from mid-April to August in southern Michigan.

Habitat: moist, forested ravines, alongside fast-flowing streams; rarely along wooded swamps.

Nesting: concealed within a rocky hollow or within a tangle of tree roots; pair builds a cup nest of leaves, bark strips, twigs and moss and lines it with animal hair, ferns and rootlets; female incubates 3–6 creamy white eggs, spotted with brown and purple gray, for about 14 days.

Feeding: terrestrial and aquatic insects and crustaceans are gleaned from rocks and debris in or near shallow water; dead leaves and other debris may be flipped and probed for food; occasionally catches flying insects over water.

Voice: song begins with 3–4 distinctive, shrill, slurred notes followed by a warbling twitter; call is a brisk *chick* or *chink*.

Similar Species: *Northern Waterthrush* (p. 278): yellowish to buff "eyebrow" narrows behind eye; underparts are usually all yellowish or buff (occasionally all white); finely spotted throat; lacks buff orange flanks. *Ovenbird* (p. 277) and *thrushes* (pp. 237–43): lack broad, white "eyebrow."

Selected Sites: Warren Woods Natural Area; Grand Mere SP; Highland SRA; Allegan SGA; Rogue River SGA; Tuscola SGA; Port Huron SGA.

KENTUCKY WARBLER

Oporornis formosus

Kentucky Warblers spend much of their time on the ground, overturning leaves and scurrying through dense thickets in search of insects. These birds are shy and elusive as they sing their loud springtime song from secluded perches. As a general rule, male warblers sing most actively in the morning, feeding only intermittently but quiet down in the afternoon and feed more actively. Once the young hatch, singing becomes rare as both the male and the female spend much of their time feeding the young. Unmated males, however, may continue to sing throughout the summer. The Kentucky Warbler's song may be confused with that of the Carolina Wren, but the Kentucky Warbler will sing the same song pattern repeatedly, while the Carolina Wren varies its song constantly. • Like waterthrushes and Ovenbirds, Kentucky Warblers bob their tails up and down as they walk.

♂

ID: bright yellow "spectacles" and underparts; black crown, "sideburns" and half "mask"; olive green upperparts.
Size: *L* 5–5½ in; *W* 8½ in.

Status: very rare migrant and breeder from May to September in southern Michigan.
Habitat: moist deciduous and mixed woodlands with dense, shrubby cover and herbaceous plant growth, including wooded ravines, swamp edges and creek bottomlands.
Nesting: placed on or close to the ground; both adults build a cup nest of plant material and hair and line it with rootlets and

hair; female incubates 4–5 cream-colored eggs, spotted or blotched with reddish brown, for 12–13 days.
Feeding: gleans insects while walking along the ground, flipping over leaf litter or by snatching prey from the undersides of low foliage.
Voice: musical song is a series of 2-syllable notes: *chur-ree chur-ree* (similar to the song of the Carolina Wren); call is a sharp *chick, chuck* or *chip*.
Similar Species: *Canada Warbler* (p. 286): dark, streaky "necklace"; bluish gray upperparts. *Yellow-throated Warbler* (p. 265): bold, white "eyebrow," ear patch and wing bars; white belly and undertail coverts.
Selected Sites: Lost Nation SGA; Warren Woods Natural Area; Grand Mere SP.

CONNECTICUT WARBLER

Oporornis agilis

Our soggy, impenetrable sphagnum bogs, dry jack pine forests and mixed woodlands are all favored breeding habitats for the mysterious and secretive Connecticut Warbler. Some believe the common denominator among its varied breeding sites is poor drainage, while others feel that a well-developed understory is mandatory. This bird's elusive nature has made it one of the most sought-after birds around. A trip to any northern bog could reveal the boisterous songs of this ground-dwelling warbler, but pinpointing this bird's location takes patience and good fortune. • Difficulty in finding active Connecticut Warbler nests means that much of this bird's breeding biology remains unknown. • Like many other North American birds, the Connecticut Warbler was named for the place where it was first collected, though this bird only visits Connecticut during fall migration.

ID: bold, white eye ring; yellow underparts; olive green upperparts; long undertail coverts make tail look short; pink legs; longish bill. *Male:* blue gray "hood." *Female* and *immature:* gray brown "hood"; light gray throat.
Size: *L* 5–6 in; *W* 9 in.
Status: uncommon migrant from mid-May to June and from late August to September; uncommon breeder from June to July in northern Michigan.
Habitat: *Breeding:* open pine forests and fairly open spruce bogs and tamarack fens with well-developed understory growth. *In migration:* dense, shrubby thickets.
Nesting: on the ground on a hummock or in a low shrub; messy nest is made of leaves, weeds, grass, bark strips and moss; female incubates 4–5 creamy white eggs, spotted with black, brown and lilac, for about 12 days.
Feeding: gleans caterpillars, beetles, spiders and other invertebrates from ground leaf litter; occasionally forages among low branches.
Voice: song is a loud, clear and explosive *chipity-chipity-chipity chuck* or *per-chipity-chipity-chipity choo;* call is a brisk, metallic *cheep* or *peak.*
Similar Species: *Mourning Warbler* (p. 282): no eye ring or thin, incomplete eye ring; shorter undertail coverts; male has blackish breast patch; immature has pale gray to yellow "chin" and throat. *Nashville Warbler* (p. 255): bright yellow throat; shorter, dark legs and bill.
Selected Sites: Indian Springs Metropark; Allegan SGA; Seney NWR; Tahquamenon Falls SP; Porcupine Mountains Wilderness SP.

MOURNING WARBLER

Oporornis philadelphia

Although Mourning Warblers can be quite common in some locations, they are seen far less frequently than one might expect. These birds seldom leave the protection of their dense, shrubby, often impenetrable habitat, and they tend to sing only on their breeding territory. Riparian areas, regenerating clear-cuts and patches of forest that have been recently cleared by fire provide the low shrubs and sapling trees that these warblers rely on for nesting and foraging. Mourning Warblers are best seen during migration, when backyard shrubs and raspberry thickets may attract small, silent flocks. • The Mourning Warbler is the only member of the hooded *Oporornis* clan—which includes the Kentucky, Connecticut and MacGillivray's *(O. tolmiei)* warblers—with a breeding area that overlaps with the ranges of all the other *Oporonis* Warblers. • This bird's dark "hood" and black breast patch reminded pioneering ornithologist Alexander Wilson of someone dressed in mourning.

breeding

ID: yellow under-parts; olive green upperparts; short tail; pinkish legs. *Breeding male:* usually no eye ring, but may have broken eye ring; blue gray "hood"; black upper breast patch. *Female:* gray "hood"; whitish "chin" and throat; may show thin eye ring. *Immature:* gray brown "hood"; pale gray to yellow "chin" and throat; thin, incomplete eye ring.

Size: L 5–5½ in; W 7½ in.

Status: uncommon migrant from mid-May to June and from August to mid-September; uncommon breeder from June to early July in northern and central Michigan.

Habitat: dense and shrubby thickets, tangles and brambles, often in moist areas of forest clearings and along the edges of ponds, lakes and streams.

Nesting: on the ground at the base of a shrub or plant tussock or in a small shrub; bulky nest of leaves, weeds and grass is lined with fur and fine grass; female incubates 3–4 creamy white eggs, spotted or blotched with brown, for about 12 days.

Feeding: forages in dense, low shrubs for caterpillars, beetles, spiders and other invertebrates.

Voice: husky, 2-part song is variable and lower-pitched at the end: *churry, churry, churry, churry, chorry, chorry;* call is a loud, low *check.*

Similar Species: *Connecticut Warbler* (p. 281): bold, complete eye ring; lacks black breast patch; long undertail coverts make tail look very short; immature has light gray throat. *Nashville Warbler* (p. 255): bright yellow throat; dark legs.

Selected Sites: Port Huron SGA; Sleeper SP; Allegan SGA; Sleeping Bear Dunes National Lakeshore; Seney NWR; Van Riper SP.

COMMON YELLOWTHROAT

Geothlypis trichas

This energetic songster of our wetlands is a favorite among birders—its small size, bright plumage and spunky disposition quickly endear it to all observers. • The Common Yellowthroat favors shrubby marshes and wet, overgrown meadows, shunning the forest habitat preferred by most of its wood-warbler relatives. In May and June, the male Yellowthroat issues his distinctive *wichity-witchity-witchity* songs while perched atop tall cattails or shrubs. Observing a male in action will reveal the location of his favorite singing perches, which he visits in rotation. These strategic outposts mark the boundary of his territory, which is fiercely guarded from intrusion by other males. • The Common Yellowthroat is certainly one of Michigan's most common warblers and, unfortunately, its nests are commonly parasitized by Brown-headed Cowbirds.

ID: yellow throat, breast and undertail coverts; dingy white belly; olive green to olive brown upperparts; orangy legs. *Breeding male:* broad, black "mask" with white upper border. *Female:* no "mask"; may show faint, white eye ring. *Immature:* duller overall.
Size: *L* 5 in; *W* 6½ in.
Status: common migrant and breeder from May to early October.
Habitat: cattail marshes, riparian willow and alder clumps, sedge wetlands, beaver ponds and wet overgrown meadows; sometimes dry, abandoned fields.
Nesting: on or near the ground, often in a small shrub or among emergent aquatic vegetation; female builds a bulky, open cup nest of weeds, grass, sedges and other materials and lines it with hair and soft plant fibers; female incubates 3–5 creamy white eggs, spotted with brown and black, for 12 days.
Feeding: gleans vegetation and hovers for adult and larval insects, including dragonflies, spiders and beetles; occasionally eats seeds.
Voice: song is a clear, oscillating *witchety witchety witchety-witch*; call is a sharp *tcheck* or *tchet*.
Similar Species: male's black "mask" is distinctive. *Kentucky Warbler* (p. 280): yellow "spectacles"; all-yellow underparts; half "mask." *Yellow Warbler* (p. 257): brighter yellow overall; yellow highlights on wings; all-yellow underparts. *Wilson's Warbler* (p. 285): forehead, "eyebrow" and "cheek" are as bright as all-yellow underparts; may show dark "cap." *Orange-crowned Warbler* (p. 254): dull, yellow olive overall; faint breast streaks. *Nashville Warbler* (p. 255): bold, complete eye ring; blue gray crown.
Selected Sites: cattail marshes or wet, shrubby thickets.

HOODED WARBLER

Wilsonia citrina

Hooded Warblers are at the northern limit of their range here, so they are rare in most of Michigan. Despite nesting low to the ground, they require extensive mature forests, where fallen trees have opened gaps in the canopy, encouraging understory growth. • Different species of wood-warblers can coexist in a limited environment because they partition their food supplies, with each species foraging exclusively in certain areas. Hooded Warblers also partition between the sexes: males tend to forage in treetops, while females forage near the ground. • Unlike their female counterparts, male Hooded Warblers may return to the same nesting territory year after year. Once the young have left the nest, each parent takes on guardianship of half the fledged young. • When Hooded Warblers leave Michigan and arrive on their wintering grounds, the males and females segregate—a practice unknown in any other warbler species—with males using mature forests, and females using shrubby and disturbed areas.

ID: bright yellow underparts; olive green upperparts; white undertail; pinkish legs. *Male:* black "hood"; bright yellow face. *Female:* yellow face and olive crown; may show faint traces of black "hood."

Size: L 5½ in; W 7 in.

Status: special concern; rare migrant and breeder from early May to September in southern Michigan.

Habitat: openings with dense, low shrubs in mature upland deciduous and mixed forests; occasionally in moist ravines or mature white pine plantations with a dense understory of deciduous shrubs.

Nesting: low in a deciduous shrub; mostly the female builds an open cup nest of fine grass, bark strips, dead leaves, animal hair, spider webs and plant down; female incubates 4 creamy white eggs, spotted with brown toward the larger end, for about 12 days.

Feeding: gleans insects and other forest invertebrates from the ground or shrub branches; may scramble up tree trunks or flycatch.

Voice: clear, whistling song is some variation of *whitta-witta-wit-tee-yo;* call note is a metallic *tink, chink* or *chip.*

Similar Species: *Wilson's Warbler* (p. 285), *Yellow Warbler* (p. 257) and *Common Yellowthroat* (p. 283): females lack white undertail feathers. *Kentucky Warbler* (p. 280): yellow "spectacles"; dark, triangular half "mask."

Selected Sites: Kensington Metropark; Waterloo SRA; Lost Nation SGA; Sarett Nature Center; P. J. Hoffmaster SP; Allegan SGA; Yankee Springs SRA.

WILSON'S WARBLER

Wilsonia pusilla

Y ou are almost sure to catch sight of the energetic Wilson's Warbler at any of Michigan's migration hotspots. This lively bird flickers quickly through tangles of leaves and trees, darting frequently into the air to catch flying insects. Birders often become exhausted while pursuing a Wilson's Warbler, but the bird itself never seems to tire during its lightning-fast performances. • This bird may make brief stopovers in backyard shrubs during spring or fall migration. Though common in migration, the Wilson's Warbler invariably moves farther north to nest, so is rarely found breeding in Michigan. • The Wilson's Warbler is richly deserving of its name. Named after Alexander Wilson, this species epitomizes the energetic devotion that the pioneering ornithologist exhibited in the study of North American birds.

ID: yellow under-parts; yellow green upperparts; beady, black eyes; thin, pointed, black bill; orange legs. *Male:* black "cap." *Female:* "cap" is very faint or absent.

Size: *L* 4¹/₂–5 in; *W* 7 in.

Status: common migrant from early May to June and from mid-August to late September; rare breeder from June to early July in Upper Peninsula.

Habitat: *Breeding:* riparian woodlands, willow and alder thickets, bogs and wet, shrubby meadows. *In migration:* wood-lands or areas with tall shrubs.

Nesting: on the ground in moss or at the base of a shrub; female builds a nest of moss, grass and leaves and lines it with animal hair and fine grass; female incubates 4–6 brown-marked, creamy white eggs for 10–13 days.

Feeding: hovers, flycatches and gleans vegetation for insects.

Voice: song is a rapid chatter that drops in pitch at the end: *chi chi chi chi chet chet;* call is a flat, low *chet* or *chuck*.

Similar Species: male's black "cap" is distinctive. *Yellow Warbler* (p. 257): male has red breast streaks; brighter yellow upper-parts. *Common Yellowthroat* (p. 283): female has darker face. *Kentucky Warbler* (p. 280): yellow "spectacles"; dark, angular half "mask." *Orange-crowned Warbler* (p. 254): dull yellow olive overall; faint breast streaks. *Nashville Warbler* (p. 255): bold, complete eye ring; blue gray crown.

Selected Sites: Holly SRA; Waterloo SRA; Grand Mere SP; Ludington SP; Seney NWR; Tahquamenon R. mouth; Whitefish Point.

285

CANADA WARBLER

Wilsonia canadensis

Male Canada Warblers, with their bold white eye rings, have a wide-eyed, alert appearance. Both sexes are fairly inquisitive, and they occasionally pop up from dense shrubs in response to passing hikers. Canada Warblers can be found in a wide variety of habitats, but you will almost always come across this "necklaced warbler" where there are dense understories. • Canada Warblers live in open defiance of winter: they never stay in one place long enough to experience one! They are often the last of the warblers to arrive on their Michigan breeding grounds and the first to leave. As the summer nesting season in our region ends, these warblers migrate to South America. Canada Warblers sing later than most warblers in the breeding season, and can even be heard singing while on migration.

ID: yellow "spectacles"; yellow underparts (except white undertail coverts); blue gray upperparts; pale legs. *Male:* streaky black "necklace"; dark, angular half "mask." *Female:* blue green back; faint "necklace."

Size: *L* 5–6 in; *W* 8 in.

Status: common migrant in May and from August to mid-September; common breeder from June to early July in northern Michigan and southwest along L. Michigan.

Habitat: *Breeding:* wet, low-lying areas of mixed forests with a dense understory, especially riparian willow-alder thickets; also cedar woodlands and swamps. *In migration:* woodlands or areas with tall shrubs.

Nesting: on a mossy hummock or upturned root or stump; female builds a loose, bulky cup nest made of leaves, grass, ferns, weeds and bark and lines it with animal hair and soft plant fibers; 4 brown-spotted, creamy white eggs are incubated for 10–14 days.

Feeding: gleans the ground and vegetation for beetles, flies, hairless caterpillars, mosquitoes and other insects; occasionally hovers.

Voice: song begins with 1 sharp *chip* note and continues with a rich, variable warble; call is a loud, quick *chick* or *chip*.

Similar Species: *Kentucky Warbler* (p. 280): yellow undertail coverts; greenish upperparts; half eye ring; lacks black "necklace." *Northern Parula* (p. 256): white wing bars; broken, white eye ring; white belly. *Kirtland's Warbler* (p. 267): black streaking on sides and flanks; broken, white eye ring; dark streaking on back.

Selected Sites: Tuscola SGA; Grand Mere SP; Waterloo SRA; Pictured Rocks National Lakeshore; Porcupine Mountains Wilderness SP.

YELLOW-BREASTED CHAT

Icteria virens

The unique Yellow-breasted Chat, measuring over 7 inches in length, is almost a warbler-and-a-half. Despite DNA evidence connecting the Chat with the wood-warbler family, its odd vocalizations and noisy thrashing behavior suggest a closer relationship to the mimic thrushes such as the Gray Catbird and Northern Mockingbird. Chats typically thrash about in dense undergrowth, and they rarely hold back their strange vocalizations, often drawing attention to themselves. • During courtship, the male advertises for a mate by launching off his perch to hover in the air with head held high and legs dangling, chirping incessantly until he drops back down. • This bird has a very localized breeding range in Michigan, and for the most part is rarely seen here in summer.

ID: white "spectacles"; white jaw line; heavy, black bill; yellow breast; white undertail coverts; olive green upperparts; long tail; gray black legs. *Male:* black lores.
Female: gray lores.
Size: *L* 7½ in; *W* 9½.
Status: rare migrant and breeder from early May to late September in southern Michigan.
Habitat: riparian thickets, brambles and shrubby tangles.

Nesting: low in a shrub or deciduous sapling; well-concealed, bulky base of leaves and weeds holds an inner woven cup nest of vine bark, which is lined with fine grass and plant fibers; female incubates 3–4 creamy white eggs, spotted with brown toward the large end, for about 11 days.
Feeding: gleans insects from low vegetation; eats berries in fall.
Voice: song is an assorted series of whistles, "laughs," squeaks, grunts, rattles and mews; calls include a *whoit, chack* and *kook.*
Similar Species: none.
Selected Sites: Pinckney SRA; Lost Nation SGA; Warren Woods Natural Area; Grand Mere SP; Gratiot-Saginaw SGA; Grand Rapids.

287

SUMMER TANAGER

Piranga rubra

The northern limit of the Summer Tanager's breeding range lies south of our state, but each year small numbers make their way here, dazzling Michigan birders. Most sightings are in spring and are the result of Summer Tanagers mistakenly traveling north past their nesting grounds. Summer and fall encounters are extremely rare, but nesting here seems possible even though it hasn't been confirmed to date. Some ornithologists think it is only a matter of time before some lucky birder confirms a Summer Tanager nest in Michigan. • Summer Tanagers thrive on a wide variety of insects, but they are best known for their courageous attacks on wasps. These birds snatch flying bees and wasps from menacing swarms, and may even harass the occupants of a wasp nest to the point that the nest is abandoned, leaving the larvae inside free for the picking.

ID: *Male:* rose red overall; pale bill; immature male has patchy, red-and-greenish plumage. *Female:* grayish yellow to greenish yellow upperparts; dusky yellow underparts; may have orange or reddish wash overall.

Size: *L* 7–8 in; *W* 12 in.

Status: very rare migrant from April to November, most frequently in extreme southern Michigan.

Habitat: mixed coniferous and deciduous woodlands, especially those with oak or hickory, or riparian woodlands with cottonwoods.

Nesting: does not nest in Michigan.

Feeding: gleans insects from the tree canopy; may hover-glean or hawk insects in midair; also eats berries and small fruits; known to raid wasp nests.

Voice: song is a series of 3–5 sweet, clear, whistled phrases, like a faster version of the American Robin's song; call is *pit* or *pit-a-tuck*.

Similar Species: *Scarlet Tanager* (p. 289): smaller bill; male has black tail and black wings; female has darker wings, brighter underparts and uniformly olive upperparts. *Northern Cardinal* (p. 310): red bill; prominent head crest; male has black "mask" and "bib." *Western Tanager* (p. 342): wing bars. *Orchard Oriole* (p. 323) and *Baltimore Oriole* (p. 324): females have wing bars and sharper bills.

Selected Sites: Lost Nation SGA; Warren Woods Natural Area; mainly Berrien, Kalamazoo and Wayne Counties.

SCARLET TANAGER
Piranga olivacea

ach spring, birders eagerly await the sweet, rough-edged song of the lovely Scarlet Tanager, which is often the only thing that gives away this unobtrusive forest denizen. The return of the brilliant red male to wooded ravines and traditional migrant stopover sites is always a much-anticipated event. • During the cold and rainy weather that often dampens spring migration, you may find yourself in the envious position of observing a Scarlet Tanager at eye level as it forages in the forest understory. At other times, however, this bird can be surprisingly difficult to spot as it darts through the forest canopy in pursuit of insect prey. • The Scarlet Tanager is the only tanager that routinely nests in Michigan. In Central and South America there are over 200 tanager species representing every color of the rainbow. The Scarlet Tanager migrates farther than any other tanager, most of which are sedentary birds in Central and South American forests.

ID: *Breeding male:* bright red overall with pure black wings and tail; pale bill. *Fall male:* patchy, red and greenish yellow plumage; black wings and tail. *Nonbreeding male:* bright yellow underparts; olive upperparts; black wings and tail. *Female:* uniformly olive upperparts; yellow underparts; grayish brown wings.
Size: *L* 7 in; *W* 11½ in.
Status: common migrant and breeder from late April to late September.
Habitat: fairly mature, upland deciduous and mixed forests and large woodlands.
Nesting: on a high branch, usually in a deciduous tree; well away from the trunk; female builds a flimsy, shallow cup of grass, weeds and twigs and lines it with rootlets and fine grass; female incubates 2–5 pale blue green eggs, spotted with reddish brown, for 12–14 days.

Feeding: gleans insects from the tree canopy; may hover-glean or hawk insects in midair; may forage at lower levels during cold weather; also takes some seasonally available berries.
Voice: song is a series of 4–5 sweet, clear, whistled phrases like a slurred version of the American Robin's song; call is a *chip-burrr* or *chip-churrr*.
Similar Species: *Summer Tanager* (p. 288): larger bill; male has red tail and red wings; female has paler wings and is duskier overall, often with orange or reddish tinge. *Northern Cardinal* (p. 310): red bill, wings and tail; prominent head crest; male has black "mask" and "bib." *Western Tanager* (p. 342): wing bars. *Orchard Oriole* (p. 323) and *Baltimore Oriole* (p. 324): females have wing bars and sharper bills.
Selected Sites: Indian Springs Metropark; Waterloo SRA; Kalamazoo Nature Center; Warren Woods Natural Area; Allegan SGA.

EASTERN TOWHEE

Pipilo erythrophthalmus

Eastern Towhees are often heard before they are seen. These noisy foragers rustle about in dense undergrowth, craftily scraping back layers of dry leaves to expose the seeds, berries or insects hidden beneath, though they also take insects and fruit from vegetation above ground. They employ an unusual two-footed technique to uncover food items—a strategy that is especially important in winter when virtually all of their food is taken from the ground. • Although you wouldn't guess it, this colorful bird is a member of the American Sparrow family—a group that is usually drab in color. • The Eastern Towhee and its similar western relative, the Spotted Towhee, were once grouped together as a single species called the "Rufous-sided Towhee." • The scientific name *Pipilo* is derived from the Latin *pipo*, meaning "to chirp or peep." *Erythrophthalmus* is derived from Greek words that mean "red eye." Eastern Towhees in Michigan have red eyes, but white-eyed Eastern Towhees are more common in the southeastern states.

ID: rufous sides and flanks; white outer tail corners; white lower breast and belly; buff undertail coverts; red eyes; dark bill. *Male:* black "hood" and upperparts. *Female:* brown "hood" and upperparts.

Size: *L* 7–8½ in; *W* 10½ in.

Status: common migrant and breeder from late March to mid-November, mainly in Lower Peninsula; scarce winter resident from December to March in southern Michigan.

Habitat: along woodland edges and in shrubby, abandoned fields.

Nesting: on the ground or low in a dense shrub; female builds a camouflaged cup nest of twigs, bark strips, grass, weeds, rootlets and animal hair; mostly the female incubates 3–4 creamy white to pale gray eggs, spotted with brown toward the larger end, for 12 to 13 days.

Feeding: scratches at leaf litter for insects, seeds and berries; sometimes forages in low shrubs and saplings.

Voice: song is 2 high, whistled notes followed by a trill: *drink your teeeee;* call is a scratchy, slurred *cheweee!* or *chewink!*

Similar Species: *Dark-eyed Junco* (p. 307): much smaller; pale bill; black eyes; white outer tail feathers.

Selected Sites: Holly SRA; Waterloo SRA; Fort Custer SRA; P. J. Hoffmaster SP; Chippewa Nature Center; Kalamazoo Nature Center; Sleeping Bear Dunes National Lakeshore.

AMERICAN TREE SPARROW

Spizella arborea

Most of us know these rufous-capped, spot-breasted sparrows as winter visitors to backyard feeders. The best time to see the American Tree Sparrow, however, is in late March and April when they are in migration. As the small flocks migrate north, they offer bubbly, bright songs between bouts of foraging along the ground or in low, budding shrubs. • Although its name suggests a close relationship with trees or forests, the American Tree Sparrow actually prefers treeless fields and semi-open, shrubby habitats. This bird got its name because of a superficial resemblance to the Eurasian Tree Sparrow familiar to early settlers. Perhaps a more appropriate name for this bird would be "Subarctic Shrub Sparrow." With adequate food supplies, the American Tree Sparrow can survive temperatures as cold as –28° F.

ID: gray, unstreaked underparts; dark, central breast spot; pale rufous "cap"; rufous stripe behind eye; gray face; mottled brown upperparts; notched tail; 2 white wing bars; dark legs; dark upper mandible; yellow lower mandible. *Nonbreeding:* gray central crown stripe. *Juvenile:* streaky breast and head.
Size: *L* 6–6½ in; *W* 9½.
Status: common winter resident from early October to early May.
Habitat: brushy thickets, roadside shrubs, semi-open fields and croplands.
Nesting: does not nest in Michigan.

Feeding: scratches exposed soil or snow for seeds in winter; eats mostly insects in summer; takes some berries and occasionally visits bird feeders.
Voice: a high, whistled *tseet-tseet* is followed by a short, sweet, musical series of slurred whistles; song may be given in late winter and during spring migration; call is a 3-note *tsee-dle-eat.*
Similar Species: *Chipping Sparrow* (p. 292): clear, black eye line; white "eyebrow"; lacks dark breast spot. *Swamp Sparrow* (p. 303): white throat; lacks dark breast spot and white wing bars. *Field Sparrow* (p. 294): white eye ring; orange pink bill; lacks dark breast spot.
Selected Sites: fields or scrubby edge habitat.

CHIPPING SPARROW

Spizella passerina

The Chipping Sparrow and Dark-eyed Junco do not share the same tailor, but they must have attended the same voice lessons, because their songs are very similar. Though the rapid trill of the Chipping Sparrow is slightly faster, drier and less musical than the junco's, even experienced birders can have difficulty identifying this singer. • Chipping Sparrows commonly nest at eye level, so you can easily watch their breeding and nest-building rituals. They are well known for their preference for conifers as a nesting site and for hair as a lining material for the nest. By planting conifers in your backyard and offering samples of your pet's hair—or even your own—in backyard baskets in spring, you could attract nesting Chipping Sparrows to your area and contribute to their nesting success. • The Chipping Sparrow is the smallest and tamest of sparrows. "Chipping" refers to this bird's call.

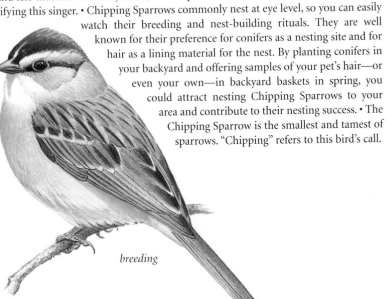

breeding

ID: *Breeding:* prominent rufous "cap"; white "eyebrow"; black eye line; light gray, unstreaked underparts; mottled brown upperparts; all-dark bill; 2 faint wing bars; pale legs. *Nonbreeding:* paler crown with dark streaks; brown "eyebrow" and "cheek"; pale lower mandible. *Juvenile:* brown gray overall with dark brown streaking; pale lower mandible.
Size: *L* 5–6 in; *W* 8½ in.
Status: common migrant and breeder from early April to early November.
Habitat: open conifers or mixed woodland edges; often in yards and gardens with tree and shrub borders.
Nesting: usually at midlevel in a coniferous tree; female builds a compact cup nest of woven grass and rootlets, often lined with hair; female incubates 4 pale blue eggs for 11–12 days.
Feeding: gleans seeds from the ground and from the outer branches of trees or shrubs; prefers seeds from grass, dandelions and clovers; also eats adult and larval invertebrates; occasionally visits feeders.
Voice: song is a rapid, dry trill of *chip* notes; call is a high-pitched *chip.*
Similar Species: *American Tree Sparrow* (p. 291): dark central breast spot; rufous stripe extends behind eye; lacks bold white "eyebrow." *Swamp Sparrow* (p. 303): lacks white "eyebrow," white wing bars and dark line behind eye. *Field Sparrow* (p. 294): rufous stripe extends behind eye; white eye ring; gray throat; orange pink bill; lacks bold white "eyebrow."
Selected Sites: open woodlands or open fields bordered by trees and shrubs.

CLAY-COLORED SPARROW

Spizella pallida

For the most part, Clay-colored Sparrows go completely unnoticed because their plumage, habit and voice all contribute to a cryptic lifestyle. Even when males are singing at the top of their "air sacs," they are usually mistaken for buzzing insects. • Although it is subtle in plumage, the Clay-colored Sparrow still possesses an unassuming beauty. Birders looking closely at this sparrow to confirm its identity can easily appreciate its delicate shading, texture and form—features so often overlooked in birds with more colorful plumage. • The Clay-colored Sparrow is a fairly recent addition to Michigan, but it is now a locally common summer resident in northern regions of the state. It is one of the few birds that will continue to sing into the heat of July.

breeding

ID: unstreaked, white underparts; buff breast wash; gray nape; light brown "cheek" edged with darker brown; brown crown with dark streak and pale, central stripe; white "eyebrow"; white jaw stripe is bordered with brown; white throat; mostly pale bill. *Juvenile:* dark streaks on buff breast, sides and flanks.
Size: *L* 5–6 in; *W* 7½ in.
Status: uncommon migrant from late April to late May and from September to early October; locally common breeder from early June to late July in northern Michigan.
Habitat: brushy open areas along forest and woodland edges; in forest openings, regenerating burn sites, abandoned fields and riparian thickets.

Nesting: in a grassy tuft or small shrub; female builds an open cup nest of twigs, grass, weeds and rootlets and lines it with rootlets, fine grass and fur; mostly the female incubates 4 brown-speckled, bluish green eggs, for 10–12 days.
Feeding: forages for seeds and insects on the ground and in low vegetation.
Voice: song is a series of 2–5 slow, low-pitched, insectlike buzzes; call is a soft *chip*.
Similar Species: *Chipping Sparrow* (p. 292): breeding adult has prominent rufous "cap," gray "cheek" and underparts, 2 faint white wing bars; all-dark bill; juvenile lacks gray nape and buff sides and flanks.
Selected Sites: Chippewa Nature Center; Kirtland Warbler tour sites; Rifle River SRA; Baraga Jack Pine Plains; Ottawa Recreation Area; Porcupine Mountains Wilderness SP.

FIELD SPARROW

Spizella pusilla

The pink-billed Field Sparrow frequents overgrown fields, pastures and forest clearings. Deserted farmland may seem unproductive to some people, but to this sparrow it is heaven. For nesting purposes, the usual pastures that these birds inhabit must be scattered with shrubs, herbaceous plants and plenty of tall grass. • Unlike most songbirds, a nestling Field Sparrow will leave its nest prematurely if disturbed. • Over time the Field Sparrow has learned to recognize when its nest has been parasitized by the Brown-headed Cowbird. Because the unwelcome eggs are usually too large for this small sparrow to eject, the nest is simply abandoned. This sparrow may be so stubborn in refusing to raise young cowbirds that affected pairs of Field Sparrows may make numerous nesting attempts in a single season.

ID: orange pink bill; gray face and throat; rusty crown with gray central stripe; rusty streak behind eye; white eye ring; 2 white wing bars; gray, unstreaked under-parts with buffy red wash on breast, sides and flanks; pinkish legs. *Immature:* duller version of adult with streaked breast and faint, buff white wing bars.

Size: L 5–6 in; W 8 in.

Status: common migrant and breeder from mid-March to mid-October in Lower Peninsula; very rare winter resident from November to March.

Habitat: abandoned or weedy and over-grown fields and pastures, woodland edges and clearings, extensive shrubby riparian areas and young conifer plantations.

Nesting: on or near the ground, often sheltered by a grass clump, shrub or sapling; female weaves an open cup nest of grass and lines it with animal hair and soft plant material; female incubates 3–5 brown-spotted, whitish to pale bluish white eggs for 10–12 days.

Feeding: forages on the ground; takes mostly insects in summer and seeds in spring and fall.

Voice: song is a series of woeful, musical, downslurred whistles accelerating into a trill; call is a *chip* or *tsee.*

Similar Species: *American Tree Sparrow* (p. 291): dark central breast spot; dark upper mandible; lacks white eye ring. *Swamp Sparrow* (p. 303): white throat; dark upper mandible; lacks 2 white wing bars and white eye ring. *Chipping Sparrow* (p. 292): all-dark bill; white "eyebrow"; black eye line; lacks buffy red wash on underparts.

Selected Sites: overgrown or abandoned fields or open areas.

VESPER SPARROW

Pooecetes gramineus

For birders who live near grassy fields and agricultural lands with multitudes of confusing little brown sparrows, the Vesper Sparrow offers welcome relief—white outer tail feathers and a chestnut shoulder patch announce its identity whether the bird is perched or in flight. The Vesper Sparrow is also known for its bold and easily distinguished song, which begins with two sets of unforgettable, double notes: *here-here! there-there!* • When the business of nesting begins, the Vesper Sparrow scours the neighborhood for a potential nesting site. More often than not, this bird builds its nest in a grassy hollow at the base of a clump of weeds or small shrub. This setup provides camouflage and functions as a windbreak and an umbrella to protect the young. • "Vesper" is Latin for "evening," a time when this bird often sings. *Pooecetes* is Greek for "grass dweller."

ID: chestnut shoulder patch; white outer tail feathers; pale yellow lores; weak flank streaking; white eye ring; dark upper mandible; lighter lower mandible; pale legs.

Size: *L* 6 in; *W* 10 in.

Status: common migrant and breeder from late March to late October.

Habitat: open fields bordered or interspersed with shrubs, semi-open shrublands and grasslands; also in agricultural areas, open, dry conifer plantations and scrubby gravel pits.

Nesting: in a scrape on the ground, often under a canopy of grass or at the base of a shrub; loosely woven cup nest made of grass is lined with rootlets, fine grass and hair; mostly the female incubates 3–5 whitish to greenish white eggs, blotched with brown and gray, for 11–13 days.

Feeding: walks and runs along the ground, picking up grasshoppers, beetles, cutworms, other invertebrates and seeds.

Voice: song is 4 characteristic, preliminary notes, with the second higher in pitch, followed by a bubbly trill: *here-here there-there, everybody-down-the-hill.*

Similar Species: *Other sparrows* (pp. 291–306): lack white outer tail feathers and chestnut shoulder patch. *American Pipit* (p. 248): thinner bill; grayer upperparts lack brown streaking; lacks chestnut shoulder patch. *Lapland Longspur* (p. 308): blackish or buff wash on upper breast; nonbreeding has broad, pale "eyebrow" and reddish edgings to wing feathers.

Selected Sites: shrubby fields and fencerows in agricultural areas.

SAVANNAH SPARROW

Passerculus sandwichensis

The Savannah Sparrow is one of our most common open-country birds. At one time or another, most people have probably seen or heard one, although they may not have been aware of it—this bird's streaky, dull brown, buff-and-white plumage resembles so many of the other grassland sparrows that it is easily overlooked. • From early spring to early summer, male Savannah Sparrows belt out their distinctive, buzzy tunes while perched atop prominent shrubs, tall weeds or strategic fence posts. Later in the summer and throughout early fall, they are most often seen darting across roads, highways and open fields in search of food. Like most sparrows, however, Savannahs generally stay out of sight. When danger appears, they take flight only as a last resort, preferring to run swiftly and inconspicuously through the grass, almost like feathered voles. • The common and scientific names of this bird reflect its broad North American distribution: "Savannah" refers to the city in Georgia, while *sandwichensis* is derived from Sandwich Bay in the Aleutian Islands off Alaska.

ID: finely streaked breast, sides and flanks; pale, streaked underparts; mottled brown upperparts; yellow lores; light jaw line; pale legs and bill; may show dark breast spot.

Size: *L* 5–6 in; *W* 6½ in.

Status: common migrant and breeder from April to October; a few overwinter from November to March.

Habitat: agricultural fields (especially hay and alfalfa), moist sedge and grass meadows, pastures, beaches, bogs and fens.

Nesting: on the ground in a shallow scrape well concealed by grass or a shrub; female builds an open cup nest woven from and lined with grass; female incubates 3–6 brown-marked, whitish to greenish or pale tan eggs for 10–13 days.

Feeding: gleans insects and seeds while walking or running along the ground; occasionally scratches.

Voice: song is a high-pitched, clear, buzzy *tea tea teeeeea today;* call is a high, thin *tsit.*

Similar Species: *Vesper Sparrow* (p. 295): white outer tail feathers; chestnut shoulder patch. *Lincoln's Sparrow* (p. 302): buff jaw line; buff wash across breast; broad, gray "eyebrow." *Grasshopper Sparrow* (p. 297): unstreaked breast. *Song Sparrow* (p. 301): triangular "mustache" stripes; pale central crown stripe; rounded tail; lacks yellow lores.

Selected Sites: open meadows or fields.

GRASSHOPPER SPARROW

Ammodramus savannarum

The Grasshopper Sparrow is named not for its diet, but rather for its buzzy, insectlike song. During courtship flights, males chase females through the air, buzzing at a frequency that is usually inaudible to human ears. The males sing two completely different courtship songs: one ends in a short trill and the other is a prolonged series of high trills that vary in pitch and speed. • The Grasshopper Sparrow is an open-country bird that prefers grassy expanses free of trees and shrubs. Wide, well-drained, grassy ditches occasionally attract nesting Grasshopper Sparrows, so mowing or harvesting these grassy margins early in the nesting season may be detrimental to these birds. Convincing local landowners and state governments to delay cutting until mid-August or September would benefit the Grasshopper Sparrow. • The scientific name *Ammodramus* is Greek for "sand runner," while *savannarum* is Latin for "of the savanna," after this bird's grassy, open habitat.

ID: unstreaked, white underparts with buff wash on breast, sides and flanks; flattened head profile; dark crown with pale central stripe; buff "cheek"; mottled brown upperparts; beady, black eyes; sharp tail; pale legs; may show small yellow patch on edge of forewing. *Immature:* less buff on underparts; faint streaking across breast.
Size: *L* 5–5½ in; *W* 7½ in.
Status: special concern; migrant and breeder from late April to early October in Lower Peninsula.
Habitat: grasslands and grassy fields with little or no shrub or tree cover.
Nesting: in a shallow depression on the ground, usually concealed by grass; female builds a small cup nest of grass and lines it with rootlets, fine grass and hair; female

incubates 4–5 creamy white eggs, spotted with gray and reddish brown, for 11–13 days.
Feeding: gleans insects and seeds from the ground and grass; eats a variety of insects, including grasshoppers.
Voice: song is a high, faint, buzzy trill preceded by 1–3 high, thin whistled notes: *tea-tea-tea zeeeeeeeeee.*
Similar Species: *Le Conte's Sparrow* (p. 299): buff-and-black-striped head with white central crown stripe; gray "cheek"; dark streaking on sides and flanks. *Nelson's Sharp-tailed Sparrow:* buff orange face and breast; gray, central crown stripe; gray "cheek" and shoulders. *Henslow's Sparrow* (p. 298): similar to immature Grasshopper Sparrow but has darker breast streaking, rusty wings and small, dark ear and "whisker" marks.
Selected Sites: Tuscola SGA; Chippewa Nature Center; Sleeper SP; Muskegon Wastewater System; Yankee Springs SRA; Sleeping Bear Dunes National Lakeshore.

HENSLOW'S SPARROW
Ammodramus henslowii

It's difficult to predict when you'll see the next Henslow's Sparrow in our region—this bird makes irregular visits here, often appearing one year but not the next. Some males have been known to occupy a field for a few weeks before suddenly disappearing, probably owing to the lack of a potential mate. The Henslow's unpredictability has made it a difficult species to study, so we have much more to learn about its habitat requirements and the reasons for its recent, widespread decline. • Henslow's Sparrows are known for their unusual habit of singing at night. In the daytime, watch the male Henslow's Sparrow as he throws back his streaky, greenish head while hurling his distinctive song from atop a tall blade of grass or low shrub. Without the male's lyrical advertisements, the inconspicuous Henslow's Sparrow would be almost impossible to observe, as this bird spends most of its time foraging alone along the ground. When disturbed, it may fly a short distance before dropping into cover, but it usually prefers to run through dense, concealing vegetation. • John J. Audubon named this sparrow after his friend John Stevens Henslow, a naturalist and one-time teacher of Charles Darwin.

ID: flattened head profile; olive green face, central crown stripe and nape; dark crown and "whisker" stripes; rusty tinge on back, wings and tail; white underparts with dark streaking on buff breast, sides and flanks; thick bill; deeply notched, sharp-edged tail. *Juvenile:* buff wash on most of underparts; faint streaking on sides only.
Size: *L* 5–5½ in; *W* 6½ in.
Status: threatened; rare and local migrant and breeder from late April to mid-October in southern two-thirds of Lower Peninsula.
Habitat: large, fallow or wild, grassy fields and meadows with a matted ground layer of dead vegetation and scattered shrub or herb perches; often in moist, grassy areas.

Nesting: on the ground at the base of a grass clump or herbaceous plant; mostly the female builds an open cup nest of grass and weeds and lines it with fine grass and hair; female incubates 3–5 whitish to pale, greenish white eggs, spotted with gray and reddish brown, for about 11 days.
Feeding: gleans insects and seeds from the ground.
Voice: weak, liquidy, cricketlike *tse-lick* song is distinctive, often given during periods of rain or at night.
Similar Species: *Other sparrows* (pp. 291–306): lack greenish face, central crown stripe and nape. *Grasshopper Sparrow* (p. 297): lacks dark "whisker" stripe and prominent streaking on breast and sides. *Savannah Sparrow* (p. 296): lacks buff breast. *Le Conte's Sparrow* (p. 299): buff-and-black-striped head with white central crown stripe; gray "cheek."
Selected Sites: no consistent sites.

LE CONTE'S SPARROW

Ammodramus leconteii

L e Conte's Sparrows are difficult to find because of their remote breeding habitat, scattered distribution and secretive behavior. These sparrows prefer to scurry along the ground in thick cover, and will only resort to flight for short distances before dropping out of sight again. Even singing males typically choose low, concealing perches from which to offer their gentle love ballads. Some skilled birders may follow the buzzy tune to its source to catch a fleeting glimpse of the singer before he dives into tall vegetation and disappears from view. • This bird's namesake, John Le Conte, is best remembered as one of the pre-eminent American entomologists of the 19th century, though he was interested in all areas of natural history.

ID: buff orange face; gray "cheek"; black line behind eye; pale central crown stripe bordered by black stripes; buff orange upper breast, sides and flanks; dark streaking on sides and flanks; white throat, lower breast and belly; mottled, brown black upperparts; buff streaks on back; pale legs. *Juvenile:* duller overall; more streaking on breast.
Size: *L* 4½–5 in; *W* 6½ in.
Status: uncommon migrant from late April to late May and from September to October; uncommon breeder from June to July in Upper Peninsula.
Habitat: grassy meadows with dense vegetation, drier edges of wet sedge and grass meadows, willow and alder flats and forest openings.

Nesting: on or near the ground, concealed by tangled vegetation; female builds an open cup nest woven from grass and rushes and tied to standing plant stems, and lines it with fine grass and hair; female incubates 3–5 grayish white eggs, spotted with gray and brown, for 12–13 days.
Feeding: gleans the ground and low vegetation for insects, spiders and seeds.
Voice: song is a weak, short, raspy, insect-like buzz: *t-t-t-zeeee zee* or *take-it ea-zeee;* alarm call is a high-pitched whistle.
Similar Species: *Nelson's Sharp-tailed Sparrow:* gray central crown stripe and nape; white streaks on dark back. *Grasshopper Sparrow* (p. 297): lacks buff orange face and streaking on underparts.
Selected Sites: Seney NWR; Sleeper Lake Bog; Tahquamenon R. mouth; Betchler Lakes; Maxton Plains; Rudyard Flats.

FOX SPARROW

Passerella iliaca

Like the Eastern Towhee, the Fox Sparrow eagerly scratches out a living, using both feet to stir up leaves and scrape organic matter along the forest floor. This large sparrow's preference for impenetrable, brushy habitat makes it a difficult species to observe, even though its noisy foraging habits often reveal its whereabouts. Its loud, whistled courtship songs are as easily recognized, and to the attentive listener they can often be as moving as a loon's wail or a wolf's howl. Though the Fox Sparrow is generally agreed to be the best singer among the sparrows, it doesn't sing while on migration in Michigan. • Unlike other songbirds, which may filter through the region in a series of lingering waves, Fox Sparrows generally appear in our region for only a few short weeks in a single effort before moving on to their nesting grounds farther north. • The overall reddish brown appearance of this bird inspired taxonomists to name it after the red fox.

ID: whitish underparts; heavy, reddish brown spotting and streaking often converges into central breast spot; reddish brown wings, rump and tail; gray crown; brown-streaked back; gray "eyebrow" and nape; stubby, conical bill; pale legs.
Size: *L* 6½–7 in; *W* 10½ in.
Status: uncommon migrant from mid-March to late April and from late September to early November; rare winter resident from November to March in southern Michigan.
Habitat: riparian thickets and brushy woodland clearings, edges and parklands.

Nesting: does not nest in Michigan.
Feeding: scratches the ground to uncover seeds, berries and invertebrates; visits backyard feeders in migration and winter.
Voice: does not sing in migration; calls include *chip* and *click* notes.
Similar Species: *Song Sparrow* (p. 301): pale central crown stripe; dark "mustache"; dark brownish rather than reddish streaking and upperparts. *Hermit Thrush* (p. 240): longer, thinner bill; pale eye ring; dark breast spots; unstreaked, olive brown and reddish brown upperparts; lacks heavy streaking on underparts.
Selected Sites: Holly SRA; Waterloo SRA; Kalamazoo Nature Center; Muskegon SP; Leelanau SP; Whitefish Point; Seney NWR.

SONG SPARROW

Melospiza melodia

The Song Sparrow's heavily streaked, low-key plumage doesn't prepare you for its symphonic song. This well-named sparrow is known for the complexity, rhythm and emotion of its springtime rhapsodies, although some people will insist that the Fox Sparrow and the Lincoln's Sparrow carry the best tunes. • Young Song Sparrows and many other songbirds learn to sing by eavesdropping on their fathers or on rival males. By the time a young male is a few months old, he will have formed the basis for his own courtship tune. • In recent decades, mild winters and an abundance of backyard bird feeders have enticed an increasing number of Song Sparrows to overwinter here. • Most songbirds are lucky if they are able to produce one brood per year. In some years, Song Sparrows in our region will successfully raise three broods. There are about 31 different subspecies of the Song Sparrow, from the pale desert birds to the larger and darker Alaskan forms. • The scientific name *melodia* means "melody" in Greek.

ID: whitish underparts with heavy brown streaking that converges into central breast spot; grayish face; dark line behind eye; white jaw line is bordered by a dark whisker and "mustache" stripes; dark crown with a pale central stripe; mottled brown upperparts; rounded tail tip.
Size: *L* 5½–7 in; *W* 8½ in.
Status: common to abundant migrant and breeder from early March to November; rare winter resident from November to March.
Habitat: shrubby areas, often near water, including willow shrublands, riparian thickets, forest openings and pastures.
Nesting: usually on the ground or low in a shrub or small tree; female builds an open cup nest of grass, weeds, leaves and bark shreds and lines it with rootlets, fine grass and hair; female incubates 3–5 greenish

white eggs, heavily spotted with reddish brown, for 12–14 days; may raise 2–3 broods each summer.
Feeding: gleans the ground, shrubs and trees for cutworms, beetles, grasshoppers, ants, other invertebrates and seeds; also eats wild fruit and visits feeders.
Voice: song is 1–4 bright, distinctive introductory notes, such as *sweet, sweet, sweet,* followed by a buzzy *towee,* then a short, descending trill; calls include a short *tsip* and a nasal *tchep.*
Similar Species: *Fox Sparrow* (p. 300): heavier breast spotting and streaking; lacks pale, central crown stripe and dark "mustache"; reddish rather than dark brownish streaking and upperparts. *Lincoln's Sparrow* (p. 302): lightly streaked breast with buff wash; buff jaw line. *Savannah Sparrow* (p. 296): lightly streaked breast; yellow lores; notched tail; lacks grayish face and dark, triangular "mustache."
Selected Sites: widespread in shrubby areas.

LINCOLN'S SPARROW

Melospiza lincolnii

There is a certain beauty in the plumage of a Lincoln's Sparrow that is greater than the sum of its feathers. Sightings of this bird, linked with the sounds and smells of its natural habitat, can bring joy to the hearts of perceptive birders. • Lincoln's Sparrows seem to be more timid than other Michigan sparrows. Males will sit openly on exposed perches and sing their bubbly, wrenlike songs, but as soon as they are approached, they slip under the cover of nearby shrubs. When they are not singing their courtship songs, Lincoln's Sparrows remain well hidden in tall grass and dense, bushy growth. Their remote breeding grounds and secretive behavior conspire to keep this species one of the least-known sparrows. • A mother Lincoln's Sparrow will have different reactions to disturbance depending on the state of her brood. If disturbed while sitting on her eggs, she will run quietly through the grasses like a mouse, hoping both she and the nest will be passed over. If the young have hatched, the broken-wing method will be employed to draw the predator away. • This sparrow bears the name of Thomas Lincoln, a young companion of John J. Audubon on his voyage to Labrador, Canada.

ID: buff breast band, sides and flanks with fine, dark streaking; buff jaw stripe; gray "eyebrow," face and "collar"; dark line behind eye; dark, reddish "cap" with gray central stripe; white throat and belly; mottled, gray brown to reddish brown upperparts; very faint, white eye ring.

Size: *L* 5½ in; *W* 7½ in.

Status: common migrant from late April to May and from September to early October; breeder from late May to June in Upper Peninsula.

Habitat: *Breeding:* shrubby edges of bogs, swamps, beaver ponds and meadows; also in jack pine plains. *In migration:* brushy woodlands and shrubby fencerows.

Nesting: on the ground, often on soft moss or concealed beneath a shrub; female builds a well-hidden cup nest made of grass and sedges and lines it with fine grass and hair; female incubates 4–5 greenish white to pale green eggs, heavily spotted with reddish brown, for 11–14 days.

Feeding: scratches at the ground to expose invertebrates and seeds; occasionally visits feeders.

Voice: song is a wrenlike musical mixture of buzzes, trills and warbled notes; calls include a buzzy *zeee* and *tsup*.

Similar Species: *Song Sparrow* (p. 301): heavier breast streaking; dark triangular "mustache"; lacks buff wash on breast, sides and flanks. *Savannah Sparrow* (p. 296): yellow lores; white "eyebrow" and jaw line. *Swamp Sparrow* (p. 303): generally lacks breast streaking; more contrast between red and gray crown stripes.

Selected Sites: Hartwick Pines SP; Minden City SGA; Tahquamenon Falls SP; Whitefish Point; Sylvania Recreation Area; Betchler Lakes.

SWAMP SPARROW

Melospiza georgiana

Swamp Sparrows are well adapted to life near water. These wetland inhabitants skulk among the emergent vegetation of cattail marshes, foraging for a variety of invertebrates including beetles, caterpillars, spiders, leafhoppers and flies. Like other sparrows, they are unable to swim, but that is no deterrent—many of their meals are snatched directly from the water's surface as they wade through the shallows. • The Swamp Sparrow must keep a lookout for daytime predators such as Northern Harriers, Great Blue Herons and large snakes. At night, the key to survival is finding a secluded, concealing perch that will keep it safe from raccoons, skunks and weasels. • Swamp Sparrows are most easily seen in spring when males sing their familiar trills from atop cattails or shoreline shrubs.

breeding

ID: gray face; reddish brown wings; brownish upperparts; dark streaking on back; dull gray breast; black stripes outline white throat and jaw; dark line behind eye. *Breeding:* rusty "cap"; streaked, buff sides and flanks. *Nonbreeding:* streaked, brown "cap" with gray central stripe; more brownish sides. *Immature:* buffy "eyebrow" and nape; faint streaking on breast.
Size: *L* 5–6 in; *W* 7½ in.
Status: common migrant and breeder from late April to late October; rare winter resident from November to April in southern Michigan.
Habitat: cattail marshes, open wetlands, wet meadows and open deciduous riparian thickets.
Nesting: in emergent aquatic vegetation or shoreline bushes; female builds a cup nest of coarse grass and marsh vegetation and lines it with fine grass; nest usually has a partial canopy and a side entrance; female incubates 4–5 greenish white to pale green eggs, heavily marked with reddish brown, for 12–15 days.
Feeding: gleans insects from the ground, vegetation and the water's surface; takes seeds in late summer and fall.
Voice: song is a slow, sharp, metallic trill: *weet-weet-weet-weet;* call is a harsh *chink.*
Similar Species: *Chipping Sparrow* (p. 292): clean white "eyebrow"; full, black eye line; uniformly gray underparts; white wing bars. *American Tree Sparrow* (p. 291): dark central breast spot; white wing bars; 2-tone bill. *Song Sparrow* (p. 301): heavily streaked underparts; lacks gray "collar." *Lincoln's Sparrow* (p. 302): fine breast streaking; less contrast between brown and gray crown stripes.
Selected Sites: cattail marshes or open wetlands.

WHITE-THROATED SPARROW

Zonotrichia albicollis

The handsome White-throated Sparrow is easily identified by its bold, white throat and striped crown. Two color morphs are common throughout our region: one has black and white stripes on the head; the other has brown and tan stripes. White-striped males are more aggressive than tan-striped males, and tan-striped females are more nurturing than white-striped females. These two color morphs are perpetuated because each morph almost always breeds with the opposite color morph. • In spring and fall, White-throated Sparrows can appear anywhere in our region in great abundance. Urban backyards dressed with brushy fenceline tangles and a bird feeder brimming with seeds can attract good numbers of these delightful sparrows. • *Zonotrichia* means "hairlike," a reference to the striped heads of birds in this genus; *albicollis* is Latin for "white neck"—not quite accurate, as it is the bird's throat and not its neck that is white.

ID: black-and-white (or brown-and-tan) striped head; white throat; gray "cheek"; yellow lores; black eye line; unstreaked, gray underparts; mottled brown upperparts; grayish bill.

Size: *L* 6½–7½ in; *W* 9 in.

Status: common migrant from mid-April to late May and from September to mid-November; common breeder from May to September in northern Michigan; rare winter resident from November to April in southern Michigan.

Habitat: *Breeding:* semi-open coniferous and mixed forests, especially in regenerating clearings and along shrubby forest edges. *In migration:* woodlots, wooded parks and riparian brush.

Nesting: on or near the ground, often concealed by a low shrub or fallen log; female builds an open cup nest of grass, weeds, twigs and conifer needles and lines it with rootlets, fine grass and hair; female incubates 4–5 greenish blue to pale blue eggs, marked with lavender and reddish brown, for 11–14 days.

Feeding: scratches the ground to expose invertebrates, seeds and berries; also gleans insects from vegetation and while in flight; eats seeds from bird feeders in winter.

Voice: variable song is a clear, distinct, whistled: *Old Sam Peabody, Peabody, Peabody;* call is a sharp *chink*.

Similar Species: *White-crowned Sparrow* (p. 306): pinkish bill; gray "collar"; lacks bold white throat and yellow lores. *Swamp Sparrow* (p. 303): smaller; gray and chestnut on crown; streaked underparts; lacks head pattern.

Selected Sites: semi-open coniferous forests or woodland edges; also backyard feeders.

HARRIS'S SPARROW

Zonotrichia querula

There are always eventful days in the natural calendar of our region. For example, during spring and fall migrations, there looms the possibility, however slim, of seeing a Harris's Sparrow. An unassuming migrant, the Harris's Sparrow passes through the region in small isolated trickles, frequently mixing with flocks of White-throated Sparrows and White-crowned Sparrows. Occasionally, a few Harris's Sparrows pick through the seed offerings at backyard feeders. • The Harris's Sparrow breeds in the far north of Canada, where the treeline fades to tundra. Because of the remoteness of its breeding grounds, there is little information about this species' breeding habits, nests and eggs. • The scientific name *querula* means "plaintive" in Latin and refers to this bird's quavering, whistled song. • John J. Audubon named this sparrow after his friend and amateur naturalist, Edward Harris, with whom he traveled up the Missouri River in 1843.

breeding

VAGRANT

ID: mottled brown-and-black upperparts; white underparts; pink orange bill. *Breeding:* black crown, ear patch, throat and "bib"; gray face; black streaks on sides and flanks; white wing bars. *Nonbreeding:* brown face; brownish sides and flanks; white flecks on black crown. *Immature:* white throat; mostly brownish crown with some black streaking.
Size: *L* 7–7½ in; *W* 10½ in.
Status: migrant from late April to May and from late September to early November in western Upper Peninsula and western shore of L. Michigan.
Habitat: brushy roadsides, shrubby vegetation, forest edges and riparian thickets.
Nesting: does not nest in Michigan.

Feeding: gleans the ground and vegetation for seeds, fresh buds, insects and berries; occasionally takes seeds from bird feeders.
Voice: song is a series of 2–4 long, quavering whistles; each series may be offered at the same or at a different pitch; call is a *jeenk* or *zheenk;* flocks in flight may give a rolling *chug-up chug-up.*
Similar Species: *White-throated Sparrow* (p. 304): grayish bill; yellow lores; black-and-white-striped crown. *White-crowned Sparrow* (p. 306): black-and-white-striped crown; gray "collar"; immature has broad gray "eyebrow" bordered by brown eye line and crown. *House Sparrow* (p. 335): male is brownish overall; gray crown; broad, brown band behind eye; broad, whitish jaw band; dark bill.
Selected Sites: Ontonagon, Keweenaw and Houghton counties; also counties bordering L. Michigan.

WHITE-CROWNED SPARROW
Zonotrichia leucophrys

The large, bold, strongly patterned White-crowned Sparrow brightens brushy expanses and suburban parks and gardens with its cheeky song for a few short weeks in spring and fall. Most birders with well-stocked bird feeders should be especially familiar with this conspicuous bird. • Many birders confuse this bird with the White-throated Sparrow, but the larger size and more erect stance of the White-crowned Sparrow helps to distinguish it. • The White-crowned Sparrow is North America's most studied sparrow. Research on this bird has given science tremendous insight into bird physiology, homing behavior and the geographic variability of song dialects. • White-crowns breed in the far north, in alpine environments or along the California coast. This bird has a widespread distribution in North America and populations in different parts of its range vary significantly in behavior and in migratory and nesting habits.

ID: black-and-white-striped head; black eye line; pink orange bill; gray face; unstreaked, gray underparts; pale gray throat; mottled, gray brown upperparts; 2 faint white wing bars. *Immature:* broad, gray "eyebrow" bordered by brown eye line and crown.

Size: *L* 5½–7 in; *W* 9½ in.

Status: common migrant from late April to late May and from mid-September to mid-November; rare winter resident from November to April in southern Michigan.

Habitat: woodlots, brushy tangles and riparian thickets.

Nesting: does not nest in Michigan.

Feeding: scratches the ground to expose insects and seeds; also eats berries, buds and moss caps; may take seeds from bird feeders.

Voice: song is a frequently repeated variation of *I gotta go wee-wee now* (not heard in Michigan); call is a high, thin *seet* or sharp *pink*.

Similar Species: *White-throated Sparrow* (p. 304): bold white throat; grayish bill; yellow lores; browner overall. *Golden-crowned Sparrow:* dark bill; golden yellow crown bordered with black.

Selected Sites: Kensington Metropark; Waterloo SRA; Kalamazoo Nature Center; Chippewa Nature Center; Wilderness SP; Whitefish Point; Peninsula Point.

DARK-EYED JUNCO
Junco hyemalis

Most juncos migrate south for the winter, but many remain in Michigan even during the coldest years. Juncos usually congregate in backyards with bird feeders and sheltering conifers—with such amenities at their disposal, more and more juncos overwinter in Michigan. • Juncos spend most of their time on the ground, and they are readily flushed from wooded trails and backyard feeders. Their distinctive, white outer tail feathers flash in alarm as they seek cover in a nearby tree or shrub. • Juncos rarely perch at feeders, preferring to snatch up seeds that are knocked to the ground by other visitors such as chickadees, sparrows, nuthatches and jays. • In 1973, the American Ornithologists' Union grouped five junco species into a single species called the Dark-eyed Junco. The five subspecies are closely related and have similar habits, but differ in coloration and range, though they interbreed where their ranges meet. Michigan is typically home to the subspecies *hyemalis*, the Slate-colored Junco.

"Slate-colored Junco"

ID: white outer tail feathers; pale bill. *Male:* dark slate gray overall, except for white lower breast, belly and undertail coverts. *Female:* brown rather than gray. *Juvenile:* brown like female, but streaked with darker brown.
Size: *L* 5½–7 in; *W* 9½ in.
Status: common migrant and winter resident from September to May; common breeder from June to August in northern Michigan.
Habitat: *Breeding:* coniferous and mixed forests, especially in young jack pine stands, burned-over areas and shrubby regenerating clearings. *In migration* and *winter:* shrubby woodland borders; also backyard feeders.

Nesting: on the ground, usually concealed by a shrub, tree, root, log or rock; female builds a cup nest of twigs, bark shreds, grass and moss, and lines it with fine grass and hair; female incubates 3–5 whitish to bluish white eggs, marked with gray and brown, for 12–13 days.
Feeding: scratches the ground for invertebrates; also eats berries and seeds.
Voice: song is a long, dry trill, very similar to that of the Chipping Sparrow, but more musical; call is a smacking *chip* note, often given in series.
Similar Species: *Eastern Towhee* (p. 290): larger; female has rufous sides, red eyes and grayish bill.
Selected Sites: Huron-Clinton Metroparks; Waterloo SRA; Kalamazoo Nature Center; Allegan SGA; Chippewa Nature Center; Leelanau SP; Whitefish Point.

LAPLAND LONGSPUR

Calcarius lapponicus

Throughout much of the year, Lapland Longspurs wheel about in large numbers over our fields. From day to day, their movements are largely unpredictable, but they typically appear wherever open fields offer an abundance of seeds or waste grain. Flocks of longspurs can be surprisingly inconspicuous until closely approached—anyone attempting a closer look at the flock will be awed by the sight of the birds suddenly erupting into the sky, flashing their white outer tail feathers. • In fall, these birds arrive from their breeding grounds looking like mottled, brownish sparrows and retain their drab plumage throughout the winter months. When farmers work their fields in spring, lingering Lapland Longspurs have already molted into their bold breeding plumage, which they will wear through summer. • The Lapland Longspur breeds in northern polar regions, including the area of northern Scandinavia known as Lapland.

nonbreeding

ID: white outer tail feathers; pale yellowish bill. *Breeding male:* black crown, face and "bib"; chestnut nape; broad, white stripe curving down to shoulder from eye (may be tinged with buff behind eye). *Breeding female:* mottled brown-and-black upperparts; lightly streaked flanks; female has narrow, lightly streaked, buff breast band. *Nonbreeding male:* similar to female, but with faint chestnut on nape and diffuse black breast.
Size: *L* 6½ in; *W* 11½ in.
Status: common migrant from March to May and from September to November;

uncommon winter resident from November to March in southern Michigan.
Habitat: pastures, meadows and croplands.
Nesting: does not nest in Michigan.
Feeding: gleans the ground and snow for seeds and waste grain.
Voice: flight song is a rapid slurred warble; musical calls; flight calls include a rattled *tri-di-dit* and a descending *teew.*
Similar Species: *Snow Bunting* (p. 309): black-and-white wing pattern. *Smith's Longspur* (p. 343): completely buff to buff orange underparts; male has black-and-white face and buff orange nape.
Selected Sites: in agricultural areas: grain stubble fields, fields with freshly spread manure; sod farms; often with Horned Larks.

SNOW BUNTING

Plectrophenax nivalis

In early winter, when flocks of Snow Buntings descend on rural fields, their startling black-and-white plumage flashes in contrast to the snow-covered backdrop. It may seem strange that Snow Buntings are whiter in summer than in winter, but the darker winter plumage may help these birds absorb heat on the clear, cold winter days. • Snow Buntings venture farther north than any other songbird in the world. A single individual, likely misguided and lost, was recorded not far from the North Pole in May 1987. • In winter, Snow Buntings prefer expansive areas including grain croplands, fields and pastures where they scratch and peck at exposed seeds and grains. They will also ingest small grains of sand or gravel from roadsides as a source of minerals and to help digestion. • Snow Buntings are definitely cold-weather songbirds, often bathing in snow in early spring, and burrowing into it during bitter cold snaps to stay warm.

nonbreeding

ID: black-and-white wings and tail; white underparts. *Breeding male:* black back; all-white head and rump; black bill. *Breeding female:* streaky, brown-and-whitish crown and back; dark bill. *Nonbreeding male:* yellowish bill; golden brown crown and rump. *Nonbreeding female:* similar to male but with blackish forecrown and dark-streaked, golden back.
Size: *L* 6–7½ in; *W* 14 in.
Status: common migrant and winter resident from late September to mid-May.

Habitat: manured fields, feedlots, pastures, grassy meadows, lakeshores, roadsides and railroads.
Nesting: does not nest in Michigan.
Feeding: gleans the ground and snow for seeds and waste grain; also takes insects when available.
Voice: call is a whistled *tew*.
Similar Species: *Lapland Longspur* (p. 308) and *Smith's Longspur* (p. 343): overall brownish upperparts; lack black-and-white wing pattern.
Selected Sites: open areas such as fields, pastures, roadsides and airports; also Great Lakes beaches.

NORTHERN CARDINAL

Cardinalis cardinalis

A bird as beautiful as the Northern Cardinal rarely fails to capture our attention and admiration: it is often the first choice for calendars and Christmas cards. Most people can easily recognize this delightful year-round neighbor even without the help of a bird field guide. • These birds prefer the tangled shrubby edges of woodlands and are easily attracted to backyards with feeders and sheltering trees and shrubs. • Northern Cardinals form one of the bird world's most faithful pair bonds. The male and female remain in close contact year-round, singing to one another through the seasons with soft, bubbly whistles. The female is known to sing while on the nest, and it is believed that she is informing her partner whether or not she and the young need food. The male is highly territorial, and will even challenge his own reflection in a window or shiny hubcap! • The Northern Cardinal owes its name to the vivid red plumage of the male, which resembles the red robes of Roman Catholic cardinals.

ID: *Male:* red overall; pointed crest; black "mask" and throat; red, conical bill. *Female:* shaped like male; brown buff to buff olive overall; red bill, crest, wings and tail. *Juvenile male:* similar to female but has dark bill and crest.
Size: *L* 7½–9 in; *W* 12 in.
Status: common year-round resident in southern half and northwestern part of Lower Peninsula.
Habitat: brushy thickets and shrubby tangles along forest and woodland edges; also in backyards and suburban and urban parks.
Nesting: in a dense shrub, thicket, vine tangle or low in a coniferous tree; female builds an open cup nest of twigs, bark shreds, weeds, grass, leaves and rootlets and lines it with hair and fine grass; female incubates 3–4 whitish to bluish or greenish white eggs, marked with gray, brown and purple, for 12–13 days.
Feeding: gleans seeds, insects and berries from low shrubs or while hopping along the ground.
Voice: song is a variable series of clear, bubbly whistled notes: *what cheer! what cheer! what cheer! birdie-birdie-birdie what cheer!;* call is a metallic *chip.*
Similar Species: *Summer Tanager* (p. 288) and *Scarlet Tanager* (p. 289): lack head crest, black "mask" and throat and red, conical bill; Scarlet Tanager has black wings and tail.
Selected Sites: brushy tangles along woodland edges in Lower Peninsula, south of a line from Traverse City to Bay City.

ROSE-BREASTED GROSBEAK

Pheucticus ludovicianus

I t is difficult to miss the boisterous, whistled tune of the Rose-breasted Grosbeak. This bird's hurried, robinlike song is easily recognized, and is one of the more common songs heard in our deciduous forests through spring and summer. Although the female lacks the magnificent colors of the male, she shares his talent for beautiful song. Mating grosbeaks appear pleasantly affectionate toward each other, often touching bills during courtship and after absences. • Rose-breasted Grosbeaks usually build their nests low in a tree or tall shrub, but typically forage high in the canopy where they can be difficult to spot. Luckily for birders, the abundance of berries in fall often draws these birds to ground level. • The species name *ludovicianus,* Latin for "from Louisiana," is misleading because this bird is only a migrant through Louisiana and other southern states.

breeding

ID: pale, conical bill; dark wings with small white patches; dark tail. *Male:* black "hood" and back; red breast and inner underwings; white underparts and rump. *Female:* bold, whitish "eyebrow"; thin crown stripe; brown upperparts; buff underparts with dark brown streaking.

Size: *L* 7–8½ in; *W* 12½ in.

Status: common migrant and breeder from May to September.

Habitat: deciduous and mixed forests.

Nesting: fairly low in a tree or tall shrub, often near water; mostly the female builds a flimsy cup nest of twigs, bark strips, weeds, grass and leaves and lines it with rootlets and hair; pair incubates 3–5 pale, greenish blue eggs, spotted with reddish brown, for 13–14 days.

Feeding: gleans vegetation for insects, seeds, buds, berries and some fruit; occasionally hover-gleans or catches flying insects on the wing; may also visit feeders.

Voice: song is a long, melodious series of whistled notes, much like a fast version of a robin's song; call is a distinctive squeak.

Similar Species: male is distinctive. *Purple Finch* (p. 326): female is much smaller and has heavier streaking on underparts. *Sparrows* (pp. 291–306): smaller; all lack large, conical bill.

Selected Sites: deciduous woodlands; backyard feeders.

311

INDIGO BUNTING

Passerina cyanea

In the shadow of a towering tree, a male Indigo Bunting can look almost black. If possible, reposition yourself quickly to a place from which you can see the sun strike and enliven this bunting's incomparable indigo plumage—the rich shade of blue is rivaled only by the sky. • Raspberry thickets are a favored nesting location for many of our Indigo Buntings. The dense, thorny stems provide the nestlings with protection from many predators, and the berries are a convenient source of food. • The Indigo Bunting employs a clever and comical foraging strategy to reach the grass and weed seeds upon which it feeds. The bird lands midway on a stem and then shuffles slowly towards the seed head, which eventually bends under the bird's weight, giving the bunting easier access to the seeds. • Only male Indigo Buntings sing, and they do not learn their musical warble from their fathers, but from neighboring males during their first spring.

breeding

ID: stout, gray, conical bill; beady, black eyes; black legs; no wing bars. *Male:* blue overall; black lores; wings and tail may show some black. *Female:* soft brown overall; brown streaks on breast; whitish throat. *Nonbreeding male:* similar to female, but usually with some blue in wings and tail.
Size: *L* 5½ in; *W* 8 in.
Status: common migrant and breeder from May to September.
Habitat: deciduous forest and woodland edges, regenerating forest clearings, shrubby fields, orchards, abandoned pastures and hedgerows; occasionally along mixed woodland edges.
Nesting: usually in an upright fork of a small tree or shrub or within a vine tangle;

female builds a cup nest of grass, leaves and bark strips and lines it with rootlets, hair and feathers; female incubates 3–4 white to bluish white eggs, rarely spotted with brown or purple, for 12–13 days.
Feeding: gleans low vegetation and the ground for insects, especially grasshoppers, beetles, weevils, flies and larvae; also eats the seeds of thistles, dandelions, goldenrods and other native plants.
Voice: song consists of paired warbled whistles: *fire-fire, where-where, here-here, see-it see-it;* call is a quick *spit.*
Similar Species: *Blue Grosbeak* (p. 343): larger overall; larger, more robust bill; 2 rusty wing bars; male has black around base of bill; female lacks streaking on breast. *Mountain Bluebird:* larger; slimmer bill; male has pure blue wings and tail.
Selected Sites: shrubby, deciduous woodland edges.

DICKCISSEL

Spiza americana

Dickcissels are an irruptive species and may be common in Michigan one year and absent the next. Arriving in suitable nesting habitat before the smaller females, breeding males bravely announce their presence with stuttering, trilled renditions of their own name. The territorial males perch atop tall blades of grass, fence posts or rocks to scour their turf for signs of potential mates or unwelcome males. Dickcissels are polygynous, and males may mate with up to eight females in a single breeding season. This breeding strategy means that the male gives no assistance to the females in nesting or brooding. • This "miniature meadowlark" has a special fondness for fields of alfalfa. Though Dickcissels eat mostly insects on their breeding grounds, seeds and grain form the main part of their diet on their South American wintering grounds, making them unpopular with local farmers. Each year large numbers of these birds are killed by pesticides in efforts to reduce crop losses, which may partially explain the Dickcissel's pattern of absence and abundance.

breeding

ID: yellow "eyebrow"; gray head, nape and sides of yellow breast; brown upperparts; pale, grayish underparts; rufous shoulder patch; dark, conical bill. *Male:* white "chin" and black "bib"; duller colors in nonbreeding plumage. *Female:* duller version of male; white throat. *Immature:* similar to female but has very faint "eyebrow" and dark streaking on crown, breast, sides and flanks.
Size: *L* 6–7 in; *W* 9½ in.
Status: special concern; irregular migrant and breeder from mid-May to September; most frequent in southern Lower Peninsula.
Habitat: abandoned fields dominated by forbs, weedy meadows, croplands, grasslands and grassy roadsides.

Nesting: on or near the ground; well concealed among tall, dense vegetation; female builds a bulky, open cup nest of grass, weed stems and leaves and lines it with rootlets, fine grass or hair; female incubates 4 pale blue eggs for 11–13 days.
Feeding: gleans insects and seeds from the ground and low vegetation.
Voice: song consists of 2–3 single notes followed by a trill, often paraphrased as *dick dick dick-cissel;* flight call is a buzzerlike *bzrrrrt.*
Similar Species: *Eastern Meadowlark* (p. 316): much larger; long, pointed bill; yellow "chin" and throat with black "necklace." *American Goldfinch* (p. 333): lacks black "bib"; white or buff yellow bars on dark wings; may show black forecrown.
Selected Sites: scattered locations statewide; southern 4 tiers of Michigan counties in normal years.

BOBOLINK

Dolichonyx oryzivorus

During the nesting season, male and female Bobolinks rarely interact with one another. For the most part, males perform aerial displays and sing their bubbly, tinkling songs from exposed grassy perches while the females carry out the nesting duties. Once the young have hatched, males become scarce, spending much of their time on the ground hunting for insects. • At first glimpse, the female Bobolink resembles a sparrow, but the male, with his dark belly and his buff-and-black upperparts, is colored like no other bird in Michigan. • Bobolinks once benefited from increased agriculture here, but modern practices, such as harvesting hay early in the season, continue to thwart the reproductive efforts of these birds. • Some people think that the name of this bird is an abbreviation of "Robert of Lincoln," the title of a poem by American poet William Cullen Bryant that captures the essence of the Bobolink, but others think it is a reference to the bird's song.

breeding

ID: *Breeding male:* black bill, head, wings, tail and underparts; buff nape; white rump and wing patch. *Breeding female:* yellowish bill; buff brown overall; streaked back, sides, flank and rump; pale "eyebrow"; dark eye line; pale central crown stripe bordered by dark stripes; whitish throat. *Nonbreeding male:* similar to breeding female, but darker above and rich golden buff below.

Size: *L* 6–8 in; *W* 11½ in.

Status: common migrant and breeder from late April to September.

Habitat: tall, grassy meadows and ditches, hayfields and some croplands.

Nesting: on the ground, usually in a hay field; well concealed in a shallow depression; female builds a cup nest of grass and weed stems and lines it with fine grass; female incubates 5–6 grayish to light reddish brown eggs, heavily blotched with lavender and brown, for 11–13 days.

Feeding: gleans the ground and low vegetation for adult and larval invertebrates; also eats many seeds.

Voice: song is a series of banjolike twangs: *bobolink bobolink spink spank spink,* often given in flight; also issues a *pink* call in flight.

Similar Species: male is distinctive. *Savannah Sparrow* (p. 296): dark breast streaking; yellow lores. *Vesper Sparrow* (p. 295): breast streaking; white outer tail feathers. *Grasshopper Sparrow* (p. 297): white belly; unstreaked sides and flanks.

Selected Sites: moist, grassy meadows or hay fields.

RED-WINGED BLACKBIRD

Agelaius phoeniceus

A birder's winter blahs may be remedied by the sound of the season's first Red-winged Blackbirds. The males get an early start on the season, often arriving in our marshes and wetlands in mid-March, a week or so before the females. In the females' absence, the males stake out territories through song and visual displays. • The male's bright red shoulders and short, raspy song are his most important tools in the often intricate strategy he employs to defend his territory from rivals. A flashy and richly voiced male who has managed to establish a large and productive territory can attract several mates to his cattail kingdom. In field experiments, males whose red shoulders were painted black soon lost their territories to rivals they had previously defeated. • After the male has wooed the female, she starts the busy work of weaving a nest amid the cattails. Cryptic coloration allows the female to sit inconspicuously upon her nest, blending in perfectly with the surroundings. • *Agelaius* is a Greek word meaning "flocking," which is an accurate description of this bird's winter behavior, when impressive flocks can sometimes be seen. The species name *phoeniceus* is a reference to the color red, which was introduced to the Greeks as a dye by the ancient Phoenicians.

ID: *Male:* all black, except for large, red shoulder patch edged in yellow (occasionally concealed). *Female:* heavily streaked underparts; mottled brown upperparts; faint, red shoulder patch; light "eyebrow."
Size: *L* 7–9½ in; *W* 13 in.
Status: abundant migrant and breeder from mid-March to November; rare winter resident from November to March in southern Michigan.
Habitat: cattail marshes, wet meadows and ditches, croplands and shoreline shrubs.
Nesting: colonial; in cattails or shoreline bushes; female weaves an open cup nest of dried cattail leaves and grass and lines it with fine grass; female incubates 3–4 darkly marked, pale blue green eggs for 10–12 days.
Feeding: gleans the ground for seeds, waste grain and invertebrates; also gleans vegetation for seeds, insects and berries; occasionally catches insects in flight; may visit feeders.
Voice: song is a loud, raspy *konk-a-ree* or *ogle-reeeee;* calls include a harsh *check* and a high *tseert;* female may give a loud *che-che-che chee chee chee.*
Similar Species: male is distinctive when shoulder patch shows. *Brewer's Blackbird* (p. 320) and *Rusty Blackbird* (p. 319): females lack streaked underparts. *Brown-headed Cowbird* (p. 322): juvenile is smaller and has stubbier, conical bill.
Selected Sites: cattail marshes statewide; alfalfa hay fields.

315

EASTERN MEADOWLARK

Sturnella magna

The Eastern Meadowlark's trademark tune is the voice of rural areas, and it rings throughout spring from fence posts and powerlines, wherever grassy meadows and pastures are found. • The male's bright yellow underparts, black V-shaped "necklace," and white outer tail feathers help attract mates. Females share these colorful attributes for a slightly different purpose: when a predator approaches too close to a nest, the incubating female explodes from the grass in a burst of flashing color. Most predators cannot resist chasing the moving target, and once the female has led the predator away from the nest, she simply folds away her white tail flags, exposes her camouflaged back and disappears into the grass without a trace. • The Eastern Meadowlark is not actually a lark, but a member of the blackbird family, even though it doesn't seem to fit in with this family. When this bird is seen in silhouette, however, the similarities become very apparent. • The Eastern Meadowlark is by far the more common of the two meadowlark species in Michigan.

breeding

ID: yellow underparts; broad, black breast band; mottled brown upperparts; short, wide tail with white outer tail feathers; long, pinkish legs; yellow lores; long, sharp bill; blackish crown stripes and eye line border pale "eyebrow" and median crown stripe; dark streaking on white sides and flanks.
Size: *L* 9–9½ in; *W* 14 in.
Status: migrant and breeder from mid-March to mid-November, common in Lower Peninsula, uncommon in Upper Peninsula; rare winter resident from November to March in southern Michigan.
Habitat: grassy meadows and pastures; also in some croplands, weedy fields, grassy roadsides and old orchards.
Nesting: in a depression or scrape on the ground, concealed by dense grass; female builds a domed grass nest with a side entrance, which is woven into surrounding vegetation; female incubates 3–7 white eggs, heavily spotted with brown and purple, for about 13–15 days.
Feeding: gleans grasshoppers, crickets, beetles and spiders from the ground and vegetation; extracts grubs and worms by probing its bill into the soil; also eats seeds.
Voice: song is a rich series of 2–8 melodic, clear, slurred whistles: *see-you at school-today* or *this is the year;* gives a rattling flight call and a high, buzzy *dzeart*.
Similar Species: *Western Meadowlark* (p. 317): paler upperparts, especially crown stripes and eye line; yellow on throat extends onto lower "cheek"; different song and call. *Dickcissel* (p. 313): much smaller; solid dark crown; conical bill; white throat; lacks brown streaking on sides and flanks.
Selected Sites: pastures and meadows statewide.

WESTERN MEADOWLARK

Sturnella neglecta

Though the brightly colored Western Meadowlark is rare in Michigan, it is one of the most abundant and widely distributed birds in other parts of the U.S. It is also one of the most popular—the Western Meadowlark is the state bird in six states. • The two meadowlark species are very similar in appearance, so birders must listen for their songs to distinguish one from the other. The song of the Western Meadowlark is more constant, while the Eastern Meadowlark varies its song during bouts of singing. • Birders are encouraged to exercise extreme caution when walking through meadowlark nesting habitat. Meadowlarks' grassy domed nests are extremely difficult to locate, and are so well concealed that they are often accidentally crushed before they are seen. • Eastern Meadowlarks and Western Meadowlarks may occasionally interbreed where their ranges overlap, but produce infertile offspring. • The Western Meadowlark was overlooked by members of the Lewis and Clark expedition, who mistakenly thought it was the same species as the Eastern Meadowlark. This oversight is represented in the scientific name *neglecta.*

breeding

ID: yellow underparts; broad, black breast band; mottled brown upperparts; short, wide tail with white outer tail feathers; long, pinkish legs; yellow lores; brown crown stripes and eye line border pale "eyebrow" and median crown stripe; dark streaking on white sides and flanks; long sharp bill; yellow on throat extends onto lower "cheek."

Size: *L* 9–9½ in; *W* 14½ in.

Status: special concern; rare migrant and breeder from mid-March to mid-November, most frequently in Lower Peninsula.

Habitat: grassy meadows and pastures; also in some croplands, weedy fields and grassy roadsides.

Nesting: in a depression or scrape on the ground, concealed by dense grass or rarely low shrubs; female builds a domed grass nest with a side entrance, which is woven into surrounding vegetation; female incubates 3–7 white eggs, heavily spotted with brown and purple, for 13–15 days.

Feeding: gleans grasshoppers, crickets, beetles, other insects and spiders from the ground and vegetation; extracts grubs and worms by probing its bill into the soil; also eats seeds.

Voice: song is a rich, melodic series of bubbly, flutelike notes; calls include a low, loud *chuck* or *chup,* a rattling flight call or a few clear, whistled notes.

Similar Species: *Eastern Meadowlark* (p. 316): darker upperparts, especially crown stripes and eye line; yellow on throat does not extend onto lower "cheek"; different song and call. *Dickcissel* (p. 313): much smaller; solid dark crown; conical bill; white throat; lacks brown streaking on sides and flanks.

Selected Sites: pastures and meadows statewide; Berrien County; Traverse City area.

YELLOW-HEADED BLACKBIRD

Xanthocephalus xanthocephalus

You might expect a bird as handsome as the Yellow-headed Blackbird to have a song as splendid as its gold-and-black plumage. Unfortunately, a trip to a favored wetland will quickly reveal the shocking truth: when the male arches his golden head backward, his struggles to sing produce only a painful, pathetic grinding noise. Although the song of the Yellow-headed Blackbird might be the worst in North America, its quality soon becomes an appreciated aspect of this bird's marshy home—together with the smell of decomposing vegetation, the insects and the overall sogginess. • A large cattail marsh is often highlighted by the presence of male Yellow-headed Blackbirds perched high atop the plants like candle flames. Where Yellow-headed Blackbirds occur together with Red-winged Blackbirds, the larger Yellow-heads dominate, commandeering the center of the wetland and pushing the red-winged competitors to the periphery. Yellow-heads often nest in small colonies of about 30 pairs.

ID: *Male:* yellow head and breast; black body; white wing patches; black lores; long tail; black bill. *Female:* dusky brown overall; yellow breast, throat and "eyebrow"; hints of yellow on face.

Size: *L* 8–11 in; *W* 15 in.

Status: special concern; rare migrant and breeder from May to September.

Habitat: deep, permanent marshes, sloughs, lakeshores and river impoundments where cattails dominate.

Nesting: loosely colonial; female builds a bulky, deep basket of emergent aquatic plants and lines it with dry grass and other vegetation; nest is woven into emergent vegetation over water; female incubates 4 pale green to pale gray eggs, marked with gray or brown, for 11–13 days.

Feeding: gleans the ground for seeds, beetles, snails, waterbugs and dragonflies; also probes into cattail heads for larval invertebrates.

Voice: song is a strained, metallic grating note followed by a descending buzz; call is a deep *krrt* or *ktuk;* low quacks and liquidy clucks may be given during breeding season.

Similar Species: male is distinctive. *Rusty Blackbird* (p. 319) and *Brewer's Blackbird* (p. 320): females lack yellow throat and face.

Selected Sites: Fish Point SGA; Tobico Marsh WA; Nayanquing Point WA; Muskegon Wastewater System; Shiawassee Flats NWR; Seney NWR; Portage Point Marsh.

RUSTY BLACKBIRD

Euphagus carolinus

The Rusty Blackbird owes its name to the rusty color of its fall plumage, but its name could just as well reflect this bird's grating, squeaky song, which sounds very much like a rusty hinge. • Unlike many blackbirds, Rusty Blackbirds nest in isolated pairs or very small, loose colonies in flooded woodlands and treed, boreal bogs, not in wetlands. These birds generally do not travel with grackles and other blackbirds in migration, but instead prefer to keep to themselves. • Rusty Blackbirds' spend their days foraging along the wooded edges of fields and wetlands, and occasionally picking through the manure-laden ground of cattle feedlots. At day's end, when feeding is curtailed, most birds seek the shelter of trees and shrubs and the stalks of emergent marsh-land vegetation. • Rusty Blackbirds are gener-ally less abundant and less aggressive than their relatives, and they generally avoid human-altered environments.

breeding

ID: yellow eyes; dark legs; long, sharp bill. *Breeding male:* dark plumage; subtle green gloss on body; subtle bluish or greenish gloss on head. *Breeding female:* paler than male; without gloss. *Nonbreeding male:* rusty wings, back and crown. *Nonbreeding female:* paler than male; buffy underparts; rusty "cheek."
Size: *L* 9 in; *W* 14 in.
Status: common migrant from early March to early May and from late September to November; very rare breeder from June to July in Upper Peninsula.
Habitat: *Breeding:* treed bogs, fens, beaver ponds, wet meadows and the shrubby shorelines of lakes, rivers and swamps. *In migration:* marshes, open fields, feedlots and woodland edges near water.
Nesting: low in a shrub or small conifer; often above or very near water; female

builds a bulky nest of twigs, grass and lichens, with an inner cup of mud and decaying vegetation, and lines it with fine grass; female incubates 4–5 pale blue green eggs, spotted with gray and brown, for about 14 days.
Feeding: walks along shorelines gleaning waterbugs, beetles, dragonflies, snails, grasshoppers and occasionally small fish; also eats waste grain and seeds.
Voice: song is a squeaky, creaking *kushleeeh ksh-lay;* call is a harsh *chack.*
Similar Species: *Brewer's Blackbird* (p. 320): male has glossier, iridescent plumage, greener body and shows more purple; female has dark eyes; nonbreeding birds lack conspicuous, rusty highlights. *Common Grackle* (p. 321): longer, keeled tail; larger body and bill; more iridescent. *European Starling* (p. 247): speckled appearance; dark eyes; yellow bill in summer.
Selected Sites: wooded and marshy wetlands statewide; cattle feedlots.

BREWER'S BLACKBIRD

Euphagus cyanocephalus

This bird of the western plains is a relatively new addition to our avifauna and is still not very common here. In Michigan, the Brewer's Blackbird often shows up along roadsides where it searches for roadkilled insects and squabbles with pigeons and starlings for scraps of food. • Unlike the more solitary Rusty Blackbird, the Brewer's Blackbird almost always nests in colonies, which often include up to 14 pairs. As fall approaches, the colonies join with other family groups to form large, migrating flocks. • The feathers of this bird show an iridescent quality as rainbows of reflected sunlight move along the feather shafts. As it walks, the Brewer's Blackbird jerks its head back and forth like a chicken, enhancing the glossy effect and distinguishing it from other blackbirds. • John J. Audubon named this bird after Thomas Mayo Brewer, a friend and prominent oologist (a person who studies eggs).

ID: *Male:* iridescent, blue green body and purplish head often look black; yellow eyes; some nonbreeding males may show some faint, rusty feather edgings. *Female:* flat brown plumage; dark eyes.

Size: *L* 8–10 in; *W* 15½ in.

Status: uncommon migrant from mid-March to early May and from late August to late November; uncommon breeder from May to June in northern Michigan.

Habitat: moist, grassy meadows and roadsides with nearby wetlands and patches of trees and shrubs.

Nesting: in small colonies; on the ground or in a shrub or small tree; female builds a bulky, open cup nest of twigs, grass and plant fibers and lines it with rootlets, fine grass and hair; female incubates 4–6 brown-spotted, pale gray to greenish gray eggs for 12–14 days.

Feeding: gleans invertebrates and seeds while walking along shorelines and open areas.

Voice: song is a creaking, 2-noted *k-shee;* call is a metallic *chick* or *check.*

Similar Species: *Rusty Blackbird* (p. 319): longer, more slender bill; iridescent plumage has subtler green gloss on body and subtle bluish or greenish gloss on head; female has yellow eyes. *Common Grackle* (p. 321): much longer, keeled tail; larger body and bill. *Brown-headed Cowbird* (p. 322): shorter tail; stubbier, thicker bill; male has dark eyes and brown head; female has paler, streaked underparts and very pale throat. *European Starling* (p. 247): speckled appearance; dark eyes; yellow bill in summer.

Selected Sites: Fish Point SGA; Nayanquing Point WA; Dead Stream Flooding; Jordan R. valley; Sault Ste. Marie; Whitefish Point; Marquette.

COMMON GRACKLE

Quiscalus quiscula

The Common Grackle is a poor but spirited singer. Usually while perched in a shrub, a male grackle will slowly take a deep breath to inflate his breast, causing his feathers to spike outward, then close his eyes and give out a loud, strained *tssh-schleek.* Despite his lack of musical talent, the male remains smug and proud, posing with his bill held high. • In fall, large flocks of Common Grackles are common in rural areas where they forage for waste grain in open fields. Smaller bands occasionally venture into urban neighborhoods where they assert their dominance at backyard bird feeders—even bullying Blue Jays will yield feeding rights to these cocky, aggressive birds. • The Common Grackle is easily distinguished from the Rusty Blackbird and Brewer's Blackbird by its long, heavy bill and lengthy, wedge-shaped tail. In flight, the grackle's long tail trails behind it. • At night, grackles commonly roost with groups of European Starlings, Red-winged Blackbirds and even Brown-headed Cowbirds.

ID: iridescent plumage (purple blue head and breast, bronze back and sides, and purple wings and tail) often looks blackish; long, keeled tail; yellow eyes; long, heavy bill; female is smaller, duller and browner than male. *Juvenile:* dull brown overall; dark eyes.

Size: *L* 11–13½ in; *W* 17 in.

Status: abundant migrant and breeder from late March to October; rare winter resident from November to March in southern Michigan.

Habitat: wetlands, hedgerows, fields, wet meadows, riparian woodlands and along the edges of coniferous forests and woodlands; also shrubby urban and suburban parks and gardens.

Nesting: singly or in small colonies; in dense tree or shrub branches or emergent vegetation; often near water; female builds a bulky, open cup nest of twigs, grass, plant fibers and mud and lines it with fine grass or feathers; female incubates 4–5 brown-blotched, pale blue eggs for 12–14 days.

Feeding: slowly struts along the ground, gleaning, snatching and probing for insects, earthworms, seeds, waste grain and fruit; also catches insects in flight and eats small vertebrates; may take some bird eggs.

Voice: song is a series of harsh, strained notes ending with a metallic squeak: *tssh-schleek* or *gri-de-leeek;* call is a quick, loud *swaaaack* or *chaack.*

Similar Species: *Rusty Blackbird* (p. 319) and *Brewer's Blackbird* (p. 320): smaller overall; lack heavy bill and keeled tail. *Red-winged Blackbird* (p. 315): shorter tail; male has red shoulder patch and dark eyes. *European Starling* (p. 247): very short tail; long, thin bill (yellow in summer); speckled appearance; dark eyes.

Selected Sites: fields, wetlands, parks, woodland edges or hedgerows statewide.

BROWN-HEADED COWBIRD

Molothrus ater

The Brown-headed Cowbird's song, a bubbling, liquidy *glug-ahl-whee*, might be translated by other bird species as "here comes trouble!" Historically, Brown-headed Cowbirds followed bison herds across the Great Plains—they now follow cattle—and the birds' nomadic lifestyle made it impossible for them to construct and tend a nest. Instead, cowbirds engage in "nest parasitism," laying their eggs in the nests of other songbirds. Many of the parasitized songbirds do not recognize that the eggs are not theirs, so they incubate them and raise the cowbird young as their own. Cowbird chicks typically hatch first and develop much more quickly than their nestmates, which are pushed out of the nest or outcompeted for food. • The expansion of livestock farming, the fragmentation of forests and the extensive network of transportation corridors throughout Michigan have significantly increased the cowbird's range. It now parasitizes more than 140 species of birds in North America, including species that probably had no contact with it before widespread human settlement.

ID: thick, conical bill; short, squared tail; dark eyes. *Male:* iridescent, green blue body plumage usually looks glossy black; dark brown head. *Female:* brown plumage overall; faint streaking on light brown underparts; pale throat.

Size: *L* 6–8 in; *W* 12 in.

Status: common migrant and breeder from late March to late October; rare winter resident from November to March in southern Michigan.

Habitat: open agricultural and residential areas including fields, woodland edges, utility cutlines, roadsides, fencelines, landfills, campgrounds, picnic areas and areas near cattle.

Nesting: does not build a nest; each female may lay up to 40 eggs per year in the nests of other birds, usually laying 1 egg per nest (larger numbers, up to 8 eggs in a single nest, are probably from several different cowbirds); whitish eggs, marked with gray and brown, hatch after 10–13 days.

Feeding: gleans the ground for seeds, waste grain and invertebrates, especially grasshoppers, beetles and true bugs.

Voice: song is a high, liquidy gurgle: *glug-ahl-whee* or *bubbloozeee;* call is a squeaky, high-pitched *seep, psee* or *wee-tse-tse,* often given in flight; also a fast, chipping *ch-ch-ch-ch-ch-ch.*

Similar Species: *Rusty Blackbird* (p. 319) and *Brewer's Blackbird* (p. 320): slimmer, longer bills; longer tails; lack contrasting brown head and darker body; all have yellow eyes except for female Brewer's Blackbird. *Common Grackle* (p. 321): much larger overall; longer, heavier bill; longer, keeled tail.

Selected Sites: cattle pastures, feedlots, fencelines and roadsides statewide.

ORCHARD ORIOLE

Icterus spurius

Orchards may once have been favored haunts of this oriole, but since orchards are now heavily sprayed and manicured, it is unlikely that you will ever see this bird in such a locale. Instead, the Orchard Oriole is most commonly found in large shade trees that line roads, paths and streams. Smaller than all other North American orioles, the Orchard Oriole is one of only two oriole species commonly found in the eastern United States. • These orioles are frequent victims of nest parasitism by Brown-headed Cowbirds. In some parts of its breeding range, over half of Orchard Oriole nests are parasitized by cowbirds. • In Michigan, the Orchard Oriole, the Yellow Warbler and the Louisiana Waterthrush are the first species to migrate following breeding and are usually absent by the beginning of August. • Orchard Orioles are best seen in spring when eager males hop from branch to branch, singing their quick and musical courtship songs.

ID: *Male:* black "hood" and tail; chestnut underparts, shoulder and rump; dark wings with white wing bar and feather edgings. *Female* and *immature:* olive upperparts; yellow to olive yellow underparts; faint, white wing bars on dusky gray wings.
Size: *L* 6–7 in; *W* 9½ in.
Status: uncommon migrant and breeder from early May to late August in southern Michigan.
Habitat: open woodlands, suburban parklands, forest edges, hedgerows and groves of shade trees.
Nesting: in the fork of a deciduous tree or shrub; female builds a hanging pouch nest woven from grass and other fine plant fibers; female incubates 4–5 pale bluish white eggs, blotched with gray, brown and purple, for about 12–15 days.
Feeding: finds insects and berries while inspecting trees and shrubs; probes flowers for nectar; may visit hummingbird feeders and feeding stations that offer orange halves.
Voice: song is a loud, rapid, varied series of whistled notes; call is a quick *chuck*.
Similar Species: *Baltimore Oriole* (p. 324): male has brighter orange plumage with orange in tail; female has orange overtones. *Summer Tanager* (p. 288) and *Scarlet Tanager* (p. 289): females have thicker, pale bills and lack wing bars.
Selected Sites: Lake Erie Metropark; Sleepy Hollow SP; Ludington SP; Rose Lake WA; Russ Forest; Kalamazoo Nature Center.

BALTIMORE ORIOLE

Icterus galbula

The male Baltimore Oriole has striking, Halloween-style, black-and-orange plumage that flickers like smoldering embers among our neighborhood tree-tops. As if his brilliant plumage was not enough to secure our admiration, he also sings a rich, flutelike courtship song and will vocalize almost continuously until he finds a mate. • Baltimore Orioles are fairly common in Michigan, but they are often difficult to find because they inhabit the forest heights. Developing an ear for their whistled *peter peter peter here peter* tune and frequently scanning local deciduous trees will undoubtedly produce enchanting views of these beloved orioles. • This oriole doesn't suffer as much as the Orchard Oriole from nest parasitism by Brown-headed Cowbirds. Female Baltimore Orioles will eject cowbird eggs from the nest and both male and female orioles will react aggressively toward any adult cowbird that approaches their nest. • The city of Baltimore was first established as a colony by Irishman George Calvert, the Baron of Baltimore. Mark Catesby, one of America's first naturalists, chose this bird's name because the male's plumage mirrored the colors of the baron's coat of arms. • "Oriole" is derived from the Latin for "golden."

ID: *Male:* black "hood," back, wings and central tail feathers; bright orange underparts, shoulder, rump and outer tail feathers; white wing patch and feather edgings. *Female:* olive brown upperparts (darkest on head); dull yellow orange underparts and rump; white wing bar.
Size: *L* 7–8 in; *W* 11½ in.
Status: common migrant and breeder from late April to mid-September.
Habitat: deciduous and mixed forests, particularly riparian woodlands, natural openings, shorelines, roadsides, orchards, gardens and parklands.
Nesting: high in a deciduous tree, suspended from a branch; female builds a hanging pouch nest made of grass, bark shreds, rootlets, plant stems and grapevines and lines it with fine grass, rootlets and fur; occasionally adds string or fishing line; female incubates 4–5 darkly marked, pale gray to bluish white eggs for 12–14 days.
Feeding: gleans canopy vegetation and shrubs for caterpillars, beetles, wasps and other invertebrates; also eats some fruit and nectar; may visit hummingbird feeders and feeding stations that offer orange halves.
Voice: song consists of slow, loud, clear whistles: *peter peter peter here peter;* calls include a 2-note *tea-too* and a rapid chatter: *ch-ch-ch-ch-ch.*
Similar Species: *Orchard Oriole* (p. 323): male has darker chestnut plumage; female is olive yellow and lacks orange overtones. *Summer Tanager* (p. 288) and *Scarlet Tanager* (p. 289): females have thicker, pale bills and lack wing bars.
Selected Sites: deciduous or mixed woodlands statewide.

PINE GROSBEAK

Pinicola enucleator

The Pine Grosbeak is a large finch that inhabits subarctic and boreal forests across North America. Every so often flocks of these birds find their way south to our region in winter and may show up at your backyard feeder. These erratic winter invasions thrill local naturalists—the Pine Grosbeak's bright colors and exciting flock behavior are certainly a welcome sight. These invasions are not completely understood, but it is thought that cone crop failures or changes to forest ecology caused by logging, forest fires or climatic factors may force these hungry finches southward in search of food. Much of their survival depends on the availability of conifer seeds, so Pine Grosbeaks are always in search of a good crop. • During nesting, adult Pine Grosbeaks develop "gular pouches," throat pouches that allow them to carry food to nestlings. • *Pinicola* is Latin for "pine dweller," and *enucleator* is Latin for "one who takes off shells."

ID: stout, dark, conical bill; 2 white wing bars; black wings and tail. *Male:* rosy red head, upperparts and breast; gray sides, flanks, belly and undertail coverts. *Female* and *immature:* gray overall; yellow or russet wash on head and rump.

Size: *L* 8–10 in; *W* 14½ in.

Status: irregular migrant and winter resident from October to March, usually in northern Michigan, occasionally statewide.

Habitat: conifer plantations, deciduous woodlands with fruiting mountain-ash, crabapple and woody nightshade; backyard feeders.

Nesting: does not nest in Michigan.

Feeding: gleans buds, berries and seeds from trees; also forages on the ground; visits feeders in winter.

Voice: song is a short, sweet musical warble; call is a 3-note whistle with a higher middle note; short, muffled trill is often given in flight; chatters when feeding in flocks.

Similar Species: *White-winged Crossbill* (p. 329): much smaller; lacks stubby bill and prominent, gray coloration. *Red Crossbill* (p. 328): lacks stubby bill and white wing bars. *Evening Grosbeak* (p. 334): female has pale bill, dark "whisker" stripe, tan underparts and broad, white wing patches.

Selected Sites: widespread across Upper Peninsula and northern Lower Peninsula; statewide in irruption years.

325

PURPLE FINCH

Carpodacus purpureus

The Purple Finch's gentle nature and simple but stunning plumage endears it to many birdwatchers. Fortunately, most bird admirers in our region have plentiful opportunities to meet this charming finch. • The courtship of the Purple Finch is a gentle and appealing ritual. The liquid, warbling song of the male bubbles through conifer boughs, announcing his presence to potential mates. Upon the arrival of an interested female, the colorful male dances lightly around her, beating his wings until he softly lifts into the air. • Flat, table-style feeding stations with nearby tree cover are sure to attract Purple Finches, and erecting one may keep a small flock in your area over winter. • "Purple" *(purpureus)* is simply a false description of this bird's reddish coloration. Roger Tory Peterson said it best when he described the Purple Finch as "a sparrow dipped in raspberry juice." Only the male is brightly colored, however, and the female is a rather drab, unassuming bird by comparison.

ID: *Male:* pale bill; raspberry red (occasionally yellow to salmon pink) head, throat, breast and nape; back and flanks are streaked with brown and red; reddish brown "cheek"; red rump; notched tail; pale, unstreaked belly and undertail coverts. *Female:* dark brown "cheek" and "jaw-line"; white "eyebrow" and lower "cheek" stripe; heavily streaked underparts; unstreaked undertail coverts.
Size: *L* 5–6 in; *W* 10 in.
Status: common migrant and winter resident statewide from September to May; common breeder from June to July in northern two-thirds of Michigan.
Habitat: *Breeding:* coniferous and mixed forests. *In migration* and *winter:* coniferous, mixed and deciduous forests, shrubby open areas and feeders with nearby tree cover.

Nesting: on a conifer branch, far from the trunk; female builds a cup nest of twigs, grass and rootlets and lines it with moss and hair; female incubates 4–5 pale greenish blue eggs, marked with black and brown, for about 13 days.
Feeding: gleans the ground and vegetation for seeds, buds, berries and insects; readily visits table-style feeding stations.
Voice: song is a bubbly, continuous warble; call is a single metallic *cheep* or *weet*.
Similar Species: *House Finch* (p. 327): squared tail; male has brown flanks and lacks reddish "cap"; female lacks distinct "cheek" patch. *Red Crossbill* (p. 328): larger bill with crossed mandibles; male has more red overall and dark "V"s on whitish undertail coverts.
Selected Sites: Tuscola SGA; Sleeper SP; Chippewa Nature Center; Sleeping Bear Dunes National Lakeshore; Whitefish Point; Seney NWR.

HOUSE FINCH

Carpodacus mexicanus

A native to western North America, the House Finch was brought to eastern parts of the continent as an illegally captured cage bird known as the "Hollywood Finch." In the early 1940s, New York pet shop owners released their birds to avoid prosecution and fines, and it is the descendants of those birds that have colonized Michigan. In fact, the House Finch is now commonly found throughout the continental U.S. and southern Canada and has been introduced in Hawaii. • Only the resourceful House Finch has been aggressive and stubborn enough to successfully outcompete the House Sparrow. Like the House Sparrow, this finch has prospered in urban environments. Both birds often build their messy nests among eaves, rafters, chimneys and other human-fashioned habitats, and both birds thrive on seeds. In the west this bird is often found in natural settings as well as urban centers; in the east it is seldom found outside of urban and suburban settings. • The male House Finch's plumage varies in color from light yellow to bright red, but females will choose the reddest males with which to breed.

ID: streaked undertail coverts; brown-streaked back; square tail. *Male:* brown "cap"; bright red "eyebrow," forecrown, throat and breast; heavily streaked flanks. *Female:* indistinct facial patterning; heavily streaked underparts.
Size: *L* 5–6 in; *W* 9½ in.
Status: common year-round resident in southern half of Lower Peninsula.
Habitat: cities, towns and agricultural areas.
Nesting: in a cavity, building, dense foliage or abandoned bird nest; especially in evergreens and ornamental shrubs near buildings; mostly the female builds an open cup nest of grass, twigs, leaves, hair and feathers, often adding string and other debris; female incubates 4–5 pale blue eggs, dotted with lavender and black, for 12–14 days.
Feeding: gleans vegetation and the ground for seeds; also takes berries, buds and some flower parts; often visits feeders.
Voice: song is a bright, disjointed warble lasting about 3 seconds, often ending with a harsh *jeer* or *wheer;* flight call is a sweet *cheer,* given singly or in series.
Similar Species: *Purple Finch* (p. 326): notched tail; male has more burgundy red "cap," upper back and flanks; female has distinct "cheek" patch. *Red Crossbill* (p. 328): bill has crossed mandibles; male has more red overall and darker wings.
Selected Sites: bird feeders in southern Michigan.

RED CROSSBILL
Loxia curvirostra

Red Crossbills are the great gypsies of our bird community, wandering through forests in search of pine cones. They may breed at any time of year if they discover a bumper crop—it's not unusual to hear them singing and see them nest-building in midwinter. Their nomadic ways make them difficult birds to find, and even during years of plenty there is no guarantee that these birds will surface in Michigan. Winter is typically the time to see crossbills here, and in some years, large flocks suddenly appear. • The crossbill's oddly shaped bill is an adaptation for prying open conifer cones. While holding the cone with one foot, the crossbill inserts its closed bill between the cone and scales and pries them apart by opening its bill. Once a cone is cracked, a crossbill uses its nimble tongue to extract the soft, energy-rich seeds hidden within. • The scientific name *Loxia* is Greek for "crooked," while *curvirostra* is Latin for "curve billed."

ID: bill has crossed tips. *Male:* dull orange red to brick red plumage; dark wings and tail; always has color on throat. *Female:* olive gray to dusky yellow plumage; plain, dark wings. *Juvenile:* streaky brown overall.

Size: *L* 5–6½ in; *W* 11 in.

Status: rare, erratic and irruptive transient and year-round resident; particularly irruptive in winter; breeds from February to June.

Habitat: coniferous forests and plantations; favors red and white pines, but also found in other pine and spruce-fir forests.

Nesting: high on the outer branch of a conifer; female builds an open cup nest of twigs, grass, bark shreds and rootlets and lines it with moss, lichens, rootlets, feathers and hair; female incubates 3–4 pale bluish white to greenish white eggs, dotted with black and purple, for 12–18 days.

Feeding: eats primarily conifer seeds (especially pine); also eats buds, deciduous tree seeds and occasionally insects; often licks road salt or minerals in soil and along roadsides; rarely visits feeders.

Voice: distinctive *jip-jip* call note, often given in flight; song is a varied series of warbles, trills and chips (similar to other finches).

Similar Species: *White-winged Crossbill* (p. 329): 2 broad, white wing bars. *Pine Siskin* (p. 332): similar to juvenile Red Crossbill, but is smaller, lacks crossed bill and has yellow highlights on wing. *Pine Grosbeak* (p. 325): stubby, conical bill; white wing bars. *House Finch* (p. 327) and *Purple Finch* (p. 326): conical bills; less red overall; lighter brownish wings; lacks red on lower belly.

Selected Sites: highly variable sites from year to year statewide; Seney NWR; Grand Marais.

WHITE-WINGED CROSSBILL
Loxia leucoptera

Although this bird's bill lacks the colorful flair of the tropical toucan or the massive proportions of the hornbill, the White-winged Crossbill's well-designed mandibles combine function with artistry. This bill arrangement is shared by only one other bird species in North America, the Red Crossbill. The White-winged Crossbill eats primarily spruce and tamarack seeds, and its bill is adapted for prying open conifer cones. • The presence of a foraging group of White-winged Crossbills high in a spruce tree creates an unforgettable shower of conifer cones and crackling chatter. Like many finches, White-winged Crossbills can be abundant one year, then absent the next. • When not foraging in spruce spires, White-winged Crossbills often drop to ground level, where they drink water from shallow forest pools or lick salt from winter roads. This salt-licking habit often results in crossbill fatalities.

IRRUPTIVE

ID: bill has crossed tips; 2 bold white wing bars. *Male:* pinkish red overall; black wings and tail. *Female:* streaked, brown upperparts; dusky yellow underparts slightly streaked with brown; dark wings and tail. *Juvenile:* streaky brown overall with white wing bars.
Size: *L* 6–7 in; *W* 10½ in.
Status: uncommon transient and year-round resident; uncommon erratic and irruptive winter resident from October to March.
Habitat: coniferous forests, primarily spruce, fir, tamarack and eastern hemlock; occasionally townsites and deciduous forests.
Nesting: on an outer branch in a conifer; female builds an open cup nest of twigs, grass, bark shreds, leaves and moss and lines it with moss, lichens, rootlets, hair

and soft plant down; female incubates 2–4 whitish to pale blue green eggs, spotted with brown and lavender, for 12–14 days.
Feeding: prefers conifer seeds (mostly spruce and tamarack); also eats deciduous tree seeds and occasionally insects; often licks salt and minerals from roads when available.
Voice: song is a high-pitched series of warbles, trills and *chips;* call is a series of harsh, questioning *cheat* notes, often given in flight.
Similar Species: *Red Crossbill* (p. 328): lacks white wing bars; male is deeper red (less pinkish). *Pine Siskin* (p. 332): similar to juvenile White-winged Crossbill but smaller, has yellow highlights on wings and lacks crossed bill. *Pine Grosbeak* (p. 325): stubby, conical bill; thinner wing bars; female very gray; male has gray sides. *House Finch* (p. 327) and *Purple Finch* (p. 326): conical bills; less red overall; lighter brownish wings.
Selected Sites: erratic and irruptive statewide, especially in winter.

329

COMMON REDPOLL

Carduelis flammea

A predictably unpredictable winter visitor, the Common Redpoll is seen in Michigan in varying numbers—it might appear in flocks of hundreds or in groups of a dozen or less, depending on the year. • Because redpolls are so small, they have only a small internal volume to produce and retain heat and a relatively large surface area from which heat can be lost. As a result, they are in constant danger of running out of fuel and dying of hypothermia in winter. This means that these birds must eat almost constantly—redpolls are continually gleaning waste grain from bare fields or stocking up on seed at winter feeders. Their focus on food helps make wintering redpolls remarkably fearless of humans. • Redpolls can endure colder temperatures than other small songbirds. These birds will sit with their highly insulative feathers fluffed out, trapping layers of warm, insulating air and keeping a circle of warmth around their bodies.

nonbreeding

IRRUPTIVE

ID: red forecrown; black "chin"; yellowish bill; streaked upperparts, including rump; lightly streaked sides, flanks and undertail coverts; notched tail. *Male:* pinkish red breast (brightest in breeding plumage). *Female:* whitish to pale gray breast.
Size: *L* 5 in; *W* 9 in.
Status: uncommon to locally abundant, erratic migrant and winter resident from October to early April.
Habitat: open fields, meadows, roadsides, utility power lines, railroads, forest edges; backyards with feeders.

Nesting: does not nest in Michigan.
Feeding: gleans the ground, snow and vegetation in large flocks for seeds in winter; often visits feeders.
Voice: song is a twittering series of trills; calls are a soft *chit-chit-chit-chit* and a faint *swe-eet;* indistinguishable from the Hoary Redpoll's songs and calls.
Similar Species: *Hoary Redpoll* (p. 331): unstreaked or partly streaked rump; usually has faint or no streaking on sides and flanks; generally paler and plumper overall; bill may look stubbier; lacks streaking on undertail coverts. *Pine Siskin* (p. 332): heavily streaked overall; yellow highlights on wings and tail.
Selected Sites: fields and backyard feeders statewide; irruptive in winter.

HOARY REDPOLL

Carduelis hornemanni

Interspersed within a group of Common Redpolls, you might see a bird that has noticeably less streaking and is lighter in color. As you compare the ambiguous field marks used to distinguish Hoary Redpolls from Common Redpolls, you may be drawn into the "Great Redpoll Debate" with fellow birders. Some say the only way to differentiate the two species is to look at the amount of streaking on the rump: Hoary's have very little and Commons are heavily streaked. By the time everyone has given their opinion on their defining characteristic, the Redpolls will have taken off! • Hoary Redpolls are well adapted to life in the cold. They possess a special pouch in their esophagus, the esophageal diverticulum, which allows them to store greater quantities of energy-rich seeds than they are able to digest at one time. Even so, when seed crops fail or icy winds become intolerably cold, Hoary Redpolls will move south into Michigan, where they occasionally "irrupt" every few years. • This bird's scientific name honors Jens Wilken Hornemann, one of Denmark's leading botanists, who helped organize an expedition to Greenland, where the first scientific specimen of this bird was collected.

ID: red forecrown; black "chin"; yellowish bill; frosty white plumage overall; lightly streaked upperparts, except for unstreaked rump; unstreaked underparts (flanks may have faint streaking); notched tail. *Male:* pinkish-tinged breast. *Female:* white to light gray breast.
Size: *L* 5–5½; *W* 9 in.
Status: very rare to uncommon, erratic irruptive migrant and winter resident from November to March.
Habitat: open fields, meadows, roadsides, utility power lines, railroads, forest edges; backyards with feeders.

Nesting: does not nest in Michigan.
Feeding: gleans the ground, snow and vegetation for seeds and buds; occasionally visits feeders in winter.
Voice: song is a twittering series of trills; calls are a soft *chit-chit-chit-chit* and a faint *swe-eet;* indistinguishable from the Common Redpoll's songs and calls.
Similar Species: *Common Redpoll* (p. 330): streaked rump, sides, flanks and undertail coverts; generally darker and slimmer overall. *Pine Siskin* (p. 332): heavily streaked overall; yellow highlights on wings and tail.
Selected Sites: fields and backyard feeders; irruptive in winter.

PINE SISKIN
Carduelis pinus

Y
ou can spend days, weeks or even months in pursuit of Pine Siskins, only to meet with frustration, aching feet and a sore, crimped neck. The best way to meet these birds is to set up a finch feeder filled with black niger seed in your backyard and wait for them to appear. If the feeder is in the right location, you can expect your backyard to be visited by Pine Siskins at just about any time of year, but particularly in winter. • Tight flocks of these gregarious birds are frequently heard before they are seen. Once you recognize their characteristic rising *zzzreeeee* calls and boisterous chatter, you can confirm the presence of these finches simply by listening. • Aside from the Pine Siskin's occasional flashes of yellow, its wardrobe is drab and sparrowlike. But for those who get to know it, this bird's behavior reveals a gentle nature that radiates the playfulness and enthusiasm of a goldfinch.

ID: heavily streaked underparts; yellow highlights at base of tail feathers and on wings (easily seen in flight); dull wing bars; darker, heavily streaked upperparts; slightly forked tail; indistinct facial pattern. *Immature:* similar to adult, but overall yellow tint fades through summer.
Size: *L* 4½–5½ in; *W* 9 in.
Status: uncommon to common, irruptive year-round resident; uncommon migrant and winter resident from October to May.
Habitat: *Breeding:* coniferous and mixed forests; urban and rural ornamental and shade trees. *Winter:* coniferous and mixed forests, forest edges, meadows, roadsides, agricultural fields and backyards with feeders.
Nesting: usually loosely colonial; typically at midheight on an outer branch of a

conifer; female builds a loose cup nest of twigs, grass and rootlets and lines it with feathers, hair, rootlets and fine plant fibers; female incubates 3–5 pale blue eggs with dark dots for about 13 days.
Feeding: gleans the ground and vegetation for seeds (especially thistle seeds), buds and some insects; attracted to road salts, mineral licks and ashes; regularly visits feeders.
Voice: song is a variable, bubbly mix of squeaky, raspy, metallic notes, sometimes resembling a jerky laugh; call is a buzzy, rising *zzzreeeee*.
Similar Species: *Common Redpoll* (p. 330) and *Hoary Redpoll* (p. 331): red forecrown; lack yellow on wings and tail. *Purple Finch* (p. 326) and *House Finch* (p. 327): females have thicker bills and no yellow on wings or tail. *Sparrows* (pp. 291–306): all lack yellow on wings and tail.
Selected Sites: fields and backyard feeders statewide; also parks, coniferous forests and woodlands.

AMERICAN GOLDFINCH
Carduelis tristis

American Goldfinches are bright, cheery songbirds that are commonly seen in weedy fields, along roadsides and among backyard shrubs throughout summer and fall. Goldfinches seem to delight in perching upon late-summer thistle heads as they search for seeds to feed their offspring. It's hard to miss the jubilant *po-ta-to-chip* they issue as they flutter over parks and gardens in a distinctive, undulating flight style. • It is a joy to observe a flock of goldfinches raining down to ground level to poke and prod the heads of dandelions. These birds can look quite comical as they attempt to step down on the flower stems to reach the crowning seeds. A dandelion-covered lawn always seems a lot less weedy with a flock of glowing goldfinches hopping through it. • The scientific name *tristis*, Latin for "sad," refers to the goldfinch's voice, but seems a rather unfair choice for such a pleasing and playful bird.

breeding

ID: *Breeding Male:* black "cap" (extends onto forehead), wings and tail; bright yellow body; white wing bars, undertail coverts and tail base; orange bill and legs. *Nonbreeding male:* olive brown back; yellow-tinged head; gray underparts. *Female:* yellow green upperparts and belly; yellow throat and breast.
Size: L 4½–5½ in; W 9 in.
Status: common migrant and breeder from April to December; less common winter resident from November to April.
Habitat: weedy fields, woodland edges, meadows, riparian areas, parks and gardens.
Nesting: in late summer and early fall; in a fork in a deciduous shrub or tree, often in hawthorn, serviceberry or sapling maple;

female builds a compact cup nest of plant fibers, grass and spider silk and lines it with plant down and hair; female incubates 4–6 pale bluish white eggs, occasionally spotted with light brown, for about 12–14 days.
Feeding: gleans vegetation for seeds, primarily thistle, birch and alder, as well as for insects and berries; commonly visits feeders.
Voice: song is a long, varied series of trills, twitters, warbles and hissing notes; calls include *po-ta-to-chip* or *per-chic-or-ee* (often delivered in flight) and a whistled *dear-me, see-me.*
Similar Species: *Evening Grosbeak* (p. 334): much larger; massive bill; lacks black forehead. *Wilson's Warbler* (p. 285): olive upperparts; olive wings without wing bars; thin, dark bill; black "cap" does not extend onto forehead.
Selected Sites: weedy fields, shrubby riparian areas and forest edges; also backyard feeders.

EVENING GROSBEAK

Coccothraustes vespertinus

One chilly winter day, a flock of Evening Grosbeaks descends unannounced upon your backyard bird feeder filled with sunflower seeds. You watch the stunning gold-and-black grosbeaks with delight, but soon come to realize that these birds are both an aesthetic blessing and a financial curse. Evening Grosbeaks will eat great quantities of expensive birdseed and then suddenly disappear in late winter. These birds are transient visitors to northern Michigan, generally encountered every two to three years in large, wintering flocks. • The massive bill of this seed eater is difficult to ignore. In French, *gros bec* means "large beak," and any seasoned bird bander will tell you that the Evening Grosbeak's bill can exert an incredible force per unit area—it may be the most powerful bill of any North American bird. • It was once thought that the Evening Grosbeak sang only in the evening, a fact that is reflected in both its common and scientific names (*vespertinus* is Latin for "of the evening").

ID: massive, pale, conical bill; black wings and tail; broad, white wing patches. *Male:* black crown; bright yellow "eyebrow" and forehead band; dark brown head gradually fades into golden yellow belly and lower back. *Female:* gray head and upper back; yellow-tinged underparts; white undertail coverts.
Size: *L* 7–8½ in; *W* 14 in.
Status: irregularly rare to locally common migrant and winter resident from October to mid-May; fairly common breeder from April to early October in northern Michigan.
Habitat: *Breeding:* coniferous and mixed forests and woodlands; occasionally deciduous woodlands, suburban parks and orchards. *Winter:* coniferous, mixed and deciduous forests and woodlands; parks and gardens with feeders.
Nesting: on an outer limb in a conifer; female builds a flimsy cup nest of twigs and lines it with rootlets, fine grass, plant fibers, moss and pine needles; female incubates 3–4 pale blue to blue green eggs, blotched with purple, gray and brown, for 11–14 days.
Feeding: gleans the ground and vegetation for seeds, buds and berries; also eats insects and licks mineral-rich soil; often visits feeders for sunflower seeds.
Voice: song is a wandering, halting warble; call is a loud, sharp *clee-ip* or a ringing *peeer*.
Similar Species: *American Goldfinch* (p. 333): much smaller; small bill; smaller wing bars; male has black "cap." *Pine Grosbeak* (p. 325): female is gray overall with black bill and smaller wing bars.
Selected Sites: erratic and irruptive; potentially any woodland or backyard feeder in northern two-thirds of state.

HOUSE SPARROW

Passer domesticus

F or most of us, the House Sparrow is the first bird we meet and recognize in our youth. Although it is one of our most abundant and conspicuous birds, many generations of House Sparrows live out their lives within our backyards with few of us ever knowing much about this omnipresent neighbor. • House Sparrows were introduced to North America in the 1850s around Brooklyn, New York, as part of a plan to control the numbers of insects that were damaging grain and cereal crops. Contrary to popular opinion at the time, this sparrow's diet is largely vegetarian, so its effect on crop pests proved to be minimal. Since then, this Eurasian sparrow has managed to colonize most human-altered environments on the continent, and has benefited greatly from a close association with humans. Unfortunately, its aggressive behavior has helped it to usurp territory from many native bird species, especially in rural habitats. • House Sparrows are not closely related to the other North American sparrows, but belong to the family of Old World Sparrows or "Weaver Finches."

breeding

ID: *Breeding male:* gray crown; black "bib" and bill; chestnut nape; light gray "cheek"; white wing bar; dark, mottled upperparts; gray underparts. *Nonbreeding male:* smaller black "bib"; pale bill. *Female:* plain gray brown overall; buffy "eyebrow"; streaked upperparts; indistinct facial patterns; grayish, unstreaked underparts.
Size: *L* 5½–6½ in; *W* 9½ in.
Status: abundant year-round resident.
Habitat: townsites, urban and suburban areas, farmyards and agricultural areas, railroad yards and other developed areas; absent from undeveloped and heavily wooded areas.

Nesting: often communal; in a human-made structure, ornamental shrubs or natural cavities; pair builds a large, dome-shaped nest of grass, twigs, plant fibers and litter and often lines it with feathers; pair incubates 4–6 whitish to greenish white eggs, dotted with gray and brown, for 10–13 days.
Feeding: gleans the ground and vegetation for seeds, insects and fruit; frequently visits feeders for seeds.
Voice: song is a plain, familiar *cheep-cheep-cheep-cheep;* call is a short *chill-up.*
Similar Species: female is distinctively drab. *Harris's Sparrow* (p. 305): gray face; black "cap"; pink orange bill.
Selected Sites: your backyard.

OCCASIONAL BIRD SPECIES

PACIFIC LOON
Gavia pacifica

These arctic-nesting birds have been spotted in Michigan, most often at Whitefish Point during spring migration. Most Pacific Loons winter along the Pacific Coast, but a few choose to winter along the Atlantic Coast, and it is these Atlantic Coast birds that are most likely to be seen in Michigan.

ID: *Breeding:* silver gray crown and nape; black throat framed by white stripes; white breast; dark back with large, bold, white spots. *Nonbreeding:* well-defined, light "cheek" and throat; dark upperparts; dark "chin" stripe. *In flight:* hunched back; legs trail behind tail; rapid wingbeats.
Size: *L* 23–29 in; *W* 3 ft.

breeding

WESTERN GREBE
Aechmophorus occidentalis

This casual transient generally breeds from the Great Plains west to the Pacific Coast and south to central Mexico, and it winters along the Pacific Coast. It is most likely to be seen in our state in fall and winter along the shoreline of Lake Michigan.

ID: long, slender neck; black upperparts from base of bill to tail; white underparts from "chin" through belly; long, thin, yellow bill; white "cheek"; black on face extends down to surround red eyes.
Size: *L* 23–24 in; *W* 24 in.

BROWN PELICAN
Pelecanus occidentalis

The Brown Pelican is a casual visitor to Michigan. Its usual range is from California and North Carolina southward. This bird generally inhabits salt water, but it occasionally ventures inland north to the Great Lakes.

ID: pale gray upperparts; black underparts; very large bill. *Breeding:* yellow head; pink around eye; reddish brown bill pouch; white foreneck; brown nape; black legs. *Nonbreeding:* white neck; head is washed with yellow; pale yellowish pouch. *Immature:* gray brown overall; white belly; brown legs.
Size: *L* 4 ft; *W* 7 ft.

breeding

TRICOLORED HERON
Egretta tricolor

This casual visitor usually breeds from New Jersey south along the Atlantic and Gulf coasts. The best place to look for this attractive bird in Michigan is in the large marshes along Lake Erie and Saginaw Bay.

ID: *Breeding:* long, slender bill, neck and legs; purplish blue to grayish blue plumage; white underparts and foreneck; pale rump; long plumes on head and back during breeding season. *Immature:* chestnut nape and wing coverts.
Size: *L* 26 in; *W* 3 ft.

breeding

YELLOW-CROWNED NIGHT-HERON
Nyctanassa violacea

The Yellow-crowned Night-Heron is a casual visitor in southeastern Michigan, as well as a rare spring and fall visitor. Its range has expanded into Michigan only relatively recently, with the first sighting recorded in 1960.

ID: black head; white "cheek" and crown; yellowish forehead; stout, black bill; pale area at base of lower mandible; slate gray neck and body; yellow legs. *Breeding:* long, white head plumes extend down back of neck. *Immature:* brown plumage with white spotting; green legs. *In flight:* legs extend well behind tail.
Size: *L* 24 in; *W* 3½ ft.

breeding

GLOSSY IBIS
Plegadis falcinellus

Your best chance of seeing this occasional transient is in the marshes of Monroe County in May, but it has also been seen in more central locales. It generally breeds along the Atlantic and Gulf coasts.

ID: long, downcurved bill; long legs; brown eyes; dark skin in front of eye is bordered by 2 pale stripes. *Breeding:* chestnut head, neck and sides; green and purple sheen on wings, tail, crown and face. *Nonbreeding:* dark grayish brown head and neck are streaked with white. *In flight:* fully extended neck; legs trail behind tail; hunchbacked appearance; flocks fly in lines or "V" formations.
Size: *L* 22–25 in; *W* 3 ft.

breeding

WHITE-FACED IBIS
Plegadis chihi

This western counterpart of the Glossy Ibis is much less likely to be seen in Michigan, an important point because the two species are almost impossible to tell apart except in breeding plumage. Only eight sightings were recorded in Michigan from 1916 to 2001.

ID: dark chestnut plumage; long, downcurved bill; long, dark legs; white feathers border naked facial patch; greenish lower back and wing covers; dark red eyes. *Breeding:* rich red legs and facial patch. *In flight:* outstretched neck; long, downcurved bill.
Size: *L* 18–26 in; *W* 3 ft.

breeding

BLACK VULTURE
Coragyps atratus

This vulture of the southern U.S. is a very rare vagrant in Michigan, but there have recently been several sightings statewide. Look for the whitish wing tip primary feathers to distinguish it from the more common Turkey Vulture.

ID: all-black plumage; grayish head, legs and feet; light gray base of primaries contrasts noticeably against otherwise dark underparts.
Size: *L* 25 in; *W* 5 ft.

ROSS'S GOOSE
Chen rossii

The Ross's Goose breeds in the high Arctic and winters in California. Its migration patterns have expanded steadily eastward over the past few decades. When sighted in Michigan, it is often among large flocks of Canada Geese. The Ross's Goose often hybridizes with the Snow Goose, so care must be taken in identification.

white morph

ID: white overall; black wing tips; dark pink feet and bill; lacks "grinning patch"; small bluish or green "warts" on base of bill; plumage is occasionally stained rusty by iron in the water. Blue morph: very rare; white head; blue gray body plumage. *Immature:* gray plumage; dark bill and feet.
Size: *L* 21–25 in; *W* 4 ft.

BRANT
Branta bernicla

This casual migrant is most likely to be found around harbors or bays along the Great Lakes, but may also be seen farther inland. There are two subspecies of Brant: the light-bellied, eastern form found in Michigan and on the East Coast is from the north-central Canadian Arctic. The western form is black-bellied.

ID: black neck, head and upper breast; dark upperparts; white "necklace"; white hindquarters; black feet; pale brown sides and flanks; white belly. *Juvenile:* less conspicuous "necklace."
Size: *L* 23–27 in; *W* 3½–4 ft.

EURASIAN WIGEON
Anas penelope

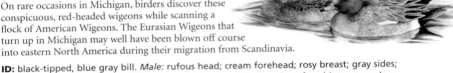

On rare occasions in Michigan, birders discover these conspicuous, red-headed wigeons while scanning a flock of American Wigeons. The Eurasian Wigeons that turn up in Michigan may well have been blown off course into eastern North America during their migration from Scandinavia.

ID: black-tipped, blue gray bill. *Male:* rufous head; cream forehead; rosy breast; gray sides; black hindquarters; dark feet; black-tipped, blue gray bill. *Female:* rufous hints on predominantly brown head and breast. *In flight:* large, white wing patch; dusky gray "wing pits."
Size: *L* 20 in; *W* 32 in.

KING EIDER
Somateria spectabilis

This casual migrant and winter visitor from the Canadian Arctic has occurred most frequently at Whitefish Point and along Lake Michigan from Muskegon south to New Buffalo.

ID: *Male:* blue crown; green "cheek"; orange nasal disc; red bill; black wings; white neck, breast, back, upperwing patches and flank patches. *Female:* mottled, rich rufous brown overall; black bill extends onto nasal shield; sides have V-shaped markings. *Immature male:* dark overall; white breast; yellow orange bill resembles female's bill.
Size: *L* 18–25 in; *W* 3–3½ ft.

BARROW'S GOLDENEYE
Bucephala islandica

The Barrow's Goldeneye is a casual migrant and winter visitor, occurring along the Great Lakes and occasionally inland. Our birds are probably strays from the far west, but possibly from northeastern Canada.

ID: medium-sized, rounded duck; short bill; steep fore-head. *Male:* dark purple head; white crescent on "cheek"; white underparts; white spotting on dark back and wings. *Female:* chocolate brown head with peaked forehead; small, orange bill is tipped with black in spring and summer; gray brown body plumage.
Size: *L* 16–20 in; *W* 28 in.

MISSISSIPPI KITE
Ictinia mississippiensis

The acrobatic Mississippi Kite makes its home in the southeastern U.S. and parts of the Great Plains, and its breeding range extends north along the Mississippi River valley. This bird has become a casual May visitor to Michigan, following a recent range expansion northward.

ID: long, pointed, swept-back wings; uppersides of secondaries are pale gray; dark gray upperparts; dark tail; pale gray head and underparts. *Immature:* dark brownish upperparts; streaky brown underparts; pale, translucent bands on dark tail. *In flight:* never hovers; first primary is shorter than the others.
Size: *L* 14 in; *W* 35 in.

KING RAIL
Rallus elegans

This endangered bird, with only four confirmed records in Michigan since 1997, has all but disappeared from the state. Pollution and the fragmentation of large shoreline and inland marshes are mostly responsible for the fragile state of this bird's population.

ID: long, slightly downcurved bill; black back feathers have fluffy or tawny edges; rufous shoulders and underparts; strongly barred, black-and-white flanks; grayish brown "cheek." *Immature:* similar plumage patterning with lighter, washed-out colors.
Size: *L* 15 in; *W* 20 in.

CURLEW SANDPIPER
Calidris ferruginea

molting

This colorful Eurasian shorebird is an accidental spring and fall migrant, occurring rarely in Monroe County's Lake Erie marshes in May and from July to September.

ID: long, black, downcurved bill; black legs; clean white undertail coverts; white rump; bold, white upperwing stripe. *Breeding:* rich chestnut over-all; dark mottling on crown and back; female is paler. *Nonbreeding:* pale gray upperparts; darker gray wings; whitish underparts; white "eyebrow"; brownish wash on head.
Size: *L* 8½ in; *W* 18 in.

RUFF
Philomachus pugnax

This striking Eurasian shorebird is a casual spring and fall migrant, occurring in mudflats, sewage ponds and flooded fields, occasionally with yellowlegs species. In breeding plumage it is Michigan's most spectacular shorebird. The female is called a Reeve.

ID: plump body; small head; yellowish green to red legs; yellow or black bill; brown gray underparts. *Breeding male:* black, white or orangy neck ruff, usually flattened, but erected during courtship; dark underparts. *Breeding female:* dark blotches on underparts. *In flight:* thin, white wing stripe; oval, white rump divided by dark central stripe.
Size: *L* 8½–12 in; *W* 16–24 in.

breeding

RED PHALAROPE
Phalaropus fulicaria

breeding

Red Phalaropes are casual migrants here, and small numbers may pass through Michigan during their fall migration to the Atlantic Coast and South America. In their dull fall wardrobe, they look similar to the more prevalent Red-necked Phalaropes. Still, the Red Phalarope's heavy bill, slightly larger size and plain, blue gray upperwings are good distinguishing clues.

ID: *Breeding female:* chestnut red throat, neck and underparts; white face; black crown and forehead; black-tipped, yellow bill. *Breeding male:* mottled brown crown; duller face and underparts. *Nonbreeding:* white head, neck and underparts; mostly dark bill; black nape; broad, dark patch extends from eye to ear. *Juvenile:* similar to nonbreeding adult, but is buff-colored overall; dark streaking on upperparts.
Size: *L* 8½ in; *W* 17 in.

LONG-TAILED JAEGER
Stercorarius longicaudus

breeding

The Long-tailed Jaeger is the rarest jaeger in Michigan. It is a casual visitor to our Great Lakes shores in May and September and is most frequently observed at Whitefish Point.

ID: long, twinned tail feathers; dark "cap"; clean white throat and belly; yellow "collar"; gray upperparts; dark flight feathers. *Subadult:* dark "necklace"; dark barring on sides, flanks and rump. *Juvenile:* dark "chin" and throat; dark barring on sides, flanks and rump; mottled underwing linings; brown upperparts; short, rounded tail streamers.
Size: *L* 20–22 in; *W* 3 ft.

breeding

CALIFORNIA GULL
Larus californicus

Unlike most of its relatives, the California Gull breeds on islands in inland lakes, often in arid regions. This visitor from the far west is a casual spring and fall migrant, principally to our Great Lakes shorelines, most frequently on Lake Michigan.

ID: yellow bill; red and black spots on lower mandible; yellow green legs; dark eyes; gray back; black wing tips. *Breeding:* white head; white underparts. *Nonbreeding:* dark spotting on head. *Immature:* mottled brown overall; pinkish legs; pale bill with black tip.
Size: *L* 18–20 in; *W* 4–4½ ft.

ARCTIC TERN
Sterna paradisaea

The Arctic Tern is a casual fall migrant along our Great Lakes shores en route to wintering grounds in the Southern Hemisphere. A few birds are accidental summer visitors in Michigan.

breeding

ID: *Breeding:* blood red bill and legs; black cap and nape; short neck; white "cheek"; gray underparts; long, white, forked tail extends to wing tips when bird is perched. *Nonbreeding* and *immature:* white underparts; black band through eyes and across nape; black bill. *In flight:* appears neckless; deeply forked tail; evenly colored gray wings with thin, dark, trailing underwing edge.
Size: *L* 14–17 in; *W* 29–33 in.

RUFOUS HUMMINGBIRD
Selasphorus rufus

Rufous Hummingbirds are more typically a western species, but several have been documented in Michigan in recent years. They turn up at backyard sugarwater feeders in September and may remain for a month or more, as long as food is provided.

ID: long, thin, black bill; mostly rufous tail. *Male:* rufous back, tail and flanks; scaled, scarlet throat; green crown; white breast and belly. *Female:* green back; red-spotted throat; rufous flanks; light underparts.
Size: 3–3½ in; *W* 4½ in.

THREE-TOED WOODPECKER
Picoides tridactylus

These northern woodpeckers are casual and very unlikely to be seen in Michigan. They usually inhabit stands of dead pines or spruces that have been killed by fire or insects. The woodpeckers leave these areas after a few years, once they have scaled the bark off the trees and eaten the insects beneath it. This species can occur in the Upper Peninsula and even more rarely in the northern part of the Lower Peninsula.

ID: black-and-white barring down center of back; white underparts; black barring on sides; predominantly black head with 2 white stripes; black tail with black-spotted, white outer tail feathers; 3 toes. *Male:* yellow crown. *Female:* black crown with occasional white spotting.
Size: *L* 8–9 in; *W* 15 in.

SAY'S PHOEBE
Sayornis saya

The Say's Phoebe is partial to dry environments and its range encompasses much of the Canadian Prairies as well as the American Great Plains and the southwestern states. This western stray is a rare spring or fall migrant that occurs mostly in May, most frequently in the Upper Peninsula, but with three Lower Peninsula records.

ID: apricot belly and undertail coverts; dark tail; brown gray breast and upperparts; dark head; no eye ring; very faint wing bars.
Size: *L* 7½ in; *W* 13 in.

SCISSOR-TAILED FLYCATCHER
Tyrannus forficatus

This beautiful, graceful, spectacular flycatcher from the Southwest is a casual migrant and summer visitor to many areas in Michigan, but occurs most frequently in the Upper Peninsula.

ID: dark wings; extremely long outer tail feathers give forked appearance in flight; whitish to grayish head, back and breast; salmon pink underwing linings, flanks and lower underparts; bright, pinkish red "wing pits." *Immature:* duller, shorter-tailed version of adult, with brownish back.
Size: *L* 13–16 in (male's tail can be up to 9 in long); *W* 15 in.

BELL'S VIREO
Vireo bellii

This small, drab, grayish olive visitor is a rarity, occasionally drifting into southern Michigan in May from its nesting range just southwest of our border. In an isolated incident, it was found nesting in Berrien County for some years.

ID: 2 white wing bars (upper bar is usually faint if present); whitish "eyebrow," whitish eye ring or lores or both. *Southwestern morph:* grayish upperparts; whitish underparts. *Eastern (Midwest) morph:* olive green upperparts; yellow underparts.
Size: *L* 4–5 in; *W* 7 in.

NORTHERN WHEATEAR
Oenanthe oenanthe

This visitor from Alaska and the Yukon is a casual fall migrant in Michigan, usually on the Upper Peninsula in October. There are only four Lower Peninsula records.

ID: white undertail coverts, rump and upper tail; lower tail forms black, inverted "T"; white forehead and "eyebrow." *Breeding male:* blue gray upperparts; black wings and triangular ear patch; cinnamon buff to whitish underparts. *Female* and *nonbreeding male:* brown upperparts; buffier underparts.
Size: *L* 6 in; *W* 12 in.

breeding

WESTERN TANAGER
Piranga ludoviciana

The colorful Western Tanager is widely distributed in the western part of the continent and is found farther north than any other tanager. In Michigan, it is a casual spring migrant with only a few records.

ID: *Breeding male:* yellow underparts, wing bars and rump; black back, wings and tail; often has red on forehead or entire head (variable); light-colored bill. *Breeding female:* olive green overall; lighter underparts; darker upperparts; faint wing bars.
Size: *L* 7 in; *W* 11½ in.

breeding

LARK BUNTING
Calamospiza melanocorys

The Lark Bunting inhabits dry prairies, plains, grasslands and areas of open sagebrush. In Michigan, it is mainly a casual spring and summer visitor to the Upper Peninsula.

ID: dark, conical bill; large, white wing patch. *Breeding male:* all-black plumage; white patch at tip of tail. *Female, nonbreeding male* and *immature:* mottled brown upperparts; brown-streaked underparts; pale "eyebrow"; whitish, partial wing patches.
Size: *L* 7 in; *W* 10½ in.

SMITH'S LONGSPUR
Calcarius pictus

This visitor from the Arctic is a rare spring and fall migrant in Michigan, often found in open fields. Look for it in flocks of Lapland Longspurs.

ID: white outer and black inner tail feathers; small, white shoulder patch (often concealed). *Breeding male:* black crown and face with white "eyebrow" and "cheek" patch; buff underparts and "collar." *Female, nonbreeding male* and *immature:* dark crown and facial markings.
Size: *L* 6 in; *W* 11 in.

breeding

BLUE GROSBEAK
Passerina caerulea

This southern grosbeak is a rare spring migrant and summer visitor in Michigan, mainly in southern counties. Care must be taken not to confuse it with the smaller Indigo Bunting, which may have brownish wing bars.

ID: large, conical, pale grayish bill. *Male:* blue overall; 2 dusty wing bars; black around base of bill. *Female:* soft brown plumage overall; whitish throat; rusty wing bars; rump and shoulders are faintly washed with blue.
Size: *L* 6–7½ in; *W* 11 in.

PAINTED BUNTING
Passerina ciris

The dramatically colored Painted Bunting has two distinct populations: an eastern population that ranges along the coastal areas of the southeastern states, and a western population that is found in Arkansas, Oklahoma, Kansas, Texas and Louisiana. It is a rare spring migrant to Michigan, occurring widely over the state.

ID: *Male:* blue head; red eye ring and underparts; green back; blackish wings and tail. *Female:* pale green upperparts; yellowish underparts.
Size: *L* 5½ in; *W* 8½ in.

SELECT REFERENCES

American Ornithologists' Union. 1998. *Check-list of North American Birds.* 7th ed. (and its supplements). American Ornithologists' Union, Washington, D.C.

Black, C.T., and C.R. Smith et al. 1994. *Bird Finding Guide to Michigan.* Michigan Audubon Society, Lansing, MI.

Choate, E.A. 1985. *The Dictionary of American Bird Names.* Rev. ed. Harvard Common Press, Cambridge, MA.

Cox, R.T. 1996. *Birder's Dictionary.* Falcon Publishing Inc., Helena, MT.

Craves, J., ed. *Michigan Birds and Natural History.* (Quarterly Journal of Michigan Audubon Society). Michigan Audubon Society, Lansing, MI.

Ehrlich, P.R., D.S. Dobkin and D. Wheye. 1988. *The Birder's Handbook.* Simon & Schuster Inc., New York.

Elphick, C., J.B. Dunning, Jr., and D.A. Sibley, eds. 2001. *National Audubon Society The Sibley Guide to Bird Life & Behavior.* Alfred A. Knopf, New York.

Jones, J.O. 1990. *Where The Birds Are.* William Morrow and Company, Inc., New York.

Kaufman, K. 1996. *Lives of North American Birds.* Houghton Mifflin Co., Boston.

Kaufman, K. 2000. *Birds of North American.* Houghton Mifflin Co., New York.

McPeek, G.A., and R.J. Adams, eds. 1994. *The Birds of Michigan.* Indiana University Press, Bloomington & Indianapolis.

National Geographic Society. 2002. *Field Guide to the Birds of North America.* 4th ed. National Geographic Society, Washington, D.C.

Sibley, D.A. 2000. *National Audubon Society The Sibley Guide to Birds.* Alfred A. Knopf, New York.

Sibley, D.A. 2002. *Sibley's Birding Basics.* Alfred A. Knopf, New York.

Terres, J.K. 1980. *The Audubon Society Encyclopedia of North American Birds.* Alfred A. Knopf, New York.

Whip-poor-will

GLOSSARY

accipiter: a forest hawk (genus *Accipiter*), characterized by a long tail and short, rounded wings; feeds mostly on birds.

air sacs: a series of air-filled spaces in a bird's body that are connected with the air passages of the lungs and which help regulate body temperature, provide buoyancy in waterbirds and assist in vocalization.

brood parasite: a bird that lays its eggs in other birds' nests.

buteo: a high-soaring hawk (genus *Buteo*), characterized by broad wings and a short, wide tail; feeds mostly on small mammals and other land animals.

cere: on birds of prey, a fleshy area at the base of the bill that contains the nostrils.

clutch: the number of eggs laid by the female at one time.

corvid: a member of the crow family (*Corvidae*); includes crows, jays, magpies and ravens.

covey: a brood or flock of partridges, quails or grouse.

crepuscular: active chiefly during twilight, before dawn and after dusk.

crop: an enlargement of the esophagus; serves as a storage structure and (in pigeons) has glands that produce secretions.

cryptic: a coloration pattern that helps to conceal the bird.

dabbling: a foraging technique used by ducks in which the head and neck are submerged but the body and tail remain on the water's surface; dabbling ducks can usually walk easily on land, can take off without running and have brightly colored speculums.

diurnal: most active during the day.

"eclipse" plumage: a cryptic plumage, similar to that of females, worn by some male ducks in fall when they molt their flight feathers and consequently are unable to fly.

endangered: a species that is facing imminent extirpation or extinction in all or part of its range.

extinct: a species that no longer exists.

extirpated: a species that no longer exists in the wild in a particular region but occurs elsewhere.

fledge: to acquire the first coat of feathers necessary for flight.

flushing: a behavior in which frightened birds explode into flight in response to a disturbance.

flycatching: a feeding behavior in which the bird leaves a perch, snatches an insect in midair and returns to the same perch; also known as "hawking" or "sallying."

hawking: attempting to capture insects through aerial pursuit.

irruption: a sporadic mass migration of birds into an unusual range.

kettle: a large concentration of hawks, usually seen during migration.

lacustrine: near or around lakes.

lek: a place where males gather to display for females in the spring.

mantle: the area that includes the back and uppersides of the wings.

molt: the periodic shedding and regrowth of worn feathers (often twice a year).

nocturnal: most active at night.

peep: a sandpiper of the *Calidris* genus.

polyandrous: having a mating strategy in which one female breeds with several males.

polygynous: having a mating strategy in which one male breeds with several females.

precocial: a bird that is relatively well developed at hatching; precocial birds usually have open eyes, extensive down and are fairly mobile.

primaries: the outermost flight feathers of a bird's wing.

raft: a gathering of birds resting on the water.

raptor: a carnivorous (meat-eating) bird; includes eagles, hawks, falcons and owls.

riparian: habitat along rivers and streams.

scapulars: feathers of the shoulder, seeming to join the wing and back.

sexual dimorphism: a difference in plumage, size or other characteristics between males and females of the same species.

special concern: a species that has characteristics that make it particularly sensitive to human activities or distur-bance, requires a very specific or unique habitat or whose status is such that it requires careful monitoring.

speculum: a brightly colored patch on the wings of many dabbling ducks.

stoop: a steep dive through the air, usually performed by birds of prey while foraging or during courtship displays.

syrinx: a bird's voice organ.

threatened: a species likely to become endangered in the near future in all or part of its range.

understory: the shrub or thicket layer beneath a canopy of trees.

vagrant: a bird that has wandered outside its normal migration range.

vent: the single opening for excretion of uric acid and other wastes and for sexual reproduction; also known as the "cloaca."

zygodactyl: feet that have two toes pointing to the front and two pointing to the rear; found in osprey, owls and woodpeckers.

crown

eyebrow/
supercilium

eye line

lore

wing bars

chin

greater coverts

throat

rump

breast

tips of primary feathers

flank

tail feathers

belly

undertail coverts

secondary feathers

CHECKLIST

The following checklist contains 415 species of birds that have been officially recorded in Michigan. Species are grouped by family and listed in taxonomic order in accordance with the A.O.U. *Check-list of North American Birds* (7th ed.).

Species recorded in fewer than 9 of the last 10 years or having fewer than 30 records during the last 10 years are in *italics*. In addition, the following risk categories are noted: extinct or extirpated (ex), endangered (en), threatened (th) and special concern (sc).

We wish to thank the Michigan Bird Records Committee for their kind assistance in providing the information for this checklist.

Loons (Gaviidae)
❑ Red-throated Loon
❑ *Pacific Loon*
❑ Common Loon (th)

Grebes (Podicipedidae)
❑ Pied-billed Grebe
❑ Horned Grebe
❑ Red-necked Grebe
❑ Eared Grebe
❑ Western Grebe

Shearwaters (Procellariidae)
❑ *Manx Shearwater*

Gannets (Sulidae)
❑ *Northern Gannet*

Pelicans (Pelecanidae)
❑ American White Pelican
❑ *Brown Pelican*

Cormorants (Phalacrocoracidae)
❑ Double-crested Cormorant

Frigatebirds (Fregatidae)
❑ *Magnificent Frigatebird*

Herons (Ardeidae)
❑ American Bittern (sc)
❑ Least Bittern (th)
❑ Great Blue Heron
❑ Great Egret
❑ Snowy Egret
❑ Little Blue Heron
❑ *Tricolored Heron*
❑ *Reddish Egret*

❑ Cattle Egret
❑ Green Heron
❑ Black-crowned Night Heron (sc)
❑ *Yellow-crowned Night Heron*

Ibises (Threskiornithidae)
❑ *White Ibis*
❑ *Glossy Ibis*
❑ *White-faced Ibis*

Storks (Ciconiidae)
❑ *Wood Stork*

Vultures (Cathartidae)
❑ *Black Vulture*
❑ Turkey Vulture

Waterfowl (Anatidae)
❑ *Fulvous Whistling-Duck*
❑ Greater White-fronted Goose
❑ Snow Goose
❑ *Ross's Goose*
❑ Canada Goose
❑ *Brant*
❑ Mute Swan
❑ Trumpeter Swan (th)
❑ Tundra Swan
❑ Wood Duck
❑ Gadwall
❑ *Eurasian Wigeon*
❑ American Wigeon
❑ American Black Duck
❑ Mallard
❑ Blue-winged Teal
❑ *Cinnamon Teal*
❑ Northern Shoveler
❑ Northern Pintail

❑ *Garganey*
❑ Green-winged Teal
❑ Canvasback
❑ Redhead
❑ Ring-necked Duck
❑ *Tufted Duck*
❑ Greater Scaup
❑ Lesser Scaup
❑ *King Eider*
❑ *Common Eider*
❑ Harlequin Duck
❑ Surf Scoter
❑ White-winged Scoter
❑ Black Scoter
❑ Long-tailed Duck
❑ Bufflehead
❑ Common Goldeneye
❑ *Barrow's Goldeneye*
❑ Hooded Merganser
❑ Common Merganser
❑ Red-breasted Merganser
❑ Ruddy Duck

Kites, Hawks & Eagles (Accipitridae)
❑ Osprey (th)
❑ *Swallow-tailed Kite*
❑ *Mississippi Kite*
❑ Bald Eagle (th)
❑ Northern Harrier (sc)
❑ Sharp-shinned Hawk
❑ Cooper's Hawk (sc)
❑ Northern Goshawk (sc)
❑ Red-shouldered Hawk (th)
❑ Broad-winged Hawk
❑ Swainson's Hawk
❑ Red-tailed Hawk
❑ *Ferruginous Hawk*
❑ Rough-legged Hawk
❑ Golden Eagle

CHECKLIST

Falcons (Falconidae)
- ❏ American Kestrel
- ❏ Merlin
- ❏ Gyrfalcon
- ❏ Peregrine Falcon (en)
- ❏ *Prairie Falcon*

Grouse & Allies (Phasianidae)
- ❏ Ring-necked Pheasant
- ❏ Ruffed Grouse
- ❏ Spruce Grouse (sc)
- ❏ Sharp-tailed Grouse (sc)
- ❏ *Greater Prairie-Chicken (ex)*
- ❏ Wild Turkey

New World Quails (Odontophoridae)
- ❏ Northern Bobwhite

Rails & Coots (Rallidae)
- ❏ Yellow Rail (th)
- ❏ *Black Rail*
- ❏ *King Rail (en)*
- ❏ Virginia Rail
- ❏ Sora
- ❏ *Purple Gallinule*
- ❏ Common Moorhen (sc)
- ❏ American Coot

Cranes (Gruidae)
- ❏ Sandhill Crane

Plovers (Charadriidae)
- ❏ Black-bellied Plover
- ❏ American Golden-Plover
- ❏ *Snowy Plover*
- ❏ *Wilson's Plover*
- ❏ Semipalmated Plover
- ❏ Piping Plover (en)
- ❏ Killdeer

Stilts & Avocets (Recurvirostridae)
- ❏ *Black-necked Stilt*
- ❏ American Avocet

Sandpipers & Allies (Scolopacidae)
- ❏ Greater Yellowlegs
- ❏ Lesser Yellowlegs
- ❏ *Spotted Redshank*
- ❏ Solitary Sandpiper
- ❏ Willet
- ❏ Spotted Sandpiper
- ❏ Upland Sandpiper
- ❏ *Eskimo Curlew*
- ❏ Whimbrel
- ❏ Hudsonian Godwit
- ❏ Marbled Godwit
- ❏ Ruddy Turnstone
- ❏ Red Knot
- ❏ Sanderling
- ❏ Semipalmated Sandpiper
- ❏ Western Sandpiper
- ❏ Least Sandpiper
- ❏ White-rumped Sandpiper
- ❏ Baird's Sandpiper
- ❏ Pectoral Sandpiper
- ❏ Purple Sandpiper
- ❏ Dunlin
- ❏ *Curlew Sandpiper*
- ❏ Stilt Sandpiper
- ❏ Buff-breasted Sandpiper
- ❏ *Ruff*
- ❏ Short-billed Dowitcher
- ❏ Long-billed Dowitcher
- ❏ Wilson's Snipe
- ❏ American Woodcock
- ❏ Wilson's Phalarope (sc)
- ❏ Red-necked Phalarope
- ❏ *Red Phalarope*

Gulls & Allies (Laridae)
- ❏ Pomarine Jaeger
- ❏ Parasitic Jaeger
- ❏ *Long-tailed Jaeger*
- ❏ Laughing Gull
- ❏ Franklin's Gull
- ❏ Little Gull
- ❏ *Black-headed Gull*
- ❏ Bonaparte's Gull
- ❏ *Heermann's Gull*
- ❏ *Mew Gull*
- ❏ Ring-billed Gull
- ❏ *California Gull*
- ❏ Herring Gull
- ❏ Thayer's Gull
- ❏ Iceland Gull
- ❏ Lesser Black-backed Gull
- ❏ *Slaty-backed Gull*
- ❏ *Glaucous-winged Gull*
- ❏ Glaucous Gull
- ❏ Great Black-backed Gull
- ❏ Sabine's Gull
- ❏ Black-legged Kittiwake
- ❏ *Ivory Gull*
- ❏ Caspian Tern (th)
- ❏ *Sandwich Tern*
- ❏ *Roseate Tern*
- ❏ Common Tern (th)
- ❏ *Arctic Tern*
- ❏ Forster's Tern (sc)
- ❏ *Least Tern*
- ❏ Black Tern (sc)

Alcids (Alcidae)
- ❏ *Dovekie*
- ❏ *Thick-billed Murre*
- ❏ *Ancient Murrelet*

Pigeons & Doves (Columbidae)
- ❏ Rock Dove
- ❏ *Band-tailed Pigeon*
- ❏ *White-winged Dove*
- ❏ Mourning Dove
- ❏ *Passenger Pigeon (ex)*
- ❏ *Common Ground-Dove*

Cuckoos (Cuculidae)
- ❏ Black-billed Cuckoo
- ❏ Yellow-billed Cuckoo
- ❏ *Groove-billed Ani*

Barn Owls (Tytonidae)
- ❏ *Barn Owl (en)*

Owls (Strigidae)
- ❏ Eastern Screech-Owl
- ❏ Great Horned Owl
- ❏ Snowy Owl
- ❏ Northern Hawk Owl
- ❏ *Burrowing Owl*
- ❏ Barred Owl
- ❏ Great Gray Owl
- ❏ Long-eared Owl (th)
- ❏ Short-eared Owl (en)
- ❏ Boreal Owl
- ❏ Northern Saw-whet Owl

Nightjars (Caprimulgidae)
- ❏ Common Nighthawk
- ❏ *Chuck-will's-widow*
- ❏ Whip-poor-will

Swifts (Apodidae)
- ❏ *White-collared Swift*
- ❏ Chimney Swift
- ❏ *White-throated Swift*

Hummingbirds (Trochilidae)
- ❏ *Green Violet-ear*
- ❏ *Broad-billed Hummingbird*
- ❏ Ruby-throated Hummingbird
- ❏ *Rufous Hummingbird*

Kingfishers (Alcedinidae)
- ❏ Belted Kingfisher

Woodpeckers (Picidae)
- ❏ *Lewis's Woodpecker*
- ❏ Red-headed Woodpecker
- ❏ *Golden-fronted Woodpecker*
- ❏ Red-bellied Woodpecker
- ❏ Yellow-bellied Sapsucker
- ❏ Downy Woodpecker
- ❏ Hairy Woodpecker
- ❏ *Three-toed Woodpecker*
- ❏ Black-backed Woodpecker (sc)
- ❏ Northern Flicker
- ❏ Pileated Woodpecker

Flycatchers (Tyrannidae)
- ❏ Olive-sided Flycatcher
- ❏ Eastern Wood-Pewee
- ❏ Yellow-bellied Flycatcher
- ❏ Acadian Flycatcher
- ❏ Alder Flycatcher
- ❏ Willow Flycatcher
- ❏ Least Flycatcher
- ❏ *Hammond's Flycatcher*
- ❏ Eastern Phoebe
- ❏ *Say's Phoebe*
- ❏ *Vermilion Flycatcher*
- ❏ *Ash-throated Flycatcher*
- ❏ Great Crested Flycatcher
- ❏ Western Kingbird
- ❏ Eastern Kingbird
- ❏ *Gray Kingbird*
- ❏ *Scissor-tailed Flycatcher*
- ❏ *Fork-tailed Flycatcher*

Shrikes (Laniidae)
- ❏ Loggerhead Shrike (en)
- ❏ Northern Shrike

Vireos (Vireonidae)
- ❏ White-eyed Vireo
- ❏ *Bell's Vireo*
- ❏ Yellow-throated Vireo
- ❏ Blue-headed Vireo
- ❏ Warbling Vireo
- ❏ Philadelphia Vireo
- ❏ Red-eyed Vireo

Crows, Jays & Magpies (Corvidae)
- ❏ Gray Jay
- ❏ Blue Jay
- ❏ *Clark's Nutcracker*
- ❏ *Black-billed Magpie*
- ❏ American Crow
- ❏ Common Raven

Larks (Alaudidae)
- ❏ Horned Lark

Swallows (Hirundinidae)
- ❏ Purple Martin
- ❏ Tree Swallow
- ❏ Northern Rough-winged Swallow
- ❏ Bank Swallow
- ❏ Cliff Swallow
- ❏ *Cave Swallow*
- ❏ Barn Swallow

Chickadees & Titmice (Paridae)
- ❏ *Carolina Chickadee*
- ❏ Black-capped Chickadee
- ❏ Boreal Chickadee
- ❏ Tufted Titmouse

Nuthatches (Sittidae)
- ❏ Red-breasted Nuthatch
- ❏ White-breasted Nuthatch

Creepers (Certhiidae)
- ❏ Brown Creeper

Wrens (Troglodytidae)
- ❏ *Rock Wren*
- ❏ Carolina Wren
- ❏ *Bewick's Wren*
- ❏ House Wren
- ❏ Winter Wren
- ❏ Sedge Wren
- ❏ Marsh Wren (sc)

Kinglets (Regulidae)
- ❏ Golden-crowned Kinglet
- ❏ Ruby-crowned Kinglet

Gnatcatchers (Sylviidae)
- ❏ Blue-gray Gnatcatcher

Thrushes (Turdidae)
- ❏ *Northern Wheatear*
- ❏ Eastern Bluebird
- ❏ *Mountain Bluebird*
- ❏ Townsend's Solitaire
- ❏ Veery
- ❏ Gray-cheeked Thrush
- ❏ Swainson's Thrush
- ❏ Hermit Thrush
- ❏ Wood Thrush
- ❏ American Robin
- ❏ Varied Thrush

Mockingbirds & Thrashers (Mimidae)
- ❏ Gray Catbird
- ❏ Northern Mockingbird
- ❏ *Sage Thrasher*
- ❏ Brown Thrasher

Starlings (Sturnidae)
- ❏ European Starling

Wagtails & Pipits (Motacillidae)
- ❏ American Pipit
- ❏ *Sprague's Pipit*

Waxwings (Bombycillidae)
- ❏ Bohemian Waxwing
- ❏ Cedar Waxwing

Wood-Warblers (Parulidae)
- ❏ Blue-winged Warbler
- ❏ Golden-winged Warbler

- ❏ Tennessee Warbler
- ❏ Orange-crowned Warbler
- ❏ Nashville Warbler
- ❏ *Virginia's Warbler*
- ❏ Northern Parula
- ❏ Yellow Warbler
- ❏ Chestnut-sided Warbler
- ❏ Magnolia Warbler
- ❏ Cape May Warbler
- ❏ Black-throated Blue Warbler
- ❏ Yellow-rumped Warbler
- ❏ *Black-throated Gray Warbler*
- ❏ Black-throated Green Warbler
- ❏ *Townsend's Warbler*
- ❏ Blackburnian Warbler
- ❏ Yellow-throated Warbler (th)
- ❏ Pine Warbler
- ❏ Kirtland's Warbler (en)
- ❏ Prairie Warbler (en)
- ❏ Palm Warbler
- ❏ Bay-breasted Warbler
- ❏ Blackpoll Warbler
- ❏ Cerulean Warbler (sc)
- ❏ Black-and-white Warbler
- ❏ American Redstart
- ❏ Prothonotary Warbler (sc)
- ❏ Worm-eating Warbler
- ❏ *Swainson's Warbler*
- ❏ Ovenbird
- ❏ Northern Waterthrush
- ❏ Louisiana Waterthrush (sc)
- ❏ Kentucky Warbler
- ❏ Connecticut Warbler
- ❏ Mourning Warbler
- ❏ Common Yellowthroat
- ❏ Hooded Warbler (sc)
- ❏ Wilson's Warbler
- ❏ Canada Warbler
- ❏ *Painted Redstart*
- ❏ Yellow-breasted Chat

Tanagers (Thraupidae)
- ❏ Summer Tanager
- ❏ Scarlet Tanager
- ❏ *Western Tanager*

Sparrows & Allies (Emberizidae)
- ❏ *Green-tailed Towhee*
- ❏ Eastern Towhee
- ❏ *Cassin's Sparrow*
- ❏ *Bachman's Sparrow*
- ❏ American Tree Sparrow
- ❏ Chipping Sparrow
- ❏ Clay-colored Sparrow
- ❏ *Brewer's Sparrow*
- ❏ Field Sparrow
- ❏ Vesper Sparrow
- ❏ *Lark Sparrow (th)*
- ❏ *Black-throated Sparrow*
- ❏ *Lark Bunting*
- ❏ Savannah Sparrow
- ❏ Grasshopper Sparrow (sc)
- ❏ Henslow's Sparrow (th)
- ❏ LeConte's Sparrow
- ❏ *Nelson's Sharp-tailed Sparrow*
- ❏ Fox Sparrow
- ❏ Song Sparrow
- ❏ Lincoln's Sparrow
- ❏ Swamp Sparrow
- ❏ White-throated Sparrow
- ❏ Harris' Sparrow
- ❏ White-crowned Sparrow
- ❏ *Golden-crowned Sparrow*
- ❏ Dark-eyed Junco
- ❏ *McCown's Longspur*
- ❏ Lapland Longspur
- ❏ *Smith's Longspur*
- ❏ *Chestnut-collared Longspur*
- ❏ Snow Bunting

Grosbeaks & Buntings (Cardinalidae)
- ❏ Northern Cardinal
- ❏ Rose-breasted Grosbeak
- ❏ *Black-headed Grosbeak*
- ❏ *Blue Grosbeak*
- ❏ Indigo Bunting
- ❏ *Painted Bunting*
- ❏ Dickcissel (sc)

Blackbirds & Allies (Icteridae)
- ❏ Bobolink
- ❏ Red-winged Blackbird
- ❏ Eastern Meadowlark
- ❏ Western Meadowlark (sc)
- ❏ Yellow-headed Blackbird (sc)
- ❏ Rusty Blackbird
- ❏ Brewer's Blackbird
- ❏ Common Grackle
- ❏ Brown-headed Cowbird
- ❏ Orchard Oriole
- ❏ *Bullock's Oriole*
- ❏ Baltimore Oriole

Finches (Fringillidae)
- ❏ *Brambling*
- ❏ *Gray-crowned Rosy Finch*
- ❏ Pine Grosbeak
- ❏ Purple Finch
- ❏ House Finch
- ❏ Red Crossbill
- ❏ White-winged Crossbill
- ❏ Common Redpoll
- ❏ Hoary Redpoll
- ❏ Pine Siskin
- ❏ American Goldfinch
- ❏ Evening Grosbeak

Old World Sparrows (Passeridae)
- ❏ House Sparrow

Red-headed Woodpecker

INDEX OF SCIENTIFIC NAMES

This index references only the primary species accounts.

INDEX OF COMMON NAMES

Page numbers in boldface type refer to the primary, illustrated species accounts.

ABOUT THE AUTHORS

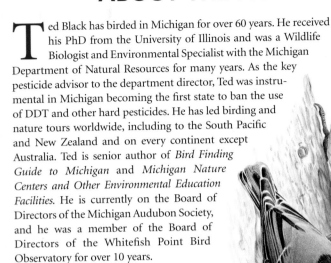

Ted Black has birded in Michigan for over 60 years. He received his PhD from the University of Illinois and was a Wildlife Biologist and Environmental Specialist with the Michigan Department of Natural Resources for many years. As the key pesticide advisor to the department director, Ted was instrumental in Michigan becoming the first state to ban the use of DDT and other hard pesticides. He has led birding and nature tours worldwide, including to the South Pacific and New Zealand and on every continent except Australia. Ted is senior author of *Bird Finding Guide to Michigan* and *Michigan Nature Centers and Other Environmental Education Facilities.* He is currently on the Board of Directors of the Michigan Audubon Society, and he was a member of the Board of Directors of the Whitefish Point Bird Observatory for over 10 years.

Gregory Kennedy has been an active naturalist since he was very young. He is the author of many books on natural history and also has produced film and television shows on environmental and indigenous concerns in Southeast Asia, New Guinea, South and Central America, the high Arctic and elsewhere. He has also been involved in countless research projects around the world ranging from studies in the upper-canopy of tropical and temperate rainforests to deepwater marine investigations.